T0316950

Africa and Economic Policy

Anthem Frontiers of Global Political Economy

The Anthem Frontiers of Global Political Economy series seeks to trigger and attract new thinking in global political economy, with particular reference to the prospects of emerging markets and developing countries. Written by renowned scholars from different parts of the world, books in this series provide historical, analytical and empirical perspectives on national economic strategies and processes, the implications of global and regional economic integration, the changing nature of the development project, and the diverse global-to-local forces that drive change. Scholars featured in the series extend earlier economic insights to provide fresh interpretations that allow new understandings of contemporary economic processes.

Africa and Economic Policy

Developing a Framework for Policymakers

Ferdinand Bakoup

ANTHEM PRESS
LONDON · NEW YORK · DELHI

Anthem Press
An imprint of Wimbledon Publishing Company
www.anthempress.com

This edition first published in UK and USA 2014
by ANTHEM PRESS
75–76 Blackfriars Road, London SE1 8HA, UK
or PO Box 9779, London SW19 7ZG, UK
and
244 Madison Ave #116, New York, NY 10016, USA

British Library Cataloguing-in-Publication Data
A catalogue record for this book is available from the British Library.

Library of Congress Cataloging-in-Publication Data
Bakoup, Ferdinand.
[Afrique peut-elle gagner sa place dans la mondialisation? English]
Africa and economic policy : developing a framework for policymakers / Ferdinand Bakoup.
pages cm. – (Anthem frontiers of global political economy)
"This book is a translated and updated version of the original French edition, L'Afrique peut-
elle gagner sa place dans la mondialisation? Pour une politique économique systémique (Paris:
L'Harmattan, 2009)."
Includes bibliographical references and index.
1. Africa–Economic policy–21st century. 2. Globalization–Economic aspects–Africa. I. Title. II.
Series: Anthem frontiers of global political economy.
HC800.B3435 2014
338.96–dc23
2014021983

ISBN-13: 978 1 78308 019 9 (Hbk)
ISBN-10: 1 78308 019 1 (Hbk)

Cover image: Anton Balazh/Shutterstock.com.

This title is also available as an ebook.

To Valerie, Brice, Elsa, Isis Maelyne, Ethan,
to my parents,
and to my brothers and sisters
for their love and unconditional support.

CONTENTS

ACKNOWLEDGEMENTS

This book is the result of the deep reflection I have, throughout my career as an economist, given to the economic situation of Africa, the complex mechanisms that influence the functioning of world economy, as well as the economic policy which African countries could implement in order to reap the advantages of globalization.

I would like to first of all thank the management of the African Development Bank. Their recent efforts to encourage the development of knowledge on African economies have created an enabling environment for the completion of this work, started several years ago.

I would also like to thank all my colleagues, a remarkable team of economists and sectoral experts with a sound knowledge of African economies, for their contribution to the realization of this book. Our frequent interactions greatly enriched and widened the scope of my thinking. I am deeply grateful.

I owe immense intellectual debt to Africans and non-Africans alike, be they public officials, researchers, actors in the private sector or in civil society. At different occasions, they have shared a number of issues with me, namely their analyses of the economic situation of the African continent, their hopes for and vision of an economic policy that will free the continent from marginalization in the global economy – which seems so inevitable, but fortunately is entirely preventable. I hereby very gratefully acknowledge them.

I wish to express gratitude to participants of the African Economic Conferences held in Addis Ababa and Tunis respectively, and particularly to those who attended the sessions at which some chapters of this book were presented. Their pertinent comments and suggestions contributed to my thinking in this book.

In the final phase of the writing of this book, a number of colleagues and friends gave me valuable assistance, including proofreading all or parts of the manuscript and making comments that enabled me to improve on a number of aspects of the book. In addition, their advice and support at such a critical phase of the work helped in its completion. I am deeply grateful to them.

I would like to thank the two anonymous referees at Anthem Press for their insightful reviews. Indeed, their comments and suggestions further corroborated my own thoughts and the feedback I had received from various readers that this book is bringing new dimensions into the debate on economic policy in Africa. Finally, I would also like to thank the editors at Anthem Press for their very able assistance throughout the production process of this book.

I remain solely responsible for the opinions expressed in this book. Under no circumstances should they be attributed to my current employer, the African Development Bank.

This book is a translated and updated version of the original French edition, *L'Afrique peut-elle gagner sa place dans la mondialisation? Pour une politique économique systémique* (Paris: L'Harmattan, 2009).

Introduction

AFRICA'S ECONOMIC GROWTH DEPENDS FIRST OF ALL ON GOOD ECONOMIC POLICY, NOT ON FOREIGN AID

"It is up to developing countries themselves and their governments to take the lead on development. They need to decide, plan and sequence their economic policies to fit with their own development strategies, for which they should be accountable to all their people."

Excerpt of the G8 Statement on Africa, Gleneagles, July 2005.[1]

The Aim of This Book

The goal of this book is to define a good economic policy for African countries within the context of globalization. It stems from the observation that Africa's current marginalization in the global scene is due to the fact that the economic policy put in place by African countries is not well oriented. Consequently, this marginalization is not an inevitable process and the implementation of a new economic policy, the main contours of which this book seeks to analyze, could enable these countries to reverse the trend and achieve sustainable growth in a rapidly globalizing world. The primary goal of this book, therefore, is to contribute to the improvement of economic policy in African countries, given that a good economic policy must necessarily take into account the constraints and opportunities that the process of globalization presents.

Thus, the question to which I am attempting to provide an answer focuses on the type of economic policies that African countries can implement in order to promote economic growth and fully benefit from globalization. To achieve this, I shall define the major elements of a good economic policy. Later, I will illustrate its implementation with examples drawn from successful African countries, and emerging and developed countries.

By focusing on the theme of economic policy, this book aims at giving a new direction to the development debate that has, for a long time, been dominated by foreign aid and the conditions of its effectiveness. Indeed, the debate on Africa's development policy seems to have been blindfolded by that of foreign aid. Thus, this book does not focus on foreign aid, or on what rich countries can or must do – or on what they must not do – to help Africa.

It is not because the subject seems of little importance, or that much has already been said about it. It is just because, beyond this assistance, it is only through their economic policy that African countries will be able to lead their economies toward prosperity and reduce poverty, which seems to be their primary goal at the moment. I began this book with a quotation taken from the communiqué that the G8 member countries published on Africa following their July 2005 meeting in Gleneagles in Scotland. In this communiqué, the G8 calls on African countries to decide, plan and organize their economic policies themselves, a stance which almost went unnoticed. Beyond promises of increased aid, this is, in my opinion, the best piece of advice the G8 could give and one of the most important contributions to reflections on the ways and means for African countries to come out of underdevelopment. In fact, to be sustainable, development in Africa should not always rely on foreign aid, even if it is important. It should rather focus on a sound economic policy that has been patiently elaborated and implemented with method, determination, creativity and voluntarism, as we shall see throughout this book.

What Is Economic Policy?

It is important to note that the concept of economic policy is one of the most widely used concepts in economic debates. But it is also one that, in my opinion, still needs to be clarified. Indeed, very few users of this concept, including even those who consider themselves experts in the domain of economics, are able to provide a clear and operational definition of economic policy. This certainly results from the fact that most of the books which deal with economic policy often assume that readers already have a good understanding of this concept and, therefore, go directly to discuss the various instruments relating to it without first of all giving an operational definition of the concept itself.[2] Therefore, it is necessary to give an operational definition of this concept, which will enable us to identify economic policy independently of the various instruments used to implement it.

Generally, I use the concept of economic policy whenever I want to refer to actions of the state that are geared toward influencing the economic performance of a country. Many attempts to define the concept of "economic policy" have approached the concept by referring to the major areas of economic activity such as production, distribution and consumption.

Thus, French economist J. Saint-Geours once defined economic policy as "a general action of the central political power, which is conscious, coherent, targeted, and implemented within the field of economics; that is, on matters relating to production, domestic or international trade, the consumption of goods and services and capital formation."[3] Although this definition contains explicit reference to some key characteristics of good economic policy measures such as coherence and being targeted, it does not pass the definitional test of a concept of economic policy since it obscures the fundamental issues at stake in economic policy. Thus, according to this definition, any government action that takes place in the economy is part of economic policy regardless of its effects: positive or negative. Moreover, the fact that this definition does not question the normative character of the purposes covered by the action of the central political power greatly reduces its scope, especially in a world where it is increasingly recognized that what the average citizen expects in the economic policy of the state is the improvement of his or her well-being.

French economist Christian de Boissieu equally suggests the following definition: "Economic policy constitutes decisions (to act or not to act) by the Government and other structures under its control whose main aims are tilted toward improving conditions related to production and distribution of resources."[4] Fairly close to the previous definition, this is wider in scope because it includes the activities not only of the central government but also those of the structures under its purview. It also includes decisions of nonintervention by the state in the definition of economic policy. Nevertheless, like the definition stated previously, the latter defines economic policy with reference to the major areas of economic activity.

A third definition, proposed by the *Lexique d'économie*, defines economic policy as "Government's deliberate actions which are manifested through the statement of economic and social goals and the adoption of related means to achieve these goals."[5] It stems from this definition that consciousness and reflection are the basic criteria for defining economic policy. Thus, in order to talk about economic policy, it is necessary to identify economic and social goals and mobilize resources to achieve them through deliberate actions of the state. This definition appears to include some of the key elements of a good economic policy, except that it makes only a weak reference to the normative aspects of the goals pursued.

In order to remedy the limitations of the definitions of economic policy currently available in the literature and with a view toward focusing attention on the desired goals of economic policy, I will define economic policy in this book as the way governments use the instruments at their disposal to influence the course of the national economy toward improving the well-being of its citizens. I will discuss in greater detail the notion of instruments of economic policy later in this book.

Justifications of Economic Policy

Is it necessary to have an economic policy? For some this question is pointless, considering that the answer is obviously yes. However, if the need for governments to intervene in the functioning of the economy (through their economic policies) is now widely accepted, we should not forget that many earlier views opposed this intervention. Thus, for proponents of economic liberalism, whose founder was the nineteenth-century British economist Adam Smith, state intervention to promote socially desirable goals is unnecessary because – thanks to the "invisible hand" – the result of individual actions of economic agents acting with their private interest as sole motivation is a collective good; that is, markets function well and produce a result that corresponds to the interest of all. However, experience has shown that, in reality, this "invisible hand" does not work as perfectly as Adam Smith thought.

In fact, observation of the functioning of economies clearly shows that economies tend to diverge away from the goals that society may fundamentally desire, such as high levels of employment and economic growth, and the reduction of poverty and of social inequality. Thus, it is now increasingly accepted that without any state intervention, every economy can sometimes generate wealth. However, it will also tend to experience prolonged periods of high unemployment and low growth, and perhaps widening social inequalities. These situations are not only sources of social instability, but may also hinder future progress.

Another justification of economic policy comes from what economists describe as situations of price rigidity. Economic theory has found in a certain number of situations factors which explain why the economy, if left on its own, will not be able to produce the results that the society wants. Among these, there are what economists call price rigidities. These are situations whereby prices in an economy are not flexible enough to allow equilibrium in the various markets to be achieved in a socially desirable manner. These price rigidities may themselves be the result of several factors such as the presence of imperfect information among economic agents or the lack of coordination between them. It is in referring to these situations of price rigidity, including wages, that the economist John Maynard Keynes advocated that government must conduct an appropriate budgetary policy to stimulate demand in a bid to boost economic growth and reduce unemployment.

A third justification of economic policy is based on the theory of externalities. Here, economic conditions are characterized by the following factors: either the existing market mechanisms fail to ensure optimal allocation of productive resources because the actions of economic agents impose costs on society as a whole and there are no market mechanisms for allocating these costs to those who cause them (negative externalities) or the actions of agents produce economic benefits for society which the agents themselves do not actually receive (positive externalities). The problem with these situations is that they generally lead to a socially suboptimal production of goods and services that are subject to externalities. Externalities, therefore, create a role for government's economic policy to the extent that governments should intervene to ensure that goods and services which the economy needs are produced in sufficient quantities and qualities.

Other situations that justify economic policy relate to public goods that enable the proper functioning of a market economy and that governments must ensure are produced in sufficient quantities and quality. The following are among the number of public goods necessary for the proper functioning of the economy: the protection of property rights, the promotion of free markets, the promotion of a competitive economic environment, the production of services such as education, health, security and national defense and other key infrastructures. As indicated above, there are therefore a number of economic theories that try to justify why the state must develop and implement a sound economic policy to guide the economy toward socially desirable goals. Even supporters of pure economic liberalism no longer challenge this stance, and therefore state intervention in the economy is indispensable, even if it is believed that such intervention should be well designed and well targeted in order to ensure the proper functioning of the market economy and the well-being of citizens.

Why This Book?

I have indicated above that the aim of this book is to contribute toward improving economic policy in Africa. But why is it important to write a new book for this purpose? My answer to this question will be two pronged: I will first argue that careful reading of recent developments strongly suggests the need for a major reorientation of economic policy in African countries if these countries are to (i) arrest and reverse their current marginalization in the globalization process and (ii) seize the opportunity offered by the recent high growth rates to lay the foundations for the structural changes needed for more durable and inclusive growth. Secondly, I will demonstrate that the current literature on economic policy destined for African countries and even developing countries in general has so far failed to adequately meet the requirements of this major economic policy renewal effort.

Three considerations underlie the need for a dramatically improved economic policy in Africa:

Firstly, it is now generally admitted that since the 2000s, African countries have been registering high growth rates, with many of them figuring among the fastest growing economies in the world. In its October 2013 *Regional Economic Outlook*, the International Monetary Fund projected that, despite a downward revision since its May 2013 report, growth was going to remain strong in sub-Saharan Africa, with output expanding by 5 per cent in 2013 and 6 per cent in 2014. Inflation was also projected to maintain its downward trend toward less than 6 per cent in 2014. This compared favorably with most of the other regions and/or country groupings, including Asia, the Western Hemisphere, emerging and developing economies and the European Union, which were projected to grow at 5.1 per cent and 5.3 per cent, 2.75 per cent and 3 per cent, 4.5 per cent and 5.1 per cent, and 0.0 per cent and 1.3 per cent in 2013 and 2014 respectively. Despite these broadly positive economic developments in Africa, many analysts have recently voiced concerns about the impact of this growth performance in terms of it leading to the structural changes which are necessary to make it self-sustained and inclusive and, therefore, durable in the long term.[6]

Secondly, uncertainties surrounding foreign aid, which has traditionally been a major factor of the African economic landscape, point to the need for a greater focus on efforts aimed at substantially improving economic policy in African countries for at least two reasons. First, research has provided ample evidence that foreign aid is only effective if economic policy put in place by recipient countries creates a conducive environment for its proper use.[7] Thus, assuming a decrease in aid flows, Africa will need a well-oriented economic policy in order to turn the limited support it will receive into tangible development results, even if there is a significant improvement in its delivery. Also, even without questioning the sincerity of promises made by donor countries, experience shows that there is always a wide gap between aid pledges and what is effectively delivered.[8] In the event that aid pledges do not materialize, there will also be a need to improve economic policy in African countries.

Finally, the view that African economic policy needs a dramatic shift seems to be gaining mainstream status in international policy discussion. Back in 2009, at the height of the financial and economic crisis, a major international conference of African finance ministers and central bankers took place in Dar es Salaam, Tanzania, to reflect on the policy actions which African countries could implement to counter the effects of the crisis. Commenting on the outcome of the conference, the London daily *Financial Times*, known for the depth of its commentaries on world economic and finance-related matters, wrote:

For a meeting billed as a chance for African policymakers to "brainstorm" responses to the global slowdown, a conference of finance ministers and central bank governors in Tanzania last month yielded slim pickings in terms of ideas. […] Its main output was a lobbying call to be made to the heads of the G20 meeting in London, the gist of which was this: Africa is not responsible for this crisis, but it is now suffering from it, so the rich countries that caused it should stump up cash to help the continent manage. [...] What the meeting did highlight, however, is how a blinkered focus on restitution from the developed world risks marginalizing the need for African policymakers to be proactive and self-reliant.[9]

Faced with these comments, two options are possible: either consider that the current state of economic policy in the continent is alright and dismiss them altogether, or see these comments as a basis for renewed thinking toward improving economic policy in the continent. The latter is the option we choose in this book.

All the above concerns bring to the fore the issue of economic policy in Africa, which, in the final analysis, is the only "magic" that can transform the economic performance of the continent in this rapidly globalizing world economy.

The above discussion clearly shows the need for a more effective economic policy in Africa. But what about the current supply of economic policy frameworks? I argue in this book that there is currently a large and widening gap between, on the one hand, the current literature on development policies for poor countries and, on the other hand, the actual needs of these countries in terms of practical guidance for the formulation and conduct of a sound economic policy for growth and social progress. In fact, the search for a good economic policy for development has always been at the forefront of economic literature on the problems of developing countries. Despite this effort, it would appear that this literature has so far been unable to build on the many results and theoretical advances it has achieved to articulate an economic policy that is both clear and intelligible for policy officials in developing countries, and effective in terms of being able to promote economic development in these countries. Although the framework once provided in the Washington Consensus[10] has been heavily criticized and is, today, widely discredited, it has been quite difficult to identify a replacement in the literature that is both innovative and conceptually and practically better. It is, therefore, the need to close this gap which provides the key foundation for the justification of this book.

On May 21, 2008, the Growth and Development Commission published its report entitled *The Growth Report: Strategies for Sustained Growth and Inclusive Development*.[11] This report, which resulted from a two-year study conducted by a team of 21 experts from the academia, government and international organizations including the United Nations and the World Bank,[12] aimed "to review the theoretical and empirical knowledge on economic growth with a view to draw policy implications for the present and future generation of decision makers." It therefore aimed to provide practical guidance for economic policy officials in developing countries and the wider development community. It was presented as containing the most current and comprehensive analysis available on the necessary ingredients for a policy of economic growth in poor countries. This report was, therefore, eagerly awaited.

Part 2 of the report is specifically devoted to the policy ingredients of a growth strategy. It will, in my opinion, immediately attract the attention of economic policy officials, who happen to be the target audience. In this section, the report identifies the policy ingredients for sustainable and inclusive economic growth as including the following: high rates of savings; investment in infrastructure, education, health, absorption of technology and knowledge from the rest of the world; promotion of competition and the structural changes which accompany it; promotion of the mobility and adequate pricing of labor; national debates which enable the recognition of bad ideas and their timely rejection; high-quality public administration; macroeconomic stability; implementation of regional development policies; equal opportunity and equity policy; financial sector development; and urbanization. The report also identifies other ingredients, which it describes as "the most controversial." Among these controversial ingredients the report includes policies to promote exports, management of exchange rates, liberalization of the current and capital accounts of the balance of payments, policy to accumulate foreign-exchange reserves, central bank independence, and adoption and implementation of fiscal rules. All in all, 18 policy ingredients for sustainable and inclusive growth are identified, and are successively discussed in more detail in the various chapters of the report.

Looking closely, the growth ingredients identified by the Commission on Growth and Development are all important, even very important, but it might not be easy for the officials in charge of economic policy in developing countries to figure out the ways in which these ingredients are combined to generate economic growth. Some of these ingredients are instruments or means of action. Such is the case with exchange rates, liberalization of capital and current accounts or the promotion of competition. Others appear to be results which are themselves obtained through the use of instruments and which, if obtained, will contribute toward the achievement of some other higher-level results or outcomes such as economic growth. This is, for example, the case with ingredients such as macroeconomic stability, financial sector development or investment. Moreover, discussions relating to employment in this report focus on what policymakers must do to facilitate labor mobility and promote its competitiveness in terms of cost. Such discussions do not reaffirm what one would expect, which is that employment creation should be seen as the fundamental goal of economic policy, one which all other actions should aim toward.

In other words, the framework of economic policy presented in the report does not show the transmission channels or intermediate results through which progress in the indicated areas will contribute toward generating growth and development in the economy. Knowledge of these transmission channels or intermediate results is important for economic policymaking because it allows the policy officials to identify with precision the key links in the chain of transmission on which it might be necessary to act to obtain the expected result of economic growth. Without a clear and explicit specification of all its intermediate results, any proposed framework of economic policy would be incomplete, and will even suffer from the problem known as the "missing middle."

This lack of specification of the transmission channels or intermediate results is not unique to the framework suggested by the Commission on Growth and Development. It characterizes almost all the frameworks for economic policy suggested in the literature on development policies. This book was written with the goal to fill this gap, to develop a credible conceptual framework for a good economic policy; that is, a framework that does not only identify the final results to be achieved, but which also specifies the transmission channels between the various results levels and, thus, identifies all the intermediate results.

For the officials in charge of economic policy, such a framework is more convenient for the formulation and conduct of economic policy than what currently exists in the literature to the extent that it provides a more practical roadmap for economic policy.

There are two particularly important intermediate economic policy results or goals that I try to highlight in this book. They are: (i) stimulating demand addressed to the economy and (ii) increasing productivity in the economy's productive base. In fact, all the growth effects of any policy measures must transit through these two intermediate results. Progress on any of the growth ingredients identified by the Commission on Growth and Development will not generate economic growth if this progress does not strengthen demand addressed to the economy or increase productivity in the country's productive base. Thus, although a development policy can also be judged in terms of the progress it achieves in the areas identified by the commission, in the end it is the quality of its effects on stimulating demand addressed to the economy[13] and improving productivity in the economy's productive base that matters. Demand addressed to the economy and the strength of its supply base are, therefore, the "inescapable route" to economic growth. This is often so because it is only when economic policy has positive effects on these two variables that it can effectively stimulate economic growth. Therefore, not only do we clearly identify these important intermediate results and fully integrate them in the framework of economic policy, we also define what we call the operating goals, operating objectives or operating results of economic policy. Operating results are the results that the officials in charge of economic policy can influence directly with the instruments available at their disposal. The attainment of these operating goals or results consequently leads to the achievement of the intermediate goals or results. Taking into account all these improvements greatly enriches the frameworks of economic policy suggested in the literature and helps to meet the real needs of economic policy officials in terms of practical orientations for the formulation and conduct of economic policy. This is the task I undertake in this book.

In addition to the inability to organize the key goals in a sound results framework, the contemporary literature on economic policy for developing countries presents another shortcoming: the list of areas considered important often seems incomplete, especially if one takes into account the very rich base of concepts and results established by the economic sciences. Let's take the example of credibility. Everyone today now knows that credibility is an extremely important concept for economic policy. Many examples show that governments in many developing countries could achieve more if they were credible to some extent. The search for credibility should therefore preoccupy economic policy, but most of the literature on economic policy destined for the developing world does not allude to this concept. The report of the Commission on Growth and Development is no exception. The same judgment could be made about many other concepts such as rational expectations, exhortation of economic agents, hysteresis effects and many others. Dani Rodrik (1999) identifies a good investment strategy and sound conflict management institutions as key conditions for a country to integrate into globalization. This book aims to close the exhaustivity gap that characterizes the policy frameworks suggested in the literature for developing countries.

Perhaps emblematic of the fact that the recent literature is still in search of a credible economic development strategy to propose to developing countries, US economist

William Easterly proposed freedom as the key to development. For him, there is no doubt that freedom is the key to economic development. Compare South Korea and North Korea, the poor and despotic Europe of yesterday to the rich and modern Europe of today, or even West Germany and East Germany, and one will understand what freedom can achieve, he notes.[14] We agree that freedom is important. We would even agree that freedom is vital to economic development. It is today widely acknowledged that one is more imaginative, creative, enterprising and therefore more productive if one feels free, or if one is not constrained by fear. Nevertheless, freedom in itself is not sufficient. Many facts would attest to the fact that freedom in itself cannot substitute for a good economic policy strategy. If freedom were the only factor to determine the growth and prosperity of a country, we would not observe the wide diversity in economic performance that we observe among countries with similar levels of freedom. Thus, in the group of countries that could be described as free, per capita income levels vary widely.[15] The same applies for per capita income levels in the group of countries that could be described as not free. This variability would suggest that freedom alone is not the only determinant of economic development. Moreover, history teaches us that economic growth and progress toward freedom happened concurrently in most of today's free and developed countries. That is to say, these countries did not focus on acquiring freedom first and then using it to develop economically. If one takes these considerations into account, then the theory of freedom as the only explanatory variable of development loses its substance.

Recently, some authors have suggested other ideas for driving African development in the future, including urbanization, demographics, the growth of the middle class and the increase of wages in China (which would lead to a delocalization of some Chinese manufacturing activities to Africa), none of which seem promising from my point of view. These ideas do not constitute in themselves an economic policy which Africa could implement to promote its economic and social development. Instead, it is a good economic policy, the broad outlines of which I try to articulate in this book, that will turn these factors into powerful growth drivers, not the other way round.

What This Book Is and What It Is Not

It is necessary to state what this book is and what it is not. This book is an attempt to define and illustrate a good economic policy which African countries can implement in order to secure a place in globalization. Although globalization offers opportunities, it also presents these countries with unprecedented challenges.

Although this book focuses on economic policy for officials in developing countries, and aims to be as practical as possible, it is not a catalog of ready-made measures of economic policy to be implemented. In fact, as we shall see throughout this book, if the main goals of economic policy are homogenous among countries, specific policy measures aimed at implementing these goals would certainly be directly linked to the particular context of each country at any given point in time. Thus, assuming that two countries A and B are pursuing the same economic policy goal at a given point in time T_0, a measure that would be relevant for country A may not be relevant for country B. Similarly, a measure which may be relevant for country A at a given point in time

T_0 might no longer be relevant at time T_1. So, instead of providing a catalog of policy measures, this book intends to suggest guiding posts for the elaboration and conduct of a good economic policy. Its sole aim is to help countries to identify policy issues that require concrete policy answers, thereby providing each country with the opportunity to find answers that better suit their own context.

In a book like this one, which is primarily destined for African countries in quest of a strategy to improve their economic policy, one is necessarily tempted, under a desire to be concrete, to suggest practical and very specific measures of economic policy. Such an approach would inevitably lead us to suggest standard measures, whereas, as it shall become clear, the wide diversity of situations requires that economic policy be tailored to the specific context of each country. In a nutshell, a one-size-fits-all policy would not work.

This book, therefore, has a two-pronged aim: it aims first to contribute to a better definition of the theory of economic policy and then to help improve the practice of economic policy in African countries. Although at the theoretical level the book relies primarily on the application of concepts which are all well known in economic theory, it is probably the first of its kind in that it attempts to develop an adequate conceptual and operating framework for an overall good economic policy for the nation that goes beyond the sectoral approach, which as we will see is based on an analysis of the main instruments of economic policy, as in most current books on economic policy. From a practical point of view, the implementation of this conceptual framework by African countries shall contribute considerably in improving their economic policy and move them away from the models used before, which consisted in defining priority sectors and allocating enough resources to them. The implementation of this conceptual framework ought to therefore enable them to renew their economic policy while rendering it more efficient in attaining their development goals. From this double point of view both theorists and practitioners of economic policy will hopefully find great interest in the analyses that are presented throughout this book.

A final point on what this book is not: This book does not focus on a discussion of the current challenges facing Africa. This book – and this is precisely one of its major strengths – aims at presenting the optimal economic policy to enable African economic growth in a globalizing world. Most current books on Africa focus on discussing the challenges facing the continent, but are very poor at highlighting policies that would reverse these challenges and are therefore of little value to policymakers. This book does the opposite and seeks to add value to current discourse, and to be helpful to policymakers.

The Main Audience of the Book

This book is aimed at officials in charge of the elaboration and implementation of economic policies in their countries. This responsibility is usually shared among many actors. However, it is the government – that is, the executive – that decides. The entire government and its head, therefore, have cause to read the analyses presented herein. In some countries, the head of government is the prime minister; in other situations, it is the president of the republic. Depending on their political systems, the prime minister or the president of the republic may be the chief officer responsible for a country's economic policy. In countries that have both a president of the republic and a prime minister, unless the first does not intervene in matters relating to the day-to-day running of the country's economic policy, the responsibility of economic policy has to be shared between these two personalities. In a bid to enhance their economic policies, they must agree and cooperate closely so as to provide stakeholders with a clear and harmonized view of the country's economic policy at any point in time. The success of the national economic policy is not the concern of its leader only, but also the concern of stakeholders such as the civil society, the private sector, consumers and even external partners. It is hoped that stakeholders of national economic policy shall find great interest in reading this book. Students in economics and researchers as well as aid agencies will also find interest in reading the analyses and conclusions presented herein.

The Structure of the Book

This book is divided into five parts. The first part questions what I call the sectoral approach to economic policy. I show that even if the said sectoral approach can yield some benefits for a given sector, its relevance is still extremely limited when it comes to a country's overall economic policy. These limits stem from the fact that the economic policy of a nation cannot be the sum of its sectoral policies. While challenging the sectoral approach, the first part of this book also relies on insights from economic theory to define a conceptual framework for good economic policy. This first part, therefore, outlines the conceptual analysis of good economic policy and shows that African countries on a quest for a genuine policy to promote their economic development can rely on this conceptual framework for the development and implementation of their economic policy.

The second part is devoted to a more detailed examination of the conceptual framework that I have outlined in the first part. In this part, I examine the various goals and instruments of a good economic policy. The analyses presented in the first two parts are quite innovative in their use of the existing theoretical concepts to build a conceptual framework for good economic policy. These analyses should help improve the quality of economic policy in African countries and consequently the continent's development. I have presented these analyses at various economic conferences, including the African Economic Conference, and audiences have found them interesting.[16] Participants at the conferences included academics, experts from international organizations and senior African government officials.

The third part deals with the theme of globalization in terms of the constraints it presents and opportunities that it offers for the formulation and conduct of economic policy according to the conceptual framework developed in the previous two parts. In this section, I characterize the process of globalization by examining its key actors and main factors. This part equally provides a summary of key findings on recent research relating to the impact of globalization on poor countries. The insight in this part is in the analysis made of the constraints that globalization presents as well as the opportunities it offers for an economic policy designed and implemented according to the conceptual framework presented earlier.

The fourth part acknowledges that foreign aid plays a major role in the economic policy of African countries. However, as is well known, foreign aid has so far failed to play its full role as an instrument to support the development efforts of developing countries, particularly in Africa, despite the efforts of the international community to improve its delivery. Based on this observation and existing literature on the effectiveness of such aid, I highlight what aid could do to contribute more to the success of a good economic policy, developed and implemented following the conceptual framework developed above.

The fifth and last part is devoted to a presentation of some successful examples of economic policy. Thus, this section describes in turn the economic policy of Tunisia and of post-apartheid South Africa. These two examples are discussed in two different chapters. In a concise manner, Chapter 16 analyzes the economic policy implemented by the West to promote its development over time (examining the cases of Western Europe and the United States). This chapter also analyzes the economic policy of some emerging Asian nations. The advantage of looking at these success stories lies in the manner in which the conceptual framework presented in this book describes each of the experiences.

By examining the successes of Tunisia and South Africa, this book is contributing to the debate on the comparative experiences of economic policy and what those experiences offer as lessons to other developing countries in general and to Africa in particular. To date, the literature on comparative experiences of development policy has concentrated largely on the examination of the experiences of Asian countries. In analyzing the experiences of countries like Tunisia and South Africa – two success stories that are not very well known in the literature of economic policy (also take note that these are both African countries) – the book expands and diversifies the literature on the comparative experiences of economic policy.

In a nutshell, this book aims at defining and illustrating the notion of good economic policy that could be implemented to accelerate the economic growth of African countries, which are among the world's poorest. Although the book is written with African countries in mind, the scope of analysis contained herein may well go beyond these countries.

Part One

THE CONCEPTUAL FUNDAMENTALS OF A SYSTEMIC ECONOMIC POLICY FOR AFRICA'S REVIVAL

The first part of this book analyzes the conceptual framework of a good economic policy and shows that African countries in search of a veritable economic policy to stimulate their development can draw inspiration from this conceptual framework to elaborate and implement their economic policy.

Chapter One

THE SECTORAL APPROACH TO ECONOMIC POLICY AND ITS LIMITS

"[…] To be sure, development economics has provided us with some remarkable insights. But as a subdiscipline of economics, it has so far been unable to provide a convincing intellectual agenda for generating and distributing wealth in poor countries, as evidenced by the persistence of poverty in many parts of the world. […] The questions before us are what to do with all these elements and how to organize them in a convincing new theory and a practical framework to help policymakers in poor countries solve the mystery of growth and sustain the dynamics of structural transformation."

Justin Yifu Lin, former chief economist and senior vice president at the World Bank[1]

Introduction

This chapter seeks to clarify and bring out the shortcomings of the sectoral approach that many African countries seem to pursue in the conception and implementation of their economic policy.

What Is Meant by a "Sectoral Approach" to Economic Policy?

Records indicate that many of the economic policies adopted by African countries to stimulate development after independence can be summarized as a succession of priorities accorded to different sectors of the economy or to certain specific thematic preoccupations considered to be of valuable importance to the economic development of the nation. This approach works as follows: once the importance of a sector or theme has been asserted, the next step is to seek sufficient resources in order to obtain the desired sectoral results, since it is projected that this would consequently produce positive effects that would in turn spread throughout to stimulate economic growth and reduce poverty. This is what I refer to in this book as the sectoral approach to economic policy. It consists in organizing a country's economic policy mainly around sectoral goals. Figure 1.1 below summarizes the sectoral approach to economic policy.

An examination of the history of economic policy in African countries indicates that among the various sectors or themes that were at one moment or the other in the course of recent history viewed as priority and placed at the center of economic concerns I may include health, education, investment, savings, population control, trade liberalization

Figure 1.1. The sectoral approach to economic policy establishes a direct link between instruments and envisaged goals

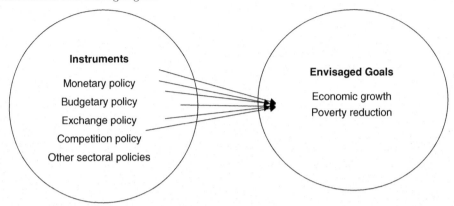

and economic liberalism in general, macroeconomic stability, promotion of gender equality, promotion of good governance, development of the infrastructure sector, etc.[2]

It is quite easy nowadays to recognize this sectoral approach in the economic policy of African countries. In many of these countries, the search for an optimal allocation of public expenditure – that is, an allocation in which the so-called priority sectors receive a significant share of public spending (both domestically and externally financed) – is very often one of the goals at the center of economic policy.

The origins of this sectoral approach are many. First of all, there is the fact that theoretically, economic policy as an entity in itself, independent of the various instruments needed to implement it, has received very little attention from scholars until now. Indeed, the concept of economic policy has so far been addressed by referring to the specific questions posed by the use of its main instruments, which are generally understood to be monetary policy, fiscal policy, exchange rate policy, foreign trade policy and that of many other sectoral policies. Thus, most theoretical work treats economic policy by always breaking it down into its main instruments,[3] which obviously does not enable a complete view of what should be the overall economic policy of a nation, and how it should be designed and implemented.

Another factor that justifies the widespread use of the sectoral approach can be attributed to the influence that the findings of empirical studies have had on economic policy in developing countries in general. Indeed, empirical studies on the determinants of various aspects of the economic performance of developing countries have today produced a voluminous, rich and very sophisticated literature. Let us take the example of the empirical literature on economic growth, a theme that has led to an intense research activity aimed at accounting for the factors that determine it in poor countries. Generally, these research efforts combine case studies to examine the experience of a country's economic growth over time and a cross-section analysis which examines the experience of a group of countries at some point in time in a bid to isolate the factors which may promote or retard a country's growth. Figure 1.2 below illustrates the main determinants of economic growth according to this literature.

Figure 1.2. Main factors influencing economic growth according to current literature[4]

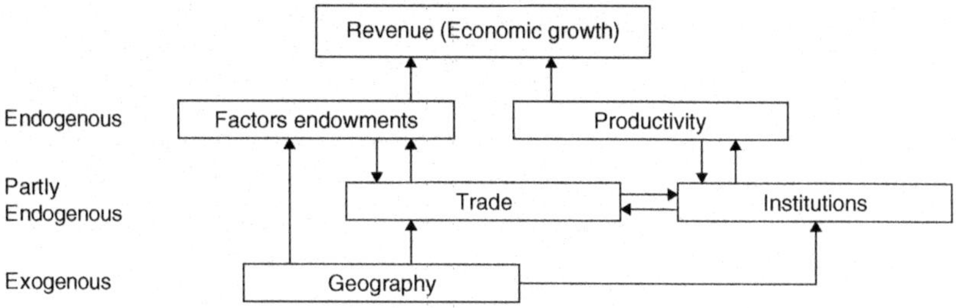

According to this empirical research, in order to influence economic growth governments should liberalize trade, improve the quality of institutions for the proper functioning of markets (including those that promote property rights and ensure the successful implementation of contracts) and seek an increase in the country's physical and human capital. As noted above, these findings, drawn from empirical studies, have often been the basis of recommendations for countries to focus more on a particular sector or theme. Although the factors identified above are important and would be part of any good economic policy strategy, in the chapter that follows and throughout this book, I shall demonstrate that good economic policy should consider many other aspects.

Elements of a sectoral approach to economic policy are also found in recent literature referred to as growth diagnostics. According to this approach, governments should try to identify the constraint that hinders economic growth and focus their attention on overcoming it. Because it recommends that economic policy should focus on the single most important constraint on economic growth, the resolution of which may set it free, this literature has all the characteristics of the sectoral approach to economic policy as defined above. I doubt if it will ever be possible to identify said constraint. As we shall see, a good economic policy requires concentration at all times on a set of concerns. Box 1.1 below describes the application of this approach by its proponents to countries like Brazil and El Salvador.[5]

Due to this sectoral approach, existing literature on economic policy appears to be a set of compartmentalized islets of structured knowledge, with each islet representing a domain of analysis of the interaction between a sector or particular theme and the overall economic performance of a country. Figure 1.3 below illustrates the compartmentalized nature of the current literature on economic policy.

Each islet in the diagram above represents a domain of knowledge which deals with specific questions that pertain to that field of knowledge. In each of these domains, the literature uses theoretical and applied models to come up with conclusions and recommendations that link this domain to the overall economic performance of a nation and whose effectiveness in the real world depends on the level of realism of the hypotheses and methods of analysis used. While this approach may be considered useful in relation to sectoral and other specific issues, it does not enable us to answer the question posed by an economic policy official concerning the overall economic policy strategy to be implemented. To illustrate this point, let us come back for a moment to the example on economic growth. The literature reveals some interesting and technically

Box 1.1. Search for the most binding constraint

To illustrate this approach, the authors took the example of two Latin American countries, Brazil and El Salvador, and tried to identify the constraints that slow economic growth the most in each of them. In line with the literature on developing countries' economic growth, these authors found that low investment and thus limited stock of physical capital in Brazil is rather due to the lack of capital to invest than to the low rate of return on investment, while in El Salvador, the reverse is true. They drew this conclusion from the fact that, according to them, growth in Brazil had evolved together with an external constraint and high interest rates, which seems to suggest that it is the availability of capital to invest which mostly hindered the economic growth of Brazil.

As for El Salvador, they observed that the country had the lowest interest rates in Latin America, and had not been able to fully utilize its external funding capacities to increase its investment rate. As for human capital, these authors discovered that the wages for skilled labor in Brazil were the highest in Latin America, while the return to education in El Salvador was below the average in Latin America.

According to these authors of the growth diagnostics approach, these results appeared to suggest that lack of human capital could be a constraint to Brazil's economic growth, while it is not the case in El Salvador. The overall conclusion was that the economic constraint that most hindered economic growth in Brazil was the lack of investment capital, while in El Salvador it was the lack of ideas.

At the policy level, the authors made the following assessments and recommendations: In El Salvador, they listed a set of factors that may explain the low return to private investment, among which the most important were high taxes, macroeconomic instability, inadequate contract enforcement mechanisms and property rights protection, political instability, poor infrastructure, labor laws and the exchange rate, but concluded that none of these was really a concern for the country. To them, the most severe constraint on economic growth was the insufficient capacity of the country to develop high-return activities that can be locally exploited. They therefore recommend that the Salvadoran government focus its economic policy on developing entrepreneurship among Salvadorans. As for Brazil, which had more ideas than resources to implement them, they observed that the business climate, the quality of infrastructure, taxes, public utilities prices, and weaknesses in contract enforcement and property rights protection were less meaningful constraints to economic growth, as they would rather contribute to making investment more profitable. Their policy recommendation for Brazil was, therefore, that the government should focus its economic policy on improving public financial management in order to increase national savings.[6]

Figure 1.3. Current literature on economic policy: Islets of compartmentalized knowledge

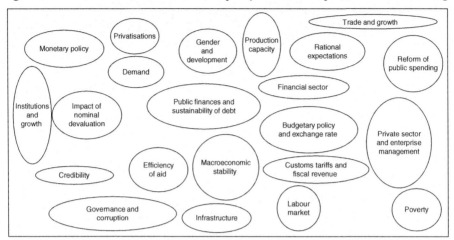

sophisticated analysis on the sectoral or thematic contributions to economic growth. But we must admit that these sectoral analyses cannot replace reflections on an overall economic policy strategy, as required by the authorities. In other words, the issue of an overall strategy for economic policy is upstream in relation to the specific and sectoral issues that are usually highlighted in the current literature on economic policy. I am now going to examine the shortcomings of the sectoral approach to economic policy.

Limitations of the Sectoral Approach to Economic Policy

The sectoral approach to economic policy can provide useful insights when the interest is sectoral in nature. However, it seems that a policy based only on a sectoral approach may not be able to stimulate sustainable economic growth and create the kinds of jobs that African countries actually need.

The main problem with the sectoral approach to economic policy is that it does not take into account all the aspects that support a successful economic policy. The sectoral approach establishes a direct link between the instruments and the final goals which are targeted by economic policy officials (see Figure 1.1 above). The establishment of this direct link fails to properly highlight the various intermediate goals of the economic policy transmission chain. Indeed, a good understanding and close monitoring of these intermediate goals is needed for the success of the economic policy. As such, the sectoral approach confines economic policy to a simple exercise whereby different sectoral instruments are manipulated without a clear overall view of the important intermediate results. Failure to take into consideration all the guideposts that determine the success of an economic policy reduces its chances of success. Generally, there is a considerable gap between the modification of an instrument of economic policy and the impact on final economic variables that count for the society. For this reason, the sectoral approach to economic policy turns out to have a very limited use for a country that is working toward designing a credible economic policy. As a matter of fact, the economic policy of a nation cannot only be reduced to a simple juxtaposition of its sectoral policies.

I participated in a discussion at the World Bank in Washington, DC on the new approach to identify economic policy priorities known as "growth diagnostics," an example of a sectoral approach to economic policy. The views expressed at the meeting broadly confirmed my skepticism that if this approach – which consists in trying to identify the single-most binding constraint whose removal would act as a magic wand to restore economic growth – may seem attractive, it nevertheless has serious limitations as a framework for a country's economic policy. As noted above, findings of researchers of this approach led to the conclusion that, in the case of Brazil, the attention of the authorities responsible for economic policy should have focused on measures to increase public savings, while in the case of El Salvador the authorities should have focused on anything that could help strengthen the spirit of entrepreneurship. Is it really possible to believe that if Brazil increases its public savings, its growth will reflect a double-digit rate? Is it conceivable that a country's economic policy can be geared solely toward increasing public savings? Assuming that the increase in public savings reduces interest rates, which in itself is not a foregone conclusion, will the increase in public savings alone restore confidence in all economic agents and lead them to increase their productive investments? Does increasing public savings suffice to increase demand addressed to the national economy, a key determinant of growth? In my opinion, these are some of the major concerns of economic policy. The various "priorities" put forward by the sectoral approach remind us of the panaceas that have throughout recent history been put forward to boost growth and development in poor countries. These panaceas ranged from the control of population growth to increasing investment (referring to the growth model of Harrod–Domar that was en vogue at one time).[7] Experience has amply shown us that the focus on a sector or on a theme as the critical determinant of economic growth and poverty reduction will not produce the desired results. Developed economies today did not develop by sector – that is, by successively developing different sectors, one after the other – but by adopting a systemic approach in their economic policy.

Summary

In the foregone chapter, I have examined what I call the sectoral approach to economic policy and I have explained its shortcomings. Hence, it can be affirmed that conducting economic policy with a sectoral approach seems to be common among African countries today. Even though the sectoral approach can effect progress in some sectors of the economy, ultimately it is least likely to achieve the intentions of a good economic policy. Good economic policy require that attention be paid on a set of fundamental concerns. In the chapter that follows, I will develop the conceptual framework from which African countries can draw inspiration to define and implement a sound economic policy that can enable them to find their place in a more and more globalized world economy.

Chapter Two

CONCEPTUAL FRAMEWORK OF A SYSTEMIC ECONOMIC POLICY FOR THE REVIVAL OF AFRICA

"Cutting through complexity to find a solution runs through four predictable stages: determine a goal, find the highest-leverage approach, discover the ideal technology for that approach, and in the meantime, make the smartest application of the technology that you already have."

Bill Gates, Harvard commencement speech, June 6, 2007[1]

"A good theory is only the summary, the substance of reality, which in turn exploits the theory. We cannot theorize a reality that was not previously observed. We cannot also practice what we do not conceive."

Joseph Tchundjang Pouemi, Cameroonian economist[2]

Introduction

I have just examined the shortcomings of the sectoral approach to economic policy. My task in this chapter is to go beyond criticism and contribute to the improvement of economic policy in Africa. I shall do this by defining a conceptual framework for a good economic policy; that is to say, a conceptual framework that is not merely a juxtaposition of sectoral policies. Although the task of defining a conceptual framework for economic policy has not so far been undertaken by current literature, which justifies the fact that the analyses are still compartmentalized (i.e., focused on specific themes and sectors), defining a conceptual framework that could inspire a revival of the economic policy of African countries is nevertheless facilitated by the fact that most of the elements of such a framework exist in the literature, though in an uncoordinated and dispersed manner.

Good Economic Policy Consists Primarily In Making the Right Choice of Credible Goals

The central argument advanced in this chapter, and this book in general, is that a good economic policy is first and foremost characterized by:

(i)   the pursuit of final goals that are clearly and sustainably anchored on achieving high levels of employment and economic growth;

(ii)   the pursuit of two intermediate goals anchored on a) national productive-capacity building and b) the stimulation of demand addressed to the national economy;

(iii) the pursuit of a set of operating goals that directly contribute to the above-mentioned intermediate and final goals; and

(iv)   the use of instruments, and of the means of implementing economic policy, to respectively design and implement specific economic policy measures, adapted to the local contexts, that target the attainment of these different goals.

It is this conceptual framework, illustrated in Figure 2.1 below, that subsequent parts of this chapter, as well as the book, will focus on to further clarify and explain.

When I had a discussion on this conceptual framework with a friend, who is presently a senior economic official in Africa, he was of the opinion that economic policy was limited to the fourth point above; that is to say, the designing and implementation of economic policy measures using available instruments. This view reflects the current practice in many African countries, where economic policy, while still dominated by the sectoral approach, seems to be highly focused on finding specific measures to be implemented to the detriment of an overall vision of the desired goals outlined above. In fact, the other three points (see points (i) – (iii) above) cannot be dissociated from a credible economic policy, as shall be revealed throughout this book.

Building on the previous definition, we will define a good economic policy as a process by which officials design a set of final (fundamental), intermediate and operating goals, and with the aid of the instruments and means of implementation at their disposal, come up with specific measures that can attain them. The following are the main challenges posed by this exercise:

(i)   select final goals that not only reflect the views of the majority of the population but those whose attainment will translate directly into improving the well-being of citizens;

(ii)   select intermediate goals whose realization will contribute directly to achieving the final goals;

(iii) select operating goals whose realization will contribute directly to the achievement of intermediate goals;

(iv)   design specific measures whose implementation will lead to the achievement of the operating goals.

Generally it is not easy to select these goals, given that there is theoretically a myriad of variables which are likely to catch the interests of economic policy officials and are therefore likely to be selected as economic goals. Among the multitude of economic variables of a nation, some are considered fundamental in economic theory in that they directly affect the well-being of citizens. Of these, one can cite the level of employment and economic growth. There are also other variables that influence the well-being of citizens, but only indirectly. These are called social variables, such as education, health, quality of infrastructure, environment and governance. Finally, there are variables that are only distantly related to the well-being of citizens, although they may be of interest to those responsible for economic policy. To this effect, one can cite examples such as the balance of payments, budget balance, investment

Figure 2.1. Conceptual framework for a good economic policy

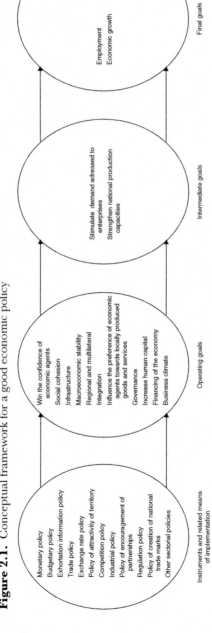

rate, savings rate, level of interest rates or the level of foreign direct investment flows. In the context of economic policy, they are referred to as call-up variables or extra variables.

In the face of this multitude of variables, the first success of an economic policy is achieved when (i) the targeted final goals are sustainably and firmly anchored on fundamental variables, and (ii) the intermediate and operating goals are selected from the social and extra variables such that their realization contributes directly to the attainment of final goals. In fact, it is advantageous for economic policy that officials have a clear and stable view that the goals they pursue should reflect the well-being of citizens, which as we have seen is essentially determined by fundamental variables such as the level of employment and economic growth. If this vision is not clear and firmly rooted in the minds of policy officials, then the risk will be that they may end up focusing either only on social variables, extra variables or on variables belonging to both categories and which are only indirectly related to the well-being of citizens. As such, economic policymakers may lose sight of the true final goals they are expected to target.

In 2006, an UNCTAD (United Nations Conference on Trade and Development) report issued a warning to leaders of developing countries, guarding them against losing sight of the goals of their countries' economic policies. The report noted: "In principle, although the reduction of inflation does not exclude that monetary policy decisions also take into account other goals, including full employment, the situation has led to the domination of other goals related to growth, employment or exchange rate by the goal of price stability."[3] This situation clearly reveals the risk faced by economic policy officials who do not view their final economic goals in terms of the fundamental variables relating to the well-being of citizens.

Although this warning was contained in an UNCTAD document written for the benefit of developing countries, the heated debate that occurred in Europe in 2009–10 and even today on the question of whether the monetary policy implemented by the European Central Bank adequately took into account concerns relating to creating jobs and stimulating economic growth – and which, in fact, is now recurrent even in many advanced and major emerging economies – shows that this call for vigilance in relation to the goals of economic policy is not just for those responsible for economic policy in developing countries. I will, in the rest of this chapter, try to identify what should be selected as the final, intermediate and operating goals of a good economic policy, as well as the relationship that should exist between these goals and between them and the instruments of economic policy.

The Final Goals of Economic Policy

It is generally admitted that employment and economic growth are fundamental determinants of the well-being of the citizens of a nation. This is due to the sovereign role of employment in determining our social status, the consideration that we may have for ourselves and others, our integration into society and in generating the income needed to satisfy our material needs. As for economic growth, it guarantees an increase in income. I therefore believe that achieving a high level of employment and strong economic growth should be the ultimate or final goal that economic policy officials should set for themselves. Social cohesion has also often been cited as deserving to be part of the final goals, but I believe that it is more of a factor promoting economic growth and employment than a final goal in itself. In addition, a high level of employment contributes to greater social cohesion. That is why I shall revisit the notion of social cohesion when discussing the intermediate and operating goals of an economic policy.

When I first published the French edition of this book in the fall of 2009, strong economic growth and job creation were already key final goals of economic policy in developed and major emerging economies, but many developing countries, including in Africa, continued to present the concept of poverty reduction as their overarching economic policy objective. Thanks to the Arab Spring, which erupted in 2011, we are now witnessing a salutary shift in economic thinking in some developing countries, who are now attempting to put strong economic growth and job creation at the center of their economic policy. Recent developments – including those in the international debate on economic policy in developing countries, to which I will come back later – would, however, lead us to observe that this trend is still in its infancy and not yet firmly anchored in the fabric of the mainstream economic policy of these countries. More work, therefore, still needs to be done to get there.

The Intermediate Goals of Economic Policy

In practice, authorities in charge of economic policy cannot directly influence the final goals that I have just identified with the aid of the instruments they possess. Hence the need to introduce intermediate goals, which are meant to relay the effects resulting from a change in instruments. Intermediate goals must have two essential characteristics: First, they must be closer to the instruments; that is to say, the effect of a change at instrument level on the intermediate goals must be more direct and therefore better understood by those responsible for economic policy, compared to the same effect on the final goals. Second, an intermediate goal must be able to influence the final goal. Monitoring the evolution of intermediate goals, therefore, allows authorities to anticipate the future of final goals. In this approach, the intermediate goals are selected so that they are influenced by the instruments and in turn they influence the final goals.

What would the intermediate goals of an economic policy be if growth and job creation emerge as the final goals of an economic policy? If the question of intermediate goals has often been raised as part of monetary policy, we must admit that it has been of least concern in terms of the overall economic policy of a nation. A quick review of economic theory reveals that economists have traditionally focused their attention on the supply side – that is to say, the national productive capacity – in discussions on economic growth and job creation.[4] Reinforcing a nation's productive capacity, therefore, seems logically to be one of the intermediate goals of economic policy. Moreover, following the work of the British economist John Maynard Keynes, the role of demand in supporting growth and job creation is now fully recognized.[5] Thus, economic policy officials should target the following two major intermediate goals: (i) strengthening local productive capacity and (ii) fostering (through noninflationary means) demand addressed to the national economy.

Operating Goals of Economic Policy

Sometimes it can be interesting, and even indispensable, to introduce operating goals which are closer to the instruments than the intermediate goals, but which influence the latter. Thus, they serve as a transmission channel linking the instruments to the intermediate goals. As with the case of intermediate goals, the issue of operating goals has often been raised in matters relating to monetary policy, but rarely in the context of the overall economic policy of a nation. What kinds of operating goals should policymakers set for themselves? Again, a review of economic theory reveals a number of variables that could serve as operating goals. These variables include gaining the confidence of economic agents, practicing good governance (a good relay factor for economic policy measures), improving the quality of infrastructure, the search for social cohesion and stability, macroeconomic stability, improving the business environment, strengthening human capital, the search for an adequate level of financing of the economy, and regional and multilateral integration.

The Instruments of Economic Policy

After identifying the final, intermediate and operating goals to pursue, the next challenge is that of selecting the appropriate instruments to be used. According to Christian de Boissieu, a leading French economist, instruments are "command variables."[6] These are essentially economic variables that have the following two basic features: Firstly, they are directly and completely under the control of the authorities responsible for economic policy. This means that they can freely choose the level of these variables as the need may be. Secondly, these variables serve as a means to influence other policy variables such as the final goals I have just discussed through the operating and intermediate goals. An instrument of economic policy must, therefore, be linked by a relation of cause and effect to a goal of economic policy. Thus, the rate of income tax, the rate of customs duty and the policy interest rate, which is controlled by the central bank, are some examples of instruments of economic policy if I consider that, on the one hand, the authorities themselves set their levels and, on the other hand, they contribute in influencing certain variables that can be goals of economic policy (operating goals) such as governance, the level of confidence of economic agents or macroeconomic stability. More generally, the major instruments of economic policy – those most commonly studied in the literature – include fiscal policy, monetary policy, exchange rate policy and external trade policy. Beyond these traditional instruments, the list of possible instruments of economic policy is infinite. Practically, all other instruments that fall within the realm of the government's authority can, in one way or another, work in the interest of national economic policy. Such is the case with information policy or even external relations policy, to cite only these two domains.

In a nutshell, the sequences of an economic policy, which result from the conceptual framework developed earlier, highlight the fact that the success of a given economic policy depends on a sustained and clear focus, on the one hand, of its final goals in the search for strong economic growth and the creation and safeguarding of jobs, and, on the other hand, of its intermediate goals on building national productive capacity and stimulating demand addressed to the national economy.

Designing and Implementing Economic Policy Measures: A Science and Art Marked by a Certain Level of Voluntarism

As stressed earlier, the ultimate aim of an economic policy is to target strong economic growth accompanied by job creation. For these results to be achieved there is a need first of all for economic agents to invest toward modernizing and expanding their production capacity, and secondly for demand to remain strong. The success of an economic policy is therefore measured not by changing the level of a particular instrument but by its ability to stimulate and catalyze production and demand from economic agents. In cases where these behaviors are the result of both rational economic calculations and subjective factors which do not respect an established economic rationality,[7] the economic policymakers must know how to combine the use of rationality – determined by economic theories and lessons learned from an examination of local contexts and realities, and the determinants of decisions made by economic agents in the rest of the world – to design and implement specific measures that build and encourage these desired production and demand behaviors. In fact, the art of economic policy actually resides in the quest for that optimal combination. In a world that is currently experiencing an increasing integration of small and big economies as a result of globalization, the decisions of economic agents around the world are also becoming an important determinant toward the performance of national economies.

The Constraints of Economic Policy

In earlier parts of this book, I defined economic policy as the way in which governments or local authorities use the instruments at their disposal to influence the course of the national economy toward the improved well-being of citizens. It should be noted that this "way" is influenced by the constraints of economic policy. Thus, constraints are an important concept for economic policy. In fact, the whole process of economic policy can be summarized as a process of optimization subjected to a number of constraints. Constraints are restrictions that affect either the selection of goals or the use of instruments, and that economic policymakers are obliged to consider. Among the constraints identified by economic theory, we can cite credibility, rational expectations among economic agents, crowding-out effects that reduce the impact of economic policy measures, the effects of hysteresis, situations of multiple equilibria, the magic square–related dilemma, insufficient knowledge of the transmission mechanisms of economic policy measures, and political cycles.[8] The entire success of economic policy is indeed based on the ability of economic policy officials to identify and overcome these constraints. Constraints influence the effectiveness of an economic policy – that is, the ability of governments to improve on the well-being of citizens through the manipulation of instruments. As a result, the effective management of these constraints is a critical determinant of the success of economic policy. Experience has shown that in the macroeconomic program supported by the IMF, the equilibrium of the balance of payments, which typically is a constraint related to the external financing to the economy, is often treated as the final goal of a government's economic policy. This item will be discussed in detail in Chapter 10, under the constraints of economic policy.

So far I have been able to show that the sequences of a good economic policy are quite complex, even though they can be structured around a set of goals that form a chain of results. The simultaneous, determined pursuit of these goals is likely to lead the economy toward better performance. The contribution of the theoretical framework developed herein does not lie within the individual concepts themselves, which are well known in economic literature. Rather, the contribution lies in the organization of these concepts into an understandable and practical operating framework for policymakers. Be they the old developed countries or the emerging nations that have recently attained remarkable levels of economic growth, as in Asia, the experiences of these countries show that they willingly pursued the operating, intermediate and final goals described above. These experiences shall be discussed in a more detailed manner in the fifth part of this book.

Summary

The aim of this chapter has been to present a conceptual framework for a good economic policy. This approach is likely to revive the economic policy of African states to earn them a place in the context of globalization. The effectiveness of economic policy toward improving the well-being of citizens depends on a clearer and more stable recognition of the role of economic growth and job creation as the final goals of economic policy. Achieving these goals also depends on a greater concentration of economic policy on improving national productive capacity and stimulating strong demand addressed to the economy. Other operating goals were also highlighted, such as the search for the confidence of economic agents, the practice of good governance (a good transmission factor of economic policy measures), improving the quality of infrastructure, the search for social cohesion, the pursuit of macroeconomic stability, improving the business environment, orienting the tastes and preferences of economic agents toward the goods and services offered by the national economy, strengthening human capital, the search for an adequate level of funding of the economy, and regional and multilateral integration. In the fifth part, I will show that the conceptual framework presented herein pretty much describes the experience of emerging economies, and even developed economies, which have made advances in the formulation and conduct of economic policy.

In the final analysis, although the conceptual framework that I have developed seems somewhat unusual and innovative, it is in actual fact nothing less than an adaptation of the successful framework widely used by central banks around the world to formulate and conduct monetary policy. In fact, for some time now, central banks have been thinking about monetary policy in terms of final, intermediate and operating goals, and instruments for implementing monetary policy. Although these goals are, in the context of monetary policy, different from those I presented above for the overall economic policy – which is normal, since monetary policy is a more restricted area as well as being an instrument of economic policy – the logical links established between them are the same as those governing them in the context of monetary policy.

In comparison, in the more restricted field of monetary policy, the final goals are often price stability, promoting employment and economic growth; it all depends on individual countries. Each country, therefore, gives these goals the importance it deems necessary according to its own values and social choices. Nevertheless, the choices are limited to these variables. In some countries the law establishes a hierarchy between these goals. In others, the law does not establish a hierarchy and thus leaves the central bank the freedom to determine how it pursues these final goals simultaneously. Intermediate goals often revolve around certain monetary aggregates, credit aggregates or long-term interest rates. As for the operating goals, they often include the monetary base or short-term interest rates.[9] As for the instruments of monetary policy, they are often categorized either as direct or as indirect instruments. Direct instruments refer to the direct regulatory power possessed by the central bank, allowing it, for example, to make decisions directly affecting their operating goals. Hence, thanks to their regulatory and administrative powers, central banks can set interest rates, fix a rate for the reserve requirements or even engage in direct lending. These actions will affect short-term interest rates or the monetary base. As concerns indirect instruments, the best known are the open-market operations and other lending policies of central banks, which aim to exert indirect influence on the operating goals, including short-term interest rates, through influencing the amount of money that the central bank injects into the financial system.

Although the act of organizing monetary policy along this framework has contributed significantly to its effectiveness, it is rather surprising that this success has so far not spurred research into ways to adapt and then apply this analytical framework to the overall economic policy. However, I must recognize that it is much more in developing countries, and perhaps especially in Africa, that the overall economic policy does not yet seem defined and implemented in accordance with a scheme of this nature. As we shall see when considering a few examples of the successful elaboration and conduct of economic policy as illustration, the revealed economic policy of developed and emerging countries show that, in general, their economic policy actions fall within this scheme. A shift by African countries toward formulating and implementing their economic policy in the light of a conceptual framework of the type developed in the first part of this book could then inject a little more rigor and method into their economic policy actions, and truly help to develop a pattern of good economic policy in a bid to promote their development in a world marked by globalization, where the challenges are enormous.

Finally, I can conclude that the conceptual framework of a good economic policy developed in this chapter seems to be closer to what a real and effective economic policy should be – that is, aiming at improving the well-being of citizens. Indeed, the facts have amply vindicated the critics of the simplistic schemes devised in the 1980s, for which the Washington Consensus was the prototype. These patterns argued that it was sufficient for those responsible for economic policy to seek the consolidation of public finances, liberalize the financial sector, liberalize foreign trade and foreign direct investment, and deregulate and privatize in order for the economy to return to a higher level of growth and well-being for all. Most of the criticism of the concept as a policy framework focused primarily on the fact that it presented liberalism as the guiding principle of economic policy. This led some observers to equate the Washington Consensus framework to an exercise in the defense of market fundamentalism. There was also the fact that countries that have implemented these requirements did not necessarily see the return of economic growth as promised.[10]

But beyond the criticism of the link with market fundamentalism, it seems that another critique is equally or even more important: that of the view of economic policy merely as an exercise in the manipulation of instruments. By referring to the concept of managing for results, it appears that the approach advocated by the Washington Consensus as well as the sectoral approach focuses on the activities and not on the results, since the fiscal consolidation, trade liberalization and other liberalization measures, although important elements of any strategy for economic policy, are at best only one of many instruments of economic policy. These instruments do not report results in terms of employment and economic growth, which enable the assessment of the effectiveness of economic policy.

Conclusion to Part One

In this first part, I have first of all tried to show the shortcomings of the current sectoral approach to economic policy. This sectoral approach consists of conceiving economic policy from an essentially sectoral angle – that is to say, by approaching economic policy through major sectoral issues and, consequently, conceiving economic policy as a mere juxtaposition of sectoral policies. To remedy the shortcomings of this sectoral approach, I have attempted to outline conceptually what seems to be a good economic policy, by building on concepts drawn from economic theory. The second part of this book will allow us to further examine this framework by specifying further the main constituents of the various goals and instruments that will form the conceptual framework I have just developed.

Part Two

GOALS AND INSTRUMENTS FOR A SYSTEMIC ECONOMIC POLICY FOR AFRICA'S REVIVAL

The second part of this book is dedicated to a more detailed discussion of the conceptual framework which could inspire a renewed African economic policy. Part Two therefore examines the goals that a good economic policy should set. It equally examines the instruments of economic policy, and the orientation that a good African economic policy should give to their use, and the means of implementing the economic policy measures selected by the authorities.

Chapter Three

FINAL GOALS FOR A SYSTEMIC ECONOMIC POLICY

"No opportunity is more important than the opportunity to work."

Joseph E. Stiglitz, Nobel laureate in economics[1]

Introduction: The Web of Goals in African Countries Still Prevent Concentration on Fundamental Final Goals

In March 2002, I was in an African country on mission under my employer, the African Development Bank (ADB). This country is one of the poorest countries in the world. There, the income per capita is about 250 US dollars per annum. Although according to official statistics the country experienced an annual average growth rate of 5 per cent from 1999–2002, I came to realize that the economic situation of the country continued to be marked by a high level of poverty. According to the same statistics, the primary sector, which is essentially agriculture, was the first economic sector of the country, both in terms of its contribution to the gross domestic product, which was about forty per cent, and its contribution to employment, given that it provided about eighty per cent of jobs in the economy. The country earned about ninety per cent of its revenue in foreign currency from the production and export of a limited number of primary agricultural products. The financial sector, which had experienced serious difficulties in the years preceding my visit, was gradually recovering after the government implemented a rehabilitation program. Infrastructure in practically all the sectors had deteriorated considerably. Socially, educational indicators were still alarming despite the positive impact on the number of children provided with education by a recent government policy instituting free primary education. The health situation had also deteriorated considerably under the effect of the HIV/AIDS pandemic. On employment, though a key variable of human well-being, the national statistics bureau did not have reliable data, despite the remarkable progress made with the help of donors to strengthen the statistical capacity of the country, which had led to an improvement of the collection of other statistical indicators. The aim of that mission was to elaborate, for this country, what we call the Country Strategy Paper (CSP).[2] To anyone familiar with the functioning of international institutions financing development, the CSP is a programming document which determines, for a period of about three to five years, the strategic scope and orientation of cooperation between a country and the ADB group. In fact, the purpose of this paper – elaborated in close collaboration with the authorities and all stakeholders in the country's development efforts –is not only to define the strategic goals that the ADB will pursue within the framework of its assistance to this country's economic development, but also to identify priority areas for financing in order to achieve these goals. The CSP is therefore a key cooperation document between the ADB and its borrowing member countries, which makes the CSP elaboration mission one of the most important missions that officials of the ADB group carry out in a member country during a programming cycle.

As is tradition, the elaboration of CSPs should always depend on the national development strategy. The CSP, elaborated by the ADB for the country, must aim at supporting efforts implemented by authorities themselves to promote the economic development and social progress of their country. Therefore, it is only natural that in my discussions with these authorities, one of my goals is to be able to seize as completely as possible efforts deployed by the authorities in this light. The government's economic program aimed at reducing poverty, which, as I described, affected a significant part of the population, and prevented several citizens of that country from fully using their productive capacities to live a happy and satisfactory life. This program was described in detail in the Poverty Reduction Strategy Paper (PRSP) that the authorities had elaborated within the framework of a participative process involving not only all the national stakeholders but also the entire community of donors to the country. The PRSP served as a reference for the actions of the government and stakeholders in the fight against poverty, making poverty reduction the ultimate goal of the efforts of the entire country. To attain this goal, the PRSP indicated that the government, with the support of stakeholders, may concentrate its efforts on three precise domains, known as priority areas, of the poverty reduction strategy. These areas included the promotion of economic growth, good governance and a number of transversal themes like science, technology and the fight against HIV/AIDS. These three priority areas were then given in a set of goals. In all, according to my deduction, poverty reduction included three priority areas (those indicated above), more than thirty subgoals and close to forty statistical indicators, which were supposed to enable the authorities and stakeholders to monitor progress made toward the achievement of the goals.

The country had also subscribed to the Millennium Development Goals that world leaders adopted in September 2000 in New York during the United Nations Millennium Summit. These goals aim at encouraging governments of developing countries to take necessary measures to reduce poverty in their countries, particularly through sustained efforts to promote access of the most vulnerable populations to basic social services – education, health, potable water and hygiene and environmental protection. These goals are in themselves praiseworthy, and it would not occur to anyone to dismiss the considerable positive changes that their achievement would represent for a country ravaged by poverty. However, I always thought that these goals should have included a specific goal on employment, given that no one denies the fundamental and irreplaceable role that employment plays in the promotion of the well-being of each of us.[3] I envisaged rightly, as during the mission to that country one of the fundamental concerns of the ordinary citizens I met was employment, but this question neither featured among the priority areas of the poverty reduction strategy of their country, nor even in the Millennium Development Goals to which their government had subscribed to.

It seemed clear to me, and I still hold the conviction that we cannot seek a solution to the problem of poverty apart from concentrating on the means to provide a job to every citizen. In fact, whether you are a citizen of a typical low-income African country, where the income per capita is (as in the country in question) about 250 US dollars per annum, or a national of an industrialized and rich country, where income per capita exceeds 28,000 US dollars per annum, it is certain that among the variables which determine your personal happiness and the level of satisfaction and fulfillment that your life brings to you (such as your health, that of your family and those who are dear to you, your capacity to benefit from adequate medical care when you fall sick, your level of education and that of your children, even the stability of your marriage and love life, the quality of the environment where you live, the quality of public services that your government can offer you, particularly water supply and hygiene, transport and the manner in which you perceive the future of your children), the possession of a job and your chances of finding another if you lose it occupy an absolutely fundamental place. Therefore, it may not be too much to say that employment constitutes a fundamental determinant of our well-being. As such, its promotion ought to be found at the center of any poverty reduction strategy in African countries.

Within the framework of the daily implementation of this poverty reduction strategy, the government also strived to apply a number of reform measures in the agricultural sector, aiming particularly at rationalizing the role of several intermediaries intervening in the marketing chain of agricultural products, reforming the parastatal sector, and also taking measures to improve public financial management, particularly the control of public expenditures. The country had experienced a series of increases in public spending, and as such, besides the support that it gave the central bank in developing and implementing monetary policy in order to ensure that inflation was controlled, the IMF also paid particular attention to public spending.[4] Although the government implemented these measures, particularly under pressure from donors, I observed that among these, one of the major concerns to which donors paid particular attention was obviously macroeconomic stability, and also the allocation of sufficient resources by the government to priority sectors for poverty reduction. To satisfy donors at this last level, the authorities had established a list of activities that they referred to as "pro-poors" and whose financing was assured no matter the budgetary circumstances. This implied that they undertook to devote a substantial level of their budgetary resources to these activities no matter the level of budgetary revenue. This list included particularly education, health and agriculture. An official of the Ministry of Agriculture asserted that the government respected its financing commitments to these priority activities, particularly that the financing would always arrive on time, which seemed a good thing to me. Practically, all the bilateral and multilateral donors insisted the priority sectors receive enough financing. Some among them made it a necessary condition for the disbursement of their aid. It is clear that the action of the authorities in their daily economic management, particularly the measures that they took in the different above-mentioned domains, would constitute indispensable elements of the economic-reforms program of any government that had the responsibility of this country in identical circumstances.

Although the above description refers to the situation of the country I visited, I think that it could also describe the situation prevailing in several African countries.

In fact, African governments undertook to make poverty reduction the main goal of their development efforts. This commitment is praiseworthy except that, practically, conceiving poverty as a multidimensional phenomenon led most of these countries to establish a multitude of goals, most often to the detriment of fundamental goals like creating and maintaining jobs and attaining a high and inclusive economic growth rate, which are the only achievements capable of catalyzing progress toward poverty reduction. Due to this multitude of goals, conceiving economic policy simply as a question of optimally allocating public expenditure among priority sectors on the one hand and lower-priority sectors on the other, all accompanied by the implementation of measures mostly from the Washington Consensus – most often without a clear and stable vision of the goals discussed in Part One – is currently a widespread practice on the continent.

Poverty Reduction: Still Operationally Ambiguous for Economic Policy

Today, the concept of poverty has become omnipresent in development policy discussions. Whether it concerns policies recommended by international consensus for developing countries or those elaborated by the countries themselves to face their economic and social difficulties, poverty reduction is invariably proclaimed as a sovereign goal. Although it is not easy to precisely situate the exact origins of the consensus on poverty in the economic policy of developing countries, we can estimate that this traces back to the 1970s, when for the first time the World Bank announced that it would raise the fight against poverty to the top of its priorities in poor countries. Several factors surely contributed to this announcement, but we cannot fail to mention the commitment of Robert S. McNamara, then president of the World Bank. In fact, deeply touched and greatly shocked by the suffering he witnessed for himself during his several trips to many developing countries, particularly in Africa, he made poverty reduction a major theme of his speech in the Annual Meetings of the World Bank held in 1974 in Nairobi, Kenya.[5]

It was the first time that the theme of poverty had taken prime position in such an important speech of a World Bank president, particularly one made on the occasion of the institution's Annual Meetings. This evolution – let's rather say revolution – not only marked the starting point of a reorientation of operational goals and priorities of the World Bank in favor of the fight against poverty in developing countries, but it also propelled this notion to the center of the international discussion on foreign aid and on economic policies that developing countries should implement to improve their situation. To affirm these changes, the World Bank made poverty reduction the central theme of its principal report, the *World Development Report*, in 1990. Following the World Bank's adoption of poverty reduction as the goal of its interventions in those developing countries soliciting its financial support, other major development actors like the United Nations Systems, regional development banks and bilateral aid agencies were also to adopt poverty reduction as the goal of their aid programs in developing countries.

This focus on poverty did not take place smoothly. Though it was relatively easy for the donor community and for developing countries to agree that poverty reduction should be the goal of their aid and economic policy respectively, a debate quickly started over the meaning of the concept of poverty. In fact, effectively fighting against poverty commanded that we agreed not only on an operational definition of poverty – that is, a definition which is useful to the conception of interventions aimed at fighting against poverty and its major determinants – but also on its measurement. A consensus on these two elements is really indispensable for the elaboration of an adequate strategy against poverty. Concerning the measurement of poverty, it is necessary for a periodic evaluation of progress made in order to proceed, in the light of this evaluation, to the necessary policy adjustments. The search for an operational definition of poverty and the indicators to measure it, which are necessary for a regular monitoring of poverty, quickly met with considerable conceptual and statistical difficulties. These still persist to date, and singularly complicate the task of African governments and their international partners in terms of the planning, elaboration, implementation and monitoring of policies aimed precisely at reducing poverty.

Conceptual difficulties emanate essentially from the fact that, contrary to intuition, poverty is an ambiguous concept, even if we think we can easily recognize it. For example, the definition of poverty is not only based on objective elements such as the level of income. Subjective considerations which depend on social contexts, even the era in which we find ourselves, rapidly intervene. It is therefore likely to vary considerably from one country to another, and even from one region to another within the same country and from one era to another. Poverty therefore varies according to the fundamental perceptions in force in the society. These perceptions are themselves influenced by the level already attained by countries on different components of well-being. As such, it is accepted that poverty will not be characterized in the same manner in a country where the average level of income is high as it will be in a country where it is very low. Similarly, poverty will not be perceived in the same way in the different regions.

Consequently, despite the preponderant role of objective elements like the level of income, a complete and rigorous definition involves resorting to conventions which themselves vary according to the conception that the considered society has of its well-being and social justice. Rigorously defining the concept of poverty necessitates making three fundamental choices, and consequently goes far beyond mere economic considerations to embrace the ethical, intellectual, political and social values which prevail in the country.[6]

The first choice is on the elements which characterize well-being in the society and, by inference, poverty. Should we be limited to income or should we consider all the elements which determine the living conditions of persons or households such as access to education, health, decent housing and the quality of the environment?[7] The second societal choice is on the definition of what is generally called the poverty line, which helps to distinguish the poor from the nonpoor. In other words, how can we determine the level of well-being below which a person or household will be considered poor? For example, should we take into consideration the size and composition of the household? The third societal choice is on the degree of the intensity of poverty – that is, the gap between the situation of persons considered poor and the poverty line. Should we therefore be concerned with the importance of this gap in the definition of poverty? And if so, what level of poverty below the poverty line is acceptable to the society?

What elements do we take into account? A monetary approach (income) or a multidimensional approach (living conditions)?

The first conceptual challenge for any attempt at finding an operational definition of poverty is that of determining the elements of well-being to be considered. Practically, it was generally calculated as the monetary equivalent of minimum nutritional needs per day for a representative individual or household.[8] However, considering the need to promote global human development, the international community progressively moved away from this conception of well-being, which it considered restrictive, and instead privileged a multidimensional conception, according to which poverty is not only characterized by an insufficient monetary income but also by an insufficient access to basic social services such as education, health, housing, access to drinking water and hygiene services, and an environment of the best quality.

This multidimensional approach was expanded by the consideration of participatory notions, according to which the absence of participation in the political process may also be one of the characteristics of poverty. It is this multidimensional approach to poverty (of which the Millennium Development Goals are the most concrete expression) that several African countries adopted within the framework of their poverty reduction strategy. However, this opposition between an approach based on income and a multidimensional approach is only visible insofar as most available studies indicate an almost perfect correlation between income and access to services linked to other dimensions of poverty. Thus, a person or household which may be classified poor in terms of its income may also be classified poor if we consider other dimensions of well-being such as access to education, health and other services.[9]

Which poverty line should we retain?

Another conceptual difficulty faced by any attempt to define poverty is on the choice of a poverty line – that is, a line of demarcation between the poor and the rich. The challenge here is twofold: the first is related to choosing between an objective approach to measuring poverty – that is, an approach based on objectively observable elements such as income or the objective elements of living conditions such as access to education, health or drinking water – and a subjective approach which depends on valuing the opinion of persons or households on their own situation. In this subjective approach, appreciating poverty is based on the opinion that individuals themselves have of their level of well-being in relation to its different determinants, if they estimate that their income makes them poor, or if they estimate that they have sufficient access to the different constitutive elements of well-being in its multidimensional sense.[10]

Once the choice between an objective and subjective approach is made, we have to then determine the level below which a person or household will be considered poor. Here also, everything varies according to the conception that the society makes of its social model. If it aims for a high level of social justice and reduction of inequalities, then the choice will be in favor of an approach known as the relative poverty line. If this is not the case, it will retain an absolute poverty line. Practically, the relative poverty line consists in classifying as poor those persons or households whose income is lower than a certain percentage of the average income or the median income of the population. There is no scientific rule enabling the determination of this percentage and it is generally established to reflect the consensus in terms of social justice. For example, the European Union retained the line at 60 per cent of the average income of the state in which the person or household lives. Thus, the poor are those whose income, after transfers, is lower than 60 per cent of the median income of the state in which they live.[11]

Establishing the absolute poverty line is much more complicated and generally starts from determining the minimum daily caloric intake necessary to keep someone alive. As we have indicated, this depends on a number of factors including geographical environment and the age of the individual. This minimum daily caloric need is then translated into a basket of minimum consumer goods. The absolute poverty line is therefore defined as the minimum level of resources necessary for procuring this minimum consumer basket. The poor, then, are defined as those whose incomes are lower than this level of minimum resources. It is this approach based on an absolute poverty line that the World Bank uses to calculate poverty rates in developing countries.[12] It is also that used by most African countries to calculate poverty rates, often indicated in their poverty reduction strategies. As already seen, the poverty lines calculated as such, and the estimates of poverty rates which result from it, are likely to vary not only in space but also in time, according to variables such as composition by age of the population and the structure of prices in force in the country.

Absolute poverty lines calculated as such suppose that we have an essentially monetary conception of poverty, in which poverty is curbed only from its monetary angle. If we place ourselves in a multidimensional approach to poverty where we consider the other dimensions of well-being beyond monetary income, less progress has been made to date toward defining the absolute or relative poverty line. However, we should take note of the work done by the United Nations Development Program (UNDP), which calculates and publishes every year, for close to two decades now, a Human Development Index (HDI) for each country.[13] This index, published in the annual *Human Development Report* (HDR), measures the opportunities that a person has to fully exploit his human potential to lead the most productive and creative life possible. In calculating this indicator, three major factors are considered to be contributing more to human development. This concerns the capacity to live the longest time possible and in good health, access to education and the capacity to earn an income that helps to lead a decent life. The HDI is thus calculated as the arithmetical average of three indices: the longevity index measured by life expectancy at birth, the level-of-education index measured on the basis of the adult literacy rate and the gross rate of schooling, and the Gross Domestic Product per capita index. The HDR also calculates other different types of indicators to measure other dimensions of human development, such as a sexo-specific human development index, which corrects the human development index to reflect the inequalities between men and women, and a women's participation indicator. All these indicators prove the success of recent efforts aimed at better apprehending well-being. One of the major limits of this important effort undertaken by the UNDP to calculate the HDI is that, although it helps to classify countries according to their level of human development, it does not still help to situate, in a given country, the proportion of the population which may be below a certain human development line. Such an indicator might be the equivalent, within the framework of a multidimensional conception of poverty, of the poverty lines raised earlier for monetary poverty.

Should we take into account the intensity of poverty?

Even after making the necessary choice to retain the different dimensions of poverty and calculate the poverty line, an important issue still needs to be resolved in order to finalize a national consensus on the definition of poverty. It is the issue of the place to give the intensity of poverty – that is, the gap which exists between the poor and the poverty line. In other words, should we be concerned about the depth of poverty? Here also, the answer varies according to the type of social justice that the society is devoted to. In a society attached to a certain social justice, this variable will be considered in the definition and monitoring of poverty. Therefore, there exist depth indicators of poverty. For example, among the indicators approved by the European Union to monitor social isolation in the union, the "Laeken" indicators contain an intensity indicator of poverty which is the ratio of the difference between the poverty line and the average income of the poor brought back to the poverty line. The higher this indicator, the greater the distance between the average income of the poor and the poverty line; to put it otherwise, the more the poor are poor. The Laeken indicators also include the calculation of the Gini index for the poor – that is, calculated only in the subgroup of the poor. This helps to build an idea of income inequalities among the poor, in other words to know to what extent some of the poor are poorer than others. Concerning African countries, most of them, following the indicators of the Millennium Development Goals, give very little attention to this issue of the intensity of poverty.

As we can see, the definition of poverty raises fundamental conceptual difficulties which can only be resolved by resorting to the value system of each country, group or society. Thus, the definition retained by each country must in principle be the result of a certain number of arbitrages and reflect the equilibrium of political, cultural, ethnic and economic influences. Therefore, we easily understand that the concept of poverty is a fundamentally complex and unstable concept, given that it varies in time and space according to the evolution of these different influences. In the meantime, African countries on their part, following the dominant position in the international community, mostly adhere to a multidimensional conception of poverty, calculate an absolute poverty line based on the definition of a minimum daily caloric need, and only give the intensity of poverty a minor role in the definition of poverty. As we will see, this conceptual difficulty is also accompanied in several African countries by measurement difficulties.

Difficulties of measuring poverty in Africa

For the concept of poverty to be useful to economic policy, it does not suffice to define it even by adopting certain conventions which are more subjective than objective. We should also be able to measure it conveniently; yet this is not the case. As asserted by the economist Angus Deaton, one of the leading world experts on poverty measurement: "Estimates of the number of the world's poor and questions about whether it has been decreasing or increasing have given rise to one of the hottest controversies in the development community."[14] Thus, experience shows that it is this other dimension of the concept of poverty which poses more problems to African countries, considering the current weaknesses of their statistical system. Generally, calculating the poverty line requires detailed statistical information on the income and food consumption of households, prices in different regions of the country, as well as other dimensions of poverty retained if we place ourselves in this multidimensional conception. This information is often generated only by household surveys, which are very costly and extremely challenging to implement.

It is for this reason that, considering the limited resources of their statistical apparatus, most African countries collect this information only in well-spaced intervals of time. Table 3.1 below presents the frequency of data collection of some variables which are usually included in a multidimensional definition of poverty and for which statistical information should, in principle, be available and regularly updated within the framework of monitoring poverty. For example, this table shows that data on the proportion of the population living on less than one dollar per day are generally available only once every 3 or 5 years. The same holds for data on the proportion of the population having access to potable water or on infant mortality rates. As it appears, statistical information on the multitude of indicators retained to monitor the evolution of poverty are not available with the regularity we may desire from the point of view of the elaboration and conduct of economic policy.

Table 3.1. Availability of poverty data in africa

	Frequency of availability of data
1. Proportion of the population living on less than $1/day	Every 3–5 years
2. Infant mortality rate	3 years
3. Prevalence of HIV in pregnant women aged 15–49	Available for 1999 only
4. Proportion of births assisted by qualified personnel	3–5 years
5. Ratio of girls compared to boys in primary, secondary and tertiary education	Annual
6. Rate of completion of primary school	Annual
7. Proportion of the population having access to drinking water	3 years

Besides the lack of regular updates, data estimates on rates of poverty and poverty lines are also fraught with significant margins of error, which are inherent in the process of designing and implementing data collection surveys. Thus, for example, studies show that by reducing the repeat period covered by surveys from one month to a week, the estimate of the number of poor people in India could be reduced to 175 million people or a reduction by half of the number of poor people.[15] Finally, conceptual difficulties coupled with difficulties of measurement make it practically impossible to find the real level of poverty which exists in a country. At the very most, we can have estimates which reflect different methodological and statistical choices, determined by the political authorities of the country. These choices themselves vary according to the political and social values of the country.

As such, despite its widespread use in the discussions on development policies, poverty proves to be a notion that is difficult to define with precision. In fact, practical difficulties start as soon as an operating definition of the notion of poverty – that is, a definition that helps to guide the conduct of economic policy with precision toward greater efficiency – cannot be found. On the other hand, faced with several limitations, which are due sometimes to the capacities of statistical systems of African countries and sometimes to value judgments inherent in it, any attempt at measuring poverty poses statistical challenges. These quickly deprive this concept of any claim to satisfy the attributes traditionally associated with the indicators used for the conduct of economic policy, such as being easily measurable and at the lowest possible costs, and being linked by a unique and identifiable relationship with the goal sought. Thus, in conclusion, one can safely posit that the conceptual difficulties linked to the definition of poverty, combined with difficulties of measurement and the irregular updating of data, singularly complicate the usefulness of this concept for the elaboration and conduct of economic policy. In such circumstances, the task is to find another variable, closely related to the goals of poverty reduction, but which lends itself more to economic policy imperatives.

Economic Growth and Job Creation: Final Goals for a Systemic Economic Policy

Work and well-being: Some perspectives drawn from social sciences

As we have already emphasized in the first part of this book, the fundamental goals of economic policy – that is, the strategic reference points which must permanently guide the actions of economic policy officials and serve as the principal criteria for evaluating the results obtained – should come from the choices of the society and its citizens. In this context, a method of finding out which goals citizens would prefer their government pursued in its economic policy may consist in directly questioning them within the framework of an exhaustive survey. However, this method comes up against some difficulties in the African context. In fact, not only are the surveys scarcely carried out in these countries, but it is also difficult to obtain, from the few surveys carried out, information on the preferences of citizens in terms of their choice of national economic policy goals.[16] For lack of credible surveys that can inform us on the preferences of citizens in terms of economic policy, the alternative is to question the different branches of social science – that is, sciences which have as their goal the study of man as a social object. Thus, it seems that throughout their development, different disciplines of the social sciences – whether sociology, philosophy, theology or economic sciences – all came to recognize the fundamental role that employment plays in the well-being of individuals.

In the antiquities and the Middle Ages, work was perceived as having an ambiguous relationship with the well-being of man. It was sometimes considered an indispensable source of well-being and even a necessity for the survival of the human species, sometimes a physical and moral constraint on man, a source of strain and impotence and therefore a factor of reduction in the well-being of man. The German philosopher and economist Karl Marx (1818–1883) saw in work a source of exploitation of man by man. However, the ambiguity which characterized the relationship between work and the well-being of man in the Middle Ages and the antiquities disappeared with the advent of the modern social sciences and made way for a more positive vision of the role of work in human well-being. Modern social sciences thus find in work an indispensable factor of individual development and social integration. This assertion of the positive role of work in well-being sprang up at the beginning of the twentieth century. As such, the French sociologist Emile Durkheim thought of work as satisfactory to man when it is carried out in an organized framework.[17] This intellectual viewpoint continued to strengthen itself in practically all the disciplines of social science.

Among sociologists, Max Weber, one of the greatest social and political thinkers at the end of the nineteenth and the beginning of the twentieth centuries, saw work as a redeeming activity and a means of salvation. In *The Protestant Ethic and the Spirit of Capitalism*, he establishes a link between Protestantism and enterprise and presents a conception of life which recognizes in work an essential dimension of oneself.[18] Thus, he asserts that "the puritan wanted to be a working man, and we are forced to be."[19] According to him, man must be entirely devoted to regular, methodical and effective work. This anchoring of professional ethics in religion will further contribute to valuing work. Some even think that it is one of the factors that sparked off the industrial revolution of the eighteenth century. Sociologists continue to mention the contribution of work to income, which is necessary for man to procure the assets he needs to preserve his living standard.

Beyond sociology, this recognition of the primordial role of work is also strongly anchored in the messages of other disciplines in social science. Thus, the famous British economist Adam Smith, in *An Inquiry into the Nature and Causes of the Wealth of Nations*, one of the founding books of classic economic thought and which many consider one of the founding books of economic liberalism, develops the theory of work value. He considers man's work as the sovereign source of the riches of nations. According to him, it is the work of a nation, which constitutes the sovereign source of all the goods and services that are indispensable to human life, and these goods and services are always either the immediate product of the nations' work or are bought from other nations with income generated by the sale of these goods and services.[20] By developing this thesis of wealth based on man and his work, Adam Smith brilliantly contradicts the thesis supported by mercantilistic economists, according to which the resources of nations depend on the accumulation of precious metals and currency, and therefore on the capacity of public authorities to implement an economic policy, which leads to a surplus of the balance of trade.

Though Adam Smith finds in work the principal source of the wealth of nations, he does not stop there. He is also interested in factors which determine the evolution of these resources in time and finds, once more, a role for work. According to him, increasing wealth depends on the proportion of productive workers in the society, and on efforts aimed at increasing the productivity of work. This increased productivity is the result of the division of labor. Summarily, labor is the principal source of wealth and the division of labor is what permits the increase in productivity of labor, the first driving force of the increase in wealth. The increase in wealth leads to the development of trade insofar as every man produces more than is necessary to satisfy his needs, and the surplus is sold on the market.

According to Smith, the free market stimulates trade, which in turn favors the division of labor, which then increases the wealth of nations. Man's natural propensity toward improving his condition thus becomes one of the major driving forces increasing the resources of a nation over time. Smith further contributed the idea that in this system of exchange of goods, each participant pursues his own interests, but there is an invisible force which guides the outcome toward an optimum, which is beneficial for all participants. This was the departure point of Smith's famous theory of the invisible hand, which has provided the intellectual basis for economic liberalism and modern capitalism. At the same time, labor is the source of wealth through which social links are woven, essentially based on trade. Smith also contributed to the theory of work value, according to which the quantity of work it commands determines the value of an asset. The civilized society is essentially a market society characterized by the interdependence of men, who are sometimes described as producers of goods, sometimes as buyers of goods, always as trade protagonists. This is the departure point of the theory of the invisible hand. Thus, Smith based harmony and social progress on three fundamental pillars: labor, trade and market.

This preponderant role attached to labor in the determination of our well-being may also be highlighted in the evolution of philosophical thought. To Greek philosophers of the antiquity, man always earns his living by the sweat of his brows. The Greeks knew that their well-being, like that of their family and their city, relied on their material activity.[21] Labor is defined as that social conduct in which every one of us participates through his function or his occupation; it plays the role of the great integrator of individuals in social life.[22] Finally, and despite some negative aspects, the economic and social value of work and the sovereign dignity attached to it as a founding element of individual and collective well-being clearly appear in the social thought of yesteryear and today. Fear of losing one's job, and the distress of most unemployed persons, proves that the place of work remains central in the life of man even if, as is often the case, the conditions of work may generate some disutility. As the French sociologist Robert Castel summarizes: "There is no choice but to realize that to date our society has not found credible alternatives which have the same force as work to ensure the recognition and social dignity of individuals. It is still through work – the idea of having it or not, the precariousness or stability of its quality and the rights inherent therein – that the essential social destiny of individuals continues to play."[23]

This truth is not only valid for developed countries; it is also valid for developing countries, and more particularly for Africa. It is mainly around employment that the economic and social destinies of individuals revolve. Even if the phenomenon of poor workers exists, those who have jobs in general cope better compared to those who have none. Finally therefore, social-science specialists assert that work is a powerful factor of development to man, of satisfaction in his family life and successful integration in society. As the eighteenth-century French writer Voltaire said, work keeps away boredom, vice and poverty.

Work: The principal determinant of well-being

All credible studies on living conditions, whether they are carried out in developed or developing countries, show that in a market economy (in which the great majority of world population lives since the collapse of the communist bloc) there exists a strong correlation between employment, income per capita and poverty – that is, between work and well-being. According to the findings of these studies, individual or household poverty is most often the consequence of a lack of employment, which itself leads to income insufficiency. In fact, in a market economy, goods and services which we need for our daily consumption are obtained on markets through a monetary income. Our access to social services is also closely linked to our level of income. In such an economy marked by the preponderance of the role of monetary income, the well-being of every one of us depends, above all, on our capacity to generate sufficient monetary income with which to acquire the goods and services we need for our present and future consumption. This capacity is mainly determined by having or not having a job. This reliance on income and on employment is further emphasized in African countries where social protection systems and social transfers are almost always inefficient.[24] Given that the state cannot single-handedly take care of basic social-service spending such as health and education, our capacity to generate sufficient income, and having or not having a job, becomes a critical element of our access to basic social services, like our well-being and the fight against poverty. Insofar as our capacity to generate this sufficient income is closely linked to our capacity to occupy a paid job, creating the necessary conditions for each citizen to occupy a paid job becomes a goal of capital importance to any effort of poverty reduction and sustainable development in Africa.

To illustrate the importance of income per capita, and also employment, in terms of access to healthcare – one of the most important dimensions of poverty reduction – Tables 3.2 and 3.3 below indicate respectively the distribution of health centers and the sources of finance for health spending in 2000 in Malawi, one of Africa's most poverty stricken countries. As it seems, healthcare expenses were jointly financed by the state and the private sector (that is ordinary citizens from their own resources) and development partners. Table 3.2 shows that the state, through the Ministry of Public Health, owned 392 of the country's 692 health centers, or about 57 per cent. Concerning the financing of healthcare spending, the state (the Ministry of Finance and the Ministry of Local Administration) contributed to the tune of about 26 per cent to healthcare spending, development partners 29 per cent, employers through health insurance funds 19 per cent and the private sector (that is, expenses paid directly by households without being subsequently reimbursed) about 26 per cent, which is very high. If we add the share paid by employers to this proportion (19 per cent), which itself depends directly on the level of employment in the economy, the share of health spending which depends directly on the level of employment attains a high level of about 45 per cent.

Thus, the share of the private sector in financing health expenses – that is, expenses considered to have a high impact on the fight against poverty – tends to be larger in

African countries that have inadequate social protection systems. In this distribution of roles, the state is very often responsible for the financing of infrastructure and personnel. This situation, characterized by a strong participation of households in the financing of services, prevails in practically all the other social services, particularly education, access to drinking water, hygiene, etc. In this circumstance, our individual capacity to generate sufficient monetary income – which only the possession of a job can guarantee, given that public social transfers are in most cases nonexistent and private social transfers are only accessible to a privileged minority – becomes an essential factor of our access to the basic social services necessary for our development and capacity to sustainably come out of poverty.

Table 3.2. Malawi: Distribution of health centers per type and property, 2000[25]

Type	BLM	CHAM	Local administration	MOHP	NGO	Total
Central hospital				4		4
Clinic	27	8	4	2	1	42
Dispensary		8	4	54		66
District hospital				22		22
Health center	1	115	12	288		416
Hospital		27		19		46
Maternity		1	12	2		15
Psychiatric hospital		1		1		2
Rehabilitation center		1			1	2
Voluntary counseling center					3	3
Total	28	161	32	392	4	617

BLM: Banja la Mtsogolo, a nongovernmental organization
CHAM: Christian Health Association of Malawi
MOHP: Ministry of Health and Population
NGO: nongovernmental organization

Table 3.3. Financing of health per source[26]

Source	US dollars (millions)	%
Ministry of Finance	28.4	23
Ministry of Local Administration	3.9	3
Donors	35.9	29
Employers	23.5	19
Households	32.2	26
Total	123.9	100

The important role of income in access to healthcare is also confirmed by most studies which use econometric techniques to estimate the determinants of access to social services. Thus, according to health economists, healthcare demand is mainly determined by the level of income (therefore implicitly by having or not having a job in countries where social transfer systems do not function properly), the distance separating patients from health centers and the quality of services provided there. Still in the health sector, after having advocated cost recovery (see the Bamako Consensus, an initiative by African ministers of health, which aimed at improving the provision of health care at health centers in Sub-Saharan Africa through increased participation of local communities) with the aim of ensuring the sustainability of finance for the health sector, African countries quickly realized that, while modest, the share borne by the patient is most often out of reach of the average citizen, especially the unemployed, and consequently constitutes a major restraint on access to healthcare.

In the educational sector, the policy of free primary schooling, instituted with the help of donors, aimed at generalizing access to education and making universal access to education a reality. However, we understand that this policy cannot, at the risk of provoking a serious financing crisis, be spread to all levels of education, particularly in secondary and higher education. Free access to education and healthcare is therefore not for tomorrow. As such, the data available for the education sector also confirm the same economic reality of the monetary contribution carried out by the poor and other populations vulnerable to educational financing. The example of Malawi, one of the most poverty-stricken countries, where the income per capita is not more than 250 US dollars per annum, is also illustrative in this regard. Thus, despite the suppression of primary school fees, poor households in Malawi continued to devote a high proportion of their meager resources to finance the education of their children, such as the purchase of school books and uniforms, transport fares to school, secondary school fees, contributions to different funds established in the institutions to ensure maintenance of infrastructure and other ongoing charges. The share of their already low income that households belonging to the poorest class devoted to financing the educational expenses of their children was estimated at 26 per cent.

The few examples mentioned above, drawn from educational and health sectors, show that as a fundamental determinant of our capacity to earn an income, employment is also at the center of our capacity to have satisfactory access to different basic social services and therefore to avoid poverty. Figure 3.1 below illustrates the central role of economic growth and employment in our well-being and the fight against poverty.

Employment and economic growth are inseparable from the improvement of well-being

I have demonstrated that even if employment fulfills significant social functions, particularly the fact that it constitutes a fundamental factor of integration, peace and social stability, it is also through its economic function as the source of income that it plays a decisive role in the well-being of a society, and that of each of its members taken individually. This results from the fact that the income earned through work provides us the means to better resolve all the other problems that society and its members can face, whether they are problems of poverty, environmental quality, social inequalities or access to basic social services.

In order to improve upon our capacity to resolve these problems over time, it is necessary that the income of the nation increases. It is the major reason for which policy officials

Figure 3.1. Employment and economic growth are at the center of the well-being of each of us and that of the nation in general

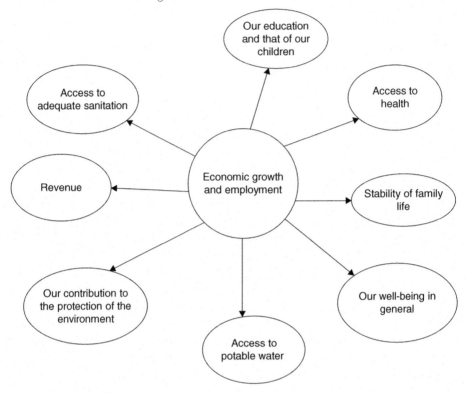

should set this continuous process of increasing the nation's income (what economists call economic growth) as a fundamental final goal. In fact, employment without economic growth may not fully improve the well-being of citizens. Let us imagine a society in which everybody works but where the income is insufficient to enable them to procure the tangible and intangible assets they need for their well-being. It is obvious that in such a society the citizens will not attain the level of well-being they desire. Similarly, let us imagine a society which experiences strong economic growth, without however being accompanied by sufficient job creation. This means that the product of this growth is the fruit of the labor of only part of the population and only this part will then benefit from the fruits of growth. In such a society, the greater part of the population does not participate in growth and therefore does not have the income necessary for its well-being. It appears, then, that economic growth and employment are inseparable in their contribution to the general well-being of the nation. It is therefore the reason for which economic policy officials should establish these two variables as the final goals of their economic policy.

The employment–economic growth correlation

If economic growth and employment are thus inseparable in their contribution to the well-being of the nation, what relationship exists between the two variables? In other words, are they compatible or incompatible variables? Fortunately, as a general rule, they are compatible; that is, they can be pursued simultaneously. In fact, from the point of view of supply, economic growth can originate from two sources: either from an increase in the productivity of factors of production, including labor, or an increase in the quantity of factors of production used, including labor also.[27] In both cases, economic growth is the main driving force of job creation, whether it is due to productivity increases or increased use of factors of production.

When economic growth is essentially the result of increases in productivity, these may be due either to technological progress or to the improvement of the quality of the factors of production. In both cases, the result is an improvement of the process of production, which helps to attain a higher level of production with the same quantity of factors. In this hypothesis, where economic growth results more from increases in productivity, we may ask whether such economic growth also contributes to the goal of full use of factors, including labor, or if, on the contrary, it destroys jobs, in which case there would be incompatibility between the two fundamental final goals of economic policy as I see them for Africa – that is, economic growth and the search for full employment of factors of production, including labor. The response here is affirmative. In fact, in a process of economic growth stimulated by increases in productivity, the sectors which record increases in productivity may experience job destructions, but the increase in income from growth generally leads to an increase in global demand which is itself satisfied by an increase in production in other sectors. This increase in production needs an increased use of factors of production, including labor, so much so that even growth stimulated by increases in productivity can finally create jobs.

When economic growth results from an increased use of factors of production the relationship that links it to job creation is more direct and unambiguous. However, such a process quickly stumbles on the fact that the labor reserves that can be exploited are obviously limited by the size of the working population of the country. That is why economists always privilege the search for growth based on increases in productivity. The search for strong and sustainable growth is therefore the best means of promoting job creation. For this reason, economic growth and job creation seem to be compatible goals and inseparable from any economic policy strategy aimed at improving the well-being of citizens. Economic policy officials should therefore establish as final goals the promotion of economic growth and the achievement of the maximum level of employment in the economy. To be really complete on this issue of final goals of economic policy, I need to review good practices in the world in order to compare them to the analysis that I have just developed, and draw lessons from it.

Overview of Practices on Fixing Final Goals of Economic Policy

When studying the experiences of African countries in setting the final goals of economic policy one can broadly distinguish two periods. The first is from the 1970s until about the early 2010s. During this period, poverty reduction, given its multidimensional meaning, was proclaimed the final goal of economic policy in most African countries. The second period runs from about 2011 until today. During this second period African economic policymakers appear to increasingly make reference to employment and inclusive growth in their economic policy discourse. Although the causes of the change may be many, the start of this second period appears to coincide with the start of the Arab Spring, the revolutions which started in Tunisia and swept the Arab World, perceived as a result of high levels of unemployment and growing inequality in these countries. It remains, however, to be seen whether this apparent shift toward employment and growth in the final goals of economic policy will be real and lasting.

An examination of good practices in both formerly industrialized North American and Western European countries and newly industrialized Asian countries shows that it is by placing employment and growth at the center of their economic policy that they found the orientation, inspiration, effectiveness and stability to make the economic success they experience today possible. When I study economic policy throughout the world, I quickly realize that countries which developed rapidly are mainly those that were able to elaborate and implement an effective economic policy based on a sustainable and stable anchoring to the two final goals of the search for full employment for their citizens and strong economic growth. On the other hand, countries whose economic policy lacked stability and vision because they pursued several varied and less clear final goals were unable to concentrate on economic growth and job creation and, consequently, often experienced stagnation and economic decline. This is particularly the case with African countries.

Thus, at the level of the European Union, the promotion of full employment has always been a fundamental goal of economic policy. The Extraordinary European Council devoted to employment, held in Luxemburg in 1997, recommended that the strategy of the EU on employment should focus on four major themes: employability, entrepreneurship, adaptability and equal opportunities. In the European Summit of Lisbon in March 2000, member countries of the EU established a new strategic goal to make the union the most dynamic and competitive economy in the world, capable of generating sustainable growth with more high-quality jobs and greater social cohesion. In order to attain the goal of full employment before 2010, established by the European Council of Lisbon, the new strategy of the union published in January 2003 established several priorities: to reduce the unemployment rate, encourage women to enter the labor market, encourage people at the age of retirement to remain in the labor market, promote apprenticeship throughout life, promote entrepreneurship and fight undeclared work. In a famous report in which it was noted that the strategy assigned several goals to the union, contributing to lack of targeting and inadequate concentration on fundamental goals, a working group presided by former Dutch prime minister Wim Kock recommended that the efforts of the union henceforth be concentrated on the promotion of employment and economic growth, which should again become fundamental goals of the economic policy of every member country. According to the recommendations of this working party, every member country of the EU should draw up an annual plan for job creation and growth recovery and be answerable to the commission for its implementation. Also, in the broad guidelines for economic policy that the European Union Commission used to guide its member countries in the elaboration and conduct of their economic policy, emphasis was placed on the promotion of employment and economic growth.

Moreover, in order to effectively contribute to the pursuit of this full-employment goal in the European Union, the monetary policy strategy adopted by the European Central Bank (ECB) in 1998, and which continues to guide the conduct of monetary policy in the eurozone today, is based on two pillars. First, a monetary analysis pillar, which aims at considering, in the projections carried out for the needs of monetary policy decisions, monetary factors affecting the outlook of inflation; second, an economic analysis pillar, which aims at considering nonmonetary factors affecting the outlook of inflation, such as employment. That is to say, the monetary policy of the ECB is not only determined by purely monetary considerations but also by the evolution of the employment situation in the union, even if the statutes of the ECB establish as the overarching goal of monetary policy the achievement of price stability. Thus, for example, if monetary factors project a slowing down of inflation, it is not impossible that the ECB will take into account the employment outlook in its monetary policy decisions.

At the level of budgetary policy, the European Union exercises an influence on budgetary policies of member countries, particularly through the Stability and Growth Pact (SGP), which was laboriously elaborated by European leaders in June 1997 during the European Council of Amsterdam. Eager to guarantee the stability of the future European currency, the euro, they imagined this mechanism to limit budgetary deficits of member countries after the single currency went into force. In 2005, European leaders reformed this important system of European macroeconomic management with precisely the aim of introducing a consideration of the budgetary impact of measures in favor of employment and economic growth in the appreciation of the budgetary position of a member state within the framework of the implementation of the SGP (see Box 3.1).

In the United States, employment also occupies a central position among the economic policy goals. The search for full employment of factors of production and strong economic growth is a constant in the history of American economic policy. Thus, from 1946, the law on employment (Employment Act 1946) provides that "it is the continuing policy and responsibility of the federal government to [...] promote full employment and production."[28] It is not only the federal government that is enjoined to search for full employment; the Federal Reserve, the American central bank, is also obliged by law to pursue a double goal: price stability and the realization of maximum employment in the economy. Reflecting this double mandate, it is almost always by referring to recent and anticipated trends of employment and inflation in the United States that the Federal Open Market Committee (FOMC; the organ that decides the monetary policy of the United States) justifies in the press releases that sanction its meetings its decisions concerning the present and future orientation of monetary policy. This means that, to anyone who fully understands the importance of monetary policy among the wide range of instruments at the disposal of the authorities in charge of economic policy, the improvement of the employment situation is one of the goals foregrounded by economic policy authorities in the United States.

Even in the newly industrialized countries of Asia, economic policy was, from the beginning of the process which resulted in their rapid industrialization, firmly anchored in the pursuit of the final goals of economic growth and employment. It was particularly the case in South Korea, where, within the framework of its first development plan, the search for economic growth was established as the only major goal for its economic policy.[29]

Moreover, the new president elected in 2007 did not depart from this orientation and baptized the government program 747 – that is, achieve an economic growth rate of 7 per cent per annum, attain a level of income per capita of 40,000 US dollars per annum and raise his country to the status of 7th world economy.

We should also consider the discussion on the introduction of a social clause in the agreements of the World Trade Organization (WTO), which in 1995 generated intense debate among experts in international trade. This clause expressed not so much the desire of developed countries to promote the rights of workers and international standards of work in developing countries, as they tried to make us think, but rather their desire to protect jobs in sectors of their economies that they considered exposed to increasing competition of exports from developing countries. In fact, under the pretext that the competitiveness of poor countries in some sectors was the result of their failure to adhere to the international standards of work adopted by the International Labor Organization (ILO), developed countries insisted during the trade negotiations of the Uruguay Round that a "social clause" be included in the WTO agreements. This clause authorizes member countries of the WTO to take restrictive measures on imports from a country if it is established that this country does not respect international standards of work.

As Final Goals of Economic Policy Are Economic Growth and Employment Exempt from Criticism?

Today, we constantly hear criticisms of the concept of economic growth as the final goal of economic policy. The criticism most often advanced is that the link between economic growth and the well-being of citizens would be weakened. Thus, some activities which contribute to economic growth may not contribute to the improvement of the well-being of citizens. The relationship between economic growth and well-being would as such be relaxed. There is also the impact of economic growth on the environment, which would not be systematically calculated and reduced from this. This means economic growth as we measure it presently would perhaps be overestimated. Some economists also think that the employment content of economic growth is reduced, alongside the beneficial effects of economic growth. And in the context of African countries, the contribution of employment to the well-being of citizens is often doubted under the pretext that practically everyone works, but that it does not alter their well-being or their relation with poverty. Despite all these criticisms, economists and political decision-makers are practically unanimous on the fact that in the present state of knowledge, strong economic growth and highest quality jobs remain the only fundamental determinants of the well-being of citizens, and on which depends its improvement.

Like any endeavor, any good economic policy needs a clear vision and orientation to be effective in its contribution to the improvement of the well-being of citizens. In this chapter, I have tried to show that the search for strong economic growth and the attainment of a high level of employment in the economy must quickly become fundamental final goals of their economic policy, if African countries are to aim at adopting an effective economic policy capable of ensuring their successful integration into globalization. In the meantime, it is not yet the case. The search for strong economic growth and job creation therefore provides this vision for the revival of African economic policy. The economic policy of African countries is still very often defined and implemented in reference to a series of sectoral goals which, though important, unfortunately do not help them to concentrate sufficiently on these fundamental elements. I equally attempted to prove that the two final goals of economic growth and job creation are compatible.

Chapter Four

INTERMEDIATE GOALS FOR
A SYSTEMIC ECONOMIC POLICY

"Let me now share with you some of our experience and initiatives. Recently, an international survey of 200 senior auto sector executives by consultancy firm, KPMG, found South Africa to be the fifth best investment choice by car makers globally. It placed us above Japan and Western European and North American countries but also above other emerging economies such as Indonesia, Turkey, Vietnam and Colombia. This is an example of the successes that are achieved where the state works closely in the economy with private sector partners. It is recognized by KPMG, which attributes the attractiveness of South Africa as an investment destination in automotive sector to the 'result of the government's commitment to retain, support and grow the existing manufacturers and component suppliers operating in the country.'"

Ebrahim Patel, South African economic development minister,
address at the Supplier Development Summit, March 14, 2013[1]

It is not enough for those responsible to merely recognize and adopt employment and economic growth as final goals of economic policy; strong economic growth and a high level of employment in the economy are not brought about by decree. Although the state can produce some services directly, and even some goods, and thus contribute directly to job creation – particularly in the civil service and in programs implemented by the government (i.e., big public sector investment projects) – it is expected, in general, that most job creation and economic growth will result from the actions of economic agents outside the public sector. The goods and services produced directly by the government, as well as the jobs created directly by it, will generally not be sufficient to generate the level of economic growth and job creation necessary for the well-being of its citizens. Economic history teaches us that the role of government in this respect is limited.

This chapter is therefore devoted to an examination of what I call in this book the intermediate goals for an effective African economic policy which strives for strong economic growth and high employment. I have, in Chapter 2, shown the need for intermediate goals and the role they play in economic policy. The main question this chapter attempts to answer is what are the intermediate variables – that is to say, the economic variables that have the most direct influence on economic growth and job creation, and that the authorities responsible for economic policy in African countries should aim to influence.

Economic growth is mainly the result of a harmonious interaction between, on the one hand, efforts to create a national network of companies able to offer a wide range of goods and services in acceptable competitive conditions and, on the other hand, efforts to establish, or strengthen as appropriate, strong world demand addressed to these companies, whether this demand is of domestic origin (domestic demand for goods and services produced locally)[2] or of external origin (export demand for goods and services produced locally). These two variables, in my opinion, constitute the two intermediate goals that those responsible for economic policy should target. I call all the measures aiming at the first goal the policies of supply because they are on the supply side, and actually aim at strengthening the supply capacity of the national economy. As to measures aiming at the second objective, I call them policies of demand addressed to the national economy because they are on the demand side and seek an increase in world demand for national goods and services – that is to say, the amount of goods and services produced locally and that world economic agents (domestic and foreign) are willing to buy. The success of any effective policy for economic growth and job creation is closely related to the extent to which the responsible authorities are able to successfully combine the policies of supply and of demand.

The creation of an enabling environment to strengthen the productive capacities of the national economy and the stimulation of demand addressed to national enterprises seem to us to be two complementary and inseparable dimensions of any effort to promote the growth of the national economy and job creation. One without the other would not be effective. The desire to only improve the business environment in order to strengthen national productive capacity without promoting demand would result in what economists call immizerizing growth – an undesirable result. Immizerizing growth is undesirable because it is characterized by output growth accompanied by falling incomes in the economy and reduced job creation. Similarly, stimulating demand addressed to national companies without creating conditions that will enable them to meet this increased demand would result in an increase in prices and consequently inflation in the national economy and high deficit of the balance of trade. Inflation is undesirable because it introduces many distortions in the economy.[3] For this reason, the intermediate goals that those responsible for economic policy in African countries should set for themselves are (i) to stimulate, through noninflationary measures, demand for goods and services addressed to national companies, and (ii) to strengthen the productive capacity and increase productivity of national companies. Achieving these goals will contribute significantly to the revival of economic growth in Africa. I will conclude this chapter by showing that stimulation of demand addressed to the economy and the strengthening of national productive capacity have not always been fully recognized as indispensable, and thus many African countries have not set them as intermediate goals in their economic policy design and implementation.

Stimulating, through Noninflationary Means, Demand for Goods and Services Addressed to the Economy[4]

Why is it important to stimulate demand addressed to the economy?

Demand is the main driving force of economic activity in a country and determines the production activity of companies. Changes in demand send strong signals throughout the economic system. It is based on these signals that companies decide to produce goods and services, recruit labor and mobilize other factors of production to meet demand. It is well known that when the demand addressed to companies is strong – when their order books are well filled – they are encouraged to invest to produce more and recruit, which starts the process of economic growth and job creation.

One of the major challenges for economic policymakers is therefore to ensure that demand addressed to the national economy remains strong. This question is of special significance in the context of African countries where national or foreign economic agents have not yet developed a natural orientation to demand goods and services produced by these countries. Indeed, the real economic problem in Africa and the main source of its marginalization in the globalization process is the insufficient world demand for its goods and services. I still remember a very interesting discussion I had with an African businessman who claimed that one of the major obstacles to the development of his production is the insufficient demand addressed to his business. Stimulating demand addressed to companies in all sectors of production, to maintain it at a high level, represents one of the most important contributions that economic policy can make to the process of economic growth and job creation, which the economy needs for the well-being of citizens. The fact that the rate of production capacity use is so low in most African companies, as we shall see, shows that in many cases the problem is not lack of investment (since an acceptable production capacity is already available), but the lack of, or insufficient, demand addressed to companies.

The economy of a country works in many ways in much the same way as a company. A company's prospects for growth and long-term development depend on the accuracy and relevance of its choices to ensure a balance between, on the one hand, improvements in its production processes to increase productivity and, on the other hand, the creation and maintenance of consumer interest in its products, and therefore the existence of strong, sustainable and solvent demand. It is much the same for an economy. In the early twentieth century, Ford, the first US producer of motor vehicles, significantly increased the salaries of its employees – justifying the increase in the need to give them the means to buy the cars they made. Creating a strong demand for its production was the essential complement to increased productivity within the company and ensured its long-term development. Ford understood that to fully realize the growth potential that advances in technology and better organization offered, it was also important to think about how production would be sold – that is, caring about the existence of demand. But beyond the specific measures taken in this case (i.e., increasing salaries of workers),[5] the most important thing in this approach is creating sustainable demand as a full-fledged component of a policy of growth for the enterprise. The same applies to the economy of a country. The existence of strong, durable and noninflationary demand addressed to national companies, along with the existence of a suitable environment to promote business productivity, is one of the leading success factors for a good economic policy to promote growth and job creation. Economic history has many examples that corroborate the importance of demand in a growth policy. All economies that have succeeded in their economic growth, in the past and today, have without exception combined reforms aimed at promoting strong growth of productivity in companies, with various measures aimed at ensuring strong demand for the goods and services of national companies.

What may, therefore, explain the lack of interest in African countries in the development and implementation of a genuine policy of demand as an essential complement to policies of supply in a growth strategy?

Would world demand addressed to African economies be infinitely elastic?

One of the reasons for the insufficient attention paid to the stimulation of world demand addressed to the national economy in African economic policy today seems to be related to the application of the assumption, very dear to development economists, that the overwhelming majority of African economies are small economies which are open to the rest of the world, also known in the economics literature as the small open economy (SOE) hypothesis. According to this hypothesis, the lack of demand addressed to African economies would not be a constraint to their growth since these economies, being small, are faced with a world demand which is infinitely elastic in relation to price. That is to say, these economies are generally "prices takers" in world markets and can therefore sell any quantity they would be able to produce at the price prevailing in these markets. According to this assumption, therefore, the problem of African economies is only at the level of supply. For those who know African economies well, it is easy to realize that this assumption does not reflect the reality of these economies. Indeed, if the SOE hypothesis has an acceptable degree of probability when it comes to primary commodities (which actually may have a high level of substitutability with the productions of other parts of the world and thus may face a perfectly elastic world demand), it is not the same for the wide range of other African agricultural and manufactured products that many African companies produce. Indeed, these other African products have a relatively low level of substitutability with foreign products.[6] These African agricultural and manufactured products, which are mostly sold in domestic, subregional and regional markets, are clearly facing insufficient demand. Under these conditions, it is quite obvious that an increase in their quality and their image, through a proactive and voluntarist policy to stimulate their demand, would provide immense opportunities for economic growth and job creation in many African countries.

Do only exports matter?

The other reason why African economic policy has completely neglected the development and implementation of a genuine policy of stimulating demand is that officials, sometimes advised by international experts, have in fact always thought that good demand, that which is able to ensure economic growth and job creation, is the demand from the rest of the world – that is to say, exports. I must say that development economists, whose advice has weighed heavily on the economic policy of African countries, until recently had insisted on demand of external origin (that is to say, exports), compared to demand of domestic origin, as a driving force of economic growth. They explained this preeminence of exports over domestic demand on two grounds. First, that exporting companies had higher productivity and a higher level of competitiveness than other companies. This higher productivity and competitiveness could be explained, they say, by the fact that exporting companies were in contact with world markets – enabling them, through the phenomenon of positive externalities, to also benefit from technology and better managerial methods of large competitive companies operating on these markets. These exporting companies then communicated to other national companies, according to the phenomenon of externalities, technology and management methods acquired on the world markets, such that, as a result of exports, the overall efficiency of the economy was strengthened. Exporting companies thus had so much more to bring to the national economy than other companies. National economic policy therefore had to focus on exporting companies and, in turn, exports. The other argument was that exports generated foreign exchange, which is very important to the national economy. Ultimately, foreign demand was therefore more valuable than domestic demand. This is how the economic policy of African countries has come to excessively give preference to exports (I could even say they have concentrated exclusively on production to satisfy export demand), to the detriment of the development and implementation of a comprehensive global policy to stimulate demand addressed to national companies. Even if the entire economy suffered from this excessive concentration on exports, the damage is most visible in the agricultural sector. Thus, African food crops, for example, of which the first demand is often domestic and regional, have not benefited from the attention they require from the authorities in charge of economic policy in African countries.

On the one hand, while acknowledging the crucial dual role that exports can play in the generation of foreign exchange earnings[7] and therefore the maintenance of external macroeconomic balance, on the other hand, we must also recognize that exports are not the only demand capable of sustaining economic growth and thus contributing significantly to job creation. This is especially true in a world where, because of globalization and the increasing integration of economies, market segmentation tends to disappear gradually. One consequence of this evolution is that producing to meet foreign demand is no longer superior to producing to meet domestic demand, as the major international companies present in the world market are now present even in local markets, making their technologies and potentially superior management practices also potentially available to all domestic companies, including those producing for domestic demand. There is also the fact that research conducted by economists did not confirm the hypothesis of the higher contribution of exports to the efficiency of the economy in relation to other components of demand, particularly domestic demand. A final point on why exports may not be the only demand that counts may be in order here: Since the financial and economic crisis which started in 2007 in the US subprime debt markets, the major world markets appear to be facing the real prospect of a long period of sustained depression due to weak domestic demand. In this context, African countries, and indeed developing countries in general, need to find alternative sources of demand.[8]

What I am saying here is that the policies of demand must be an essential component of economic policy in African countries and should aim at increasing both external demand and domestic demand. The important role that domestic, subregional or regional demand can also play as a source of growth, if African companies fully exploited all these possibilities to sell their outputs, was not sufficiently recognized. In saying this, I am not defending regionalism at the expense of multilateralism. Of course,

African countries should play their role in the globalization process and continue efforts to stimulate strong foreign demand addressed to their economies. But we cannot deny the immense possibilities of development offered by national, subregional and regional markets as a source of demand and thus economic growth and job creation, especially for products which, due to their strong local or regional content, will find opportunities in these regional and subregional contexts.

A study carried out by the Boston Consulting Group (BCG) in 2006 confirms the potential role of domestic demand to economic growth.[9] Studying globalization strategies implemented by a number of companies that have played an important role in the economic growth of their countries, BCG arrives at the conclusion that it is actually the domestic market which most often serves as a base and training ground for national companies before they venture onto the export market. This study examines six key strategies of globalization that were used by 100 leading companies in emerging countries in Asia, Latin America and North Africa, namely: (i) export to the world market of brands well established in the local market; (ii) the valorization on the world markets of a technological advantage; (iii) exploiting a niche; (iv) development of the comparative advantage of their home countries based on natural resources; (v) the worldwide implementation of various growth models such as mergers and acquisitions already well tested in the local market; and (vi) the acquisition of natural resources which are essential for their local market. Of the 100 companies surveyed, 28 used the first strategy, 22 the second, 12 the third, 13 the fourth, 13 the fifth and 12 the sixth. As can be seen, the most commonly used globalization strategy – that is to say, strategy (i) – is based on full exploitation of growth opportunities in the local market to later on embark on a process of globalization. If one adds to this strategies (iv), (v) and (vi), which rely in one way or another on the valorization of an aspect of the local market, we realize that the contribution that the valorization of domestic demand can bring about should not be underestimated. The search for export should not be carried out at the expense of the full exploitation of growth opportunities in the domestic market, as is currently the case in most African countries.

Is a policy of demand stimulation necessarily inflationary?

A third reason why policies of demand were not given enough attention in economic policy in African countries is certainly the fear of increasing inflation, which has often been presented as the inevitable consequence of a policy of demand in developing countries. Let us give some credence to this argument. In the context of African economies which are still very open to the rest of the world, a policy of demand which is not well calibrated – that is to say, implemented through expansionary macroeconomic instruments such as expansionary fiscal policy or monetary policy – would actually be counterproductive. It would trigger a process of macroeconomic imbalances that would be detrimental to the goal of economic growth and job creation. But the stimulation of demand addressed to the economy that I advocate in this book is rather to seek, by noninflationary means, increased demand for goods and services addressed to African companies in order to encourage those who are already running at full capacity to invest in the expansion and modernization of their production, and for those who still have

Table 4.1. Malawi: Rate of utilization of capacity in the manufacturing sector[10]

Subsector	1997	1998	1999	2000
Agro-industries	65	54.6	47.5	50
Drinks	60	55	60	43
Textiles	53.5	50.5	46	46
Wood processing	63.3	68.3	67.5	85
Paper and packages	60	65	62.5	61.5
Chemical industries	90.9	74.2	78.9	74.3
Manufacture of metals	12.7	23.1	21.5	30
Mining products	42	55	62	63

unused capacity to undertake the necessary expenditure to increase utilization of their production capacity. Table 4.1 below shows the utilization status of productive capacities in various subsectors of the manufacturing sector in Malawi.

As shown, the utilization of installed production capacity is often very low, generally below 60 per cent, meaning that companies would have no difficulty meeting increased demand. The fact that in many African countries companies operate below the installed capacity clearly reflects an insufficiency in demand and the possibility of increasing it without incurring the risk of inflation, especially if the newly created demand is addressed to companies with unused production capacity. The economic policy that I advocate in this book should aim at succeeding in this task.

Officials of African economic policy, contrary to what is happening in other parts of the world, have not yet fully exploited the potentials of a truly global, targeted and voluntarist policy aimed at winning a higher share of world demand for goods and services. Some results obtained by stimulating potential demand addressed to African companies, even if initially minimal, would represent a huge reservoir of noninflationary economic growth for the continent.

Ultimately, the insufficient attention given to measures to create and maintain strong and sustainable demand addressed to African companies seems today to be one of the key missing structural elements in the necessary sequence of actions needed for the stimulation of African economic growth. In this context, the development and implementation of a policy to create and maintain strong noninflationary demand for goods and services addressed to companies seems to be one of the major intermediate goals of the systemic economic policy that I advocate in this book.

Strengthening Production Capacity and Increasing Productivity in African Companies

Creating favorable conditions for strengthening the national production capacity must be another major intermediate goal of economic policy in African countries. Indeed, as mentioned, increasing the production capacity of the national economy by fostering the emergence of a national network of companies capable of producing a wide range of

Figure 4.1. Africa: Factory-floor costs comparable to those of China and India (cost in us dollars)[11]

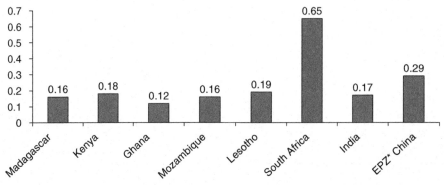

goods and services in acceptable competitive conditions is an indispensable component of any effective economic policy. It would serve no purpose to stimulate demand for goods and services addressed to national companies if at the same time they do not have sufficient production capacity to meet this increasing demand. Generally, increasing the production capacity of the national economy may be the result of either improving efficiency with which the factors of production are used, resulting in an increase in the productivity of factors of production, or an increase in the amount of factors of production used. In the first case, the objective is to ensure that national companies produce more with the same level of inputs, without having to increase the installed production capacity. In the second case, it entails increasing the installed production capacity. The new African economic policy that I advocate in this book should aim at both scenarios – that is to say, encourage companies to improve productivity and increase their installed production capacity.

Unlike demand, production capacities in African countries are currently experiencing progress, although the progress can still be described as timid. Indeed, the World Bank conducted as part of an evaluation of the business climate in its borrowing countries, a survey of manufacturing firms.[12] The survey covered 15 countries, including 9 in sub-Saharan Africa, plus India, China, Morocco, Bangladesh, Bolivia and Nicaragua, and about seven thousand manufacturing firms, including two thousand seven hundred manufacturing companies in sub-Saharan Africa, and seven sectors of activity. Information was collected on the turnover of the companies, costs and other more subjective issues. Figure 4.1 above compares the factory-floor costs in some African and Asian countries.

As indicated in this graph, the factory-floor costs in some African countries can fairly well be compared with Asian countries. This study also showed that gross factory-floor total factor productivity in countries such as Kenya and Senegal reached about 80 per cent that of China. But despite this progress, much remains to be done to increase productivity in African companies. For example, when indirect costs are taken into account, the net productivity of Senegalese companies drops to about 40 per cent of that of Chinese companies. Indeed, the indirect costs in most African companies are between 20 and 30 per cent of the total cost against 13 to 15 per cent in Chinese and Indian companies. In addition, the study also showed that African countries were the least active in terms of reforms. In 2004, the average number of reforms per country was 0.6 in sub-Saharan Africa against 0.9 in Latin America, 1.4 in South Asia and 1.6 in member countries of the Organization for Economic Cooperation and Development (OECD). In addition, one needed 64 days in sub-Saharan Africa to start a business compared to the standard 2 days (i.e., the performance of countries with the best rating on this indicator), 118 days to register land compared to the standard 1 day, and had 41 taxes to pay compared to the standard 1.

Despite these early stages of progress, we should not conclude that the current economic policy of African countries has better recognized the importance of an effective concentration on strengthening the production capacity of the economy as compared to the stimulation of demand. As discussed above, these two key intermediate goals have not often been on the radar of economic policy in these countries. With the food crisis which started in 2007 I have, however, observed a new beginning that these countries now to need concretize. Indeed, Senegal launched the Great Agricultural Offensive for Food and Abundance (GOANA), which set the goal of increasing agricultural production in Senegal. The government mobilized all stakeholders and its budgetary and other resources to achieve this goal. The second-generation agriculture program that the government of Cameroon is currently implementing is also a step in the right direction and should be supported. The challenge now is to ensure that these initiatives become permanent features of economic policy in these countries.

Failing to Stimulate Demand Addressed to the Economy and to Build Productive Capacity

When looking at economic reform efforts implemented since the early 1980s by African countries, we quickly realize that even if the measures implemented could affect demand and supply, they would do so indirectly. Stimulating demand addressed to the economy and the reinforcement of productive capacities were not really at the heart of the economic policies that were implemented. Table 4.2 below summarizes some of the main economic policy measures implemented by African countries together with their respective targeted goals as envisaged by the authorities. The major areas of economic reform concerned the stabilization of public finances, financial liberalization, liberalization of foreign trade, and liberalization of prices and marketing channels for agricultural exports.

As it appears, the goals targeted by these measures were mainly to increase public saving rates, improve macroeconomic stability and reduce inflation, reduce government intervention and liberalize the economy, and open it up to the rest of the world. Virtually all the economic reforms undertaken by African countries, along with other low-income countries in other regions of the world, have aimed at these conceptual goals since the 1980s. These goals are laudable, but it is clear that the two *sine qua non* goals of economic growth and job creation that I have just seen – that is, a high demand addressed to the

Table 4.2. Major economic reforms implemented by African countries[13]

Reform measures put in place	Goals
Stabilization of public finances • Reforms of tax system • Reforms of public expenditure	• Increase the rate of public savings and investment • Ensure macroeconomic stability • Reduce inflation
Reforms of exchange regime • Liberalization of exchange rate so that it can be determined by the market • Suppression of exchange restrictions	• Liberalize the economy and open it up to the rest of the world
Reforms of foreign trade policy • Reduction of tariff and nontariff barriers to external trade	• Liberalize the economy and open it up to the rest of the world
Reforms of the financial system	• Increase the private savings rate
Reforms of public enterprise sector and privatization	• Reduce the intervention of the state in the economy • Increase the rate of public savings • Stabilize public savings
Reforms of price policy of agricultural exports commodities (mainly coffee and cocoa) and marketing structures of these products	• Reduce the intervention of the state in the economy; stabilize public finances and macroeconomy
Reforms of the labor market	• Reduce the cost of labor
Public debt management • Search for measures of debt reduction (obtaining rescheduling from creditors, payment of arrears)	• Mobilize external resources

economy and reinforced productive capacity – were not very present in the conceptual schemes of the policies implemented. It is also because these two goals were not firmly rooted in these policies that in some countries we witnessed combinations of measures, such as deep depreciation of the national currency combined with the suppression of demand. Such combinations could of course contribute to the macroeconomic stability these countries sought, but they could only reduce demand excessively since they did not seek to stimulate it. It is the same with strengthening the supply capacity of the economy. Indeed, the theory stated that reducing the role of government, ensuring macroeconomic stability and, especially, liberalizing trade would increase the competitiveness of the national productive apparatus. This will not do: we cannot assume that the national productive apparatus will become competitive by pursuing other goals. It must be explicit in economic policy; therefore it requires concrete and specific means. It is difficult, then, to detect a specific concentration on the two intermediate goals discussed above among the plethora of measures that were implemented. Economic growth and job creation could not, therefore, be achieved.

Summary

Ultimately, a good mastery of the distinction between policies of demand and policies of supply is critical to the revival of economic policy in African countries. Each category of policy exerts its effects on a specific area of the economy. At the level of supply, the policies of supply are designed to act directly on the production capacities of the national economy in view of increasing them. At the level of demand, policies of demand aim at increasing demand addressed to companies for their production. The policies of supply alone have limitations regarding their ability to generate economic growth and job creation. Without strong and vigorous demand for their products, companies have no incentive to produce. Indeed, as we have seen, a policy of demand seems to have been the major missing link in the efforts made so far by African countries in their economic policies. My argument in this book is that policies of demand and policies of supply are inseparable in a growth strategy and must be pursued concurrently. It is important to emphasize the concurrent nature of this effort as many authors often appear to argue either for demand-side policies or for supply-side policies, as if one could work without the other. This has given rise to unnecessary controversy in the literature.[14]

In his famous *Treatise on Political Economy* (1803), the French economist Jean-Baptiste Say stated his law of markets, where supply creates its own demand. Stated in the context of economic policy, the law maintains that policymakers should focus their attention only on the conditions of supply; demand is never a constraint as it always exists whenever supply exists. In 1936, John Maynard Keynes, no doubt one of the leading economists in the history of economics, showed that a lack of demand can sometimes be the main constraint on the expansion of economic activity. Stimulating it must be central to the concerns of economic policy. This discovery inspired economic policies that virtually all developed countries implemented. Economic policy must focus on stimulating supply and demand to promote a harmonious expansion of economic activity. African countries did not really concentrate on one or the other and have not thus implemented the economic policy that would have made economic growth and social progress possible. There is still time to change course.

Chapter Five

OPERATING GOALS FOR A SYSTEMIC ECONOMIC POLICY

"Growth demands a stable, but flexible, political and social framework, capable of accommodating rapid structural change and resolving the conflicts that it generates, while encouraging the growth-promoting groups in society."
Simon Kuznets, Nobel Prize laureate in economics, prize lecture, 1971

"In countries operating a largely capitalist system, there does not seem to be a wide understanding among its actors and overseers of either its advantages or its hazards. In the past, ignorance of what it can contribute led some countries to throw out the system or clip its wings. Ignorance of the hazards made imprudence in markets and policy neglect all the more likely. Regaining a well-functioning capitalism will require re-education and deep reform."
Edmund Phelps, Nobel Prize laureate in economics,
Financial Times, April 15, 2009

Introduction

In the first part of this book, I demonstrated the role of operating goals in the conceptual framework of economic policy. My goal in this chapter is to point out the operating goals that the officials in charge of economic policy in African countries should target. The operating goals are tactical targets that the officials in charge of economic policy can best influence in order to achieve the intermediate goals. They are closer to the instruments, which are the means of action directly in their hands. They are also linked to intermediate goals by a relationship of cause and effect, which is easier to understand than that which may exist between the instruments and intermediate goals. In fact, officials in charge of economic policy cannot use instruments in their hands to directly influence the intermediate goals, but they can use them to influence the operating goals that in turn influence the intermediate goals.

In this chapter I consider three categories of operating goals. First, there are those which, if achieved, will contribute simultaneously to the two intermediate goals of strengthening demand addressed to the economy and strengthening its productive capacity. There are also those which, if achieved, will contribute to achieving the intermediate goal of strengthening the supply capacity of the national economy. Finally, there are those that, if achieved, will contribute to stimulating demand addressed to the economy. These categories of operating goals are not watertight categories, but this classification has the merit to retain some of the conceptual coherence needed to guide the actions of officials in charge of economic policy. Before examining the operating goals, two precisions are worth mentioning here: firstly, unlike the final and intermediate goals, which are supposed to remain relatively stable from one country to another, the operating goals should, in principle, reflect more the specific context of each country and therefore have some variability from one country to another. Secondly, beyond the expected cross-sectional variability, it seems to us that it should be possible to identify a set of concerns that should form the core of operating goals of economic policy. It is this core of operating goals that I will review in the rest of this chapter.

Operating Goals that Contribute Both to the Stimulation of Demand Addressed the Economy and to the Strengthening of Productive Capacity

Gain credibility among economic agents

The level of credibility enjoyed by the officials in charge of economic policy from economic agents is a fundamental determinant of the success of all the efforts they can deploy either to stimulate demand addressed the economy or to strengthen the productive apparatus. When the officials in charge of economic policy are not credible, economic agents spend most of their time and energy on unproductively searching for ways to circumvent economic policy decisions announced by the authorities, instead of making the decisions on production and demand which alone can revive the economy, as I have extensively demonstrated in the previous chapter. Indeed no economic policy can be successful if economic agents do not consider that policy credible.

In 2004, two leading economists – Finn Kydland, professor at the School of Economics and Business Administration, and Edward C. Prescott, professor at the American University of Carnegie-Mellon – won the Nobel Prize in Economics for having demonstrated that when officials in charge of economic policy do not enjoy a high level of credibility among economic agents, economic policy faces a problem of time inconsistency, which destroys its effectiveness.[1] This results from the fact that since economic agents do not believe in economic policy announcements made by the authorities, they engage in behaviors which are contrary to those sought by these announcements. This forces the authorities to reconsider their economic policy plans and the outcome is that the economy moves into a suboptimal equilibrium precisely because of their lack of credibility and, consequently, the low level of trust they enjoy among economic agents. This lack of credibility is a costly situation for the national economy. This result is, in my opinion, one of the most important contributions by economic theory to the formulation and conduct of economic policy since Keynes. This new discovery of the role of credibility has greatly influenced the reforms implemented in most developed countries to increase the independence of central banks, whether they are institutional reforms that ensure the formal independence of the central bank or reforms to fix a target for inflation.

Armed with this theoretical result, it is therefore better understood why the search for credibility must be one of the major operating goals of economic policy. Indeed, this credibility determines the effectiveness of all actions undertaken by the authorities to stimulate demand for goods and services addressed to the national economy as well as actions to strengthen its supply capacity.

Maintain the confidence and morale of economic agents

The level of confidence of economic agents is also an important determinant of their demand and production behaviors. Confidence that economic agents have in the national economy, its current functioning and its anticipated future performances is a fundamental determinant of economic performance of any country. Regarding demand, a high level of confidence on the part of economic agents stimulates it. On the other hand, if the confidence level is low, the result is that economic agents will become cautious, which will result in lower demand addressed the national economy and a slowdown in growth. The same applies to supply. A low level of confidence on the part of economic agents (producers) reduces investment and hinders the development of the supply capacity of the national economy. The search for a high level of confidence among economic agents, therefore, appears to be among the key operating goals that those responsible for economic policy must set in all circumstances.

Promote good governance

Several meanings have often been attributed to the concept of good governance. For example, according to a commonly used definition, governance refers to how power is exercised in society. A complete sense to me seems to be that which the African Development Bank, in 1999, adopted as part of its policy of promoting good governance in African countries. According to this definition, governance encompasses essentially transparency and accountability, the involvement of stakeholders in governance, the fight against corruption, and an adequate legal framework and judicial system. As we notice, the concept of governance refers simply to the quality of all institutions of the country and to the respect of a code of conduct by public authorities.

The main reasons why the authorities in charge of economic policy should take as their operating objective the promotion of good governance are twofold: First, good governance contributes substantially to the credibility of the authorities and, therefore, the maintenance of trust which they need to ensure the effectiveness of their economic policies, including policies to stimulate demand and strengthen the national productive fabric. Second, good governance is a factor in the transmission of the impulses given by economic policy measures. Indeed, in a system of poor governance, all channels of transmission of the effects of economic policy are cut, so that the announced policy and actions have no effect on their targets. It is therefore necessary that those responsible for economic policy aim at a high level of governance. Recent research has also shown that the quality of institutions of a country counts in promoting economic development.

Improve the quality of infrastructure and other public goods

The quality of infrastructure in the areas of transport, communications and energy is crucial both for the strengthening of the national production base and for the stimulation of demand for goods and services addressed to the national economy. As regards the strengthening of the production base, numerous research carried out in development economics today confirm the role of infrastructure in productivity gains to the extent that they facilitate the coordination of production activities, helping to save time and reduce drudgery. Indeed, in the agricultural sector, we now know that the productivity of farms is closely related to the quality of rural infrastructure, including transport. If the role of infrastructure in enhancing the production base is now known and generally accepted, it is not the same in terms of stimulating demand for goods and services in the national economy. Indeed, the quality of transport infrastructure in particular contributes to lower production costs and consequently lower prices of goods and services. As we will see, price is an important determinant of demand; lower prices resulting from improved quality of infrastructure will stimulate the demand for goods and services addressed to domestic companies. Improving the quality of infrastructure contributes directly to strengthening the national production base and stimulating demand for goods and services addressed to the national economy. This is why improving the quality of infrastructure must be among the key operating goals of the authorities responsible for national economic policy.

Therefore, for it to contribute fully to economic growth and job creation, infrastructure improvements would have to lead not only to the improvement of the quality of services, but also to a significant decrease in costs for consumers. If the consumer costs do not decrease significantly, the positive effects for the supply side of the economy, and thus for economic growth, resulting from the improvement of the quality of services are neutralized by the adverse effects on growth that high prices have on demand addressed to the economy. One sector where these negative effects were mostly felt in many African countries is telecommunications. If the liberalization policies implemented by these countries have in fact contributed to an improvement in the quality of services, thanks to the arrival of numerous international operators, the prices charged to consumers, however, are still too high to have positive effects on growth in these countries. Let's take the example of cellphones, a sector where Africa is often presented as the fastest-growing market in the world. Calculations by the OECD show that the average monthly cost in countries in sub-Saharan Africa of a standard basket of mobile phone use, including twenty-five calls and thirty SMS messages, represents about 26.37 per cent of gross national income per capita. In comparison, and to illustrate the possibilities that exist for lower prices, the same percentage for South Africa was 3.11 per cent, for the countries of North Africa it is 5.16 per cent (2.98 per cent in Algeria, 6.33 per cent in Egypt, 1.24 per cent in Libya, 12.59 per cent in Morocco, and 2.67 per cent in Tunisia). The average cost of a cellphone call during peak period was, in 2007, 30 cents for countries in sub-Saharan Africa, and 21 cents for the five countries of North Africa above.[2] If the cost of using mobile phones alone absorbs such an important portion of the income of economic agents in sub-Saharan Africa, it is not surprising that demand addressed to the economy is depressed and therefore that economic growth does not follow, at least at the pace that is expected, the improvement of the quality of services that is often presented as having resulted from competition. All the possibilities of falling prices must still be fully exploited, especially in an industry where production technology is well mastered.

In addition, as part of the implementation of its economic policy, the government will very often be responsible for the adequate supply of some public goods such as education, health, transport, sanitation and drinking water, and for the security of goods and persons. It is the responsibility of officials in charge of economic policy to ensure that the provision of such services is at an appropriate level in relation to operating goals. The government can ensure adequate supply either by taking over production itself (direct production), or by entrusting their production to the private sector through various forms of mutually beneficial partnerships with the private sector (indirect production).

Promote social cohesion

The search for social cohesion, which can be defined as the harmony between the different components of society, must also be an operating goal at the forefront of economic policy. Indeed, the social stability and confidence economic agents have in both the political and economic institutions of the country depend on this social cohesion. An economy characterized by latent or actual tensions between the different components of society will find it difficult to achieve the economic goals it has set. Indeed, when such tensions exist, economic agents adopt mistrust vis-à-vis the authorities, resulting in wait-and-see behavior on the part of investors and an increase of precautionary savings by private economic agents. The wait-and-see behavior of investors has a negative impact on investment, delaying efforts to strengthen the productive capacity of the economy. The excessive increase in precautionary savings slows private demand (domestic and external) addressed to the national economy and chokes growth and job creation.

In the context of African economies, it is precisely the achievement of this goal of social cohesion which is one of the most formidable challenges for economic policy. The combination of unfavorable physical geography (in fact, in addition to certain risks that are inherent in the tropical climate, most African countries could be classified as either rich in natural resources, or poor in natural resources and located near the coast, or poor in natural resources and landlocked) and unfavorable human geography (most African countries have small populations and large ethnic diversity) increases the challenges for social cohesion and the practice of good political and economic governance.[3]

The size of the challenges should not lead to abandonment. Even if the trend in literature has often been rather to present these characteristics as factors explaining the poor economic performance of Africa, which may be the case, I think that in a situation where these characteristics are there to stay, economic policy should explicitly recognize the challenges that these characteristics create and anchor one of its operating goals on overcoming them. These countries do not, however, have a monopoly on these handicaps. Virtually all of today's developed countries have experienced, and still experience throughout their development process, challenges of social cohesion which they have tried with varying degrees of success to overcome, thanks to their economic policies.[4]

Promote and maintain a stable macroeconomic framework

Although the concept of macroeconomic stability is one of the most used in circles of development experts, it has rarely been the subject of a rigorous definition. Today, economists use the concept of macroeconomic stability to characterize the situation where the key macroeconomic variables in the national economy are at a compatible level with its fundamentals. Economists agree that such a situation is characterized by a low and stable inflation rate, balanced public finances and a viable external position. We have long spoken about the major distortions that a high rate of inflation introduces to the economic system of a country. Although a debate still exists about the meaning of low inflation, some countries have adopted policy frameworks that are based on a predetermined level of inflation. Thus, the European Central Bank considers a level of inflation below 2 per cent low.

Macroeconomic stability is an outcome of economic policy that economic agents observe directly and it is a powerful determinant of credibility. It determines the confidence that economic agents have in the entire economic system of the country. Indeed, in a country plagued by high and chronic inflation, for example, or a serious imbalance of public finances to the point that the state is unable to meet its financial obligations, economic agents find it difficult to properly plan their production and demand expenditures. High and chronic inflation is often accompanied by the high variability of prices. This instability of the price system contributes to a loss of confidence on the part of economic agents, which, as we have seen, inhibits the stimulation of demand and the strengthening of productive capacity. For this reason, the maintenance of macroeconomic stability should be sought as a key operating objective of economic policy (Box 5.1 below describes the various channels through which inflation has negative effects on demand and supply capacity).

Maintaining a stable macroeconomic framework is a challenge that is not easy for officials to meet because the risk of accelerating inflation is inherent in the process of interaction between supply and demand. In this interaction, the economy tends toward its maximum supply capacity,[5] producing goods and services in greater and greater quantities in response to the increased demand for goods and services it receives. If in the process of interaction, the increase in demand is permanently higher than supply, the result will be an increase in the general price level in the national economy – in other words, inflation or an external deficit and a devaluation of the currency. This means that the main challenge for economic policymakers is to ensure that the increase in demand in the economy is not higher than the long-term supply capacity of the economy to the risk of letting inflation set in. In practice, the management of the interaction between supply and demand to achieve noninflationary economic growth is more art than science. In fact, it is not often easy to determine when demand has already permanently exceeded supply, necessitating measures to contain inflation. This difficulty complicates the conduct of economic policy. If the authorities responsible for economic policy act too soon as demand is sustainably outstripping supply, they run the risk of prematurely halting the increase in demand and therefore preventing the economy of attaining its point of maximum supply capacity, which is also the point where the economy reaches its full potential to create jobs. If they act late, they run the risk of letting inflation increase in the economy.[6] In practice, economic policy officials in the United States have used the concept of NAIRU (Non Accelerating Inflation Rate of Unemployment; an unemployment rate which does not bring about higher inflation)[7] to guide their actions. In this model, the authorities take measures to stop the expansion of demand, and thus slow economic growth if unemployment falls below the NAIRU. As noticed, there exist potential tensions between economic growth and inflation. This is why economic policy should aim at noninflationary economic growth.

Box 5.1. The negative effects of inflation

Thanks to economic research, we now know that inflation has a negative impact on the functioning of the economy. This negative impact is mainly due to the five types of distortion it introduces into the economy. The first is linked to the lack of transparency that it introduces in the evolution of relative prices. Indeed, when inflation is high, it becomes difficult for economic agents to readily identify changes in relative price[8] – that is to say, the price of a good or service compared to that of another – meanwhile it is these relative prices that play a key role in decisions of resource allocation (decisions of production and demand) that economic agents take on a daily basis to enable the national economy to function. The second major distortion that inflation introduces in the economic system of a country is that it helps to increase the risk premium related to inflation – that is to say, the compensation that creditors demand to guard against the risk of higher prices when they are repaid in liquid assets. This increase in risk premium is itself an increase in the nominal interest rate and weighs on demand for business investment. The result is that an economy that is experiencing a high inflation rate also experiences an investment rate that is structurally below its optimal level and consequently economic growth and job creation rates that are also structurally below their potential. Inflation is also a source of development of unproductive activities, in that, when it occurs, economic agents waste a significant proportion of their resources to undertaking activities which will enable them to guard against its effects. One of the distortions that inflation introduces into the economic system, which is more prevalent in popular imagination, is that it encourages an unjust, immoral and involuntary redistribution of wealth and income for debtors to the detriment of creditors. Finally, inflation can also enhance other distortions that are already introduced in the economy, such as those related to the imposition of taxes. It is therefore because of all these distortions that inflation undermines the morale of economic agents, reduces the credibility of officials in charge of economic policy, reduces both supply and demand, and ultimately slows economic growth and job creation. It is therefore important to come up with a stable macroeconomic framework.[9]

The freedom to choose one's own economic policy

Freedom to choose one's economic policy implies that those responsible should strive to eliminate, or at least severely limit, all forms of external interference on the choice of national economic policy. Experience has shown that these outside influences are not always favorable to the aspirations of the countries in relation to their economic policies. The international community fully recognizes this fact. It is for this reason that it is committed, particularly in the context of the Paris Declaration (see Chapter 13), to put the ownership of aid at the heart of efforts to improve its quality; that is, to allow more flexibility to countries in defining their development policies. But since the adoption of the Paris Declaration this commitment has seemed more difficult to implement than to adopt.

Today, many countries of Africa, Asia and Latin America greatly resent the impact that outside influences have had on their economic policies, especially those from international financial institutions, the IMF and the World Bank. This resentment is now such that virtually all countries in these regions, at a point in the recent past, were doing everything to stop borrowing money from these institutions and thus stop them from dictating their economic policies. Thus, the London daily *Financial Times* describes an episode where during the 2007 presidential election campaign in Argentina, while the candidates clashed on almost everything, the only point on which they were able to agree was that the era in which the IMF defined the economic policy of their country was over. A campaign commercial for the victorious candidate, Cristina Fernandez Kirchner, showed children playing in the courtyard of a daycare center, to whom it was asked what the IMF meant. One of them says, "Horses"; another says, "Satellite"; a third adds, "... that crashed into the moon"; and a fourth says, "No, a country where everything goes wrong." It is then that a voice off-screen explains that the purpose of this campaign element is to make sure that generations of Argentine children have no idea of what the IMF is.[10]

There are increasing calls for the international financial community to give more freedom to developing countries in determining their economic policies. This would allow them to experiment with different solutions to their economic problems and select those that best suit their context. But instead of conceiving this freedom to choose their economic policies as a possibility that the aid providers have to offer them, it seems that African countries and the developing countries in general would be better advised to seek this freedom themselves, recognizing that such a search must be one of the major operating goals of economic policy. This means that the authorities have to, in making decisions, also evaluate them in terms of the present and future impact on their freedom of action. In this quest, the conduct of fiscal policy is crucial, for it is usually the first gateway to outside interference. I will come back to this point in the next chapter when I examine the instruments of economic policy. As many developing countries are realizing every day, significantly reducing external influences on economic policy will not be easy, but it must be tackled with great determination and method.

As we shall see later on, when we look at some success stories of economic policy as examples of the ideas in this book, countries that have succeeded in their economic policies are those which were able to define it and carry it on, specifically having in mind the search for a certain freedom in choosing their policy options as an objective. This was very clear in the case of South Africa, for example, and even Tunisia, two success stories in economic policy which will be discussed in greater detail in Part Five.

The economist John Maynard Keynes, whom I quote at length in this book, believed in the virtues of the independence of national economic policy and had even written about it. But during his time, when still very little was known about the experience of developing countries, since they had not yet acceded to international sovereignty and therefore had no economic policy to be implemented, it was much more in relation to the constraints arising from membership in supranational entities that he explained the virtues of independence in the choice of economic policy.[11] Today, for many countries in the developing world, particularly in Africa, the reasons for loss of independence in economic policy are manifold. To those already identified by Keynes, we add influences from the world of development aid, which I have talked about, and international geopolitics. In such a context, gaining independence will require extraordinary imagination.

Prices that reward production

Price indicates the value of a good or service in a given currency. Although the notion of price means for the average person the price he must pay to purchase various goods and services which are necessary for his daily use, it is possible for the purposes of economic policy to distinguish five types of prices in an economy, namely the interest rate, the exchange rate, the price of labor, the prices of raw materials (i.e., those used in the production of virtually all other goods and services produced in the national economy, such as oil), and the prices of other goods and services produced by the national economy for the current consumption needs of economic agents.[12] I shall come back to the concepts of interest rates, exchange rates and the general price level in the discussions of monetary policy and exchange rate policy in Chapter 6.

I would love to say that prices are a final variable in an economy since they are so important. However, having already reserved this status for economic growth and employment, I would say rather that prices play an extremely important role in the economy. There is no economic policy without a good understanding of the role that one wants to assign to prices. For proponents of economic liberalism, prices must reflect the result of the free interaction between supply and demand in a competitive environment. In doing so, prices should give signals to guide the allocation of resources in the economy. Price freedom should therefore be the rule. But there are no rules without exceptions, and economic policy is no exception to this principle. Economic liberalism, invented by the classical economists who dominated economics in the eighteenth and nineteenth centuries and even today, advocates price freedom. "Get prices right" has long been synonymous with liberalization. At the other end, Karl Marx predicted that a system of organization of economic life based on economic liberalism would not live long. To replace such a system, he imagined another system that communism that part of the world experienced for some time would be the prototype. In such a system, prices are set by a central public authority. Experience has now amply demonstrated that neither of these extremes can function sustainably.

The communist experiment collapsed before our eyes, and two leading economists, Kenneth Arrow (Nobel Prize in Economics, 1972) and Gerard Debreu (Nobel Prize in Economics, 1983), have shown that the conditions for obtaining the competitive equilibrium needed to produce an optimal price system rarely exist in the real world. The optimal system of prices for an economy, that which economic policy must seek, is therefore somewhere between these extremes. It is only through the pragmatism and creativity of economic policy that it will prevail.

It is the recognition of the non-optimality of the two extreme systems described above which, in reality, justifies public intervention. If there must be intervention, however, it can only be very limited. It could not be otherwise because it is easy to see the daunting challenges that will inevitably arise if the state attempted to broaden the scope of its intervention on prices.

Under these conditions, what should a good economic policy aim at in relation to the price system? Which operating objective should be sought? If prices affect both demand and supply, should economic policy aim at putting them at the service of demand or at the service of supply? Low prices encourage demand and discourage supply, while high prices[13] encourage supply and discourage demand. Here, in my opinion, lie the stakes of one of the most critical issues of economic policy in African countries. In these countries, economic policy has implicitly or explicitly chosen to put price at the service of demand and not at the service of supply, as a good economic policy would have recommended and as is practiced in all countries that have successfully promoted economic development. One area where this choice was most costly for African countries is the agricultural sector. The absence of a genuine policy of prices for agricultural products – in other words, a policy that has as its result prices that remunerate production and not just prices that encourage consumption – has blocked agricultural development in these countries and, in short, economic development.

In 2007, when prices of agricultural commodities increased rapidly in global markets, virtually all observers saw it as a risk of increased poverty for vulnerable populations but above all as an opportunity for a revival of agricultural production in African countries. Indeed, the hope was that the combination of changes in demand and the substitution of imported products with local and less expensive ones would revamp the agricultural sector. African countries did not fully seize this opportunity because most of them once more preferred demand to the detriment of production, especially by implementing policies of lower prices to favor demand. High prices were a good thing for local production, but not for demand, especially the consumption demand of urban populations which occupy an important place on the chessboard of political economy. This is one reason why low prices were quickly sought.

Is the political cost of a price system that remunerates production and not consumption too high for African governments? I do not think so. They have already demonstrated their ability to implement reforms that required a high level of political courage. The measures that most governments put in place in the 1980s and 1990s, during which structural adjustment programs were en vogue, were far more difficult politically. Perhaps that was the twentieth century, and in the freer and more democratic Africa of the twenty-first century the equilibrium level of political courage is structurally much higher. Whatever the case, it is also on this ground (that of the capacity of governments to reform while facing opposition from various segments of society), that the fate of economic policy in Africa – in short, its economic destiny – is decided. The economic development of the West today, of which many Africans dream, was achieved at the cost of successive courageous reforms. Margaret Thatcher entered the history of British economic policy for knowing how to deal with resistance from trade unions in order to implement the bold measures which today have given Britain one of the most successful and flexible economies in Europe. Africa will only achieve the development it aspires to if it succeeds in placing production at the center of its economic policy, and this can only be achieved through a price system that remunerates it.

To conclude this important issue, prices should aim at remunerating production and not demand. That said, and given the context of globalization in which we live, the prices offered by the national economy must of course aim at stimulating production, while at the same time being reasonable for demand. This is what economists mean by the concept of price competitiveness. Situations like these, which involve many requirements that do not converge in the same direction, are many in economic policy. All this shows that the concept of "get prices right" requires more imagination, and cannot be limited to liberalization, as a certain literature has for a long time made many believe.

Faced with the difficulty of reconciling goals that can sometimes be difficult to pursue simultaneously, especially price stability and growth, the countries of the eurozone invented an ingenious formulation of the ECB's goals during its creation. They said that the primary objective of monetary policy of the ECB was price stability, but without prejudice to this, that monetary policy should provide support to other economic policy goals of the union. I will refer to the same structure and suggest that the primary objective of a price system must be to encourage production and without prejudice to this objective, it must also aim to be reasonable to demand.

Ensure adequate financing of the economy

The financial system is to an economy what blood is to the human body. Like blood, which provides nutritive elements to the various organs of the body without which they cannot function, the financial system provides the different actors of the economy, mainly producers and consumers, the essential means to carry out their respective activities. The financial system thus plays an irreplaceable role in enhancing the supply capacity of an economy and in stimulating demand in the economy. Indeed, it is the financial system that provides national companies the means of financing their production. This role of the financial system in the development process has already been highlighted by the Austrian economist Joseph Schumpeter. Recent theoretical research work has confirmed the role of the financial system in economic development. The financial system plays an important role in stimulating demand. Officials of economic policy, then, should also set as an operating objective the attainment of a regular and adequate level of financing of national companies and consumers through the financial system. Optimizing the contribution of the financial system to the financing of supply and demand is an essential operating goal for economic policy. This requires a proactive effort to encourage financial institutions, especially banks, to play their role. The current situation prevailing in many African economies – where banks keep a great share of cash at their disposal and draw their income mainly from fees levied on services rather than on their activity of financial intermediation – does not contribute to the efforts that these countries are making to integrate into the global economy.[14]

Build capacity, especially the level of economic expertise of those involved in economic policy

The success of economic policy depends on the analytical skills and imagination of all its stakeholders. It must, therefore, in its own interest, seek an ever-increasing improvement of the capacities of the latter. One of the first aspects of this capacity is to increase economic expertise within the public administration. This of course can be achieved through development within the various public administrations of their capacity to analyze, develop and review economic strategies, but also a substantial improvement in the capacity of national statistical systems so that they can produce the reliable and pertinent statistical information that this process requires.

It is true that African countries have undertaken many efforts, often with support from development partners, to strengthen their statistical systems. Although these efforts have been particularly useful for the production of statistical information used to track important indicators of poverty, they have not, in my opinion, succeeded in guiding the work of national statistical systems toward their true role in supporting economic policy.

In my opinion, apart from producing statistics on aspects of poverty as it is now, most statistical systems in African countries must at least also provide information to enable the monitoring of the following variables: the status and trends of employment in all its dimensions; changes in demand for goods and services in the national economy; the situation of the productive capacity of the national economy; the confidence level of economic agents and of the rest of the world vis-à-vis those responsible for national economic policy and the institutions of the national economic system, as well as the main determinants of these variables; and the confidence level of economic agents and the rest of the world toward goods and services offered by the national economy and its main determinants. In the following I will discuss the variables and the need to collect them in detail.

One of the most obvious manifestations of the lack of consideration toward preoccupations related to employment in the economic policy of African countries is the lack of tracking employment statistics. There are no (or very few if any) African countries that have acceptable updated statistics on the employment situation. This, of course, makes it impossible to integrate employment in the analysis and development of economic policy. It is therefore necessary that African countries dedicate resources for the regular collection of statistics on employment. These statistics could, for example, provide on virtually a monthly basis the evolution in the employment situation both nationally and regionally, by sector of activity, gender, age, type and level of qualifications as well as seasonal variations. They are essential for monitoring the goals that will be set.

Information on changes in the level of confidence of consumers and producers and their determinants are valuable and necessary to understanding the perceptions of economic agents, whom, as we have seen, influence the performance of the economy. In the European Union for example, the statistical services of the commission systematically calculate these indicators and updates them before each meeting of the Economic and Financial Affairs Council (Ecofin), which brings together the finance ministers of EU member countries. In the United States, such indicators are also calculated and widely used. Thus, the Conference Board Consumer Confidence Index (see Box 5.2 below) measures each month, since June 1997, the level of confidence that economic agents have in the health of the US economy. Experience has shown that the evolution of this index indicates a high correlation with that of demand, gross domestic product and employment in the United States. This is certainly the reason why the Federal Reserve, one of the main actors in economic policy in the United States, is also among the first users of this index. A similar indicator calculated in Germany is the IFO index, which calculates and publishes a regular index of consumer confidence in business leaders in Germany. The Japanese authorities are monitoring this variable through the Tankan survey.

Regarding the demand for goods and services addressed to the national economy, we must distinguish this concept from that of aggregate demand, whose evolution is monitored and controlled within the macroeconomic framework. As already indicated in Chapter 4, demand addressed to the national economy is the sum of exports and domestic demand for goods and services offered by the national economy, while the concept of aggregate demand refers to the sum of domestic demand for consumer and capital goods and imports. Without denying the importance of aggregate demand that determines absorption and can cause internal and external imbalances, if its evolution is not controlled, my purpose here will be to insist that demand addressed to the economy should be a variable of the focalization of economic policy and, consequently, should also be monitored by the national statistical systems. The monitoring of this variable seems critical because, as we have seen, it is this demand which is at the basis of all economic activity and dynamism. The evolution of demand addressed to the economy plays a central role in explaining the economic performance of a country. Despite this importance, it is noticed that this statistic has not always been monitored by the statistical systems in most African countries. It is a gap which ought to be filled.

Another whole section of the statistics needed for the development and monitoring of the implementation of economic policy advocated here relates to the productive capacity of the national economy. This category includes statistics on installed capacity by the productive sector, the utilization rate of installed capacity, etc. For now, this type of statistic is not regularly produced by African countries. This is also a gap which should be filled fairly quickly. Finally, knowledge of the attitude of national economic agents and the rest of the world toward goods and services offered by the national economy is of paramount importance to guide efforts to boost demand addressed to the national economy. The statistical information available should also inquire about this variable.

The state plays a central role in the process of developing and implementing economic policy. Its behavior determines that of all other actors in the system. The strengthening of its own internal capabilities as I have described must occupy a prominent place

Box 5.2. The conference board consumer confidence index

The Conference Board, whose headquarters are in New York, now calculates a monthly index that measures the confidence of economic agents in the US economy. The idea behind this calculation is that changes in the level of confidence of economic agents determine the behavior of consumption and investment, which are the main engines of the economy. In the case of the United States, consumption only represents about two-thirds of economic activity. Any improvement in consumer confidence thus results in an increase in consumer demand, which in turn leads to increased production and employment. So, there is a high correlation between this index and GDP. This is why the Federal Reserve (the US central bank), as well as many other departments of the US government, closely follows the evolution of the index.

The Consumer Confidence Index is calculated on the basis of the results of a survey of a representative sample of 5,000 US households. The questionnaire focuses on the assessment of five criteria considered important for present and future evolution of economic activity, namely: (i) the appreciation of the current business climate, (ii) expectations about the business climate in six months, (iii) assessing the current situation of employment, (iv) the employment situation in six months, and (v) the total family income in six months. The average of the answers of the five questions is used to calculate the index of consumer confidence. The average of answers to questions (i) and (iii) is used to calculate the index of the current situation and the average of responses to questions (ii), (iv) and (v) is used to calculate the index of consumer expectations. The Conference Board also calculates indices of the confidence level, the assessment of the current business climate and the expectations of business leaders.

among the operating goals of economic policy. But the state cannot be regarded as the only actor in economic policy. Indeed, to the extent where economic policy must be able to influence the behavior of all economic agents, producers and consumers in order to be effective, the civil society must also be taken into account because it also has the ability to influence the behavior of economic agents. A special effort should be made to strengthen the capacities of all these major actors in economic policy.

Some actors are more organized and better structured than others. This is especially true for producers. Indeed, it exists in virtually all countries employers' organizations in their efforts to present in a unified way the points of view of business leaders. For consumers, their role, though extremely important in the economic performance of a country, as I have demonstrated at length in this book, have so far not been fully recognized and exploited by those responsible for economic policy. Thus, through the demand they express, they determine the total dynamics of the entire economic system of the nation. They are generally less structured and less visible than the producer organizations. It is the role of economic policy to strengthen the capacity of consumer organizations so that their participation in national economic policy becomes more effective.

The sustainability of economic policy choices

Economic policy cannot accomplish anything if it is not sustainable – that is to say, if the authorities are not able to honor on time and on the agreed terms the obligations arising from measures implemented, be they commitments with financial implications or not. This is why the concept of sustainability, which will be discussed when I tackle the issue of fiscal policy, is an important operating goal that economic policy should seek continuously. It is only when policy measures are sustainable that they can be implemented fully, with patience and independence, and consequently successfully.[15] The independence of economic policy choices, which I have identified here as an important operating goal of economic policy, is partly supported by sustainability.

Regional and multilateral economic integration

It is necessary to seek, through regional and multilateral economic integration efforts, access to the markets of countries or geographical areas experiencing strong growth momentum. The growth momentum of foreign countries determines the overall demand expressed by economic agents around the world, part of which (see β in Box 5.3) is destined to the national economy. Generally, although officials in charge of economic policy have very little opportunity to influence global growth, they must nevertheless ensure that the country has as trade partners countries or parts of the world experiencing rapid growth. This will ensure that the export demand addressed to the country (which, as we have seen, is an important component of demand) is high.

In this perspective, a first step is to exploit the full potential of regional integration and subregional cooperation to increase demand for goods and services addressed to the national economy. Indeed, given the generally small size of African economies, everyone now admits that the pursuit of economic integration at the regional and subregional level offers great potential for increasing market size and thus the demand for goods and services addressed to the national economy. Given the generally low level of income in regional and subregional markets directly accessible to African countries, the increase in demand will come initially from the substantial increase in the number of potential consumers of goods and services offered by the national economy. It is more realistic to anticipate this increase in demand as the tastes and preferences of the regional and subregional demand are generally quite close to those prevailing in the national market, which national producers have mastered quite well. They will, therefore, have little difficulty in meeting this new regional demand.

The question has often been asked how to reconcile the pursuit of regional economic integration and the need for integration into the global economy. Integration should be pursued in accordance with the provisions of Article XXIV of the Agreement of the World Trade Organization, which recognizes regional economic integration arrangements when they do not lead to trade diversion. The risk of trade diversion can be considered negligible in the integration efforts among African countries to the extent that the progress already made by these countries to liberalize trade with the rest of the world reduces the risk of trade diversion. I demonstrated this in a research paper on the process of economic integration among member countries of the Economic and Monetary Community of Central Africa (CEMAC).[16]

Still in the area of regional integration, an area where efforts would be particularly promising is the putting together of resources to develop an information tool in order to truly put information at the service of developing the continent. I will demonstrate at length in this book how the information policy is an important instrument of economic policy if it contributes to the formation of perceptions, which ultimately also determine the behavior of economic agents. By improving knowledge of African markets and products, first with national economic agents, but also among economic agents around the world, such an information tool will significantly increase the effectiveness of efforts to increase demand addressed to African economies and, consequently, would contribute to economic growth and job creation on the continent. The search for markets should not be limited to countries which are geographically closer, particularly in the context of regional integration. It is also necessary to target all the other growing areas by participating actively in multilateral trade liberalization efforts.

Although regional integration has most often been seen as a means of enlarging markets, it should also be seen as a means to strengthen efforts to build productive capacity. Countries would pool their resources together to develop their supply capacity of key goods or infrastructure. Current efforts in various parts of Africa to jointly develop energy production and other key infrastructures are examples of the use of regional integration to strengthen supply. These initiatives should be pursued and strengthened.

Operating Goals Specifically Contributing to Productive-Capacity Building

Improve the business environment and corporate governance

Continuously improving the business environment and corporate governance equally seems to me to be among the operating goals that those responsible for economic policy must set. Indeed, the ability of the national economy to supply goods and services in competitive and acceptable conditions, which I have identified reinforcement as being a key intermediate goal of economic policy in the previous chapter, obtains mainly in domestic companies. This means that the national companies, their operations and their prosperity should be a central operating goal if economic policy is to achieve the intermediate goal of strengthening the supply capacity of the national economy. Officials of economic policy must constantly ask themselves whether they are doing everything that can be done to ensure national companies have the means to meet the demand addressed to them, and if they invest enough either to expand their production capacity or to improve production processes and consequently productivity. They must not only ensure they do what is necessary, they must also ensure that national companies respond effectively and positively to their efforts by making the necessary investments. The monitoring of the investment of companies is a critical task of the operating goals of economic policy. French president Nicolas Sarkozy once said that a country which abandons its companies is a country that has no economy.

In this context, care must be taken to facilitate the creation of companies on the one hand and the operation of existing ones on the other. Indeed, as the company is central to the creation of wealth and jobs, authorities must do all they can to remove obstacles to the emergence of a national network of competitive companies, including removing administrative barriers, reducing real and perceived risks by investors and promoting corporate profitability. Those responsible for economic policy must set all of these elements as operating goals and they must establish indicators to measure progress. No economic prosperity will be possible as long as companies do not take their place at the heart of the goals of economic policy.

Intimately related to the concentration on companies is the promotion of good corporate governance. Corporate governance refers to the whole question of who has the power of decision and management within the company, if shareholders have the means to control the actions of managers, etc. The organization of power within the company is important because it determines the extent to which companies contribute, to the maximum extent of their capabilities, to the development of the economy. Even if one can assume that the normal functioning of companies, in the absence of any regulation, would lead them to contribute to the economy, particularly through the payment of taxes and the hiring of part of the local workforce, the establishment of a framework of good corporate governance is essential to sustaining their functionality and maximizing their contribution.

Build human capital

The concern here should be to ensure good health and better education of the national workforce. Since the important work of the American economist G. Becker, Nobel laureate in economics in 1992, economists agree that human capital consisting of knowledge and a healthy workforce enters the production function in the same capacity as physical capital made up of machinery and other physical assets. This reflects the important role now attributed to human capital in the production function and consequently in the productive capacity of an economy. It is this human capital that determines innovation, productivity and the quality of goods and services, which determine the supply of the economy.

Increase the attractiveness of the national territory

Another key operating objective in the reinforcement of the supply capacity of the economy is to increase the attractiveness of the country. Indeed, the process of globalization we are experiencing is primarily a fierce competition where countries are engaged in attracting economic activities to their areas. Globalization is ultimately a competition of territories. It is a competition of countries to win the hearts and minds of consumers and producers so that they choose to locate their production activities on the national territory, but the hearts and minds of consumers must also be won so that they purchase the various goods and services offered by the national economy. It is clear that progress on the various other operating goals that I have just mentioned will do much in terms of promoting the attractiveness of countries, but this should not lead African countries to minimize the need for a real national policy that specifically targets their attractiveness. The focus areas of this policy should of course include objective elements that influence the region's attractiveness to investors, such as improving the quality of infrastructure, but also actions that can influence the perceptions that economic agents have about the country, as it is now well known that economic agents act with their hearts (that is to say, on the basis of subjective or psychological factors) as well as with their heads (that is to say, on the basis of objective rationality). To be effective, a real policy of attractiveness for the territory must include far-reaching actions that can positively attract the attention of economic agents to the country.

On another point, a policy of attraction should not only target nonresident economic agents, as was the case for most previous attempts to improve the attraction of the territory undertaken by African countries. It must also focus especially on resident economic agents because it is they who are the first actors in the economic growth and job creation that I am targeting through the economic policy framework described in this book. A particularly important target that I see for a policy of attractiveness is the population of nationals who have left their country to settle abroad (the diaspora). This population is often a considerable potential for a well-trained workforce that these countries need to give life to their development efforts. In spite recent research, sponsored especially by the World Bank, which tends to show the importance of remittances from migrant workers, experts are increasingly recognizing that the departure of the highly educated population has a negative impact on developing countries. The rate of return of the well-educated diaspora could be an important measure of the success of a policy of attractiveness.

Operating Goals that Contribute Specifically to the Stimulation of World Demand Addressed to the Economy

Equation 4 in Box 5.3 below describes in a basic mathematical form the four major determinants of world demand addressed to the economy. It is based on this equation that I will identify the specific operating goals contributing to the stimulation of demand addressed to the economy.

World demand addressed to the economy consists of a fraction of the demand expressed by resident economic agents[17] and a fraction of the demand expressed by nonresident economic agents (respectively called α and β in Box 5.3). I use the word fraction because not all demand expressed by resident economic agents is addressed to the economy. Similarly, it is obviously not all the demand expressed by nonresident economic agents which is addressed to the economy. In the context of African countries where effective policies to stimulate demand addressed to the economy do not yet exist, much (we would say most) of this demand goes to importation – that is to say, turns into demand addressed to the rest of the world.

Box 5.3. Demand in the economy

Demand addressed to the economy is a more useful concept for analyzing growth than the concept of absorption or aggregate demand in that it aims to measure the amount of goods and services offered by the national economy that resident economic agents and the rest of the world wish to acquire. This concept can be illustrated from the fundamental equation of gross domestic product.

That is:
Y = gross domestic product (GDP)
C = consumption of durable and nondurable goods and services by households
I = investment by companies
G = demand for goods and services by government
X = exports of goods and services
M = imports of goods and services
DG_{RoW} = aggregate demand for goods and services expressed by the rest of the world
DANC = demand addressed to resident companies
α = average proportion of demand addressed to resident companies in the aggregate demand for goods and services expressed by resident economic agents
β = proportion of demand addressed to resident companies in the aggregate demand for goods and services expressed by the rest of the world

With:
$0 < \alpha < 1, 0 < \beta < 1$
(1) $Y = C + I + G + (X - M)$
(2) $X = \beta \times DG_{RoW}$
(3) $M = (1 - \alpha) \times (C + I + G)$
(4) $DANC = \alpha \times (C + I + G) + \beta \times DG_{RoW}$

Demand expressed by resident economic agents has three main components: the first is from households that express demand for durable and nondurable consumer goods and services of various kinds. There are also companies that express a demand for goods and services in connection with their investment operations. Finally, there is the government that also expresses a demand for goods and services as part of their ongoing operations and for the implementation of public investment programs. Of these three components, consumer demand expressed by households is very often the largest component. In most economies, it is usually more than sixty per cent of the aggregate demand for goods and services expressed by resident economic agents. This means that genuine efforts to boost demand addressed to the economy should focus especially on it. Various economic theories have identified factors that influence it. Some are stable and change little over time, especially households' propensity to consume (identified by the Keynesian theory), the size and age structure of the population (identified by the theory of the life cycle by the Italian-born American economist Franco Modigliani) and household wealth (whose role has been developed by the American economist Milton Friedman). Regarding demand from companies' investment needs, it is determined by various factors including the perspectives of demand for their products as perceived by business leaders, or the profitability of production. Demand for goods and services by the government is primarily determined by the government's economic policy. In addition to these factors, the stable monetary and financial environment prevailing in the economy, which is mainly to say the availability of means of payment in the economy, also determines the demand that resident economic agents can address to the economy. Competitiveness – prices of domestic products – also come into play. Demand expressed by nonresident economic agents is determined by price and nonprice competitiveness factors. The following must therefore constitute the operating goals whose attainment will certainly stimulate demand addressed to the economy.

A macroeconomic framework that stimulates, in a noninflationary manner, demand addressed to the economy

So far, the quality of the macroeconomic framework has almost always been assessed in terms of stability, this stability itself being assessed primarily by the level of some standardized aggregates. The Growth and Development Commission, whose work I have referred to at the beginning of this book, said that if a stable macroeconomic framework is good for economic growth, not all stable macroeconomic frameworks fully support growth. I think we have here a theme that economic research should actually look into in the years to come. While waiting for this research to one day shed light, it seems to us that besides being stable, a good macroeconomic framework should fully exploit the possibilities of stimulating demand addressed to the economy. Each element of the macroeconomic framework must therefore be evaluated not only on its contribution to the stability of the entire system, but also on its contribution to the stimulation of demand addressed to the economy. Is a stable fiscal policy also characterized by a full exploitation of possibilities to strengthen demand addressed to the economy? Does the composition of credit to the economy – consumer credit, for example – reflect an optimum in terms of demand addressed to the economy, given the available information on the spending patterns of beneficiaries of these credits? These are some of the questions that should be asked when assessing the quality of the macroeconomic framework in terms of stimulating demand addressed to the economy.

What is advocated here is a shift in approach in the analysis of macroeconomic aggregates and frameworks from an approach which sees C, I and G as part of *absorption* and therefore needing to be controlled and reduced,[18] to an approach which focuses on the notion of *demand addressed to the economy* and which seeks instead to strengthen it by identifying economic policy measures which would substantially increase α and β (see Box 5.3). This approach requires a more thorough analysis and understanding of the determinants of the spending behaviors of economic agents both domestic and foreign.

The quality of goods and services

Economic policy must encourage companies to improve the quality of goods and services they produce. Demand addressed to an economy is also sensitive to the quality of goods and services it offers – very sensitive even, since we live today in a world of globalization. In such an environment, the products offered by the different countries are competing not only in price but in quality. It is so much so that good quality can, in some cases, compensate for a disadvantage in terms of price. This idea has been known for some time, but three economists studying the experience of countries in Central and Eastern Europe have demonstrated it empirically; they have shown that these countries expanded their exports and gained market shares in export, despite an appreciation of their real effective exchange rate.[19] Although this example deals with countries of Central and Eastern Europe, I have no doubt that the effects of quality that have been demonstrated are also valid in the case of African countries. It is therefore legitimate that one of the operating goals of economic policy is to encourage companies to improve the quality of their products and to achieve results in this regard. Tunisia, for example, did it very well, having developed a program that worked in this direction and that works well (I shall come back to the economic policy of Tunisia). The effects of an improvement in quality can be very powerful.

Tastes and preferences of economic agents

Economic policy should aim at guiding the tastes and preferences of economic agents to demand for goods and services produced locally. Factors such as price and quality of goods and services that determine demand can be grouped into the category of objective factors. Thanks to advances in the field of marketing research on consumer behavior, we now know that the objective determinants enumerated above are only one of the determinants of demand among others. In addition to these objective factors, there is also another category of factors that I can describe as subjective factors. These are the tastes and preferences of economic agents – that is to say, perceptions by economic agents on the goods and services provided by resident companies. These preferences also contribute to determining the fraction of total demand of resident and nonresident economic agents (α and β in Box 5.3) addressed to the economy. Tastes and preferences of economic agents are ultimately, if not the largest, at least one of the most critical determinants of demand addressed to resident companies and thus of the economic activity and economic growth rate of a country. These tastes and preferences are influenced by the following factors: (i) the cognitive processes of economic agents that refer to beliefs they have developed about the goods and services offered by the national economy, which are usually the consequences of the information they have stored; (ii) affective processes that refer to the attachment that economic agents have on goods and services offered by the national economy – overall opinion and feelings, positive or negative, that consumers have developed in respect to goods and services offered by the national economy; and (iii) conative processes that refer to the intentions that economic agents have to buy or not to buy goods and services offered by the national economy.

In the logical process of demand for goods and services offered by the national economy, the cognitive processes of consumers determine their affective processes, which in turn influence their conative actions. Today we know that this chain of processes is a predictor of consumer behavior. If it is positive, it stimulates demand; otherwise, one can expect that it has a depressive effect. Tastes and preferences are thus an important determinant of demand addressed to the national economy. It is for this reason that officials must ask themselves at any moment the question of whether they are doing everything that can be done to develop a positive attitude (chain of cognitive, affective and conative processes) toward goods and services produced locally. The fierce battle between Western and Asian countries on the issue of the image of products among their respective customers is proof of the important role these subjective factors can play in a good economic policy.[20]

For African countries, the task of developing a positive attitude toward local products is more difficult since most African economies are characterized by an image gap that has helped to develop both in domestic consumers and the rest of the world a negative attitude vis-à-vis domestically produced goods and services in African countries. In fact, marketing experts tell us that once consumers have developed an attitude, they hardly change. They tend to distort any contrary information so that it fits into their original cognitive structure and it takes a significant amount of contrary information to get them to change their attitudes. This is the phenomenon of "distorted perception," which is well known in research on consumer behavior. This means that those responsible for economic policy in Africa face a daunting task if they want to reverse the negative perceptions and unfavorable consumer attitudes in order to stimulate demand for goods and services addressed to national companies. Much remains, therefore, to be done on the side of demand to create a conducive environment for inclusive economic growth in Africa. Admittedly, this is a very difficult task, since it demands in democratic and free societies a change in people's behavior so that their demand, which is naturally destined for the rest of the world, is transformed into demand addressed to the national economy. Observing the behavior of household demand in Nigeria, the London daily *Financial Times* noted this:

> Locals say that, far from being regarded as inferior quality, Chinese shoes and those from other Asian countries such as Indonesia can in fact sell for more than theirs, being seen as a premium imported products. "Chinese shoes are more expensive, but Nigerians do not value their own goods," says Mike George, who runs a workshop of six shoemakers in Ariaria, the vast, sprawling market in Aba, which acts as the factory for much of west Africa. [...] "If your price is N200 they will buy a Chinese pair for N1,200. Then if we drop our prices to N180 or N160, they cut theirs to N600." [...] He reckons about half the market has been taken by Chinese and other east Asian imports. Other estimates have market penetration even higher. [...] Cheaper power may help bring down Nigerian costs, but absent a big change in productivity or tastes, for some of the country's traditional manufacturers it is too late, and for many it seems likely to be too little.[21]

This observation, which, beyond Nigeria, could describe the situation in any African country, illustrates the constraints that inappropriate management of demand imposes on African growth. The example described above relates to manufactured goods, but the development of African agriculture, especially food and staple products, face substantially the same constraints: lack of demand for local food products and economic agents often preferring imported foreign products. Faced with such a situation, one of the critical tasks of economic policy is to act both on objective factors and subjective factors to stimulate demand addressed to national companies. The analysis of consumer behavior, its motivations and attitudes toward goods and services produced by local companies must become one of the central concerns of any well-planned economic policy. The mastery of all aspects of the behavior of the potential consumer of national products provides information which is essential to the development and conduct of economic policy.

In this chapter, I have suggested the key operating goals that African countries could set within the framework of a new economic policy. What I can note is that some of these operating goals correspond to the priorities that are often identified in the current literature on development policies and on which African countries are making significant efforts. This is the case, for example, with research on macroeconomic stability, which virtually all studies and reports on developing countries mention and on which progress is being made. This is also true of the improvement of human capital, including education, training and health, and promoting good governance, which are also very present in the literature and on which African countries and their development partners invest most of their joint efforts. I have also identified here other operating goals which are generally less mentioned but which seem very important, and on which African countries do not pay enough attention and have made less progress than is necessary. These are, respectively, the need for a macroeconomic framework that is not only stable but also fully exploits the possibilities to stimulate demand addressed to the economy, changes in tastes and preferences of economic agents to goods and services offered by the national economy, the search for social cohesion, the search for credibility, and the search for a high level of confidence among economic agents. To be complete on the operating goals, a final word is in order at this point. As much as the final and intermediate goals seem to be the same from one country to another, the operating goals are highly dependent on the specific context of each country. I have, therefore, developed in the preceding lines only those which seemed truly fundamental. Each country can identify operating goals that are best suited to its context and that contribute toward achieving the intermediate and the final goals, which I have presented in the book.

This discussion of operating goals closes my examination of the structure of goals for a good economic policy for Africa in a globalizing world economy. What is noteworthy here is that in this structure no goal is more important than another. They are all important, and, therefore, must all constantly appear on the radar screen of economic policy if African countries want to gain their place in globalization. Ultimately, the innovation I bring in this book is, of course, to insist on certain goals, but also to organize them into a conceptual framework clearly showing the results chain of economic policy. This has not often been achieved in current literature since the different goals are almost always presented in a disparate and unstructured manner, making it difficult for the policymaker to comprehend. According to their sensitivities, each author emphasizes an important objective he or she considers important and recommends to be placed at the center of economic policy.[22] Of course, the well-being of citizens does not come about that way. What I have demonstrated is the existence of a set of important concerns which are located on a chain of results in which they contribute to each other. The possession of a conceptual framework like the one I have developed in this book enables a better design and implementation of economic policy.

Summary

Although they are all important, the concerns of economic policy that I have examined since Chapter 3 remain. They are worth nothing without the right tools to implement them – that is to say, to transform them into reality. That is why I will now proceed to examine the instruments of economic policy – the means that officials in charge of economic policy possess to achieve these final, intermediate and operating goals I have identified.

Chapter Six

INSTRUMENTS FOR A SYSTEMIC ECONOMIC POLICY

"Although pressures to use the government's tools of economic management to achieve one or another short-term aim are always present, the tools of government are, in fact, most appropriately used to create an environment in which private economic activity can flourish over the longer run."

Alan Greenspan, chairman of the US Federal Reserve, October 26, 2005[1]

Introduction

Economic policy is a science and an art. Its success lies both on a scientific process founded on the consideration of established laws and rationalities, particularly concerning the behavior of economic agents, and on a pragmatic process made of creativity, inventions, innovations and adaptations to particular and the ever-changing situations to which the officials must adapt. In the foregoing chapters, I examined the first component of what, in my opinion, falls under the scientific component of economic policy – that is, choosing the final, intermediate and operating goals of economic policy. These goals serve as guideposts on the long, winding and complex road that any good economic policy must necessarily take. These goals determine the overall orientation of economic policy and inspire the specific measures which will eventually be taken to implement it. Without a clear, stable and sustainable vision of these goals in the minds of economic policy officials at all times, they run the risk of reducing themselves to a simple visual navigation, a simple manipulation without conviction and coherence of instruments, lacking motivation, failing to mobilize the key actors, and consequently, failing to achieve the successes on which the lives and well-being of millions of citizens rely. I can therefore convincingly affirm that the choice of pursuing these goals conditions the success of economic policy and constitutes the first phase of the scientific process.

This chapter is devoted to examining the instruments of economic policy and the manner in which they can be used to better contribute to the goals examined in the foregoing chapters. In particular, I may say that it is in this manner of using the instruments to attain the final, intermediate and operating goals identified in the preceding chapters that the second part of the scientific component but also and most importantly the artistic aspect of economic policy are found – that is, the pragmatic, creative, inventive and innovative minds of the officials in charge.

Instruments are tools directly under the control of economic policy officials that they can use, either at their discretion or by following preset rules, to orient the economy toward the different goals that they have established. When officials modify the level of one or several instruments, it produces an impact on the goals by influencing the behavior of economic agents. The effects of a modification of the instruments are transmitted through a change in either the volume, composition and/or direction of financial assets in circulation in the economy.[2] The instruments to be discussed in this chapter are: monetary policy, tax policy, budgetary policy, exhortation of economic agents, exchange rate policy, competition policy, industrial policy, foreign trade policy, regulations, partnerships in the economy, information management policy, public debt policy, trademark creation policy, social security policy and other sectoral policies. This is not a comprehensive list of instruments that economic policy officials may wish to use to accomplish their mission, but it contains the major ones.

To conclude this introduction, three elaborations seem necessary:

Firstly, the relationship which exists between instruments of economic policy and the operating and intermediate goals pursued by authorities is not a one-way relationship. As much as instruments are used to pursue goals, the progress made in achieving these goals in turn strengthens the capacity of the authorities to further make progress on the goals with the help of the instruments. Thus, if I take the example of budgetary policy, which I will examine below, it must enable the authorities to strengthen their credibility toward economic agents. However, as immediately as this credibility is achieved it will in turn provide maneuvering margins in the use of budgetary policy, by facilitating, for example, a better recovery of tax yields, or by contributing to the drop in the price of public borrowings.

Secondly, among the different categories of goals that I have just examined, operating goals are those that the authorities responsible for economic policy may directly influence with their instruments.

Finally, and most importantly, the fact that Chapter 6 of this book discusses the instruments of economic policy each in turn does not mean that the book returns to the sectoral approach that it criticizes. The thrust of this book is a proposal for a new framework for the global economic policy of the country, of which the various instruments I discuss in this chapter are only a part. The key point I make is that the way in which policymakers would use the instruments discussed in this chapter in the context of the proposed global framework is very different from the way in which they would use them if they did not have a solid command of the framework, as is currently the case in many developing countries, and Africa in particular. So there is no inconsistency in proposing a global framework and discussing each of the various instruments in turn.

Monetary Policy

To public authorities, monetary policy consists in acting on the conditions under which the economic agents acquire means of payments. It therefore aims at controlling the quantity of the means of payments that circulate in the economy.[3] Thanks to progress made in economic science, we know today that inflation, whose effects on the economy can be devastating, is mainly a phenomenon of monetary origin. That is, it is the result of an excessive creation of the means of payment, faster than is required by the needs of the economy. As I have already said in this book, when inflation is high it introduces distortions in the economy which are harmful to its effectiveness. One of the major distortions resulting from inflation is the fact that it undermines the morale of economic agents and the confidence they may have in all the elements of the economic system of their country. This confidence is a fundamental determinant of the demand for goods and services addressed to the economy on the one hand, but also the capacity building of supply on the other, and it is therefore one of the key operating goals of economic policy officials.

I fully subscribe to the present consensus, according to which the best use of the monetary policy instrument in pursuing operating, intermediate and final goals is to promote price stability – that is, maintain a low rate of inflation. Economic policy officials must, therefore, continue to allocate to this instrument its special role, that of maintaining price stability. Price stability enables economic agents to concentrate their reflections, multiple talents and energies on thinking and planning their production and consumption activities, which are indispensable for economic growth and the creation of jobs. From this point of view, African countries made significant progress compared to the situation that prevailed about three decades ago. Presently, inflation rates are somewhat low in most African countries. According to the statistics of the IMF, the average inflation rate of sub-Saharan African countries has dropped considerably from 39.5 per cent in the mid-1990s to 6.9 per cent in 2013 and was projected to 6.2 per cent in 2014.[4] This trend is moving toward the right direction and should be pursued.

In this perspective, monetary policy officials must also ensure that credit to the economy, to support the production activity of companies and consumer demand, progresses adequately. Stiglitz and Greenwald strongly emphasize this point of view: "We argue for a shift in focus from money to credit, and from thinking about the interest rate as determined in the money market, by the demand and supply for money, to an examination of the determinants of credit."[5] In this context, the monitoring of credit aggregates also becomes as important as the monitoring of monetary aggregates. In fact, in several African countries where the financial system is still characterized by an insufficient development of financial markets, the role of bank credit in financing the economy, particularly the financing of companies and household consumption, acquires major importance, though it is still insufficiently developed.[6] Indeed, for multiple reasons, sometimes pertaining to the absence of collaterals that banks judge satisfactory, due to insufficient development of land property or the absence of satisfactory accounting by companies, banks are still too timid and do not lend much for economic development.[7]

Has monetary policy a role to play in growth and employment, beyond price stability?

To some, the answer to this question is clear: the role of monetary policy is to maintain price stability. It has nothing to do with economic growth and job creation. However, things are not all that simple. Indeed, can I conceive that monetary policy (which, at the bottom line, is one of the most powerful instruments of economic policy) is totally exonerated from all responsibilities concerning the pursuit of the final goals of inclusive economic growth and job promotion? I do not think so. Monetary authorities should feel an obligation to contribute toward promoting economic growth and job creation. I have discussed the monetary policy strategies of some of the major central banks of the world, be they the US Federal Reserve, the European Central Bank or the Bank of England, and have shown that economic growth and employment occupy an important place.

However, some will say that if the central banks of developed countries have human resources and hence the analytical capacity necessary to coherently integrate growth and job preoccupations in their monetary policy strategy without risk of inflation, it is not the same for monetary officials of African countries. Here, according to them, the risk is high that clear recognition of growth and job creation as goals leads rapidly to money printing and the acceleration of inflation. Even if there is a small amount of truth in such an argument, it may not be able to completely exonerate monetary authorities from all responsibilities concerning job creation. This does not mean that monetary authorities should be bound by growth and the employment goals of the government, but simply that they should, while adopting these goals, preserve their independence concerning the means and manner in which they contribute to them, since these are the goals of the entire nation. In other words, monetary authorities must feel an obligation to contribute to these goals, but feel an obligation of means and not an obligation of results. They must prove that they do all they can to support economic growth and job creation.

Economic science however recognizes this double mandate and has formalized it through the well-known Taylor rule for central banks. This rule indicates how the central bank can consider the evolution of inflation and economic growth respectively in its monetary policy decisions.[8] It offers a useful frame of reference, and African economic policy officials, particularly central banks, should explore the possibility of adapting it to their specific contexts to make it a useful instrument for the conduct of economic policy. Some are already doing so – the Central Bank of West African States (BCEAO), for example. As such, it has been shown that, from 1987–99, Taylor's rule somewhat described the behavior of the BCEAO with respect to fixing short-term interest rates.[9]

In favor of a liquidity policy?

Liquidity is an extremely important concept to monetary policy. It is the interbank market, on which banks exchange their liquidity in high-powered money among themselves, which constitutes the entry point for the monetary policy action of the central bank. If the recent financial crisis amply confirmed what we already knew – that the functioning of the interbank market depends on the level of confidence that prevails among banks – it also demonstrated a fact on which officials up to then paid little attention: that this confidence depends not only on banks' solvency but also on their level of liquidity. In fact, some observers think that the crisis was worsened by the fact that the banks' liquidity had reached very low levels, resulting in the fact that, besides solvency, there might also be a need to regulate bank liquidity within the framework of a global policy to better prevent systemic risk.[10] The Basel Committee has prepared directives on bank liquidity risk management.[11]

The present financial crisis highlighted the role that confidence plays among banks for the good functioning of the interbank market. In most African countries, this lack of confidence is permanent,[12] thereby making the inadequate functioning of interbank markets a structural problem. In most of these countries, a reflection on the liquidity of banks therefore doubles with another important thought on the functioning of interbank markets, which has been long postponed. When these markets function well, the transactions that take place therein, and the interest rates that these transactions produce, indicate the general climate of the economic activity in the country. The informational content of these transactions is therefore very rich for the Central Bank and the conduct of monetary policy. That is, considering the role of monetary policy in economic policy in general, establishing the adequate functioning of interbank markets must be a priority of the first order in these countries.

Budgetary Policy

Budgetary policy can be defined as the practices of the authorities in collecting taxes and determining the level of public expenditure. It is said to be expansive when the budget balance – that is, the difference between public revenues and expenditures – is negative. In this case, we talk of a budget deficit. On the contrary, it will be characterized as restrictive if the budgetary balance is positive – that is, if public revenues are higher than public expenditures. In this case, we talk of budget surplus. Budgetary policy as an instrument is totally in the hands of officials responsible for economic policy to the extent that they have certain latitude to establish the level of revenues and public expenditure.

Budgetary policy and credibility

Budgetary policy can contribute to the operating goals of economic policy I discussed earlier. First, fiscal policy has an enormous potential to contribute to the credibility of economic policy and to the confidence of economic agents, which as we have seen are among the operating goals at the forefront of stimulating demand addressed to the economy and building its productive capacity. It can contribute to credibility by reducing pressures for monetary creation. In fact, studies have proven that, in most African countries, one of the major sources of excessive monetary creation liable to end in high inflation is linked to excessive budgetary deficits, financed by inflationary means. Considering this reality, and where maintaining price stability is necessary for credibility and confidence of economic agents, budgetary policy must contribute to this credibility and confidence by limiting the excessive deficits.[13] Incidentally, limited budgetary deficits also contribute to the sustainability[14] of the budgetary policy, which is a key factor of economic policy credibility in the eyes of economic agents. Among the other budgetary measures that may contribute to the credibility of officials of economic policy and increase the level of confidence which they enjoy from economic agents, I can cite the adoption and implementation of budgetary rules and reforms which contribute to the promotion of budgetary transparency. In this perspective, the efforts presently made by a certain number of African countries must be pursued and encouraged, particularly those of the

West African Economic and Monetary Union (WAEMU)[15] and the Central African Economic and Monetary Community (CEMAC), within the framework of their respective programs of multilateral convergence and budgetary policy monitoring of their member states.

Budgetary rules are commitments that the authorities in charge of budgetary policy undertake to respect a certain number of budgetary practices. These practices may either concern certain quantitative and qualitative indicators characteristic of budgetary policy (different budgetary balances), the composition of public expenditure, or certain practices related to the budgetary process. As illustration, Box 6.1 below summarizes the budgetary rules retained by member states of WAEMU within the framework of their convergence, stability, growth and solidarity pact.

Several countries in the world have adopted and now implement budgetary rules to promote the transparency of their budgetary management and credibility. In 2007, Nigeria adopted a law on fiscal responsibility which aimed at promoting macroeconomic stability, transparency and responsibility in the preparation and execution of the budget. Since 2008, Great Britain has implemented a budgetary rule which in my opinion is very sensible. According to this rule – better known in the literature as the "golden rule" – budgetary deficit, if it exists, must finance investments and not consumption. Also, public debt must remain lower than 40 per cent of GDP and the return expected from investment must be able to finance initial investment spending.[16] This imposes on public investments the same profitability constraints as for private investments. If African countries adopted and respected such budgetary rules, the situation would be different from those existing today on the continent where many countries face difficult budget sustainability challenges. The Stability and Growth Pact, which European eurozone member countries adopted in 1997 at the Amsterdam Summit, constitutes one of the most cited examples of budgetary rules. In the wake of the sovereign debt crisis facing many eurozone countries, Europe has adopted other budgetary rules aimed at better preventing the risks of unsustainable public finances among their members.

For them to be useful to the conduct of budgetary policy, budgetary rules must present a certain number of characteristics; in particular: being clear in their definition, simple in application, flexible, significant in relation to the targeted goals, and coherent with all the other commitments undertaken.[17]

Has budgetary policy a role to play in directly stimulating demand?

Traditionally, most studies of budgetary policy have concentrated on its role as instrument of direct stimulation of demand addressed to the economy. This approach expresses the influence of the Keynesian thought, which, in the 1930s, popularized budgetary policy as a major instrument of economic policy. I began the discussion of budgetary policy by insisting on its contribution to the search for credibility of the economic policy authorities, not that its contribution to the stimulation of demand is less important to me. In African countries, public spending averagely constitutes about one-third of GDP. It is, thus, potentially a non-negligible source of demand for goods and services addressed to the economy. Everything must be set up to fully exploit this potential. Budgetary policy must, therefore, also contribute directly to goals related to stimulating demand addressed

---

Box 6.1. West African Economic and Monetary Union (WAEMU) budgetary rules of the convergence, stability, growth and solidarity pact

In 1999, member states of WAEMU adopted a pact of convergence, stability, growth and solidarity, the goal of which is to strengthen the convergence of the economies of member states, strengthen macroeconomic stability, accelerate economic growth and increase solidarity among member states. The pact specifies eight criteria of convergence among which four are first-class criteria and four are second-class criteria.

First-class criteria:

• Ratio of the basic budgetary balance to nominal GDP (key criterion) higher or equal to 0 per cent in 2002.
• Average annual inflation rate maintained at 3 per cent maximum per annum.
• Ratio of outstanding domestic and external debt to GDP should not exceed 70 per cent in 2002.
• Payment arrears: non-accumulation of internal payment arrears in the current period and non-accumulation of external payment arrears in the current period.

Second-class criteria:

• Ration of the wage bill to tax revenues should not exceed 35 per cent in 2002.
• Ratio of the public investments financed from internal resources to tax revenues should attain at least 20 per cent in 2002.
• Ratio of current-account deficit (excluding grants) to nominal GDP should not exceed 5 per cent in 2002.
• Tax pressure rate should be higher or equal to 17 per cent in 2002.

Originally programmed for 31 December 2002, the period of convergence was postponed to 31 December 2008. According to the evaluation of convergence for 2007 conducted in June 2008 by the WAEMU commission,[18] Benin and Niger respected the four first-class criteria, Burkina Faso and Côte d'Ivoire one, and Guinea-Bissau none. Concerning the second-class criteria, Senegal respected three, Benin, Mali and Niger two, Burkina Faso and Côte d'Ivoire one, and Guinea-Bissau none. The same report projected that in 2008, the year of convergence, Benin, Mali and Niger could respect the four first-class criteria.

---

to the economy and building the productive capacity the national economy. The level and composition of public spending may and must be commissioned to the pursuit of these goals (see Chapter 5). In fact, for the same level of budgetary balance, the impact of budgetary policy on demand addressed to national companies will not be the same depending on whether public spending composition is more oriented toward goods and services produced by the national economy or not. In several African countries, the productive base has already attained an advanced stage of diversification. In these countries, there exists a non-negligible potential for stimulating demand addressed to national companies through an action on the composition of public spending.

In fact, the authorities responsible for budgetary policy must ensure that public spending composition in terms of goods and services produced by the national economy and goods and services from the rest of the world reflects the preoccupations of stimulating demand addressed to the national economy. Although this aspect is a constant in developed and emerging countries, African countries have not often fully recognized this special role of budgetary policy. The practice of tied aid, which has been a dominant practice in the community of donors and which consists in granting aid in exchange for the purchase of goods and services from donor countries, better illustrates the use of fiscal policy to stimulate demand for goods and services within the economy of donor countries.

If I first insisted on the role of budgetary policy in the search for credibility,[19] it is because despite the weight of public spending in the GDP, it remains lower compared to private demand, and I first expect that the most important source of sustainable demand addressed to the economy should be private. The expansion of public deficit, a phenomenon which may increase risks of macroeconomic instability, is certainly not the best way of stimulating demand addressed to the economy. Keynes himself did not think otherwise. He saw an increased role for budgetary policy in the stimulation of demand addressed to the economy only during times of crisis, marked by a significant drop in private demand. It is in this case that budgetary policy could be useful in stimulating demand, by increasing public demand to at least compensate for the drop in private demand. Recent studies have also shown that a budgetary policy deemed credible and sustainable by economic agents can stimulate demand addressed to the economy, even if it is restrictive.

That said, contemporary African economies are most often characterized by a relatively low utilization rate of productive capacities (I raised this point previously), an increased integration into the global economy and a better mastery of monetary policy, factors which limit the upward flexibility of prices. These characteristics create an environment favorable to a significant potential role of budgetary policy in stimulating demand addressed to the economy, if budgetary stimulation is implemented hand in hand with adequate efforts to increase the value of the multiplier coefficient $1/(1-c+m)$.[20] These efforts involve actions aimed at reducing m, given that c is normally high in these countries, considering the low level of income. The search for useful levers for a satisfactory reduction of m is, therefore, a prerequisite for calibrating budget stimulation so that it results in an increase in demand addressed to the economy and thereby increases the rate of economic growth. Among these levers, I can cite the composition of the stimulation in terms of the origins of the goods and services financed and of spending patterns of those benefitting from the budgetary stimulus, taking into account the spending behaviors of different categories of economic agents.[21] If these conditions are met, then without prejudice of the goals of credibility and macroeconomic stability, budgetary policy must also be commissioned to the stimulation of demand addressed to the economy.

Budgetary instruments and other operating and intermediate goals of economic policy

Budgetary policy is, if not the most important, at least one of the most important instruments of economic policy. It is also one of the instruments whose manipulation is the most visible in the eyes of economic agents. Authorities must therefore fully exploit all the possibilities offered by its use to pursue the different operating and intermediate goals of economic policy examined in the foregoing chapters. Thus, the sectoral composition of public spending must reflect a particular emphasis on spending liable to contribute to the productivity of factors of production by granting a significant share toward developing the country's human capital, particularly education, health, innovation and infrastructure, and strengthening governance in the management of public affairs, improving the business climate and strengthening social cohesion. Concerning public revenues, they must be charged in a way that reduces the negative impact they may have on the system of incentives facing economic agents and, therefore, the distortions usually introduced by taxes in the economic system.

Budgetary policy also bears an important responsibility in the search for a greater freedom and independence of economic policy, for it is the profound imbalances of public finances that generally constitute the first gateway of foreign interference. When the imbalance of public finance is such that foreign aid, instead of financing investment, finances a non-negligible part of current expenses (as is often the case in several African countries), we quickly end up in a situation where the state must depend on foreign resources to get through the month. These resources are generally supplied in exchange for considerable influence on the orientations of national economic policy. It is for this reason that for African countries, which are still mostly in imbalanced and fragile situations and which must therefore depend on foreign budgetary contributions, reducing foreign influences will need much determination and competence in budget management to progressively readjust budgets.

That is why, when I hear officials of the European Union affirm that they will grant aid to compensate the enormous losses of tax revenues that the proposed Economic Partnership Agreements will generate, I say that Africans and their Europeans counterparts should think twice before implementing them, particularly if we have an idea of what African countries want as far as the independence of their economic policy is concerned. In fact, though the estimates are still preliminary in several cases, available figures show that losses in customs receipts will be enormous. Citing a study of the Center for Studies and Research on International Development (CERDI), President Abdoulaye Wade of Senegal revealed that tax revenue losses for his country may range between 38 and 115 billion CFA between 2008 and 2015 if his country applied the agreements, representing 23 per cent and 69 per cent respectively of foreign aid.[22] Concerning Nigeria, this country may lose about 800 million euros per annum. In these conditions, even by admitting that the European Union is ready, as it affirms, to compensate these fiscal losses, this situation will increase the budgetary dependence of African countries to such an extent that their freedom in terms of economic policy would be compromised for some time. The quality of the economic policy of a country also depends on its independence vis-à-vis foreign interference.

Should we seek automatic stabilizers of public finances in African economies?

In developed Western economies, economists have observed an empirical regularity. The budget tends to exercise automatically – that is, without any discretionary intervention of public authorities – a stabilizing effect on the economy. As such, the budgetary deficit tends to grow (thereby exercising an upturn effect) when the economy slows down and to shrink (thereby exercising a contractionary effect) when the economy overheats. This is what is called automatic stabilizer of the budget. This phenomenon is linked to public-spending composition: some public expenditures automatically tend to increase when the economy slows down and to fall when the economy is in a favorable situation. As we may realize, the functioning of automatic stabilizers requires that the structure of public revenue and spending be such that public revenues increase while public spending reduces or increases more slowly during a boom, and that public revenues reduce while public spending increases or reduces more slowly during a recession.[23] The advantage of automatic stabilizers is that they enable the budget to automatically play the role of demand-management instrument without the need of conjunctural budgetary measures from the state. These conjunctural budgetary measures may at times require long political debates liable to retard action. Not having to pass through that, therefore, may in some circumstances constitute a non-negligible advantage. In my opinion, ensuring that the structure of public revenues and spending facilitate the functioning of automatic stabilizers is therefore a task worth undertaking. In fact, the observation shows that in African countries deficits have the tendency to grow hollow during periods of boom instead of reducing during these periods. This is what happened during previous boom periods. This situation then obliges states to implement more restrictive measures during periods of recession, thereby increasing it.

Despite the attraction that automatic stabilizers may exercise from a theoretical point of view, their role in practice can be limited. However, this is what empirical studies realized in some Western countries where the structure of public revenues and spending favor the functioning of these mechanisms. For the eurozone, estimates converge on the hypothesis according to which automatic stabilizers may cushion about 30 per cent of the initial shock when it is a shock in demand. That means if, for an exogenous cause, demand drops by a point of GDP, the GDP growth rate will drop by about only 0.7 instead of 1 per cent.[24] In spite of the limited size of these mechanisms in practice, there is no reason to deprive oneself of the few countercyclical effects that they contribute.

Tax Policy and Administration

The power of the state to tax – that is, to appropriate itself a fraction of the income and/or wealth generated by private economic agents – has a long history in economic policy. Tax administration refers to the administrative machinery put in place by the state toward ensuring that the agreed taxes are collected efficiently and at minimum cost. Because taxation influences the incomes of economic agents, tax policy and administration is one of the most powerful instruments that economic policy officials have at their disposal to influence the behavior of economic agents.

In a nutshell, the contemporary debate on tax policy has emphasized the need for a sound tax system to achieve many goals, including: (i) revenue generation,[25] to enable the state to adequately fund its sovereign prerogatives; (ii) progressivity, ensuring that those who earn more should also pay more in taxes; (ii) encouraging voluntary compliance, and limiting opportunities for avoidance and evasion; (iv) reducing opportunities for corruption; (v) having a broad base; and (vi) not being distortionary. African tax systems should also seek to reflect these principles in their design and administration. In the context of African countries, much more should be required of a sound tax system, especially considering the importance of taxation as a tool in the policymaker's toolkit to influence the behavior of economic agents. In this context, a key question immediately comes to mind, considering that I have defined a good economic policy as one that is able, at the end of the day, to influence the two intermediate goals of strengthening demand addressed to the economy and building productive capacity. That question is the following: on which one of these two key intermediate goals should the tax system focus?

The economic literature and policy discussions have traditionally focused on the role of taxation as a productive capacity-building tool. Policymakers have thus tried to pursue this goal by granting various exemptions and tax holidays as incentives to support businesses' development. Although these practices have been widespread, their efficacy is being questioned. A recent study jointly conducted by the Nairobi-based Tax Justice Network – Africa and the Johannesburg-based Action Aid International, which assessed the effectiveness of tax incentives in Kenya, Rwanda, Tanzania and Uganda, showed that these countries had granted substantial tax incentives (amounting to 3.1 per cent of GDP in 2007/08 in Kenya, 4.7 per cent of GDP in 2009 in Rwanda, 6 per cent of GDP in 2008 in Tanzania and 2 per cent of GDP in 2009/10 in Uganda), but the return in terms of additional investments had been quite disappointing.[26] An earlier 2006 study by the IMF had reached similar conclusions. It can therefore be said that if extortionate taxes can significantly stifle private investment efforts, the effectiveness of tax breaks toward productive-capacity building can be limited. Where necessary, governments should therefore carefully study them toward ensuring that they will have positive effects before granting them.

The contribution of the tax system to stimulating demand addressed to the economy toward strengthening the framework for growth has not always been explicitly mainstreamed in the literature and policy discussions, although this is very important. As we will see below in the discussion on trade policy, it is through import tariffs that the tax system has traditionally contributed toward strengthening demand addressed to the economy, since import tariffs increase the domestic price of imported goods and services relative to the price of locally produced goods and services. But the successive waves of trade liberalization, which in essence have meant that import tariffs in African countries have been substantially reduced, have also considerably weakened the contribution of the tax system to one of the major intermediate goals of economic policy, which is to strengthen demand, as we have seen. In many African countries, the advice often tendered by donors was to adjust other domestic taxes such as value-added tax to make up for lost revenues stemming from the reduction of import tariffs. Although revenue considerations are very important, the remaining key issue for African countries is to find another demand-stimulating instrument in their tax system or elsewhere in their economic system to make up for the lost demand occasioned by the sometimes necessary[27] reduction in import tariffs. This is, in my view, the next big challenge that African economic policy officials will have to address, because the current situation cannot continue without permanently jeopardizing their growth and employment creation prospects.[28]

Public Debt Policy

The first contribution of budgetary policy to the pursuit of the goal of stimulating demand addressed to the economy and building supply capacity is to promote the confidence of economic agents. It may achieve this by ensuring that public debt is not excessive, or anyway not beyond the capacity of public authorities to reimburse. An excessive public debt undermines the confidence that economic agents may have in the capacity of economic policy officials to manage the economy, brings about capital flight and reduces investment. All these factors contribute not only to a loss of confidence (and therefore reduces demand addressed to the economy) but also to a reduction of the productive base.[29] Some types of spending are normally financed by loans, while others must be financed by taxes. Thus, economists today agree that recurrent spending like healthcare, educational and infrastructural maintenance spending must be financed by taxes, while investment spending, particularly in fields like infrastructure for example, should be financed by loans. This principle is also known as one of the golden rules of budgetary policy.

Communication Policy

As I have earlier discussed in this book, the role of psychological factors is as critical as that of objective variables in the explanation of the decisions of economic agents and therefore in the determination of a country's economic performance. This psychological dimension is influenced by the manner in which economic policy officials communicate with economic agents. All acts of communication matter, including what officials say and what they do not say, what they do or what they do not do. Economic agents constantly scrutinize all the declarations, acts and gestures of authorities responsible for economic policy with the aim of gleaning information which can orient their own economic behavior. In such a context, we must realize that besides traditionally studied instruments (i.e., monetary policy, budgetary and tax policy, trade policy, etc.) we will also find all the instruments that officials of economic policy can use to influence the psychology, perceptions and even behaviors of economic agents. The possibility of influencing the perceptions of economic agents and their behavior gives to economic policy officials a very powerful instrument – that is, their policy concerning information. They can, thanks to an information policy designed for purposes of a well-oriented and well-targeted cause, obtain from economic agents favorable behaviors in pursuit of the economic goals of the nation. Up to this point, African countries have not fully placed information at the service of their economic policy, whereas, if well used, it offers considerable potential to stimulate economic growth.

Recent progress in economic science – particularly the rise of neuroeconomy, which places the role of psychological factors at the forefront, besides other more traditional determinants – in explaining the rationality behind the decisions of economic agents certainly increases the importance that should be given to information as an instrument of economic policy. As such, the economic results of a country are as much the result of well-oriented economic fundamentals as the result of the behavior of economic agents influenced by psychological factors which, at times, go beyond what the level of fundamentals imply. Moreover, we do not only have theory to demonstrate the role of these psychological factors, economic facts also point in this direction. As such, in 1998, Alan Greenspan, then chairman of the US Federal Reserve, realizing that these psychological factors were probably the main explanation for the rally in financial markets in the United States, called the actors to order by qualifying this increase as "irrational exuberance,"[30] a famous expression today. Several observers also estimate that these same psychological factors played a lead role in starting and propagating the financial crisis which shook Asian countries toward the end of the 1990s.[31] This highlighting of the importance of psychological factors in determining the behaviors of economic agents gives an important place to an efficient information policy in influencing these psychological factors. Eventually, what I advocate here is a more efficient use – more efficient than it has ever been the case up until now – of information policy as an instrument of economic policy.

Despite the promising perspectives provided by neuroeconomy for the conduct of economic policy, it should be acknowledged that economic science has not waited for its accession to establish the role and importance that communication plays for the effectiveness of economic policy, particularly when this communication effort doubles with efforts to strengthen the credibility of economic policy officials and of the messages they communicate. As such, the formulation in the 1960s of the hypothesis that economic agents are rational in their expectations, and its later use in the theory of time inconsistency in economic policy choices (two major theoretical advances that I evoke in this book) demonstrated the cost linked to the absence of an effective information and communication policy in economic policy. An effective policy on informing economic agents contributes to anchor expectations on the goals pursued by the authorities and, by so doing, contributes to their realization. This was demonstrated empirically in the case of monetary policy for example,[32] but is also valid in all the other domains of economic policy.

Exhortation of Economic Agents

Exhortation refers to efforts that economic policy officials can deploy to persuade economic agents to adopt certain behaviors deemed favorable to the pursuit of economic policy goals. As a general rule, exhortation uses nonbinding, informal means and counts only, for its success, on the good disposition of economic agents to adopt the required behaviors. At times, it works. While economic policy has often resorted to exhortation in some countries, particularly developed countries, African countries generally have not been able to create the conditions for the profitable use of this instrument, which may however prove very efficient in some circumstances. However, some recent examples justly show that exhortation works and that African countries would do better by creating the conditions for the effective use of this instrument.

Can exhortation be an effective instrument of economic policy in Africa?

Although exhortation has not always been used effectively in African countries, its potential may be non-negligible when it comes to influencing the behaviors of economic agents in a way favorable to the final, intermediate and operating goals pursued by national economic policy officials, particularly when it is implemented in a methodical and sustainable manner. The effective use of exhortation occurs through the development of a message on the national economy and its productions, a message which must be convincing enough to encourage the adhesion of economic agents. One of the major axes of this message should be to incite economic agents to strengthen their demand addressed to the economy by illustrating national successes and the qualities of national productions to illustrate the message. As such, it is thanks to a well-conducted exhortation campaign that the poultry sector, which was completely devastated in Cameroon, progressively recovered (see Box 6.2).

Several other examples of successful exhortation certainly exist on the continent. They demonstrate that thanks to small actions, at times less expensive, great successes may be achieved in economic policy. In the foregone example, where insufficient demand was the major constraint on the growth of this sector of the Cameroonian economy, the stimulation of this demand by an effective exhortation campaign significantly contributed to the recovery of the sector and to job creation.

Competition Policy

Public authorities must also use their power to regulate the conditions of competition in the economy, particularly to limit infringements on it – abuse of position, monopoly power, concentrations and collusion between firms and other unfair competition practices. In fact, the free exercise of competition is an important factor in increasing the efficiency of the process of production in national companies and thus strengthening the national productive tissue. It is also a factor of development of demand addressed to the national economy to the extent that it is a factor of price reduction, thereby contributing to the increase in demand. The obstacles to competition that emanate from market structures – monopolies, oligopolies and duopolies – have well-known negative effects, amply illustrated by economic analysis. They result particularly from the fact that companies, in a situation of absence of competition, are tempted to fix selling price at a high level, which helps them to make high profits. Of course when prices are so high, it discourages demand addressed to the economy. Non-competing companies also implement actions to prevent any potential entrant from efficiently penetrating the market, thereby stopping the development of the national productive tissue.

Who benefits from competition? Demand or supply

During the debate that took place in France, a key European country, within the framework of the 2005 referendum on the European constitutional treaty, some supporters of the 'no' camp relied heavily on the article which stipulated that the objective of the union was to promote undistorted competition. To them, competition presented risks.

Box 6.2. An example of successful exhortation in Africa: The recovery of the poultry sector in Cameroon

The poultry sector in Cameroon experienced a real disaster following the massive importation of frozen chicken, particularly from Europe. According to the statistics of the Association citoyenne pour la défense des intérêts collectifs (ACDIC), a local NGO, poultry imports in Cameroon galloped from 59 tons in 1994 to more than 22,000 tons in 2003. This development had significant negative consequences on the economic activity and employment in this sector. It is thanks to an exhortation campaign successfully carried out since 2004 by the private sector in partnership with civil society organizations, particularly to discourage the local demand for imported frozen chicken to the advantage of local production, that the poultry sector in Cameroon experienced an extraordinary recovery. Commenting on the success of this campaign, Bernard Njonga, president of ACDIC, declared:

If we won the fight of the chickens, it is because consumers adhered. […] We realized an awareness of the citizens. Poor families abandoned frozen chicken, though cheap, for local products. It is a giant step. We also realized that actors of the domain reoriented themselves toward local production, realizing that the activity could be profitable. The best route to the future is dialogue and engagement with political and economic actors as well as the citizens.[33]

These words of an actor on the field join those I have made in this book on the importance, for the success of economic policy, of efforts aimed at stimulating the demand for local products. If the local production succeeded in recovering in Cameroon, it is thanks to the reorientation of local demand toward local production.[34]

Finally, during the European Council in Brussels, a consensus was reached among European leaders under which the promotion of competition would not be a fundamental objective of the treaty, but simply a means among others to attain its goals.

In fact, whether competition benefits consumers, particularly through the price drops that it generates, has never been an object of controversy. Concerning supply (that is, producers), the impact of competition is the subject of the most heated controversies. Indeed, for some, it stimulates creativity and innovation, which in turn contribute to improve the quality of products and services. For others, though it presents these positive effects, it may also lead to widening inequalities, the strongest crushing the weakest, resulting in their disappearance from production chains. It is undeniable that in an economic context where unbridled competition reigns, some companies are bound to disappear. Partisans of economic liberalism refer to this process of destroying companies that perform less well as "improvement of the allocation of resources in the economy."

The effects of competition are at the center of all the debates on the liberalization of international trade. If no one contests the fact that the price drops it enables are beneficial to the consumer, developing countries fear for their productive base. I think these fears are founded. From the point of view of a good economic policy, the promotion of undistorted competition in the domestic market among resident firms must be sought first before the promotion of unbridled competition between resident and nonresident economic agents. It is also the approach implemented by some Asian countries like India or China,[35] or even the European Union, where the setting up of the single internal market within the union is very much advanced compared to the liberalization of trade with the third countries.

Partnerships in the Economy[36]

Information exchanges, the attitude of collaboration and cooperation among the different economic actors in analyzing economic perspectives and making the decisions that these require, are an important instrument of economic policy. As such, economic policy officials must strive to promote these partnerships. In the business world, when these partnerships function well, they contribute toward creating a social climate which is favorable to the productivity of companies and therefore contribute to strengthen the productive tissue of the economy. All developed countries implement different arrangements, adapted to their particular contexts, to promote partnerships within companies. In Japan, for example, these partnerships are such that the future of employees is closely linked to that of their companies. These partnerships not only contribute to productivity but also to demand addressed to the economy by restoring the confidence of workers in general. In fact, for the private sector to move – that is, for it to undertake the investment projects – it needs sustainable and stable assurance on the part of public authorities. Economic policy should therefore ensure that mechanisms of an active and productive partnerships fully function among the different actors of the national economy. President Olusegun Obasanjo of Nigeria often liked to say that one of the lessons he drew from the development experience of South Korea was that the economic and industrial power of this country, today the 11th world economic power, was constructed by some six individuals, great entrepreneurs, working closely with the public authorities. We could moreover say the same thing of all the other industrialized countries which owe their economic success to their capacity to promptly identify and encourage, within the framework of a well-targeted and effective industrial policy, national businessmen and entrepreneurs with exceptional talents, in order that they fully deploy their creativity to implement actions that contribute to the strengthening of the national productive tissue. When we find ourselves in this perspective, the criticisms made by some Western commentators during the crisis which hit Asian countries toward the end of the 1990s – in respect of the partnerships between the public and private sectors, which had contributed to the previous economic success of these countries and which they qualified as "crony capitalism" – are perfectly unfounded. Moreover, Western policy officials are almost always accompanied on visits abroad by a strong delegation of businessmen of their countries. These official trips as such offer the opportunity to make industrial contacts which are beneficial to their countries. Is that not an example of partnership between the public authorities and the private sector?

Besides these company partnerships, another form of partnership must also be encouraged. This is what is conventionally called public–private partnership (PPP). They are generally defined as the association between public and private entities constituted with the view of conceiving, realizing and managing a project of public interest, under the auspices and the total or partial financing of the private sector. The advantages such partnerships present for African countries are in the optimization of the respective performances of the public and private sectors in the realization of key public infrastructures. It is therefore with the aim to sustainably develop the private sector through better participation in state projects that economic policy officials in African countries must fill one of the major gaps in the present business environment by intensifying reforms aimed at setting up the legal and institutional framework required for the increase of PPPs.

Industrial Policy

Industrial policy, which entails the selective granting of aid by the state under different forms for the development of certain activities, is a very important instrument for pursuing the intermediate objective of building productive capacity. This instrument has in the past, and to some extent still today, given rise to heated controversies. Detractors of this policy assert that the state has neither the capacity nor the necessary information to identify the most promising activities. But no one today truly contests the important role that a good industrial policy may play in the development of the productive capacity of an economy. Whether it is the formerly developed countries of Western Europe or North America or the recently developed countries of Asia, all these countries have had and continue to make recourse to a well-conceived and well-implemented industrial policy to promote the development of the productive machinery of their economy.

The debate is no longer on the necessity of an industrial policy. Generally, it is accepted today that no economic development is possible without a strong, stable and sustainable partnership among public authorities and the actors of the private sector within the framework of an effective industrial policy. However, some think, and perhaps rightly so, that for institutional arrangements to work effectively and in the interest of the society, they must be studied carefully. In fact, a great risk is that some less scrupulous investors will exploit public aid for private purposes. We should immediately realize that, faced with these risks, there is no one-size-fits-all solution that may fully satisfy all countries in all contexts. It is up to every country to create and execute the institutional arrangements which will guarantee the success of its industrial policy. It is also in this creation that the imagination and the innovation which economic policy needs to succeed should express themselves.

In one of his articles on industrial policy, Dani Rodrick, a US-based economist, studies the question of institutional arrangements for positive collaboration between the public and private sectors.[37] He states certain general principles which may contribute to the success of these arrangements. These principles include the fact that these arrangements must benefit from the support of political leadership of the highest level, being based on the existence of coordination and reflection mechanisms, which will guarantee regular exchanges of information between the public and private sectors, as well as mechanisms to guarantee transparency and accountability in decision making. Box 6.3 below summarizes the

10 principles which, according to Dani Rodrik, should govern the implementation of a good industrial policy. A country like France devotes about sixty-five billion Euros[38] of its budget – that is, about four per cent of its gross national income – to public aid for its companies.

Box 6.3. Ten principles for the implementation of an industrial policy[39]

(i)   Incentives should be provided only to "new" activities

(ii)   There should be clear benchmarks/criteria for success and failure

(iii) There should be a built-in sunset clause

(iv) Public support must target activities, not sectors

(v)   Activities that are subsidized must have the clear potential of providing spillovers and demonstration effects

(vi) The authority for carrying out industrial policies must be vested in agencies with demonstrated competence

(vii) The implementing agencies must be monitored closely by a principal with a clear stake in the outcomes and who has political authority at the highest level

(viii) The agencies carrying out promotion must maintain channels of communication with the private sector

(ix) Optimally, mistakes that result in "picking the losers" will occur

(x)   Promotion activities need to have the capacity to renew themselves, so that the cycle of discovery becomes an ongoing one

---

Discussions on industrial policy have so far focused on broad outlines, falling short of ideas on how to identify specific products to target for public support. In what, in my opinion, is one of the best books recently published on development policy, Chinese economist Justin Yifu Lin, former chief economist of the World Bank, has closed this gap. He has outlined six critical steps for identifying which specific products industrial policy should target. Box 6.4 below summarizes these steps.

Trade Policy

Economic policy officials also have at their disposal a number of instruments usually grouped in what is conveniently called instruments of foreign-trade policy or trade policy in short: customs duty, subsidies, quantitative restrictions and voluntary exports restrictions. The debate concerning the most adequate use of trade policy to effectively contribute to economic growth and job creation in the developing countries has given rise to one of the most heated controversies in the entire history of economic policy.

The literature on trade policy has the tendency to present trade policy as an instrument to stimulate or strengthen the supply capacity of an economy. The idea being that trade

Box 6.4. Industrial policy in action: Six steps by Justin Yifu Lin[40]

(i)   Policymakers should select dynamic growing countries with similar endowments structures and with per capita incomes that are about one hundred per cent higher. They must then identify tradable industries that have grown well in those countries for the past 20 years.

(ii) If some private domestic firms are already present in those industries, they should identify constraints to technological upgrading or further firm entry and take action to remove those constraints.

(iii) In the case of industries in which no domestic firms are present, policymakers may try to attract foreign direct investment from the countries listed in step 1 or organize new firm incubation programs.

(iv) In addition to the industries identified in step 1, the government should also pay attention to spontaneous self-discovery by private enterprises and support the up-scaling of successful private innovation in new industries.

(v)   In countries with poor infrastructure and business environments, special economic zones or industrial parks may be used to overcome barriers to firm entry and foreign direct investment and encourage the formation of industrial clusters.

(vi) The government should be willing to compensate pioneer firms in the industries identified earlier with tax incentives for a limited period, co-financing for investments, or access to foreign exchange.

policy helps to influence the level of competition in the domestic market between local productions and imported goods and services, competition which in turn influences the allocation of resources in the economy, and therefore the level of productivity. It is based on this reasoning that, within the framework of structural adjustment programs in the 1980s and 1990s, international financial institutions pushed developing countries, including those in Africa, to adopt policies to liberalize their trade regime, with a view toward encouraging this competition, and as such favoring the entry into their domestic markets of goods and services from the rest of the world.

In fact the direct and immediate effect of trade policy is to modify the relative price of locally produced goods and services compared to goods and services from the rest of the world. Therefore, since it first influences prices, trade policy can be considered an instrument which first influences demand addressed to the national economy. It is only indirect to the extent that, in an economy, all the variables end up in one way or another being linked among themselves, and as such, movements of demand also end up being movements of supply, so we may say that trade policy indirectly influences supply.[41] As such, the reduction of customs duties, for example, is expressed by a drop in the relative prices of imported products, thereby tending to orient demand toward these goods. Similarly, an increase in customs duties tends to orient demand toward locally produced goods and services since it increases the relative prices of imported goods, all things being equal.

The instruments of trade policy must be used such that they contribute to demand addressed to the national economy and to the strengthening of its productive base. In a perspective of contribution to demand, trade policy must first seek to stimulate exports which are an important component of demand. To attain this goal, it should ensure that there are no taxes or other restrictions on exports, except if it can be proved that the imposition of such a tax is in the interest of the national economy. Concerning consumer goods, it should be ensured that the rate of customs duties and other taxes and measures are at a level where they orient demand toward goods and services supplied by the economy, without necessarily being excessive. In fact, excessive levels generate governance problems in their management. In order to maximize the contribution of trade policy to the building of supply capacity, it must aim at favoring the efficiency of productive facilities by ensuring that customs duties on inputs and capital goods are low enough in order not to increase the structure of production costs in the economy. It is this strategy of liberalization of foreign trade that countries like Mauritius, South Korea and Tunisia followed successfully. I will come back later to the Tunisian experience concerning liberalization of trade.

Besides relative prices, another goal through which trade policy can contribute to the intermediate goals is the confidence of economic agents. When customs duties and other trade barriers are excessive, they destroy the confidence of economic agents and contribute to the development of fraud and corruption, thereby perpetuating the vicious cycle of losing the confidence necessary for the good performance of the economy. In certain circumstances, particularly when an acceptable goal of public revenue is at stake, officials my explore the possibility of compensating the impact of low-level import duties on tax revenues (when such a low level is justified) with an appropriate domestic tax reform.[42] However, we also know that a tax reform in poor countries is never easy, considering the limited administrative capacities.

Public Procurement Policy

Public procurement refers to the purchase of goods and services by the government toward delivering the various services for which it is responsible. Public procurement can represent a substantial amount of resources. In this context, officials should carefully explore and fully exploit opportunities to use public procurement as a tool to strengthen demand addressed to the economy. This may involve giving preference to local suppliers in the public procurement of some goods and services, although international competition should be explored toward getting value for money. Some countries have even designated some goods and services which should be procured locally only. To be effective, these local procurement efforts should be accompanied by well-targeted and effective efforts to build the capacity of local suppliers. The above orientations should be part of a public procurement policy. In this context, I think African countries, and indeed developing countries in general, should think twice before agreeing to the inclusion of government procurement in the current negotiations of the World Trade

Organization, otherwise they risk considerably weakening one of their key instruments of demand stimulation.

Regulation

Although regulation is a domain of intense activity by economic policy officials, and is also one of the most studied domains, the concept of regulation is still imprecisely defined. In this book, I consider regulation as "control exercised by the government on prices, conditions of entry and exit in a given sector or industry."[43] The goal pursued by the public authorities through regulation is to coercively orient the behaviors of economic agents (companies and consumers) in a way that generates less-harmful negative effects for the society. In fact, experience has amply shown that in the absence of an adequate regulatory framework, companies and consumers may adopt behaviors which, while being beneficial to them, may risk having a negative impact on society. Although the success of regulation depends on the credibility of the authorities, successful regulation may also contribute to strengthening the credibility of authorities and the confidence that they enjoy from economic agents, and may therefore contribute toward the strengthening of demand addressed to the economy and of the investment necessary for building productive capacity.

Exchange Rate Policy

Foreign exchange is an operation which consists in exchanging the currency of a country with that of another country. The exchange rate is the price of foreign currency in national currency.[44] This rate varies from day to day according to the supply and demand of currencies on foreign-exchange markets (if the country adopted a floating exchange rate regime) or is fixed (if the country adopted a fixed exchange rate regime). Thus, in Tunisia, a country that has adopted an exchange rate which fluctuates from day to day, on 28 December 2013, 1 US dollar was equivalent to 1.6412 (buy) and 1.6445 (sell) Tunisian dinars and 1 euro was equivalent to 2.2588 (buy) and 2.2634 (sell) Tunisian dinars.[45] In the eurozone, we will say that, on 27 December 2013, 1 euro was worth 1.38140 US dollars and 0.83665 GB pounds, and on 23 December 2013, 1 euro was worth 1.37020 US dollars and 0.83770 GB pounds.[46]

Exchange rate policy – that is, that which consists in attempting to determine an appropriate level of exchange rate between the national currency and foreign currencies – constitutes another major instrument of economic policy. As the price of foreign currency in national currency, the exchange rate is a price that influences, and in turn is influenced by, all the other prices in the national economy. It determines prices in national currency of goods and services bought in the rest of the world and imported into the national economy and prices in national currency of goods and services produced by the national economy and sold to the rest of the world. Thus, the lower the exchange rate – that is, the less foreign currency the national currency buys – the lower the prices in foreign currency of goods and services produced by the national economy and sold to the rest of the world, thereby stimulating demand addressed to the national economy by foreign economic agents. In the domestic market, a low exchange rate also stimulates domestic demand addressed to the national economy to the extent that it increases price in national currency of foreign goods and services compared to prices of locally produced goods and services, thereby stimulating demand addressed to the national economy by national economic agents to the detriment of demand that these same economic agents address to the rest of the world.

In another situation, if the exchange rate is high – that is, if a given quantity of national currency buys a significant quantity of foreign currencies – the prices of goods and services produced by the national economy and sold to the rest of the world will be high, thereby discouraging their demand on world markets. Given that it determines prices in a significant manner, exchange rate is an important instrument to stimulate demand addressed to the national economy.

However, even if the exchange policy is thus used purposefully as an instrument to influence demand addressed to the economy, it also acts indirectly on productive capacities of national companies to the extent that they ineluctably respond to variations of demand, themselves stimulated by the variations of prices which result from those of exchange rate movements. Due to this indirect link, exchange rate policy is also a powerful instrument of a good policy of supply. The important role that the exchange rate exerts on productive capacities was illustrated by the impact that the rise in value of the euro in the latter part of the 2000s had in European industries. The aircraft manufacturer Airbus estimated that the continuation of the drop in the dollar and therefore the rise in value of the euro would lead to delocalization of part of its activities from France to the dollar zones. It estimated that the rise in value of the Euro could put to question the industrial scheme contained in its restructuring plan.[47] Before the drop of the US dollar, the exchange rate of the Chinese currency, the yuan, was at the center of tensions between China and the United States first, then between China and the European Union later. The United States and the European Union accused China of maintaining the exchange rate of its currency at such a low level that it became undervalued, in a bid to stimulate the demand of Chinese products on American and European markets and, by ripple effect, procure a competitive advantage for its productive system to the detriment of those of the United States and Europe. More recently, "Abenomics," the new economic policy conceived by the Japanese prime minister Shinzo Abe to pull his country out of a long deflationary period, has also relied on a substantial depreciation of the Japanese yen in most of 2013. If variations in the exchange rate have the potential to affect well-established industrial groups with sound technological and managerial know-how to this extent, we can imagine at what level the exchange rate must be important to the health of the fragile industrial tissue of many African countries.

If the exchange rate policy thus offers a powerful instrument to increase demand addressed to the economy, particularly where it results in a depreciation of the exchange rate, the question that immediately comes to mind is why a country would not lead a profound depreciation policy of its exchange rate to obtain a competitive advantage at the level of demand. The response to this question is twofold. First, there is the risk that this depreciation may lead to an acceleration of inflation – the well-known depreciation–inflation spiral. The difficulty in the definition and implementation of an exchange policy stems from the latter's influence on the inflation rate – that is, the general level of prices in the economy and, therefore, the macroeconomic stability. However, as we have seen, macroeconomic stability is an important factor in the confidence of economic agents in the economic system. As such, an exchange policy which considerably reduces the exchange rate with the goal of stimulating demand addressed to the national economy may result, from a certain level of depreciation, in accelerating inflation as the prices of imported goods and services which enter into the local production and consumption processes rise. This high inflation will destroy the confidence of economic agents in the national economy and introduce the distortions that I raised in the foregoing chapter. The authorities must therefore seek an appropriate level for the exchange rate in order to avoid spiraling depreciation and inflation.[48]

Finally, a country cannot indefinitely depreciate its exchange rate to obtain a trade advantage without provoking a reaction from its trade partners. In the absence of coordination, the country runs the risk of triggering a scenario of competitive devaluations, which in the final analysis will not benefit any country. This is what economists call a beggar-thy-neighbor policy. The reaction that Americans and Europeans had concerning the level of the exchange rate of the yuan, which they judged undervalued, better explains the type of reaction to which I am alluding. Speaking on this issue in 2007, the French president Nicolas Sarkozy evoked the risk that such a situation can lead to an economic war.[49] During the annual meeting of the World Bank and the IMF held in Singapore in 2006, Americans sought to obtain the support of major industrialized countries to put pressure on China to revalue its currency. Later that year, the IMF, under pressure from the United States, which wanted China to modify its foreign exchange policy, adopted a new enhanced framework for monitoring countries' practices concerning the exchange rate.[50] However, China expressed its opposition to this new framework, with its representative in the IMF declaring that the policy should not be directed against a particular country. It is in its practical implementation that we realize what this new framework means exactly in terms of the international monitoring of exchange rates.

The history of international monetary relations shows different mechanisms established at different moments to conjure the risk of competitive devaluations by attempting to fix exchange rates among currencies. These mechanisms include the gold standard in which the exchange rate of the currency of each country was defined in terms of gold and the country had to convert its currency into gold on demand. This system functioned from the end of the nineteenth century until its replacement, in 1944, by the gold-exchange standard. This system was one of the major results of the International Monetary Conference held from July 1 to 22, 1944 at Bretton Woods, New Hampshire in the United States. In the gold-exchange standard, which progressively became a gold–dollar exchange system given that the dollar became a reserve asset of the same level as gold, the exchange rates of other currencies were to be fixed in terms of the dollar and the dollar was in turn convertible into gold. This gold–dollar exchange system functioned until August 15, 1971 when the United States officially announced the suspension of the convertibility of their currency into gold. Since then, every country has been free to choose the most convenient method to determine its own exchange rate, the only requirement being that it informs the other countries of the method chosen and avoid the practice of multiple exchange rates. Since then, all countries have effectively exercised this freedom to choose their exchange rate system.

As such, the systems chosen by countries show a great diversity ranging from irrevocably fixed exchange rates to perfectly floating exchange rates. Generally, however, we notice a movement toward flexible exchange rates. Research carried out by Andrea Bubula and Inci Ötker-Robe, two IMF economists, on the evolution of exchange rate systems since 1990 confirm this trend.[51] Based on exchange rate systems effectively implemented by member states of the IMF, as opposed to the officially adopted systems, this study shows that, if we take all the member countries of the IMF, the proportion of countries implementing a flexible exchange rate system increased from 15 per cent in 1990 to 35.5 per cent in 2001. This trend can be observed both in developed countries as well as in developing countries. In the first group, the proportion of countries practicing a flexible exchange rate system increased from 26 per cent in 1990 to 41.7 per cent in 2001,[52] while in the second group, this proportion increased from 13.2 per cent in 1990 to 34.6 per cent in 2001. Figure 6.1 below illustrates these evolutions.

If the exchange rate is such a powerful instrument for a policy of demand stimulation and, by ripple effect, of productive-capacity building of the national economy, the first question that comes to mind is that of knowing which is the best exchange rate for a country. Generally, authorities face a certain number of difficult choices in the definition of their foreign exchange policy. They must first determine which is appropriate for the national economy: an exchange rate which is fixed or is not fixed.[53] If they opt for the first, they must then determine the currency peg, in terms of which the exchange rate of the national currency will be expressed. This question does not come up in the case of an exchange rate which is not fixed. The choice of the currency peg is made between pegging to a currency and what economists refer to as pegging to a currency basket.

Thus, generally, the question is to know whether the country needs a fixed or floating exchange rate. Whatever the case, when a country has a fixed exchange rate, the economy must be flexible enough to be able to adjust to the exchange rate; in the case of floating exchange rate, it is the exchange rate that has to adjust to the economic situation of the country. From the point of view of stimulation of demand addressed to the economy, it appears that where the economy of a country is often under internal and external disturbances, it is necessary to have an exchange rate which is adjustable when necessary to maintain a high demand for the national economy.[54] As such, when for one reason or the other demand tends to drop, the exchange rate adjusts to re-establish the price competitiveness of national products. With a fixed exchange rate, as I have mentioned, the real variables of the national economy, such as wages and other prices, have to adjust to re-establish the price competitiveness of national supply and can, as such, maintain demand addressed to the economy. It is well known that when the economy has to adjust to a fixed exchange rate it is much more painful. In fact, in this case, the national economy is finally at the service of the chosen exchange rate instead of the contrary.

That said, an economic policy which is lax on other elements that determine the price competitiveness of national productions, such as the improvement of the processes of production in companies toward improving the quality of national productions, and which seeks to rely only on an adjustment of exchange rate to stimulate demand addressed to the economy, may not be viable. In other words, the exchange rate must be flexible and

Figure 6.1. Trend in exchange regime per group of country[55]

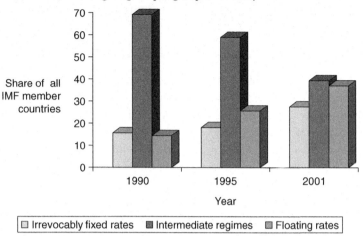

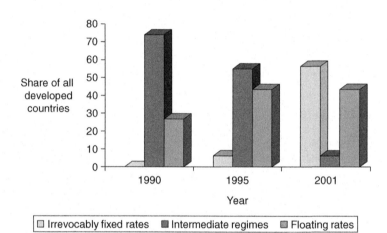

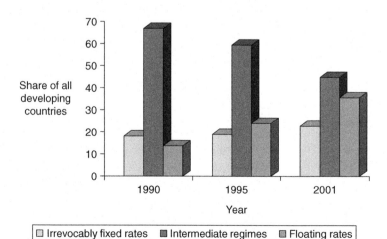

used together with other instruments to stimulate demand addressed to the economy and build productive capacities, and not in isolation from the other instruments.

Creating trademarks to stimulate demand addressed to the economy

Where tastes and preferences of economic agents are an important determinant of their decisions, economic policy officials must also develop means to influence them directly. Creating trademarks can, in some cases, prove an effective means to influence these tastes and preferences. All developed countries have, at one moment or the other, depended strongly on creating and developing trademarks to establish customer loyalty and as such guarantee the existence of a sustainable market for their products. This is valid for developed countries like France, Germany, Japan, England. It is also valid for the new generation of major emerging economies like South Korea, China, Taiwan and Hong Kong. Some will say that creating and maintaining a trademark is not yet within the reach of African countries, but the example of Ethiopia – a very poor country, dependent on the production and exportation of coffee, which attempted to have its coffee trademark recognized in the United States with the aim of increasing demand and the income of Ethiopian farmers (see Box 6.5) – shows that it is possible, even for African countries, to depend on trademarks to increase demand addressed to the economy and obtain a higher share of the value incorporated in national production.

Social Security Policy

Economic agents best develop their potentialities and their innovation capabilities and creativity when they are reassured that at least part of the multiple risks they run (sickness, accident, old age, etc.) is covered by society. Social coverage of risks is therefore a powerful instrument to give confidence to economic agents, reassure them, and as such liberate the productive energies needed by the productive capacity–building efforts of the national economy, a key intermediate goal of economic policy. It also contributes to growth by stimulating demand addressed to the economy. Economic policy must therefore develop an effective instrument of social insurance. Within the context of African countries, I know that several obstacles bar the implementation of effective social-insurance programs, but it is indispensable. Approaches helping to surmount the difficulties must be sought.[57] Modest services can accomplish much from the point of view of the confidence that economic agents need to liberate their productive and demand energies.

Other Sectoral Policies

I have partly founded this book on the questioning of the sectoral approach of economic policy. That does not mean that purely sectoral policies do not have their place in a good economic policy. What the systemic economic policy developed in this book proposes is that sectoral policies be elaborated and implemented by aiming at attaining sectoral goals, obviously, but also by aiming at contributing clearly to the operating, intermediate and final goals of the economic policy I have raised. Thus, achieving social cohesion,

Box 6.5. Ethiopia wishes to create trademarks for its coffee[56]

Ethiopia is one of the poorest countries of the world. About fifteen million people live on coffee farming, which contributes between 40 and 60 per cent of the country's exports. Between 2000 and 2003, world coffee prices dropped and revenue from coffee farming dropped by about 59 per cent. Ethiopia produces three of the most demanded types of coffee in the world: Sidamo, Harar and Yirgacheffe. Estimates show that coffee lovers are ready to pay up to 26 dollars per pound for Ethiopian coffee due to its quality and taste. However, the farmers earn only a small portion of the value that their coffee represents, about 10 per cent, because this value is monopolized by foreign coffee importers, the roasters. With coffee brands recognized for their quality and taste, and particularly when we know that consumers are ready to pay a higher price for them, it was clear that Ethiopians could obtain a higher share of the price of their coffee than they had previously. To obtain this high share, in 2005 the Ethiopian government filed an application with the US Patent and Trademark Office. The application actually aimed at creating an Ethiopian coffee trademark and, therefore, make it known that the use of the name is exclusive to Ethiopia. Despite several obstructive attempts, the American coffee giant Starbucks finally agreed to work in collaboration with the Ethiopian government for a solution which guaranteed the protection of the intellectual property of Ethiopian coffee names. After meeting with Starbucks president Jim Donald, Ethiopian prime minister Meles Zenawi said, "The right to possess a name for our coffee is the only means for us to protect our rich coffee heritage. Ethiopia has an obligation toward consumers in the world to protect and preserve our unique coffee." Ron Layton, president of Light Years IP, an organization based in Washington, DC working on intellectual property, said: "The ownership of intellectual property today constitutes an important proportion of the total value of world trade, but the rich countries and world companies confiscate a greater part of these incomes. Ethiopia, the place where coffee is born and one of the poorest countries in the world, tries to affirm its rights and obtain more values for her products."

contributing to good governance, confidence of economic agents, credibility of economic policy, stimulating demand addressed to the economy and building productive capacities of the economy toward growth and employment are also goals to which even a policy for the educational, agricultural or infrastructural sector – just to cite these few examples as sectoral policies – must demonstrate concretely the manner in which it contributes, besides targeting specific goals in the sector.

Summary

To conclude Chapter 6 on economic policy instruments, I will say, as already emphasized, that it is in the handling of instruments that we find the art of economic policy.

The success of economic policy officials in using instruments is not measured by this or that instrument reaching a particular level, but first, and foremost, by the progress toward the intermediate and final goals targeted by the authorities. In using instruments, it is often in the judicious choice of the moment of intervention, the direction and the level of the instrument that the art of economic policy manifests itself. It is often on these three decisions that the skills of economic policy officials are judged. These decisions must be taken in a way to positively influence the operating goals of economic policy.[58]

A last point on which I wish to particularly insist here is the fact that the authorities that manage economic policy must not see the different instruments that I just described as ends in themselves. The success of economic policy is measured not by the capacity of authorities in manipulating the instruments, but obviously by the progress toward achieving the operating, intermediate and final goals that I discussed lengthily in the foregoing chapters. It is convenient, henceforth, that besides indicators related to commonly available instruments, African countries develop appropriate indicators which measure the progress toward the operating and intermediate goals, thereby helping to better judge accomplished progress.

Chapter Seven

MEANS OF IMPLEMENTING
A SYSTEMIC ECONOMIC POLICY

Introduction

Once officials have agreed upon the economic policy – that is to say, when they have agreed upon the operating goals to pursue during the chosen period, the orientation for each instrument to achieve these goals, and the specific measures to be taken – all that is then left for them is to implement the measures. If I make reference to operating goals, it is because the final and intermediate goals should generally be fairly stable from one period to another. It suffices to simply reiterate them in the elaboration of economic policy. It is essentially in the selection of operating goals and the determination of changes to bring to the instruments that the action of economic policy is found from day to day. I will, in this chapter, examine the means that the officials in charge of economic policy have to implement the chosen measures.

The Legal and Regulatory Framework as a Means of Implementing Economic Policy

When it concerns the means of implementing economic policy, one might at first think of financial resources. Most often, we hear officials saying that they would have accomplished more if they had more financial resources. This may be true, except that the resources at their disposal for the implementation of economic policy are mainly from taxes on the income and/or wealth produced by the economy. The financial resources are not exogenous, but are, as economists say, endogenous in relation to economic activity. I discussed this relationship in Chapter 6 in the context of tax policy and administration. If financial resources are endogenous in relation to the economic activity that economic policy seeks to stimulate, and especially if this relationship is concave as we have seen, then a high level of financial resources should not be the criteria for the means of implementing economic policy.[1]

Beyond the endogeneity between public resources and economic activity, modern methods of public management focus on managing for results. In this approach, the goal is not to seek the highest possible means, but to get the best results with the available resources.

If the level of financial resources should thus not be seen as the main determinant of the means of implementing economic policy, on what are these means based? Since economic policy works primarily through its effects on the behavior of economic agents, its most powerful means are first of all the legal rules that organize the interactions between economic agents and between them and the state. Legal scholars distinguish four types of legal rules according to their importance in the hierarchy of legal norms: the constitution, supranational rules (resulting from commitments made by countries under the international treaties they have ratified), laws and regulations. These are the main means of implementing economic policy. The quality of the legal framework of a country is therefore essential for the implementation of its economic policy. It is important to ensure that it enjoys respect from economic agents, but also that it is adapted to the economic and social context of the country. Achieving this should be the purpose of the operating goal in relation to good governance as I identified in Chapter 5.

Faced with this multitude of legal norms, the question then arises of the respective roles of the constitution, supranational rules, laws and regulations in economic policy implementation. In other words, what means for what goals or measures? This is the question that I will now try to answer.

The Constitution

The constitution is at the top of the hierarchy of legal norms. Usually, it organizes the exercise of political power in a country. It also sets out the fundamental rights of citizens. From the standpoint of economic policy, the constitution could set the final goals of the economic policy of the nation, which are supposed to be stable even in the long term. It can, for example, clearly set these final goals as being a high level of employment and economic growth. Using the constitution for the purpose of economic policy could make these goals credible in the eyes of economic agents. Such an approach would have the advantage of encouraging a wide, enriching and productive debate within the country on government's economic policy. In fact, everything related to the constitution is generally widely debated. Although this debate is already in itself a good thing, the fact that these final goals are enshrined in the constitution would give citizens a way to remind the state at any time of its constitutional duty to promote economic growth and safeguard employment. This would be a way to ensure that all acts of the state are evaluated on their contribution to these fundamental goals.

In addition to these two final goals, it seems to me that broad orientations in terms of the use of fiscal policy, especially the search for a position that tends toward a medium-term balance between public expenditure and domestic resources, could also be included in the constitution, as this orientation in the use of this instrument seems important to the success of economic policy. Indeed, a movement toward this balance not only contributes to macroeconomic stability, but also strengthens the country's independence in its economic policy choices, which seems to me to be one of the determining considerations for the success of economic policy.[2]

However, we must admit that the practices regarding operating goals are varied. There was a debate in the US whether or not to compel the federal government to meet a balanced budget by including a provision to that effect in the constitution. This constitutional amendment was not finally adopted. In fact, although it is still possible to regulate the use of instruments in the constitution, some believe that the use of instruments may require some flexibility, which would be lost if the terms for their use were defined in a less flexible tool like the constitution. That is why they are of the opinion that only the final goals should be subject to treatment in the constitution. Intermediate and operating goals and instruments, because they should be more responsive to conjunctural economic trends, can be reserved for laws and regulations. I think I should remain open on this issue and leave it to each country to make the choices that best suit its political and social values. I can distinguish between two types of laws of economic policy: framework laws on economic policy and other laws of economic policy.

Framework Laws of Economic Policy

A framework law would aim to define the main directions of the medium-term economic policy of the nation.[3] It can take many forms, depending on the practices and values of each country. Whatever the form chosen, it is important that it be given a level of authority which is sufficient enough to enable officials in charge of economic policy feel the obligation to respect the parameters it has set. In some countries, the framework law for economic policy is, for example, in the form of five-year development plans, produced every five years and adopted as a law passed by parliament. The fact that these five-year plans are approved by parliament gives them a sufficient level of authority and they act as a force to remind the government of its intermediate and operating goals of economic policy.

Until the 1990s, the economic policies of African countries, which were limited to the Washington Consensus (whose limits I have amply illustrated), were most often described in the policy framework papers (PFPs) that they, as well as other developing countries, had to prepare in collaboration with international financial institutions, particularly the IMF and the World Bank, in order to receive financial assistance. In response to growing criticism from civil society and in some quarters of the developing world, and in order to give the fight against poverty a central part in their aid programs to low-income countries, during their annual meetings in September 1999 the World Bank and the IMF jointly launched a new approach to their financial relationships with them.

A key element underpinning this new approach was that each low-income country seeking financial assistance from the Bretton Woods institutions was to draw up, every three or five years, a poverty reduction strategy paper (PRSP), which was supposed to present the national consensus on policies most likely to contribute to the pursuit of poverty reduction.[4] The country was also to report annually on progress in the implementation of this strategy. The process of the PRSP was also expected to follow a number of principles, including (i) aiming at a high level of ownership by the country, which implies that the strategy is prepared with a participatory approach involving all stakeholders in the fight against poverty, including government, parliamentarians, civil society and the private sector; (ii) being directed at achieving results in reducing poverty; (iii) having a comprehensive approach to poverty that recognizes its multidimensional nature; (iv) being based on a strengthened partnership between countries and donors; and (v) having a long-term vision of poverty reduction. As for the content of the strategy proposed in the PRSP, expectations emphasized the need to present (i) a clear diagnosis of the situation of the country in terms of poverty, based on a poverty profile where it is available; (ii) priorities for the macroeconomic, structural and social policies that the country intends to implement to reduce poverty; (iii) appropriate medium- and long-term goals as indicators of progress in this area; and (iv) appropriate monitoring and evaluation of the results of poverty reduction. Since its introduction in 1999 by the World Bank and the IMF, other development partners have immediately adopted it, such that the PRSP is not only used by the World Bank and the IMF but by other donors, including other multilateral development banks, as part of their support to development efforts in these countries. The development of a PRS has become one of the essential steps in the process of economic policy in African countries.

After the adoption in September 2000 of the Millennium Development Goals (MDGs), the expectations of the international community vis-à-vis this document focused on its role as an instrument of reflection at the national level on a strategy to achieve the MDGs. According to the report of the Millennium Project of the United Nations, a good strategy for poverty reduction must have the following four characteristics: the goals of poverty reduction must be aligned with the MDGs and the strategy should aim to achieve them all; they must be defined based on a sound analysis of resource requirements; they must be based on an analysis of long-term needs; finally, the strategy must present a budget that is commensurate with the resources necessary to achieve the MDGs.

In July 2004, the World Bank and the IMF published the results of a study to evaluate the process of developing and implementing what I can now call the first generation of PRSPs.[5] The study aimed at assessing both the policy content of these strategies and the effect that PRSPs had had on policies and institutions, as well as the links between the PRS and the budgetary and decision-making processes of countries. In general, this study concluded that an approach based on PRSPs had the potential to promote a country's ownership of its own economic policies, particularly in the areas of growth and poverty reduction, since the first experiments showed that the PRSPs generally laid emphasis on greater participation, even if the level of participation was not equal in all segments of society. This approach could also contribute to a better understanding of the multidimensional nature of poverty, and development strategies contained in the PRSPs generally appeared better than previous strategies in that they were more focused on poverty reduction and granted greater attention to results.

Despite this initial progress, an area where much effort is still needed to improve the quality of PRSPs, and which the study also noted, is that of economic policy. Indeed, as noted in the study, most PRSPs did not succeed in developing a real road map for economic policy that takes into account the country's specificities and its initial conditions toward proposing original and well-targeted economic policies that can both promote strong and sustainable economic growth with particular focus on the productive sectors[6] and contribute toward reducing poverty while maintaining macroeconomic stability. This, in my opinion, remains the major challenge that African countries must surmount in order to achieve growth and poverty reduction. Indeed, beyond the commitments made to reduce the budget deficit, containing inflation and ensuring the balance of external accounts, which are all necessary policy options, the policy measures contained in PRSPs developed by African countries are most often limited to the composition of public expenditure in order to increase the share of social expenditure and other so-called pro-poor expenditures in the budget.

In addition to the absence of a real and clearly articulated development strategy, another common weakness of most strategies to reduce poverty prepared by African countries is linked to the fact that these strategies fail to establish adequate strategic priorities to guide development actions. Thus, most simply list the progress that the government intends to achieve over the next three to five years. The desired progress generally covers virtually all sectors of the economy, particularly the social sectors like education and health, access to potable water and improved sanitation, transport, energy, environment, agriculture, industry and handicrafts, and also include the commitment of the authorities to implement policies that can enable the country to achieve the Millennium Development Goals. It is this trend that has prompted some observers to say that, where PRSPs are concerned, *everything* is a priority. But we must recognize that establishing the priorities for achieving the MDGs is not an easy task in a country where everything needs to be done. This difficulty is confirmed by the fact that even aid organizations, which have virtually all adopted a new approach to developing their country strategies based on the results (I will come back to this point later), still fail to develop country strategies that are sufficiently selective and focused on concrete and clear results.

I think it necessary to go beyond current practice in many African countries, where for now the PRSP takes the place of an economic policy document and is developed and adopted by the government in various forms which do not seem to really reflect a real commitment. It may be necessary that these documents actually define the medium-term economic policy of the country and constitute a framework law of economic policy. Such a law could include the intermediate and operating goals the country aims to achieve in the medium term in order to move toward the final goals of economic growth and job creation I have lengthily discussed in this book. Setting for the state, within a framework law of economic policy, clear intermediate and operating goals in relation to those I have examined would have the advantage of concentrating the state's attention on the results that matter in the search for the well-being of citizens, and reduce the risks associated with a diversion of attention onto certain economic goals that may actually turn out to be only quasi goals or instruments and therefore do not reflect the fundamental well-being of citizens. We have seen that this risk exists.

Other Economic Policy Laws and Regulations

In addition to the constitution and framework laws, ordinary laws and regulations that lay down the more detailed rules governing the behavior of economic agents can also be used as means of implementing economic policy. Thus we could have a law on social stability, another on the promotion of confidence among economic agents, another on the promotion of financing of the economy, or many sectoral laws on education, infrastructure, and so on. These laws should be concrete and well-adapted to the country in question in order to promote the various goals mentioned above. It is within this category of legislation that the well-known finance act on the state budget belongs. Some would say that the economic policy of the state is reflected in its annual budget voted by parliament. The budget should be seen as a law that allows the state to implement an economic policy previously defined in an economic policy framework law, for example.

The choice of a law as a way to set for the state the final goals of economic policy is a practice that also exists. Thus, in the United States, a law dating from 1946 requires the federal government to seek full employment.[7]

International Agreements and Treaties

Agreements and international treaties ratified by the country can also be effective ways to implement an economic policy. Compared with internal means as I have just described, international treaties have the advantage of preserving some important goals of economic policy from domestic pressures.

Summary

I have examined in this chapter the means that officials in charge of economic policy have to implement it. It emerged from this analysis that it is through legislative and regulatory means that officials implement economic policy. These means include the country's constitution, laws and their decrees of application, as well as regulations. An intelligent mixture, which takes into account the values and circumstances, enables the authorities to optimize the use of these different means.

Chapter Eight

ECONOMIC POLICY IN PARTICULAR CONTEXTS: ECONOMIC CRISES AND NATURAL RESOURCES–BASED ECONOMIES

In everything I have said so far, I have, at least implicitly, remained within the hypothesis of ordinary times – that is to say, in circumstances where the economy is not going through moments characterized by exceptional events. But it is not always the case. We are quite often in extraordinary times – moments when the economy is disturbed. These exceptional times are often called, in common parlance and even in economics, periods of economic crisis. Which economic policy should we pursue in times of crisis?

There is also the case of countries exceptionally blessed by nature, which has endowed them with abundant natural resources that may be exploited, to be sold to the world and make enough income to continuously improve the well-being of their citizens. Does the issue of economic policy have the same meaning in these countries in the same way it does for others – that is to say, those who do not have this privilege and who constitute primarily those I had in mind in the previous chapters?

It is on these two questions, which seem relevant in the context of African countries, that this chapter will primarily focus. Discussing economic policy in times of crisis, I will successively lay emphasis on the manifestations of economic crisis (for the first thing is to identify and recognize the crisis when it is there), the origins of the crisis and the approach to adopt through economic policy in order to contain it. Finally, I will talk about economic policy in countries which depend on their abundant natural resources to improve the well-being of their citizens. As in previous chapters, the goal here is not to prescribe specific measures of economic policy to be implemented in times of crisis (they depend fundamentally on the characteristics of the crisis and contexts of different countries), but to state some general policy guidelines that I believe should guide the search for measures to be implemented.

Manifestations of Economic Crisis

Recognizing the signs of an economic crisis is in principle an easy exercise. This is when the performance of the national economy deteriorates. For example, growth slows down, unemployment rises and the various macroeconomic and microeconomic indicators (such as fiscal balance, balance of payments, corporate profitability, demand addressed to the economy, spending on investments by companies, and monetary aggregates and credit, for example) deteriorate. In general, the deterioration of economic indicators is accompanied by a worsening of social tensions. Anyway, it is really through its impact either on demand addressed to the economy, or on the productive capacity of the latter that an economic crisis becomes acute. It is therefore when there is deterioration in one or the other of these two intermediate variables that an economic crisis begins to have a real impact on economic growth and creating and safeguarding jobs.

If recognizing a crisis through its manifestations is relatively easy, the most important, and the most difficult, however, is predicting it – that is to say, anticipating it and taking precautionary measures in time. Experience has shown that predicting an economic crisis has so far proven to be an extremely difficult task, even in countries that have an established economic expertise, as is the case in developed countries. Economic crises have almost always surprised officials in charge of economic policy.

The Origins of Economic Crises

The origins of economic crises are many and varied. Some are tangible. This is the case, for example, when natural disasters (floods, drought, etc.) or unnatural disasters (an internal or external conflict) destroy part of the production tool of a country. Negative shocks to productivity can also be the cause of economic crises. Others, however, are less tangible and more virtual, but are no less important in the magnitude of their effects. This is the case with confidence, for example. When the level of confidence of economic agents declines, this may affect demand addressed to the economy and the productive capacity and thus economic growth. Experience even shows that the decline in confidence has been at the center of the origin of most crises that have marked the history of the world economy. This was the case during the crisis of 1929, when a simple reversal of confidence caused the bursting of a speculative bubble that had formed around call loans, leading to the fall of the New York Stock Exchange and panic among small depositors, marking the beginning of the crisis. One can also attribute the origins of the financial crisis that began in the summer of 2007 in the United States to a loss of confidence in subprime loans,[1] the high-risk mortgage loans that had developed in the country since the 1980s.[2] The decline in confidence due to an economic crisis can be either sudden (due to the occurrence of sudden events, but which are great enough to influence the drop in the expectations of economic agents),[3] or the result of a more or less long process. When it is the culmination of a process, a drop in confidence is as a result of the combination of objective factors, such as certain important economic variables whose values rise gradually to unsustainable levels, and the occurrence of a triggering event. The crisis of confidence at the origin of the 2007 financial crisis was triggered by the excessive and unsustainable levels of mortgage debts by households.

Finally, whatever their origins, the economy of a country can be affected by a crisis in the rest of the world which spreads and affects it or by a crisis it created itself. Figure 8.1 describes the transmission channels to the national economy of an economic crisis born in the rest of the world.

Crises arising from the rest of the world can affect many variables of interest to the national economy such as foreign direct investment flows, remittances from nationals

Figure 8.1. Transmission channels to the national economy of economic crises arising in the rest of the world

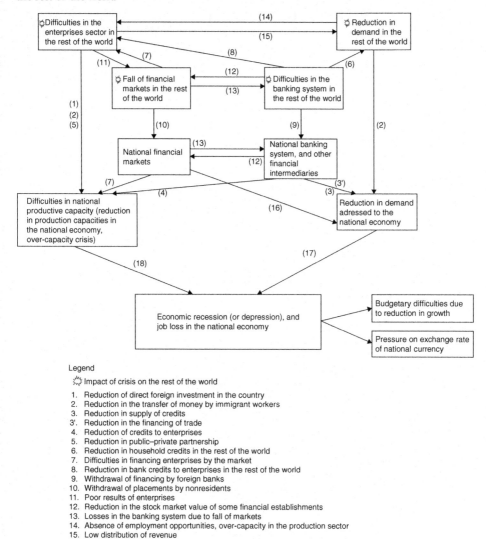

Legend

☼ Impact of crisis on the rest of the world

1. Reduction of direct foreign investment in the country
2. Reduction in the transfer of money by immigrant workers
3. Reduction in supply of credits
3'. Reduction in the financing of trade
4. Reduction of credits to enterprises
5. Reduction in public–private partnership
6. Reduction in household credits in the rest of the world
7. Difficulties in financing enterprises by the market
8. Reduction in bank credits to enterprises in the rest of the world
9. Withdrawal of financing by foreign banks
10. Withdrawal of placements by nonresidents
11. Poor results of enterprises
12. Reduction in the stock market value of some financial establishments
13. Losses in the banking system due to fall of markets
14. Absence of employment opportunities, over-capacity in the production sector
15. Low distribution of revenue
16. Negative wealth effects linked to the fall of the national financial market
17. Reduction in growth due to insufficient demand
18. Reduction in growth due to difficulties in national supply

working abroad, the national banking and financial system, the mechanisms for trade financing, or the performance of the domestic financial market. But ultimately, as Figure 8.1 indicates clearly, it is through demand addressed to the national economy and its productive capacity that these crises weigh on what matters to citizens – that is, economic growth and job creation. The decline in foreign direct investment flows is harmful because it hinders the development of national productive capacity. The decrease in financing trade is damaging because it leads to a decline in demand addressed to the national economy.[4] Part of the decline in remittances from nationals working abroad (that which is destined for consumption) results in a decrease of demand addressed to the economy, while another part (that from those who wish to invest in their country of origin) results in a negative impact on the national productive capacity. The impact on the banking and financial system results in a reduced ability to distribute loans to economic agents, which affects national demand and supply.[5] Be it that it arose from the rest of the world or from within the country, a crisis indeed only affects the national economy if it leads to a reduction in demand addressed to the economy or if it affects the productive capacity of the economy.

What Should Be Done in Times of Crisis?

Does a crisis put to question the pattern of economic policy that I have developed in previous chapters? No. As we have seen, crisis consists either in a reduction of demand addressed to the economy or a narrowing of its productive capacity. Restoring these two key variables, especially in times of crisis, can require substantial exceptional financing. But financial means must be sought while respecting the broad guidelines of economic policy developed in this book. These means are themselves conditioned by the quality of economic policy implemented before the crisis and thus the country's economic performance before the crisis.

The pattern of economic policy that I developed earlier does not change in times of crisis, especially the final and intermediate goals. We must stay focused on economic growth and job creation as the final goals of economic policy. And since it is through demand addressed to the economy and the state of its productive capacity that everything that happens affects economic growth and job creation, priority must also be given to encouraging demand addressed to the economy and to protecting its productive apparatus. These should be the two key priorities in times of economic crisis. The final and intermediate goals, therefore, do not change.

What about the operating goals and instruments? Here, adaptations will certainly be necessary, depending on the characteristics of the crisis. If, as was the case in the recent financial and economic crisis, the financing of the economy proves to be an important channel of transmission of the crisis, restoring the financing of the economy must become an utmost operating priority. This explains the concentration that was observed in Western countries on this variable throughout the search for solutions to the crisis.

From the 1980s, a literature on developing countries sprung up in which the choice that exists in times of crisis would be between adjustment (meaning reduced demand, economic austerity, slowdown in economic growth) and financing (meaning finding resources to finance demand and build productive capacity). This literature advocated adjustment for these countries. Following this logic, Ricardo Haussmann, a Harvard economist, suggested that to overcome the crisis, the US must reduce demand rather than stimulate it.[6] Americans did not agree with him, with a good reason. They preferred to stimulate demand and, at the same time, invest heavily to increase the competitiveness of their economy and increase the production capacity, which made more sense. Several of the measures implemented to fight the crisis in the US in effect involved supporting household incomes toward strengthening demand and implementing key supply-side measures such as, for example, providing support to the key US firms.[7] Having the decline and loss of jobs as an economic horizon with a view to ending the crisis is not imaginative and shows, in my opinion, a lack of ambition and creativity. No country should follow this path.

Economies Based on the Exploitation of Natural Resources

Provided that the natural resources they possess are available to them in sufficient quantity and quality to be exploitable for long periods and, be they natural resources whose demand will always exist, economies based on natural resources have, in principle, sufficient income to ensure the well-being of their populations. Their economic growth and job creation performance is tied in a mechanical way to that of those countries seeking the natural resources they possess. If such a country chooses to rely solely on its natural resources, the key issue of economic policy is to strengthen productive capacities in the field of exploitation of natural resources in order to ensure continued exploitation of their natural resources. For such a country, building human capital and good governance become first-hand priorities.[8] However, obtaining concrete results in these areas in order to put the resources at the service of the well-being of the population is often problematic, resulting in a deterioration of the well-being of citizens despite the abundance of natural resources. Thus, even for a country that chooses to focus on exploiting its natural resources, experience has shown that, despite these gifts of nature, things are never easy. This has given birth to the phenomenon now known in the literature as the natural resources curse.

But the challenges of governance and internal economic management are not the only issues facing a country with natural resources and which has chosen to focus on its exploitation to ensure the well-being of its citizens. In fact, nothing is so sure in life. Foreign demand for natural resources is never guaranteed. Take the example of oil: only ten or fifteen years ago, no one would have bet on the growth currently being experienced by bioenergy. In 2006, US president George W. Bush asked his countrymen to reduce their dependence on oil. The reduction of the dependence of the United States, one of the world's largest consumers of oil, on oil imports was at the center of the 2008 election won by Democratic candidate Barack Obama. He made a new energy policy based on lesser dependence on oil imports, an important goal of his mandate. In this way, the United States and Europe are investing heavily in the search for alternative energy sources to oil. The United States has already invested more than 80 billion dollars to develop ethanol, a fuel produced from corn, and has also taken steps to encourage automakers to build vehicles that consume less fuel. Although ethanol currently represents less than six per cent of oil consumption in the United States, with the pace of research advances, its share in oil demand from developed countries in general could grow rapidly. According to figures from the US Department of Energy, the dependence of the United States on foreign oil is expected to decline from 60 per cent to 50 per cent by 2015. This discussion shows that foreign demand is never guaranteed in the long term, even for a natural resource like oil.

For a country with natural resources that has made the decision to diversify its economy away from natural resources, the challenges are significant. To those elements of governance already discussed, I may add what has become known in the literature as "Dutch disease" This is the risk that the appreciation of the exchange rate due to inflows of natural resources revenues hinders efforts to diversify the economy.

Finally, therefore, either because adequate demand cannot be taken for granted forever, or because the diversification of the productive base of the economy is not easy, countries with natural resources should look at the improvement of the well-being of their citizens as a similar challenge to that faced by countries which do not. They may, therefore, very well base their economic policy strategy on the pattern that I have developed in this book.[9]

Conclusion to Part Two

The second part of this book has enabled me to outline what seems to be a new approach to economic policy for African countries. This new economic policy is not only necessary, it is essential if Africa wishes to use its immense potential to earn its place in globalization and improve the living standards of its citizens. This economic policy contains new elements for most countries, such as a greater focus on economic growth, creating and safeguarding jobs, the search for strong demand addressed to national companies, the strengthening of the productive capacities of the economy, and greater consideration of expectations and perceptions of economic agents. The most difficult issue, however, remains implementing this policy in an orderly, methodical and sustainable manner to ensure success. Some will find the framework developed in this book so far away from the current practices of African countries in economic policy that it has no chance of being implemented. I believe otherwise. Some countries are already implementing the new approach. However, I recognize that all countries are not at the same level of preparedness for the implementation of economic policy under the framework advocated here. Some are more advanced than others, especially countries that have managed to make peace with themselves and with their neighbors, those who are also trying to consolidate their democratic processes. These countries are in a better position to target the key operating and intermediate goals that I have identified above, including the confidence of economic agents and the credibility of their policies. I believe the proposed framework is accessible to all African countries, except those who are currently engaged in armed conflicts that hinder concentration on final, intermediate and operating goals, as well as using the instruments I have just examined in a state-of-the-art fashion.

Many apparent signs indicate that African countries have started to see the need to redefine, within the framework of their strategies for poverty reduction, the conception and implementation of economic policy in light of a clear reaffirmation of the place that economic growth and employment must occupy at the heart of final goals. Even if much remains to be done for this trend to be generalized, which would enhance the quality of economic policy implemented by African countries, I can only note with interest that the PRSPs of a growing number of African countries, which could be referred to as second-generation PRSPs, recognize the need to focus on strong growth and greater job creation. When the French edition of this book was first published in 2009, only a handful of African countries had clearly focused on growth and job creation in their PRSPs.[10] But since then many more countries have made the shift. Thus, Cameroon prepared a growth and employment strategy paper in 2009, followed later by many other countries. These changes of attitude clearly reflect a more fundamental change in terms of visions and desires that now guide the economic policy of a growing number of African countries. The challenge now is not to leave these paradigm shifts at the stage of intentions.

At the continental level, the United Nations Economic Commission for Africa, for nearly two years, has carried out a remarkable job which aims at giving issues concerning employment promotion a central place in the economic policies of African countries. It is in this context that the second meeting of the African Ministers of Finance on this topic was held in Ouagadougou, Burkina Faso in May 2006. The United Nations Office for West Africa also recommended that employment should be at the center of development policies. Although the 39th Conference of African Ministers of Finance, Planning and Economic Development and the United Nations Initiative for West Africa have not produced concrete policies, the fact that this topic features for the second time on the agenda of this meeting reflects the progress being made. The challenge now is to consolidate this reflection.

Beyond the proper use of available instruments as well as the appropriate institutional reorganization it requires, the full implementation of the new economic policy advocated in this book raises other major difficulties. It involves, on the one hand, the constraints imposed by the globalization process, which constitutes the context in which economic policy must take place and which, therefore, must be taken into account, and, on the other hand, the existence of a number of purely economic constraints that may act either individually or by combining their effects to substantially reduce the scope of economic policy measures that governments can implement. It is thus by reviewing these constraints and their interactions with the process of globalization that I am now going to tackle the third part of this book.

But first, I will mention two final points to complete the main issue of the second part of this book, which covered the structure of the desirable goals and instruments of the systemic economic policy for Africa. These relate to the Tinbergen rule and Mundell rule respectively. First, the Tinbergen rule. In 1969, two leading economists, the Norwegian Ragnar Frisch and the Dutchman Jan Tinbergen, jointly obtained the first Nobel Prize in Economics for their contribution to the application of mathematics and statistics to the study of economic phenomena. They had contributed much to the development of the construction of models and also pioneered the development of the branch of economics known as econometrics today. Among the many works of Tinbergen that the Nobel Foundation rewarded was the economic policy rule he enunciated in 1956, which, in my opinion, remains valid today. This rule, which is well known in the theory of economic policy as the Tinbergen rule, states that the officials in charge of economic policy must have as many instruments as goals. Now the Mundell rule. I have in this book identified a set of operating goals that those responsible for economic policy must pursue to achieve the final and intermediate goals. By applying the Tinbergen rule, these leaders must ensure in all circumstances that they have enough instruments for the goals they have set. In this process, another important rule must be observed: each instrument must be allocated for the attainment of the operating goal for which it has a comparative advantage – that is to say, that it can influence the most compared to other goals (this is the Mundell rule).

Part Three

GLOBALIZATION: CHALLENGES AND OPPORTUNITIES FOR AFRICAN ECONOMIC POLICY

The purpose of this book is to clearly situate the economic policy of African countries within the context of globalization and to examine the manner in which globalization should be considered in conceiving and implementing economic policy. In Part Three, I will therefore look at globalization in terms of formulation and conduct of economic policy according to the conceptual framework developed in the first two parts of this book. Although economic policy and globalization may appear as two distinct themes that may each deserve separate treatment, Part Three is out to show that these two themes are so interwoven that it will be very difficult to completely treat one without the other.

In Africa, as well as in other continents of the world today, where countries are called upon to build their development, economic policy and globalization are not two distinct realities which could be treated in two separate works. In fact, to decision makers of economic policy, globalization, its ramifications and implications are everyday concerns. For literature on economic policy to be pedagogic and truly useful to decision makers, the major challenge is to bring together these two realities in an integrated concept of economic policy. It is this integration that I will try to achieve in Part Three.

From this integrative perspective of globalization and economic policy, Part Three initially characterizes the globalization process by examining the major actors and factors which determine it (Chapter 9). This chapter also contains a summary of key findings of recent research on the impact of globalization on poor countries. Chapter 10 in turn analyzes the major constraints that globalization has on an economic policy designed and implemented according to the conceptual framework developed earlier, as well as the opportunities that it offers from this same point of view.

Chapter Nine

GLOBALIZATION: A VARIABLE GEOMETRY PROCESS

Introduction

A book which strives to contribute to a renewed economic policy in Africa, in view of helping the continent to accelerate its progress toward the achievement of its aspirations for economic development, would not be complete without an adequate treatment of globalization from the point of view of its implications for the elaboration and conduct of economic policy. As a matter of fact, globalization, in my opinion, presents the greatest challenge which officials of economic policy in Africa today must handle. This challenge is greater than all the challenges that developed countries have had to face during their development process. What effects may globalization have on the elaboration and conduct of economic policy in Africa? How can African countries better consider globalization in the elaboration and conduct of their economic policy? These are some of the questions to which I will try to find answers in Part Three. As such, I will start by examining the main aspects of the process of globalization. This will be the aim of Chapter 9. The next chapter will enable me to examine in greater detail the constraints and opportunities that globalization represents for the new African economic policy I am calling for.

Today, most, if not everyone, would define globalization as both a process and a result. As a process, globalization is seen as the acceleration of international trade in goods and services, ideas and knowledge, and increase of capital movement involving developed countries as well as developing countries. Globalization is also the result of this acceleration – that is, the situation characterized by increased integration of national economies among them. Although some situate the origin of this movement before the modern era, most observers think that it is actually after the Second World War that globalization grew rapidly, mainly influenced by technological developments, particularly in the fields of transport and communications, and by the economic policies implemented by governments to liberalize cross-border trade. Before examining these elements, let us pause a moment to briefly describe some results of globalization.

Brief Overview of Some Important Facts about Globalization

Trade in manufactured goods and agricultural products: Support to globalization

International trade in goods, one of the measures of the process and results of globalization, has increased greatly. According to the United Nations Conference on

Trade and Development (UNCTAD), in 1960, exports of goods constituted about 10 per cent of world GDP. In 2006, this figure reached close to 35 per cent.[1] As indicated in Table 9.1 below, from 2000–2007, growth in the volume of world export of goods reached 5.5 per cent in annual rate. During the same period, world GDP was growing at an annual rate of 3 per cent. In fact, world exports tend to increase twofold higher than world GDP, indicating that to some extent an increasing share of wealth produced in the world enters trade among countries. The development of world trade seems to be pulled by trade in manufactured goods, which is normal because trade in agricultural products generally face more restrictions than trade in other products.

Table 9.1. Increase in world exports of goods (in volume) 2000–2007 (annual percentage change)[2]

	2000–2007	**2005**	**2006**	**2007**
World export of goods	5.5	6.5	8.5	6.0
Agricultural products	4.0	6.0	6.0	4.5
Fuels and mining products	3.5	3.5	3.5	3.0
Manufactured goods	6.5	7.5	10.0	7.5
World GDP	3.0	3.0	3.5	3.5

The economic dynamism of Asia

According to UNCTAD statistics on the distribution of world GDP and its growth dynamism per region, in 2006, 72.9 per cent of world GDP was produced in developed countries. This percentage dropped compared to 1992 when it stood at 79.5 per cent. This drop is explained particularly by the emergence of Asia. In fact, during this period, Asia increased its share of world GDP. As such, the share of developing countries in Asia – that is, mainly Asian countries except Japan, including particularly China, India, South Korea and Thailand – rose from 10.1 per cent in 1992 to 15.6 per cent in 2006. If we add the share of developed countries in Asia to this (that is, mainly Japan), Asia's share in world GDP may reach 26.7 per cent. Today, foreign exchange reserves accumulated by Asian countries stand at about 3,500 billion US dollars.

A marginalized Africa

Africa seems to be a continent which is still to gain its place in globalization. Africa (North Africa and sub-Saharan Africa) represents about 14.5 per cent of the world's population, yet only 2.9 per cent of world GDP in 2012 (GDP at market prices). Though this share increased lightly compared to 1992, when it stood at 2.1 per cent, it still holds that Africa is the most underdeveloped compared to the requirements for successful integration into the globalization process. In terms of growth, during the period 2003–07, Africa experienced one of the highest increases up to 5.8 per cent, behind East, South East and South Asian countries (8.3 per cent) and West Asia (6.9 per cent), but this performance remains highly insufficient to significantly improve the standard of living on the continent.

Over the period 2008–12, Africa registered an average annual GDP growth of 3.6 per cent, while the above two groupings grew by 6.8 per cent and 4.0 per cent respectively. However, Africa is not homogenous. North African countries like Egypt, Morocco and Tunisia had been able (before the political turmoil they are currently experiencing), thanks to the mastery of their economic policies, to obtain performances which enabled them to profit from globalization. GDP per capita in North Africa was thus 2,382 US dollars in 2006, against only 617 dollars in sub-Saharan Africa (excluding South Africa). South Africa stood out as a major economic power not only in the continent but beyond.

Decoupling or globalization?

Are we witnessing a decrease in interdependence among economies, thereby reducing globalization? Recent research seems to defend the standpoint of decoupling. According to this view, economic cycles in the world, particularly those of developed and emerging economies, may no longer be interdependent and convergent as the belief in globalization would suggest, but rather divergent, meaning a slow down in the process of globalization. In fact, in a study of the behavior of three important macroeconomic variables (production, consumption and investment) in 106 countries divided into three groups (industrialized countries, emerging countries and other developing countries), three IMF economists proved that, from 1985–2005 – the period they refer to as having accelerated globalization – there has been a convergence of economic cycles in each group of countries and a divergence (decoupling) among the groups. In other words, there are factors peculiar to each group which may explain the greater part of fluctuations of the economic cycle in the group and not world factors common to all the sample countries.[3] These results were particularly exact for the groups of developed and emerging countries. They therefore tend to credit the standpoint which holds that different groups of countries may have separate business cycles. Despite this trend, the financial crisis has also proven that the concept of decoupling may have limitations. Actually, although it started in the United States, this crisis had negative effects which have been felt in practically the whole world.

While waiting for research to further elucidate the reality of interdependent forces in action in the global economy, other interconnection indicators among economies show that interdependence among world economies is today a reality. Whether it is foreign direct investments, development assistance, capital flows or transfers from the diasporas, sources of economic interdependence among world economies are very many today.[4]

Actors of Globalization

By actors of globalization, I mean public or private, national or supranational entities whose actions influence the pace and direction of the globalization process. Today, we may admit that the key actors of the process of globalization are (i) firms producing goods and services sold in different markets around the world; (ii) international institutions trying to define the rules of globalization, which everybody must respect (among these, one may cite the most important, which are the Bretton Woods institutions – that is, the

International Monetary Fund and the World Bank – the World Trade Organization); (iii) civil society organizations, which also play an important role in the globalization process; and (iv) consumers, who through their purchasing decisions play an important role on the volume and flow of goods and services and capital that define globalization, and have not often been fully and explicitly recognized in the literature among actors of globalization. In the following lines, I will show that, in the final analysis, consumers are the primary actors of globalization.

Many other international organizations have been created over the course of history and have considerable influence on the process of globalization in various important domains such as health, education, etc., but I will limit myself here to those whose actions exert more influence from a point of view which is of interest to us – the conditions of elaboration and conduct of economic policy.

Consumers

I start my examination of the key actors of globalization with a group which plays an extremely important role in the development and sustainability of the process but, maybe because they are not as well organized as the others, is often not explicitly recognized in the literature. This concerns consumers. World consumers represent the group of economic agents with the highest influence on the process of globalization. This reality is confirmed by the high share of final consumption in GDP (see table 9.2 below).[5] As a matter of fact, as we may have noticed, this share was close to 61 per cent of GDP in developed economies over the period 1981–90, if we consider the final consumption of households. In the US economy, the biggest economy in the world, the corresponding figure was 66.8 per cent. In China and in developing economies, household final consumptions were a bit lower, but significant, at 53.5 per cent and 58.3 of GDP respectively over the period 1981–90. As for Africa, household final consumption constituted 61.7 per cent of GDP over the period 1981–90. What is equally interesting to note is the fact that these proportions remain fairly stable enough with time.[6]

These statistics indicate the significant role of consumers as globalization actors of the first order. In fact, more than three quarters of total goods and services produced in the world economy aim at satisfying the demand expressed by consumers – that is, responding to consumer-oriented demands. As a group, this means world consumers represent the most important economic agents through their economic weight. As such, the economic activity directly linked to household consumption demand occupies an important place in the entire economic activity, as well as employment at world level. This important role of consumers in global economy remains valid at the level of individual national economies. The immediate conclusion that one can draw from these statistics is that one of the major goals of economic policy must be an in-depth analysis of consumption to identify the key factors that can contribute to its strengthening with a view to boosting economic activity. In my opinion, this does not seem to have been fully considered by African economic policy. Moreover, it is worthy to note that in the African context, where economies are generally outward looking, the current account balance generally constitutes a stronger constraint than in industrialized countries to a strategy of stimulating economic activity

Table 9.2. GDP and its components, 1981–2011[7]

GDP components (in GDP %)	1981–90	2008–11
Developed Economies		
Household consumption expenditure	60.7	62.7
Government consumption expenditure	20.7	19.0
Investment	18.9	18.5
Exports	13.3	26.5
Imports	13.2	26.8
United States		
Household consumption expenditure	66.8	70.9
Government consumption expenditure	20.4	16.5
Investment	15.4	15.7
Exports	6.5	13.1
Imports	7.9	16.2
China		
Household consumption expenditure	53.5	35.9
Government consumption expenditure	14.5	13.2
Investment	38.3	46.4
Exports	9.7	39.9
Imports	9.4	35.3
Developing Economies		
Household consumption expenditure	58.3	52.9
Government consumption expenditure	16.1	13.6
Investment	24.3	30.8
Exports	22.2	42.0
Imports	19.6	39.6
Africa		
Household consumption expenditure	61.7	62.8
Government consumption expenditure	16.0	16.0
Investment	21.4	22.3
Exports	29.3	35.7
Imports	27.3	36.3

based on the strengthening of global demand, or absorption as this variable is often called in the economic literature. To take account of this stronger constraint, demand should rather be oriented toward locally produced goods and services. It is this component of global demand which will have the highest influence on economic activity.

International Institutions

The International Monetary Fund

Among all international institutions which exist today, the IMF is surely, from the point of view of many African countries, the one whose actions have exerted the most determining influence on the progress of the process of globalization. In fact, it has the greatest influence on economic policies implemented by most African countries, particularly through different forms of conditionality which accompany the balance-of-payments loans it grants to these countries. Created in 1944, and pursuant to Article I of its statute, the IMF has as one of its goals: "To facilitate the expansion and balanced growth of international trade, and to contribute thereby to the promotion and maintenance of high levels of employment and real income and to the development of the productive resources of all members as primary objectives of economic policy."[8] This interest that the founding fathers of the Bretton Woods institutions attached to the promotion of high levels of employment and the building of productive capacities of economies, justify, if the need arises, the importance of the place that these strategic variables must occupy in the economic policy of states. The IMF achieves its goal through a certain number of activities; the major ones are related to the surveillance of the economic policies of its member states,[9] its loan operations and its technical assistance activities. The IMF works within the confines of periodic consultations existing between the IMF and each member state. To the IMF, surveillance consists in reviewing the economic policy of a member state to evaluate its impact on its own economic prosperity and that of the global economy. At the end of this evaluation, the IMF issues recommendations which aim at improving the economic performances of countries and increasing its contribution to the well-being of world economy. These recommendations are not obligatory and the country is not forced to implement them. The scope of the monitoring has increased and presently includes consultations carried out with regional institutions and economic groupings of its member countries. Thus, the IMF carried out consultations with the eurozone, the Central African Economic and Monetary Community (CEMAC), and the West African Economic and Monetary Union (WAEMU), for example. Concerning loan activities, they constitute the main means through which the IMF influences the economic policies of countries which resort to its resources, where these resources are placed at the disposal of the country on condition that the country implements a number of policies defined by mutual agreement. Monitoring and technical assistance activities, which have become an important part of IMF activities and even the research works it carries out, also play a role in the IMF's influence on the economic policies of countries, but the influence of other activities is less, compared to those which have to do with loans.[10]

Since the beginning of the 1990s, the IMF's action concerning the promotion of the process of globalization, particularly in low-income countries, has provoked serious criticism from several observers of the process and results of globalization. Nobel Prize winner in economics Joseph Stiglitz is today one of those who have tried to better structure their criticism, and who argue that the IMF's actions, according to them, may not have contributed to a globalization process which is harmonious and beneficial for all. Among these criticisms, those that are most often cited refer to the role that the IMF might have played in the financial crisis of the late 1990s, by encouraging countries to take precipitated measures of financial liberation even though their supervisory and regulatory infrastructure were not yet developed fully enough to enable an efficient management of the risks which accompany increased capital flows. There is also the insufficient attention that the IMF pays to the impact on employment and growth of the policies that it recommends to developing countries (despite the fact that its statutes show that employment is one of the major goals of economic policy),[11] the pro-cyclical fiscal austerity policies[12] that it might have imposed on countries in crisis that resorted to its resources, and the fact that it might also have given priority to the reimbursement of foreign creditors to the detriment of settling the economy of countries seeking its financial assistance.[13] According to the authors of these criticisms, this preference leads to the nationalization of private debts if the country has repayment difficulties, thereby increasing the problem of moral hazard for private creditors. The criticisms are also on an internal governance structure which does not promote the accountability of the institution toward the countries to which it lends most, and which are theoretically better placed to assess whether the institution has fulfilled its mandate as it should.[14]

To these criticisms is added another which is often made to all donors, that the IMF often "imposes" its point of view and its policies on countries, thereby making ownership something of an empty concept. In fact, many countries appear to resent what they most often consider as a very strong interference, similar to intrusion, in their economic policy. Some African economic officials with whom I have had the opportunity to exchange ideas on this subject have often confirmed that they shared this point of view. I can actually see the reluctance some countries, particularly in Latin America, Asia and Africa, have had in borrowing from the IMF as a manifestation of their desire to no longer be under its yoke.[15] According to the *Global Monitoring Report*, a joint IMF–World Bank publication, the IMF recorded a significant reduction of its loans to developing countries. These countries reimbursed more than 7 billion US dollars to the IMF in 2007, giving a total of 135 billion US dollars reimbursed during the five years to 2007. At the end of 2007, outstanding loans to developing countries (what is known in the jargon as outstanding debt owed by these countries to the IMF) hit its lowest in twenty-five years – that is, 15 billion dollars.[16] With the economic crisis which started in the United States and whose effects spread to other countries of the world, we observed a surge of IMF loan activities, granted particularly to Eastern European countries, and since the sovereign debt crisis in Europe to many eurozone countries (Greece, Ireland and Portugal). Iceland, Ukraine and Hungary also asked for loans from the IMF to solve their economic difficulties.

Other critics hold that the IMF is very much influenced by great powers[17] in its policies and decisions, instead of maintaining a certain balance in considering the points of view of all its member states. In fact, it should be observed that the IMF sometimes behaves in a way that credits the critics. As such, when the United States had a problem with the exchange rate of the Chinese yuan, the IMF hurriedly placed the monitoring of exchange rates at the center of its activities. Similarly, it was important that sovereign funds of emerging countries obtain a fraction, however small, of the capital of some companies in developed countries such that governments of developed countries decided that the elaboration of a code of good conduct for these sovereign funds was necessary. It did not take long for the IMF to take hold of the issue and announce that it would intensify its work on sovereign funds. The result was the elaboration and publication in October 2008 of the Santiago Principles, which outline a set of 24 principles intended to promote good governance and accountability in investment decisions of sovereign funds. In my opinion, elaborating these principles constituted progress, particularly considering the increasing role of sovereign funds in international financial transactions and implications of these transactions for economic stability in several countries. Nevertheless, one can note that within the framework of privatization, when companies of developed countries massively took control of most of the companies in developing countries, including companies of strategic sectors, the same eagerness of the IMF to support the elaboration of a code of conduct for these acquisitions would have reduced criticisms based on the excessive influence of developed countries in the activities of the IMF. It was not the case.

Following this avalanche of criticism, the IMF initiated a debate on a set of reforms which aimed at affecting the manner in which it carries out its operations as well as its internal governance structure. Concerning its operations, the reforms aim at strengthening the IMF's multilateral surveillance. At the level of governance, emphasis was placed on a revision of the structure of quotas and the voting rights of its member countries in a bid to give more weight to emerging economies like China.[18] African countries must take active part in these reforms, because the IMF's policies have a considerable impact on the manner in which they may be integrated in the process of globalization and how they benefit from it. This participation must be inspired by efforts made by Africa to be heard during debates on the United Nations reforms. On this occasion, African countries demonstrated their willingness to exercise ownership of this debate and had even elaborated African propositions for the UN reform. We realize that Africa was not prepared with the same diligence to play a key role and influence the reform of the Bretton Woods institutions, whereas it constitutes a stake as important to Africa as the reforms of the UN Security Council. However, things have evolved, and a meeting of African ministers of finance and planning which took place in Tunis in November 2008 promised to elaborate concrete proposals on the reform of the Bretton Woods institutions.

Drawing from its past experience and from the criticisms it faced, the IMF also implemented a number of other measures to improve their surveillance activities and lending operations. Thus, there was the creation in 2001 of an Independent Evaluation Office (IEO), a department in charge of carrying out retrospective evaluations independently from IMF policies and operations. The IEO is supposed to be independent of the management of the IMF and work in close collaboration with the Board of Directors.[19] A number of studies were also conducted, some by the IEO, to examine aspects of policies that the IMF had advised the countries seeking funds. Among these studies, I may cite those on the liberalization of capital accounts of the balance of payments, the practice of conditionality in loans, and the role of the IMF in determining and giving assistance to sub-Saharan Africa, particularly within the framework of the economic programs of these countries supported by the Poverty Reduction and Growth Facility (PRGF). I will raise the issue of the practice of conditionality later, when discussing the role of foreign aid in economic policy. The question of the liberalization of capital accounts became central, particularly after the financial crisis which hit Asian countries at the end of the 1990s. In a special study, the analysis carried out by IMF economists concluded that, although the liberalization of capital accounts is a good goal to pursue, there are cases, however, where this can prove premature and risky. Authorities must assess the position of their countries well in relation to the requirements of such a policy before engaging in such an action. Concerning the mobilization of assistance to sub-Saharan African countries within the framework of programs supported by the PRGF, the IMF was criticized for not accepting the use of all available aid, but also for being too restrictive in its projections of future levels of aid. The evaluation conducted by IEO concluded that, in general, the IMF favored the use of available additional aid in countries where the rate of inflation was low and where reserves were at a satisfactory level. In other countries, the programs were intended to allocate additional aid to constitute additional reserves,[20] which in my opinion was not too bad, especially in a context where several countries still needed to make much effort to guarantee lasting stability and sustainability of public finances.

The World Bank

The World Bank was created at the same time as the IMF during the Bretton Woods Conference. Originally, its role was to help in reconstructing European economies devastated by the Second Word War by granting them long-term loans to fund specific projects in different sectors such as infrastructure. After the reconstruction of Europe, it focused on development assistance to developing countries through the same projects loans. In the 1980s, in order to assist developing countries in coming out of the economic crises caused by the debt crisis, the World Bank launched structural adjustment programs, loan instruments whose objective is to promote economic reforms in these countries in exchange for fast-disbursing financing. It is mainly through this instrument that the World Bank has played an increasing role in the development of the process of globalization and the conditions of integration of developing countries in this process. In fact, the fast-disbursing loans were initially granted to support reforms aiming at liberalizing the trade system, according a key role to prices and markets in the allocation of resources, reforming the public and parapublic sectors. An evaluation of World Bank support to liberalize trade from 1985–2004 concluded that this support succeeded in making economies more outward looking.

Besides the World Bank, which intervenes on the five continents, there are also regional development banks which function almost on the same line as the World Bank – that is, they give loans and grants to their member states to finance development projects, support the implementation of economic reforms and build technical capacities in these countries. Created mostly after the independence of developing countries, these regional development banks play a non-negligible role today in international financial intermediation. Today, there exist four major regional development banks: the African Development Bank, the Asian Development Bank, the European Bank for Reconstruction and Development and the Inter-American Development Bank. Perhaps, because they are less important than the World Bank and the IMF in terms of the funds they raise or because they are a little less visible, regional development banks are usually less central to debates raised by the process of globalization compared to the World Bank and the IMF.

The World Trade Organization

Trade in goods and services among countries is one of the most important aspects of the process of globalization. It is also mainly through these exchanges that the citizens of different countries participate in the process of globalization, or feel its effects. It is not surprising, therefore, that the WTO, the international organization in charge of promoting the liberalization of world trade, is also one of the main actors in the process of globalization. Created within the framework of the Uruguay Round of multilateral trade negotiations, which lasted from 1986 to 1994, it was on January 1 1995 that the WTO was officially created. As such, it took over from the General Agreement on Tariffs and Trade (GATT), which, from 1948, served as the framework for negotiations toward liberalizing world trade. Under the auspices of GATT, eight series of multilateral trade negotiations were concluded, from the Geneva cycle in 1947 to the Uruguay Round, and resulted in the reduction of the rate of customs duties on imports of goods as well as on progress toward reducing nontariff barriers on the importation of goods.[21] While the mandate of GATT covered only trade in goods, the mandate of the WTO also covers trade in services and areas such as property rights. The WTO strives to fulfill its mandate by mainly constituting a place where member states come and negotiate toward concluding multilateral trade agreements by depending on a number of basic principles. Multilateral trade agreements form the basis of the functioning of the WTO. These agreements, better known by the agreement name, are the legal rules of world trade which, negotiated and signed by member states of the WTO, force governments to maintain their trade policies within the limits fixed in these agreements.

There are four basic principles on which the WTO agreements lie: firstly, to promote trade without discrimination thanks to the application of the clause known as the Most Favored Nation (this clause aims at ensuring equality in the treatment of foreigners and nationals in world trade); secondly, to liberalize trade progressively through negotiations; thirdly, to make agreements more predictable thanks to transparency and application of the consolidation of commitments taken by every country; and finally, to promote fair competition and encourage development and economic reforms in WTO member states.

Trade in goods and services are of primary importance in each individual's everyday life. In fact, we consume imported goods and services, and a high number of jobs in economies where we live depend directly or indirectly on the latitude of competition from imported products and export demand addressed to the national economy. This double dependence enables the development of trade with the rest of the world and offers considerable income-generating opportunities, thereby enhancing economic growth, but is also a source of adjustments which may at times be painful. Box 9.1 below gives the advantages of a multilateral trade system characterized by a liberalization of trade according to the WTO.

The actions of the WTO have often been criticized, particularly by civil society organizations and even by the governments of several developing countries. This is one reason why the WTO is one of the most controversial international organizations in the world. As such, the WTO meetings for some time have become forums for (sometimes violent) protests from organized groups that criticize the liberalization of trade upheld by the organization. One of the criticisms often leveled against the WTO is that its actions have led to a variable geometry liberalization in which developed countries have succeeded in having developing countries open up their markets to products for which they have a comparative advantage and which constitute a sure trade interest to them, while, thanks to a number of measures which create distortions, keeping their markets closed to products which constitute a sure trade interest to developing countries,

Box 9.1. The 10 advantages of the trade system promoted by the WTO[22]

1. The system helps promote peace
2. Disputes are handled constructively
3. Rules make life easier for all
4. Freer trade cuts the cost of living
5. It provides more choice of products and qualities
6. Trade raises incomes
7. Trade stimulates economic growth
8. The basic principles make life more efficient
9. Governments are shielded from lobbying
10. The system encourages good government

particularly agricultural products. Some economists, of whom the American free trader Jagdish Bhagwati may rightly be considered as the leader, believe that, on the contrary, developed countries have liberalized their trade with the rest of the world the most. However, the analysis that he has given in support of this point of view seems debatable. As a matter of fact, his analysis consists in showing that the average rate of *ad valorem* customs rights practiced by developed countries on manufactured goods, textiles and agricultural products respectively are inferior to those practiced by developing countries.[23] Of course, such an analysis does not take into account nontariff measures applied by developed countries, even though most economists agree on the fact that these nontariff measures are restrictive and consequently create more distortions on trade compared to tariff measures. Joseph Stiglitz also proves that the tariff structure of developed countries comprises tariff escalations that are harmful to the development of economic activity in developing countries. Thus, a Zambian trade minister declared during a ministerial meeting of the WTO in Hong Kong that "in ten years of tariff reform, we have de-industrialized Zambia literally," and Duncan Green, director of research of a British NGO, discussing the outcome of the Uruguay Round affirmed: "The developed world has obtained a free trade cycle. There is a little here for developing countries."[24,25]

It was by recognizing this bias and the need to reinstate an acceptable balance in the process of world trade liberalization that the WTO member states, at the start of negotiations at the Doha Round in December 2001, decided to make a special effort in favor of developing countries. The Doha Round of negotiations, also called the "development cycle" was supposed to result in an agreement that was especially favorable to developing countries. In this context, one of the goals of the Doha Round was that developing countries obtain a free trade-negotiation cycle – that is, they may not have to appease developed countries to obtain trade advantages from them, particularly in the area of trade in agricultural products through the reduction of subventions to their exports of agricultural products. After divergences among major trade powers like the United States, the European Union and Japan, negotiations of the Doha Round were suspended in July 2006 in the context of reciprocal accusations; the United States and the European Union mutually rejected responsibility. Discussing the American position in the negotiations, Peter Mandelson, then European commissioner for trade, said, "What they are saying is that for every dollar reduced from their agricultural subventions which create trade distortions, they want to receive a corresponding dollar of access markets of developing countries"; while Susan Schwab, the American trade representative, confirmed on her part that her country would remain "fully committed to the multilateral trade system. [...] Having attained an advanced stage, a number of developed countries and developing countries were looking for less ambitious means, to make less ambitious contributions."[26]

After more than 12 years of inaction, trade ministers met in Bali, Indonesia, on December 5–7, 2013 for the WTO's 9th Ministerial Conference to try to revive the Doha Round. They agreed on what is known as the Bali Package, which focused on trade facilitation, agriculture and cotton, some market access measures for least developed countries, and on the WTO's work program going forward. Although many praised the Bali Package, it remained clear that it fell short of the development commitments of the Doha Round. The chairman of the conference, Indonesia's trade minister Gita Wirjawan, said, "Now we must complete the Doha Round"; while WTO director general Roberto Azvêdo said, "The decisions we have taken here are an important stepping stone toward the completion of the Doha Round." South Africa's minister of trade and industry Rob Davies expressed his concerns:

The Members of the World Trade Organisation have not been able to establish an adequate balance between the three pillars that have made up the Bali Package, namely Development and LDC issues; Agricultural issues; and Trade Facilitation. The LDC pillar remains weak, again postponing the legitimate demands of the poorest countries with uncertain promises of delivery in the future. The Agriculture pillar contains nothing more than best endeavour on the critical issues of export subsidies and an "opt out" clause for an important member on the issue of tariff rate quotas. The proposed Trade Facilitation text is expansive and contains many new obligations for most developing countries, which will disproportionately bear the burden of implementation. There is also no certainty that the capacity building and assistance that would be necessary for implementation would be forthcoming. For this reason, South Africa proposes that this Ministerial Conference focus its efforts not just on concluding the so-called Bali Package, but also on providing political guidance on the development of a post-Bali work programme. This programme should prioritise turning the best endeavour undertakings that we have in the draft package on LDC issues and Agriculture into effective, time-bound programmes of delivery. We should also reaffirm that the fundamental principle of special and differential treatment in favour of developing countries. Balanced outcome on this early harvest Package would be an essential basis for re-starting negotiations under the wider Doha Round that places development at the centre of the process.[27]

To summarize, the IMF, the World Bank and the WTO, which constitute the main framework of what is appropriately called the "international financial architecture," were created in the 1940s – more than sixty years ago. There is no doubt that this architecture as it is today will continue to evolve. In fact, since the end of the international monetary system established at Bretton Woods, the smooth functioning of which was the responsibility of the IMF, calls to reform the international financial architecture are heard from time to time and are intensified in moments of crisis. Thus, this theme was raised with some force during the financial crisis that hit Asian countries at the end of the 1990s. During that period, these Asian countries argued forcefully in favor of setting up an Asian Monetary Fund. At the time, the United States did what it could to discourage this initiative. What is certain is that one of the major changes of the international monetary architecture will probably come from Asia. Thai finance minister Suchart Thadathamrongvech affirmed as much in the London daily the *Financial Times*: "The first stage will be a sort of Asian IMF, such that when we are in difficulty, we can obtain aid from such a multilateral organization. [...] Thus, if there is no crisis, there will be money in the system and it may act as a sort of development bank, like the World Bank."[28] This suggestion is a continuation of that of another Asian senior official, who estimated that debtor countries had too much weight in the present governance structure of the IMF, whereas in normal situations the creditors should have the highest powers. During a ministerial meeting in February 2009, the ASEAN (Association of South East Asian Nations) countries as well as China, South Korea and Japan took measures to strengthen the Chiang Mai Initiative by increasing its resources from 80 billion to 120 billion US dollars. During the same meeting, they decided to transform this initiative, which until then was just a mechanism based on bilateral currency swap agreements, into a real multilateral agreement.

During a meeting held on November 12, 2008 in Tunis under the auspices of the African Development Bank, in preparation for the G20 Summit, African finance and planning ministers and central bank governors also launched an appeal for an in-depth reform of the architecture of the international financial system.[29] The African Union is also working on the project of creating an African Monetary Fund.

On November 15, 2008 and April 2, 2009, two summits of the G20 were held in Washington and London successively to regroup the most industrialized and major emerging countries. The aim of the summit, whose theme was "financial markets and global economy," was to find solutions to the financial crisis born of the United States subprimes and which had been shaking the world economy since 2007 in the run-up to these summits. Some observers had wished that these meetings would take the form of a Bretton Woods II and lead to in-depth reform measures of the functioning of the international financial architecture.[30]

The question of the governance of international financial institutions, mainly the IMF and the World Bank, and the representation of African countries in these institutions is important. This theme plays on many people's minds and is often debated in current news. In 2009, the then South African minister for finance Trevor Manuel submitted a report to the managing director of the IMF on these issues. However, other problems also appear important concerning Africa. First, there is the economic policy that these institutions impose on the countries concerned. Even by admitting the need for reform, this will not lead automatically to a new vision of the economic policy that these institutions advocate. However, it is this new vision that constitutes the most important change that Africa must strive to obtain in this international debate. In fact, it is in Africa that the economic policy advocated by international institutions has the highest influence. And since this change will not come from a governance reform,[31] it is therefore important that Africa institutes a specific debate on this issue. It must therefore ensure that this debate on economic policy is a separate debate from that on governance and representation in these institutions.

Civil society organizations

Civil society today regroups a complex and heterogeneous number of interests. These civil society organizations experienced a sharp increase from the 1990s and have since then become key actors of the international society. The most visible among these entities are generally those based in developed countries. They are active in practically all areas concerning the process of globalization, such as trade in goods and services and capital, protection of the environment, poverty reduction and development in poor countries and gender promotion. Their actions play an important role in the process of globalization to the extent that they try to influence policies implemented by governments as well as international organizations which have an impact on globalization. Their main means of action is to lobby political and economic officials and those of the business world to implement measures which, according to them, will promote a more humane globalization – that is, one which leads to shared progress and not to increasing inequalities and exclusion.

Practically all social categories are represented in this group of actors of globalization: workers, religious personalities, consumers, students and local actors. Although it is difficult to evaluate the level of influence of civil society organizations on the process of globalization, experience demonstrates the influence they can exert on public policies and key actors of the process of globalization, even if they do not have any veritable means of action apart from efforts to mobilize support through different means. For example, in 2006 a simple student movement in France forced the French government to withdraw a reform which, according to the movement, increased insecurity on the labor market; NGOs have enjoyed some success recently in guiding the actions of rich countries on the debt of poor countries; and a Cameroonian NGO played a key role in reducing the importation of frozen chicken (see Box 6.2).

However, it may be hasty to generalize the capacity of NGOs to influence public policies which contribute to globalization. In fact, if NGOs of developed countries can, due to the democratic nature of their countries, contribute through their effective participation in democratic debates to the elaboration and implementation of policies that shape globalization, it is not the same for NGOs in most developing countries, Africa in particular. In fact, in most African countries, due to the insufficiency of democratic debate, the capacity of African NGOs to contribute effectively to policies implemented by their respective governments and which shape globalization is still limited. African countries should encourage effective partnership among NGOs and other national stakeholders because it is obvious that there exists a possible division of labor among the different stakeholders which optimizes public policies. As a matter of fact, governments and NGOs have different mandates. In some cases, NGOs can provide considerable support by defending certain positions that governments, because of their mandate and statute, cannot meaningfully defend.[32]

Multinational companies

Multinationals are today one of the major driving forces of the process of globalization. Their number increased sharply from 7,000 at the beginning of the sixties to more than 77,000 in the mid-2000s. They have about 777,000 branches distributed all over the world and made profits of up to 4,500 billion dollars in 2005. It is believed that they are at the origin of about two-thirds of international trade, one-third being what economists refer to as intrafirm trade. Their operations impact doubly on the process of globalization. On the one hand, they are the origin of the major causes of globalization such as technological progress in domains as varied as telecommunications and information management, and on the other hand, their operations contribute to the rapid development of various transnational flows such as trade in goods and services, capital flows (in diverse forms such as foreign direct investments, portfolio investments, loan activities of financial institutions and different forms of partnerships), and even international labor movements, which link economic agents of different countries the world over. It is through these different types of movements that the globalization process is most visible to some of us.

Several theories have been advanced to try to explain the fast development of multinational companies. One of the major explanations is related to the economic rationale that the quest for profit justifies their development. Firms may break down their production process into relatively independent segments and localize each segment where it may be produced at a lesser cost. In this process, manufacturing output activities which use abundant and less-qualified labor are often transferred to developing countries,[33] while developed countries control the designing and marketing of products where the use of skilled labor is required. This division of labor helps them to retain the most lucrative activities. The other explanation is policy related and identifies in the development of multinational companies the result of voluntary policies implemented by developed countries. Although, up to recent times, multinational firms were mostly from developed countries, we should note that an increasing number of these firms stem from emerging countries. Thus, South Africa is famous for being an important source of foreign direct investment in a number of African countries and beyond.

In the present context of globalization, the activities of multinational companies and their impact on the development of poor countries, particularly in Africa, have been a source of heated debate between supporters who see a positive impact and those which, on the contrary, think that multinational companies have a negative impact. For some, multinational firms bring technology and modern methods of management and organized production to poor countries and practice conditions of work which, though open to criticism, constitute an improvement compared to the situation in the rest of the economy of countries where they are implanted. On the contrary, to others, multinational companies often benefit from exorbitant advantages of different kinds, particularly at the level of taxes, which limit the scope of their contribution to the development of host countries. They also have a lot of negotiating power, linked to their connections with the governments of their countries of origin as well as with international financial organizations which impose policies on poor countries, thereby enabling them to always obtain more advantages; they may also not be subjected to the same ways of functioning as those observed in their host countries and which render them socially, economically and environmentally accountable in the full sense of the words.

What is certain is that several recent developments, particularly the sometimes difficult relations between multinational companies on the one hand, and local stakeholders in a number of African countries as well as elsewhere on the other, reflect the increasing uneasiness created by the existing gap between the potential impact of the activities of multinational firms on the development of host countries, and the real impact.[34] According to the authorities, because of the unfair nature of contracts, the Bolivian government even took the decision to denounce contracts with multinationals which exploit the country's natural resources in the field of oil and gas, a decision which came to strengthen this perception of uneasiness.[35] More recently, Argentina also took similar steps against Repsol, an oil company with Spanish ties. Commenting on this resurgence of nationalism observed in most developing countries with subsoil resources, a European resource person on energy issues had this to say:

> The outburst of energetic patriotism is linked to the fact that international companies had the tendency to take advantage, in a scandalous manner, of producing countries when the price of oil was low, particularly weak states. Multinationals are only interested in the short term, such as the reaction of markets to their quarterly profits. The era of industrial leaders enlightened by an exceptional stature which established a partnership with the producing country is unfortunately over. The wave of nationalism observed today, which is sometimes aggressive, stems from the short-sightedness of these companies. During the rise in the price per barrel, producing countries had the impression that these agreements (production-sharing agreements according to which oil companies provide the financial and technical resources necessary for drilling and exploiting hydrocarbon resources of an area and in return receive a share of the future production)[36] were not as beneficial to them as expected.[37]

These comments increase the feeling of exploitation which developing countries claim to have suffered at the hands of multinationals, particularly in the oil sector. Box 9.2 below further illustrates these difficult relationships.

After his re-election in December 2006, the late Venezuelan president Hugo Chavez said that his economic goal would be to obtain "total sovereignty" of his country on oil and gas resources in the country. The Bolivian president Evo Morales also passed an act to restore the sovereignty of his country on gas resources. In Africa, Algeria instituted a tax on profits linked to rising prices and demanded that Sonatrach, a national company in charge of oil and gas, held 51 per cent of all future explorations.

Box 9.2. The Sakhalin-2 Project[38]

The problems between the Anglo-Dutch oil giant Royal Dutch Shell and the Russian authorities better illustrate the comments above and also express another episode of the sometimes difficult relations existing among multinational companies and the emerging and developing countries in which they operate. In fact, at the beginning of the 1990s, Shell joined two Japanese companies and signed an agreement with the Russian authorities to exploit Russian oil and gas within the framework of the Sakhalin-2 project in Russia. This project, which was Shell's fourth biggest oil project in the world after Pearl Gas to Liquids in Qatar, Athabasca Oil Sands in Canada and Kashagan in Kazakhstan, targeted the exploitation of about 1,400 billion barrels of oil equivalent and was to generate an internal rate of profitability of about seven per cent and an actual net value of about 4.85 billion dollars. All in all, the Sakhalin-2 project aimed at constructing two offshore platforms for exploiting gas and oil, a 1,600 km pipeline, four billion barrels of oil and gas equivalent, creating about 17,000 jobs and, during its peak, producing about 340,000 barrels of oil equivalent per day. The contract rested on production sharing between Russia and Shell and stipulated that Shell and its partners would provide the technology and financing necessary for the exploitation, but would first recover all these investments before the Russians received their own share of the benefits.

The contract more or less worked out until Shell decided to double the cost of the project from 10 billion dollars to more than 20 billion dollars. This doubling would have significantly delayed Russia's collection of its own share of the benefits. Coincidentally, Shell's announcement of this cost overrun coincided with another announcement, made by Russian authorities, that the project did not respect Russian environmental norms and as such was causing serious environmental problems. On the basis of these accusations, Russian authorities threatened to stop the project; moreover, these difficulties had considerably slowed progress. In December 2006, following pressure from Russian authorities, an agreement was reached. Gazprom, the Russian state company which controls the energy sector, was to take control of the project by paying the sum of 7.5 billion dollars (Shell and the two Japanese partners had to reduce their share by half so that Gazprom would retain most of the shares). Shell was to continue to be the project operator. Even if some observers felt that this price was a little bit higher than what the market anticipated, the Russian authorities did not hide their satisfaction at achieving their main goal, which was to take full control of the exploitation of their oil and energy resources. The Russian president Vladimir Putin asserted after the conclusion of this agreement, "I am very pleased that our environmental agencies and our investors have agreed about the resolution of the questions which have arisen."

Shell is also present in Nigeria in two important projects: OK LNG and Bonga, which target the exploitation of reserves to the tune of 931 million and 631 million barrels of oil equivalent respectively. The internal rate of profitability of these projects stands at fourteen per cent and twenty-five per cent respectively and the actual net value at 1,792 and 6,759 billion dollars respectively.

Considering all these developments in the world, I would wish to have seen the same renewal of relations with multinational firms take place in Africa, in order to increase their contribution to the economic development of the continent. Though still tentative, recent initiatives taken by some African countries (Niger, for example, has renegotiated a uranium-exploitation contract signed in the 1960s which linked it to the French nuclear energy giant AREVA, and, Nigeria has renegotiated oil-exploitation contracts with companies like Royal Dutch Shell, ExxonMobil, Chevron, Total or Agip) demonstrate the fact that they are not free from the controversies raised at times by the actions of multinational companies in emerging and developing host countries. Some years ago, when oil prices increased to their peak, Donald Kaberuka, president of the African Development Bank, expressed a wish that multinational companies operating in the oil sector would contribute to ease the oil bill of African countries.[39] This is an excellent idea. It would be a considerable manifestation of the solidarity for development that developed countries continue to espouse.

National governments

An enumeration of the actors of globalization would not be complete without mentioning the role of governments. Obviously, governments, through the measures they put in place, are the first to facilitate or, contrarily, slow down the process of globalization. However, at times the affirmation of this role does not fail to incite debate. To some analysts, governments follow the trends more than they initiate or trigger them. As such, measures announced and implemented by governments very often only consecrate and legitimize in law (i.e., grant *de jure* recognition to) facts of globalization that have already entered into practice. This point is commonly used to explain the acceleration of financial globalization which took place in the 1990s. For this point of view, financial liberalization measures applied at that time simply came to legitimize an intensification of capital movements that was difficult to oppose.

Factors of Globalization

I have just looked at the key actors of globalization – that is, major agents that participate in the process of globalization and, by their daily actions, determine the pace and direction of this movement. By factors of globalization, I mean major parameters whose progress and values condition the decisions of actors of globalization and, finally, simply condition globalization. I have three, namely: technological progress, psychological factors and public policies.

Technological process

As already mentioned in this book, the process of globalization manifests itself mainly through an increase in the trade in goods and services, capital, ideas and knowledge (and to a lesser extent, the movements of persons) among nations of the world. From this definition, it is simple to account for the important role played by technological progress, particularly in the fields of transport and communication, in facilitating this process. The fact that it is more and more easy and less expensive to displace considerable quantities of goods, and effect and receive payments to and from any part of the world in total security, does not only make the development of these exchanges possible, but stimulates them. In fact, these technological processes reduce distances and greatly improve coordination, indispensable conditions of a harmonious development of trade. As such, most Africans at least know of Western Union, which they use for their money transfers. The rise and development of these mechanisms, which contribute to the globalization of capital, are partly due to the technological processes which have helped to carry out these transactions in total security. Table 9.3 below shows, for example, the spectacular drop in the cost of a telephone call from 1930 to 1990.

Table 9.3. Changes in the cost of air transport and telephone calls, 1930–90 (US dollars of 1990)[10]

Year	Average income of air transport per passenger mile	Cost of a three-minute telephone call between New York and London
1930	0.68	244.65
1940	0.46	188.51
1950	0.30	53.2
1960	0.24	45.86
1970	0.16	31.58
1980	0.10	4.8
1990	0.11	3.32

Psychological factors

As aforementioned, demand for goods and services by consumers and demand addressed to a country in the context of globalization are highly determined by objective factors such as the price and income of consumers, but also by subjective factors like tastes and preferences. In a global economy where price differences among producers are often minimal and negligible, consumers' tastes and preferences determine to a large extent the demand for goods and services addressed to a country by economic agents all over the world and, therefore, also determine production opportunities offered by the country, and its capacity to take advantage of its integration in globalization. In this context, any country that succeeds in winning consumers' preferences and confidence will receive high demand and also benefit consequently from more production opportunities and economic growth. This demand may come from outside; in this case, it will be an expansion of exports. It may also be internal. In this case, it will be growth powered by domestic demand. In this line of reasoning, no demand is considered superior to the other in terms of its impact on the economic results of the country, particularly on economic growth, macroeconomic stability and job creation. What is important is that demand is directed to locally produced goods and services.

On the contrary, a country that does not succeed in winning the preferences of world customers will observe a drop in the demand directed to it as well as the opportunities of growth it may draw from globalization. Thus, I remember that one day in November 2003, while I was watching a televised news bulletin, a department supervisor in one of the most important supermarkets in France explained that, in some cases and for certain categories of products, just mentioning the name of the country of origin on the product may constitute negative publicity, independent of the quality of the product. Such negative publicity may consequently discourage the buying behavior of this product and slow down the benefits that the country may derive from the process of globalization. This example clearly shows that consumers' preferences are an explanatory factor of globalization whose importance is at times more than that of price and other factors linked to the fundamentals of the economy in question.

As such, any country wishing to increase its share in world trade in order to maximize profit from globalization must not only act on objective factors such as price to increase its price competitiveness, but must also win the battle of consumers' preferences and their confidence. Here, the image that the media gives of a country and its products acquires major importance as a factor of successful integration into the process of globalization. Attraction and demand of goods and services offered by a country depend obviously on quality, but also on the way the country is presented to consumers. The image of the country is projected onto its goods and services. Out of these determinants of demand, Africa does not occupy a favorable position compared to other regions of the world, whether Europe, North America or Asia. I may reasonably affirm that the preferences of customers in goods and services go first to those produced in the other regions. Thus, in a paper for the International Media Summit on Re-branding Africa, Cameroonian journalist Eric Chinje wondered:

How many entrepreneurs working outside extractive industries think of Africa as a place where they may invest in and do business? How many potential tourists go to other destinations because they do not know whether they will find decent hotels and restaurants in Africa? How many potential visitors even refuse to plan a trip to Africa because of the perception according to which famine and sickness are omnipresent? How many declared and non-declared rules and regulations against importation in Europe, Asia and America targeted African products simply because of their origin? [...] Progress is registered far from world television camera images: the growth rate of the GDP of Africa stands at 2.6 in 1994; in 2003, it rose to 3.7%; in 2005, the regional economic growth was more than 4%, rate far higher than demographic growth. In 1994, the average inflation rate was 41%; in 2003, 40 countries of the region reduced their inflation rate to a single digit, now the trend in 2005 despite great fluctuations suffered by the global economy. Africa's foreign debt constituted 77% of the GDP in 1994; this rate dropped to 48% at the end of 2003. Substantial debt reduction during these two periods has further improved the situation. The progress observed in many parts of the continent is real. From every indication, these developments are submerged in the frenzy of world media coverage, in a bid to publish negative information on Africa in international media.[41]

In this context, the battle to conquer market shares, in order to boost demand, to stimulate growth in Africa and to fight against poverty, is first of all a battle to redress the image of Africa in the present process of globalization.

Public policies

The acceleration of the process of globalization is also the result of policies implemented by public authorities in many countries of the world to foster the demand and supply of globalization in their respective economies. Some observers believe that these policies most often follow rather than influence the process of globalization. This is why measures taken by Western governments to liberalize capital movements in the 1990s were mostly presented as a response by authorities to the increasing importance of capital flows which had developed at a sharp rate since the 1970s. In spite of this reality, most observers agree today that the process of globalization, whether capital flows or trade in goods and services, could not reach the present rate and particularly could not be sustainable if it were not accompanied by policies implemented to favor their global development. Typically, public policies may be conceived to influence either the demand of goods and services produced in the country or the degree of attraction and competitiveness of the country in order to develop its productive capacity. As noted earlier, influencing global demand addressed to a country calls for action on subjective factors such as consumers' perceptions and preferences, by resorting to different economic policy instruments such as exhorting economic agents to change their behavior in favor of the country within the framework of an effective communication effort, or on the relative prices offered by the country compared to the rest of the world. Public policies aimed at influencing the country's supply of globalization will seek to develop the productive capacity of the country through strengthening its attractiveness and competitiveness.

What Is the Impact of Globalization on Poor Countries?

Much has been said and written on this important theme of globalization. Discussions on its real or speculative effects on the growth of global wealth and its distribution are far from coming to an end. In developed countries, which have long understood that promoting and safeguarding economic growth and employment should be at the center of economic policy goals, it is mainly in the field of employment and economic growth that the debate among supporters and opponents of globalization has taken place. As such, the main debate topics are (i) whether the increase in the trade of developed countries with developing countries, and the resulting competition, will lead to the displacement of workers of high-wage jobs in industry to low-wage jobs in services, thereby exerting pressure on the reduction of the standard of living in industrialized countries; (ii) whether globalization will reduce the demand for unskilled labor in rich countries, thereby deteriorating the distribution of income by creating a gap between the wages of unskilled workers and those of skilled workers, but also by increasing unemployment among the unskilled. Most studies carried out on these issues have concluded that the impact of globalization on the labor market of rich countries, whether through accrued trade in goods and services or through delocalization or immigration from low-income countries, was negligible.[42] Concerning the economic policies of rich countries, particularly their monetary, budgetary and trade policies, studies carried out on these topics also concluded that globalization had an impact on the sovereignty of authorities in the definition and implementation of their policies. From this point of view, I can affirm that research carried out to date seems to indicate that developed countries, as a whole, know how to take advantage of the process of globalization to further increase their standard of living.

Concerning developing countries in general and Africa in particular, the analysis of the present balance sheet of globalization on the economic performances of these countries has given birth to one of the most heated controversies that the contemporary world has ever experienced on an economic question. It is the question of the impact of globalization on poor countries, which is the origin of all debates on legitimacy and reform of institutions in charge of the management of globalization. In fact, I think it no exaggeration to call it a trench war between two camps whose positions are radically opposed. To some, globalization may have had a positive effect on the economic development of poor countries; to others, globalization may, on the contrary, have increased poverty in developing countries. In an article published in 2002, leading economist Pierre-Richard Agénor expressed the idea that globalization may have effects on poverty in the form of a J-curve, according to which it will first aggravate poverty because of the development of unemployment (which may result from the low intersectoral mobility of labor), before contributing to poverty reduction during the expansion of exports in sectors that benefit from globalization.[43] We may be happy that globalization ends up having a positive impact on poverty reduction, but if, as this research seems to show, it has to first aggravate poverty before reducing it in the long term, then there is cause for concern. As John Maynard Keynes, one of the greatest economists of our time, observed: in the long term we will all be dead.

In fact, to study the effects of globalization in poor countries, economists usually distinguish the short term and the long term. Let's start with the long-term effects. In the long term, the most advanced point of view by economists is that globalization has dynamic effects on the economic growth in low-income countries. They obtain this result by showing that there exist several channels through which globalization, and the openness to trade that it implies, increases the growth rate of an economy. This is due particularly to the fact that openness to trade enables a country to adopt modern management methods thanks to several contacts with the outside world, especially with multinational firms which are supposed to be taking the lead in technology and modern management methods. Globalization can also enable a country to benefit directly from the technical progress incorporated in production inputs that they import from abroad. Armed with this positive effect of globalization on growth, economists also support the point of view that growth is an important factor in reducing poverty and, from there, reach the conclusion that globalization, being good for growth and growth being good for poverty reduction, will itself be good for poverty reduction.

As for analyzing the effects of globalization on short-term poverty – that is, what they call the static effects of globalization – economists have so far used a scheme of theoretical analysis developed in the 1950s, the model of trade known as Hecksher–Ohlin.

This model studies the effects of openness to trade by using the hypothesis that the world is composed of two economies, one developed and the other developing, each producing two goods with the help of two factors of production available in different proportions in the two countries. As such, the model presupposes that one of the factors of production is abundant in one of the countries, while the other factor is scarce. Finally, the model also presupposes that the production of each of the goods requires an intensive use of one of the factors of production and a less intensive use of the other factor. When this model is used to analyze the effects of globalization, the two factors of production often identified in this model are capital and labor. Economists further make the hypothesis that developing countries have abundant labor and a low capital, while the reverse is true for developed countries. Finally, they make the hypothesis that the poor are the major holders of labor,[44] while the capital is supplied by the rich.

Armed with this theoretical framework and these simple hypotheses, economists demonstrate that the openness of the two countries to trade within the framework of growing globalization results in the specialization of developing countries in the production and exportation of the goods whose production require a relatively intensive use of labor and a relatively less intensive use of capital input. As for the developed country, economists show that globalization results in a specialization of this country in the production and export of goods whose production requires a relatively intensive use of capital input and a relatively less intensive use of labor. The other result drawn from this line of thinking by economists is that an increase in production of the labor-intensive good will result in an increase in the demand for labor, a factor that the poor have in abundance, and consequently results in an increase in the income of the poor in developing countries. This other result is better known in economic literature as the theory of Stolper–Samuelson, from the names of the two American economists who first advanced it. It is on the basis of this theoretical result that economists base their arguments, according to which the process of globalization inevitably leads to poverty reduction in low-income countries.

Thus, according to theoretical schemes outlined by economists, globalization should have a positive impact on poverty reduction in the world. However, as I have indicated, things are not all that easy in the real world. As such, a heated debate has arisen between those who believe that the beneficial results of globalization on poverty reduction are not automatic and that in all cases globalization as it has functioned to date has not reduced poverty (and even that it may have aggravated it in low-income countries), and those who, on the contrary, think that globalization has contributed to poverty reduction. Among the first group, we find the renowned economist and Nobel Prize laureate in economics Joseph Stiglitz.[45]

However, several economists are today unanimous in admitting that analyzing the effects of globalization on poverty in low-income countries by far outweighs the existing theoretical frameworks and that such analysis should depend more on an empirical analysis, on a case-by-case basis, which conveniently integrates the real characteristics of each economy. Consequently, these economists, whom I may call skeptics, believe that one should not be content with simple generalizations emanating from theoretical models. It is in this context that a group of American scholars and economists belonging to different institutions undertook an empirical study on the impact of globalization on poverty.[46] This comprehensive work depended on a re-examination of the theoretical fundamentals of models currently used to study the effects of globalization on poverty reduction in the world as well as on empirical case studies depending on microeconomic data and referring to the impact of trade liberalization (particularly the reduction of tariff barriers on imports) and capital movements in different countries like India, Colombia, Ethiopia, Mexico, Zambia, South Africa, China, Poland and Indonesia. The goal of these authors was to once more study the links existing between globalization, measured by the liberalization of trade in goods and services, capital movements and poverty. In this work, the authors questioned firstly the validity of theoretical models in analyzing the effects of globalization on poverty and the distribution of income, particularly the Hecksher–Ohlin model and the Stolper–Samuelson theorem cited above. How adequate are the hypotheses of these models compared to the characteristics of the real world in which we live? How reliable is the statistical data on which most studies and conclusions on the impact of globalization on poverty depend? Secondly, these authors studied, from a direct observation of episodes of trade liberalization and foreign direct investment flows, the impacts of these developments on the evolution of poverty in the above-mentioned countries.

The conclusions of their work seem very interesting to me. Let's first remember what these conclusions are before looking at how they fit into my comments in this book on the manner in which Africa can carry out its economic policy with the hope of coming out of poverty and attaining the Millennium Goals. These authors proved first of all that the conclusions obtained from theoretical models that globalization unavoidably benefits the poor in low-income countries to the extent that they have a comparative advantage in the production and exportation of unskilled labor-intensive goods, and that consequently the poor will benefit more than the rich from the liberalization of trade, do not generally match what is going on in the real world. The main reason for this difference between theory and reality is due, according to these authors, to the fact that some of the hypotheses suggested by these models, particularly that relate to the intersectoral mobility of labor – that is, the fact that workers may easily move from sectors experiencing a contraction due to trade liberalization to sectors experiencing growth – are not obtained in the real world. In fact, if unskilled workers – that is, mainly the poor – cannot move from contracting sectors (due to an increase in imports and an intensification of competition resulting from the drop in protection, for example) to expanding sectors, then they will lose their jobs, thereby aggravating poverty and provoking a deterioration of the distribution of income in the country. Other factors that mitigate the theoretical models are linked to the fact that, in the real world in general, countries protect sectors that intensively use skilled labor and export sectors more, that foreign companies generally use skilled labor more than unskilled labor, and finally, that access to international markets of goods manufactured with unskilled labor – that is, the main asset of the poor – is often dependent on important additional investments. The first factor renders unskilled workers more vulnerable to the elimination of protection and increase of imports and the intensification of competition. Concerning the two other factors, they cut down the capacity of unskilled workers – that is, mainly the poor – to benefit from an expansion of exports to the extent that this will benefit skilled workers first.

Concerning the impact of globalization on poverty, the conclusion of the empirical study carried out by these authors based on statistics disaggregated at the level of households and sectors in the countries cited above is mainly the following: the impact of globalization on poverty is not homogeneous. This is determined by a certain number of factors such as the characteristics of the labor market, the level of protection of the sector where the poor work before the liberalization of trade, the importance of foreign direct investment flows in the sector where the poor work, and the level of increase in exports of the sector where the poor work following the liberalization of trade.

As such, according to the study, the reduction of customs duties in India was associated with slower poverty reduction in regions where labor regulations were more restrictive (less liberal), whereas it had no impact on poverty in regions where regulation facilitated a greater mobility of labor. The study of Poland's case showed that globalization benefited unskilled workers in sectors that had a comparative advantage in the export of unskilled labor-intensive goods to rich countries as well as workers of sectors that received important foreign direct investment flows. This role played by foreign direct investment flows in determining the impact of globalization on poverty is also illustrated by studies on the cases of Mexico and India. Generally, the three case studies mentioned above (Poland, Mexico and India) showed that globalization profits low-wage workers if they are in sectors experiencing growth in exports. The case study of Colombia showed that the urban poor who worked in previously protected sectors saw their situation worsen due to globalization resulting from the liberalization of trade through the reduction of tariff barriers.

One of the most important conclusions of this significant research work is therefore the role played by the expansion of exports in determining the direction and magnitude of the impact of globalization on poverty reduction in poor countries. In fact, beyond the role played by exports, what these results seem to show is that the success of the integration of a country in the process of globalization depends on the vigor of world demand of goods and services addressed to it and the capacity of its productive machinery to respond to this demand. In a global economy, world demand directed to a country is mainly composed of two major components: a foreign demand, which economists currently call exports, and that of domestic origin. It is extremely important to note that these empirical studies confirmed that, for a particular country, the success of globalization in contributing to poverty reduction depends on the extent to which it leads to the expansion of exports. In fact, it puts to question the theory according to which the benefits of integration into globalization appear when the increase in imports leads to a contraction of less competitive sectors under the effect of an increase in competition on the local market, this leading to an improved allocation of resources in the economy. According to this theory, it is from this contraction of less competitive sectors that productivity gains stem. This line of reasoning is based on a conception of increased integration into globalization, particularly through a trade liberalization policy as an instrument for a supply policy. However, I have noticed that integration into globalization is first and foremost an instrument for a demand policy.

Finally, to improve the functioning of globalization in order that it should better contribute to the development efforts of poor countries, Joseph Stiglitz has proposed reforms which aim at improving the functioning of the international financial system, the multilateral trade system and development assistance. Concerning the international financial system, the idea is to promote an international financial system that will equilibrate the interests of creditors and those of debtors, which will ensure the adequate and regular financing of companies toward creating jobs, including during times of financial crisis, and in which costs linked to excessive movement of capital may be reduced. To achieve these goals, targeted reforms are on (i) the need to recognize that the liberalization of capital accounts, though it may be profitable, involves serious risks (consequently, the IMF, which has often insisted that developing countries liberalize their capital accounts, has accepted that these countries can intervene to reduce the instability and costs that it imposes on weak economies);[47] (ii) the establishment of an international mechanism to resolve the insolvency of sovereign debtors, similar to existing mechanisms at the national level in cases of private bankruptcy; (iii) a lower recourse to bailouts to save indelicate private creditors; (iv) an improvement of the banking regulations in both developing and developed countries, such that banks are more rigorous in their lending practices; (v) an improvement of risk management linked to variations in exchange and interest rates; and (vi) an improvement of safety nets, particularly in the field of unemployment insurance.[48]

Chapter Ten

GLOBALIZATION: A FACTOR OF WORSENING ECONOMIC POLICY CONSTRAINTS, BUT ALSO A SOURCE OF OPPORTUNITIES?

"We start from the belief that prosperity is indivisible; that growth, to be sustained, has to be shared; and that our global plan for recovery must have at its heart the needs and jobs of hard-working families, not just in the developed countries but in emerging markets and the poorest countries of the world too. [...] We believed that the only sure foundation for sustainable globalization and rising prosperity for all is an open economy based on market principles, effective regulation, and strong global institutions."

G20, Leaders' Statement, Global Plan for Recovery and Reform,
London, April 2, 2009

Introduction

The economic policy outlined in this book will reposition Africa on the road to economic prosperity for all its citizens. But in life, nothing is easy. Our capacity to execute the plans that we elaborate for our life is constantly under diverse constraints. Some constraints even limit the actions that we can undertake. Others, on the contrary, limit the effects of the actions that we take. Economic policy is no exception to this rule. I will say that it is even more submissive to it than any other thing. Its implementation will therefore require much skill, determination and creativity on the part of officials in charge, especially to manage and remove a number of constraints.

A Resource Constraint?

In the first part of this book, I started off by stating the constraints which economic policy must handle. Some will say that the most important constraint is the lack of financial resources to implement the orientations proposed. Although the problem of financial resources may be real in some cases, it is not among my most important points. In fact, as affirmed by an African finance minister, during a meeting of African finance and planning ministers held in Ouagadougou in May 2006 under the auspices of the United Nations Economic Commission for Africa on the promotion of employment in Africa, the problem is not that of resources, but a problem of ideas. If you have ideas, you will have resources to implement them, this minister said.

I are convinced that African countries can themselves generate from their domestic resources the non-negligible share of resources necessary to implement the strategic and systemic economic policy developed in this book. This is moreover what the conference on financing development held in 2002 in Monterrey, Brazil recommended to developing countries. An increase in public resources is predictable to the extent that I have identified an improvement in governance as inherent in a good economic policy. As a matter of fact, such improvement will be felt in public expenditure by economies and in public revenues by an increase in inflows. There is also the fact that a firm, visible and credible commitment to implementing an economic policy following what I have proposed in this book may once more instill confidence in economic agents, which can have a positive impact on the repatriation of part of the capital withheld abroad. Finally, despite the difficulties of procedures linked to the mobilization of external resources, a determined government can find the means to mobilize the external resources needed to finance its economic policy. During a conference held at the African Development Bank, Michel Camdessus, former IMF managing director and representative of the French president for Africa, said that the G8 ensured that a country which elaborated a good economic policy would not lack the resources to implement it.[1] Though one should not underestimate the constraints of resources, it does not seem to be one of the most critical for the implementation of the systemic economic policy outlined in this book. In addition, there are private capital inflows that can be mobilized if the country has a good economic program.

Do Those Governing and the Governed Pursue the Same Goals?

Another constraint, perhaps a more serious one, seems worthy of examination. The effective implementation of the orientations contained in this new economic policy presupposes that governments, the first actors of implementation, truly have in their hearts the search for general interest. Economists have long debated the issue of adequacy between the search for general interest – that is, the search for collective well-being – and the goals effectively followed by policy officials in power. Though this issue may have been debated in developed as well as in developing countries, it retains a particular attention within the context of African countries, where failure in development and insufficiency in governance seem *a priori* the most obvious. I acknowledge that the response to this question is largely beyond the scope of this book, which focuses on desirable orientations of an economic policy targeting general interest. I allow experts in political science the duty to one day find the form of political organization which may facilitate the adequation between general interest and the interest of political officials in power and, thus, the implementation of the economic policy I advocate.

If the question of availability of resources is not a first-hand constraint, and if that of political will to adopt a veritable economic policy oriented toward the search for general interest will not be decided here, what then are the constraints that may limit the scope of actions undertaken if I assume that governments effectively adopt the proposed systemic economic policy? I see mainly three types of constraints. First, there are those I will call constraints of compatibility between goals. Furthermore, there are constraints that affect the use of instruments. Finally, there are constraints which are linked to the behaviors of economic agents. I will examine these three categories of constraints successively.

Are Economic Policy Goals Compatible?

In the first part of this book, I defined a good economic policy mainly as a set of goals that the public authorities fix and use the instruments described in Chapter 7 to attain. To streamline ideas and better clarify the concept of a good economic policy, I have structured the goals which constitute it around the concepts of final/fundamental, intermediate and operating goals. The first question I ask, therefore, is whether these goals are compatible among themselves.

The dilemma of economic policy linked to the magic square

What economists call the magic square refers to the set formed by economic growth, unemployment, inflation and external equilibrium. The existing relationship between these four economic variables, according to which it is impossible to have good results on all these four variables simultaneously, leads to what economists call the dilemma of the magic square. For example, good performances in economic growth and employment are often associated with risks accrued from the acceleration of inflation and the deterioration of external equilibrium. As such, stronger and faster growth, an important final goal, may be accompanied by a threat to price stability. Conversely, rising tension on prices eases when growth slows down. This incompatibility has often been presented as one of the major constraints confronted by the elaboration and conduct of economic policy. This constraint is explicitly considered in all the economic and financial programs that African countries implement with the support of international financial institutions. Generally, these programs retain the maintenance of external equilibrium as a priority goal.

Globalization has different effects on the constraint linked to the dilemma of the magic square. In fact, the increased integration of world economies has the tendency to restrain price increase for the same level of growth (i.e., all things being equal, the same level of growth would generate less inflation compared to a situation without globalization), thanks particularly to the effect of accrued competition. Therefore, globalization reduces the level of inflation compatible with a given level of growth. Globalization worsens the risk of deterioration of the balance of trade of an economy on a high-growth trajectory. This effect is, however, more probable in the context of African economies that generally have a very high rate of openness to the rest of the world and, thus, economic growth in African countries tends to generate a higher level of imports compared to other regions. Faced with this constraint, a clear political choice is to be made between the different priority goals. During the discussion of final goals, I advocated the creation of jobs and economic growth as final priority goals of economic policy. Eventually, price stability must be at the service of economic growth and job creation and not the contrary. It is a political choice that the society must make.

Growth and inequality

As suggested by Kuznets, economists had long thought that economic growth and the reduction of inequality were not compatible. To grow rapidly, countries had to accept an extension of inequality because, as they thought, the share of capital holders – the rich in society, those who have the highest savings rate and therefore contribute most to investment and, hence, economic growth – had to increase faster than that of the poor, who, due to their low savings rate, do not contribute much to investment and growth. If such reasoning is true, economic growth, the final goal of economic policy, is incompatible with one of its important operating goals: social cohesion, one of the factors of which is a reduction of inequality. Recent economic history has proven that Kuznets was wrong. A policy of reducing inequality to contribute to social cohesion stimulates economic growth. It is even one of the essential conditions. This is what the growth experience of the Asian Tigers has shown. These countries knew how to elaborate and implement policies to promote social cohesion; strong economic growth went hand in hand with the reduction of inequality. Commenting on this performance, Nobel laureate Joseph Stiglitz said that the miracle of the Asian Tigers was first a political miracle before being economic, thanks to its management of social cohesion.[2]

Constraints that Affect the Use of Instruments

Economic policy action may also be submitted to constraints affecting the use of some instruments, either because the instrument is no longer in the hands of the authorities or because the use of the instrument is submitted to constraints that the authorities must respect. Belonging to a monetary zone, for example – in which monetary policy is conducted at the level of the union by a supranational entity – is an example of the first case, given that monetary policy totally escapes the control of the public authorities of each member state. If the country is a member of a customs union, its trade policy vis-à-vis nonmember countries may not be under its control if the trade policy is defined and implemented at the level of the union. An example of the second case is when the use of the instrument is guided by specific provisions that the country has adopted. As such, budgetary policy may be guided by adopted budgetary rules. Some principles guiding budgetary policy may even be written in the constitution.

The impossible trinity

Beyond these constraints linked to external or domestic commitments, there exists another constraint which is linked to what economists call the impossible trinity, which designates another well-known inconsistency in economic policy. It designates the incompatibility that may arise if a country tries, at the same time, to seek some degree of independence in its monetary policy, practice a fixed exchange rate and liberalize movements of the capital account of its balance of payments. Thus, for the monetary policy to be independent – that is, for authorities to freely choose its orientation[3] – one of the following must obtain: either they adopt a flexible exchange rate and thereby enable free capital movements between the country and the rest of the world, or they decide to exercise control over the movements of capital and as such adopt a fixed exchange rate.

This constraint of the impossible trinity is exercised with even greater force in the context of a world economy characterized by both significant and volatile capital movements. Experience shows that the actions implemented by countries to control this constraint are highly heterogeneous. But in general, these actions combine according to proportions which reflect strategic options peculiar to each country, an independent monetary policy, and certain flexibility in the management of their exchange rate combined with a certain dose of control on capital movements, and capacity building in the forecast of capital movements and in liquidity management.[4]

Do the rules of the WTO constitute constraints?

A point of view commonly defended by some observers argues that the rules which govern the multilateral trade system constitute a formidable constraint to the economic policy of developing countries. They may prevent these countries from resorting to the same instruments which present developed and emerging countries have resorted to in order to promote their industrialization. As such, according to this point of view, WTO rules prohibit subventions, whereas East Asian and even developed countries have massively resorted to subventions and moreover continue to resort to them to support their productive machinery. The same is true for different WTO agreements, including those contained in the Agreement on Trade-Related Aspects of Intellectual Property Rights (TRIPS) and the Agreement on Trade-Related Investment Measures (TRIMS), presented as binding on economic policies of developing countries.[5]

If it is true that to have all possible instruments, without any limitation, is always superior to submitting to any sort of constraint whatsoever (economists express this by saying that an optimum without constraint is always superior to an optimum with a constraint), it also seems to me that to remain stuck in the past is not the best way for developing countries to achieve the creativity and imagination that their economic policies so badly need to succeed. After all, nothing condemns these countries to seek to use exactly the same instruments that developed countries have used in the past. In fact, the history of international economic policy shows that developed countries, on different occasions in their history, invented these instruments to adapt their economic policy to the challenges it faced during those moments. For example, voluntary exports restraints were not recognized among instruments of trade policy until the United States introduced them in the 1970s to manage imports from Japan. The multi-fiber agreement (which regulated trade in textiles for close to thirty years), the cultural exception successfully defended by France in the WTO within the framework of negotiations for the liberalization of trade in cultural products, and the consideration of international labor standards in international trade may also be seen as some of the innovations used by developed countries to better adapt their economies to the continuously changing requirements imposed by globalization. The reciprocity that the European Union is trying to make ACP countries accept within the framework of the Economic Partnership Agreements (EPA), even though reciprocity is not a WTO requirement as Europe pretends, is another recent example of this innovation. More recently again, before the dollar began to drop, the United States was committed to a tug of war with China on the issue of the exchange rate of the yuan, which they claimed to be undervalued. After several efforts to make the Chinese revalue the yuan, they ended up launching the idea (until then not aired) that the undervaluation was a disguised subsidy to exports, and the United States began to acquaint the IMF and the WTO on this issue. Only after the dollar began to drop on the exchange market did the United States take a backward step on this innovation.

Discussions on the extension of the protection of geographical indications on products, undertaken in Doha on the initiative of the European Union to protect and strengthen the demand of European products, offer another example of innovative measures of economic policy. Economic officials of developing countries, particularly Africa, may demonstrate the same imagination in order to elaborate and implement innovative measures to ensure the integration of their economy into globalization.

Finally, the WTO rules seem to impose constraints. No one can deny this reality. However, it is when we remain focused on the past, and fixed on instruments formulated in the past by today's developed countries to meet their own economic policy needs and afterward try to restrain their use by developing countries, that these constraints have more effect.[6] A forward-looking attitude, which seeks to innovate by identifying possible actions that are compatible with the multilateral framework, is surely more promising. In short, what is needed is forward-looking, creative and fertile thinking on economic policy, not a backward-looking attitude. Some countries have started to think about the immense opportunities that a little bit of creativity in economic policy may offer. Thus, thanks to a pilot and a well-managed subvention program, Malawi, one of the poorest countries of the continent, doubled its agricultural production between 2004/05 and 2005/06 (See Box 10.1 below).[7]

Box 10.1. Malawi: Program of subventions of agricultural inputs

Malawi is one of the poorest countries on the African continent. The country depends predominantly on an agriculture dominated by smallholders. In order to improve the productivity of these smallholders and increase production of food crops and export, the government implemented, from the 2005/06 season, a program of subsidizing agricultural inputs. Within the framework of this program, about one hundred and seventy-five thousand tons of fertilizer and forty-five thousand tons of improved maize seeds were distributed to farmers. These inputs were supplied to farmers against the payment of 28 per cent of the cost. The total cost of the program stood at about ninety-one million dollars and was financed to the tune of 87 per cent from the government's resources. Thanks to the program, the proportion of households which indicated having suffered price hikes of agricultural products dropped from 79 per cent to only 20 per cent, which seems to indicate that food insecurity dropped.[8]

Constraints Linked to the Behaviors of Economic Agents

Constraints linked to the behaviors of economic agents are essentially the following: the present low level of credibility that African economic policy officials enjoy and that of productions of African economies; the existence of rational expectations of economic agents; the possible existence of crowding in and crowding out inherent in some economic policy measures; the effects of hysteresis; and the insufficient knowledge of the model of the economy. Finally, there are rules of globalization as enacted by institutions managing the process and which some find more and more binding on poor countries. I will examine these constraints and their interactions with globalization in the following paragraphs.

Means to increase the credibility of authorities responsible
for economic policy must be sought absolutely

Lack of credibility toward economic agents constitute, in my opinion, one of the major constraints that officials of African economic policy must first seek to remove if they wish to gain a minimum of success in implementing the economic policy whose main contours have been described in this book. Without this minimum credibility, all attempts at implementing this economic policy can be summarized as a simple manipulation of instruments without any chance of a real success in attaining the expected economic results.

I have already raised the notion of credibility when discussing the operating goals of economic policy. The role of credibility in economic policy has today generated a voluminous literature since two brilliant economists, F. E. Kydland and E. C. Prescott, pioneered this concept, which won them the Nobel Prize in Economics in 1973. Credibility is defined as the anticipation that the authorities responsible for economic policy will implement the policy and actions they have announced. An authority is therefore credible if economic agents anticipate that it will implement its policy. Defined as such, credibility may appear a trivial concept, but this triviality is only apparent. As I have demonstrated by discussing the goals of economic policy, lack of credibility is an important factor in the failure of economic policies to the extent that economic theory and practical experience demonstrate that economic policies which are not credible are most often abandoned midway. In this context, it therefore becomes important to know what the determinants of credibility are. Economic research today shows that there are two main determinants of credibility: namely, the reputation enjoyed by the authorities responsible for economic policy and the social cost of economic policies themselves. The reputation of the authorities responsible for economic policy is linked to their past performance in the implementation of economic policies. As such, a good past performance contributes to building a reputation of credibility among economic agents, while a mediocre performance contributes to a lack of credibility. Another determinant of credibility, the impact of policies, refers to the fact that a policy whose implementation economic agents see as expensive is not generally credible because it runs the risk of undermining the base of its political support. Economic agents do not expect that the government will implement an expensive economic policy even if it has positive spillovers for society.[9]

Defined and understood as such, the present low level of credibility enjoyed by officials of economic policy in Africa will not facilitate the pursuit of the operating and intermediate goals mentioned above – for example, the search for good governance and improvement of the business environment. Let's take the example of good governance. If a government announces its intention to improve governance (for example, by fighting against corruption), economic agents will not believe that it will implement the required measures because the government has not established a reputation of credibility in the implementation of policies contributing to good governance. This is either because in the past it has not volunteered enough toward the improvement of governance in the management of public affairs, and therefore has not established positive antecedents on its performance in this domain, or because economic agents claim that pursuing such policy may have a price for the government itself, to the extent that it is not unheard of for some influential members of government to be worried by a real policy targeting the improvement of governance.

It is for these reasons that efforts at improving governance initiated by most African governments have not been sufficiently credible in the eyes of economic agents. However, without this credibility and change of behavior implied on the part of economic agents, policies of improving governance cannot have the expected results. This is why most governments of African countries, even among the well intentioned, face the difficulties we know of in their efforts to improve governance. As such, the low level of credibility projected toward economic agents seems to be one of the constraints that authorities responsible for economic policy in Africa should remove primarily. It is for each government to elaborate an improvement program of its credibility.

The lack of credibility not only handicaps the implementation of economic policy measures linked to improving governance in the management of public affairs. It may also thwart the pursuit of other goals of economic policy that I have identified in this book. The same holds for efforts aimed at establishing an adequate regulatory framework to the extent that, if economic agents do not judge credible the intentions of authorities to orient their behavior toward a desirable standard for the national economy, they will not undertake the necessary investments and behavioral changes. But there almost always exist some economic agents to fully apply the regulations targeted by the authorities. However, the results will be a failure.

Lack of credibility may also thwart the effectiveness of actions aimed at creating brands of products and geographical locations, which I have identified as one of the instruments of economic policy in the previous chapter. Here, the weight of past reputation is the major determinant of the lack of credibility. In fact, to date, consumers' attitudes toward goods and services produced by African economies has not led to an increase in their demand. This negative attitude should therefore be reversed in order to encourage the consumption of goods produced in Africa. Lack of credibility is also a factor in weakening the link among measures of economic policy and the behavior of economic agents. In fact, if officials of economic policy are credible, the behavior of economic agents not only takes into account the present level of instruments of economic policy, but also the anticipation of their future level as announced by the authorities. This increases the efficiency of economic policy.

If credibility is so important for the implementation of economic policy, how can the authorities responsible for economic policy in Africa establish their credibility or at least regain it, if we assume they have already lost it? As much as it is easy to lose credibility, so extremely difficult and demanding is it to regain a lost credibility, which calls for an approach which is voluntary, methodic, determined and creative, as well as a real will on the part of the authorities responsible for economic policy. It will demand much patience, a change in government relations with the economic agents, not only from the point of view of government actions, but also in the manner in which the government, the head of state, ministers and other national economic officials at all levels communicate with domestic and foreign economic agents. Regaining this credibility will also depend on the manner in which economic agents perceive through their acts of communication that the authorities express some degree of respect for them and demonstrate a real commitment to fully implementing the policies they have announced. This change in the perception that economic agents have of economic policy officials will certainly not come from a sporadic program of credibility implemented during a given period. Evidently, economic agents, individuals who are so frequently more intelligent than authorities think, realize that such a sporadic program does not reflect a real change of paradigm in the credibility of authorities and will not give any credibility to such a program. As already mentioned, gaining credibility is a long-term action. Where reputation is an important determinant of credibility, it is almost certain that any government which seriously strives at regaining a certain level of credibility shall work to establish good performance in a field deemed important by economic agents, for it is well known that having succeeded previously strengthens the credibility of your commitment to succeed again in future. In fact, the initiatives that authorities may undertake to regain a small amount of credibility toward economic agents are many. They depend on the particular context of each country, its system of values and the circumstances of the time. In some cases, just appointing credible national personalities with an impeccable reputation and high level of credibility in posts of responsibility and in a visible manner, and giving them the means to carry out the responsibility bestowed on them, may accomplish much in terms of restoring the credibility of authorities. This leads us to say that any government wishing to accomplish something should take the reputation of officials into account when making appointments to responsibilities in economic policy.

In other circumstances, particularly when the credibility of the authorities and the national economic system is at a very low level, it may be necessary to implement institutional reforms aimed specifically at strengthening the credibility of institutions. These reforms may include the elevation of some final, operating or intermediate goals in the hierarchy of the country's legal instruments,[10] or the ratification of some international and regional treaties. It is up to each country to identify its operating or intermediary goals, which will be redefined within the framework of legal instruments at a higher hierarchical level. Practices within this domain greatly vary according to country, but the goal everywhere is the same: to increase the credibility of economic policy commitments toward economic agents. The following examples illustrate these practices: in the United States, goals of full employment and price stability are contained in the law, which defines the mandate of the central bank. There also exists a law, voted on in 1998, which mandates full employment. In Brazil, a law obliges the government to respect budgetary equilibrium. As already said, in the 1980s, several countries also implemented institutional reforms aimed at conferring more independence on the Central Bank with the aim of strengthening the credibility of the commitment taken by authorities to fight against inflation by promoting price stability. When the North American Free Trade Agreement (NAFTA), which regroups the United States, Canada and Mexico, was signed in 1992, some observed that the great advantage of this agreement to Mexico came not from a certain intensification of trade, but more from the strengthening of the credibility of Mexican economic policies to the extent that one could not envisage Mexico reneging on its commitments taken with the United States and Canada within the framework of NAFTA. In fact, this opens up new perspectives for the contribution of regional integration to the success of economic policy in Africa. African countries must fully exploit the opportunities offered by regional integration agreements to strengthen the credibility of their economic policies.

Evidently, this search for credibility becomes more complicated in the context of globalization. In fact, to the extent that economic agents deal with varied and diversified offers, they have the opportunity to compare the performances of goods and services offered by the country to those of goods and services offered by the rest of the world, and also to compare the performances of economic policy officials to those of officials of other countries; winning the confidence of economic agents, therefore, becomes a more difficult exercise in a rapidly globalizing economy. In this context, globalization increases the constraints of credibility faced by officials of economic policy in Africa.

Can an agreement with international financial institutions foster the search for credibility?

According to economic theory, the fact that officials of economic policy cannot turn down their commitments increases their credibility, which is likely to strengthen the efficiency of economic policy. This is not new; I have already amply mentioned it in this book. As such, to the extent that it was thought that the authorities responsible for economic policy would choose not to renege on the commitments undertaken within the framework of a program they agreed with international financial institutions, particularly the IMF, an agreement on such a program was often presented as a potential mechanism for strengthening credibility. Some also raised this argument within the framework of discussions on EPAs between European and African countries, the Caribbean and the Pacific.[11] If this perception that an agreement with international financial institutions and other external partners would instill credibility was widespread in the 1980s and 1990s, I believe that things have begun to change, to the extent that such agreements today reduce more than they increase the credibility of authorities. As a matter of fact, governments and even citizens of developing countries regard these agreements as a form of control carried out by international financial institutions on their countries, as proof that they are incapable of managing their economy alone. Citizens and governments do not often live in this situation, and possibly hope that their countries will not be at the mercy of international financial institutions.[12]

Some time ago, and even recently, developing countries almost everywhere were increasingly reluctant to conclude financing agreements with international financial institutions or to reimburse in advance outstanding loans.

For a long time, it was believed that the increasing resentment about what is perceived as the heavy involvement of external financial partners in national economic policy matters and, therefore, the weakening of links between agreements with international financial institutions and the credibility of economic policy officials was a phenomenon peculiar to developing countries. This is not the case. It is a feeling also present in developed regions. Recent developments in relation to the financial crisis corroborates this observation. When the financial crisis expanded, born of excessive risk taking in financial systems of developed countries, it was first the US Treasury, the US Federal Reserve and different European capitals that elaborated and implemented bailout plans for the financial systems and for the protection of companies of the real sector. The role of the international financial institutions, particularly the IMF, in all these initial rescue efforts was not very visible. When the crisis reached Europe as a sovereign debt crisis, Europeans were initially very reluctant to allow an IMF role in the bailout programs for European crisis countries. This position was most vehemently defended by the European Central Bank, which first argued that the problems in Europe were not of a monetary nature, and therefore there was no justification for the intervention of the IMF, which is first and foremost a monetary institution. But most analysts believe that the true reason for the initial opposition to IMF intervention in European crisis countries was more than this and reflected the opinion among European leaders that such an intervention would diminish their credibility, and therefore the confidence of economic agents in European economic management capabilities. One European leader later revealed that Europe finally accepted IMF involvement because the head of the IMF is a European.

The implementation of their economic programs, designed with international lenders, including the IMF, also proved challenging in many European countries, further highlighting the increasing resentment of international involvement in national economic matters. After passing a 2014 budget which international lenders had not agreed to, Greek prime minister Antony Samaras said in parliament in December 2013: "We all want to be released from the bailout program and this budget marks the first step. We are on the road to securing our national independence."[13]

A fact that highlights this evolution is, however, the difference in opinions that exist on this issue between countries making recourse to international financial institutions and those that do not. The former do not believe that agreements with international financial institutions improve credibility, whereas the latter believe they do. In fact, most developed countries that do not seek international financial assistance continue to link the disbursements of their aid to the existence of an agreement between the recipient country and the international financial institutions, most notably the IMF. It is certainly to this difference in perception that the *Financial Times* commentator Martin Wolf was alluding when he asserted, "Summarily, the Fund is powerless where it is cherished and powerful where it is not cherished."[14] What conclusions can we draw from these contrasted appreciations? The ideal is that there should be harmony between the two points of view. However, in this controversial situation, I believe that by means of synthesis it may be logical to work with the hypothesis that the conclusion of an agreement with an international financial institution is no longer the precious key that provides access to credibility, to the extent that credibility projected toward national economic agents is more important to the success of a country's economic policy than credibility projected toward external parties.

To be rigorous in the analysis, I shall make a distinction between the Bretton Woods institutions (the IMF and the World Bank) and regional development banks. It seems that the issue of loss of confidence mostly concerns the Bretton Woods institutions and to a lesser extent the regional development banks, for example. Recent experience shows that in developing countries in general, and in African countries in particular, there are no exceptions to this observation; regional development banks tend to benefit from a higher level of preference as partners to development, and of course a higher level of potential credibility in public opinion compared to the Bretton Woods institutions. A recent study carried out under the auspices of the UK Department for International Development by the Overseas Development Institute, a British research center based in London, confirmed this hypothesis.[15] The fact that in 2005, Brazil, which needed resources to support the implementation of its economic reforms program, went to the Inter-American Development Bank instead of first going to the Bretton Woods institutions (with the Inter-American Development Bank co-financing as was the practice then), was also an emblem of this change in the perception of the role of financing agreements concluded with the Bretton Woods institutions in the search for credibility.

Though a whole book should be dedicated to an analysis of the reasons for breaking off links between agreements with international financial institutions and the credibility of and confidence in developing countries' policymakers,[16] the issue that retains our interest here is that of the implications of this break for the credibility of economic policy officials in Africa. Certainly, if there could exist an easy mechanism to strengthen credibility, such as an agreement with a foreign party, it may not be better for these countries. In the absence of such a mechanism, the task of seeking out credibility becomes more demanding, difficult and time consuming, but not impossible. It suffices to get to work.

Rational expectations of economic agents

Rational expectations of economic agents constitute another major constraint that requires particular attention from officials of economic policy in Africa if they wish to improve the elaboration and conduct of economic policy in the manner described in this book. With this term, economists designate the capacity of economic agents, whether consumers or producers, to correctly anticipate future decisions of officials responsible for economic policy and consequently adjust their own decisions. I have already demonstrated the impact of these rational expectations during the discussion of the operating goals of economic policy. When rational expectations combine with lack of credibility, they may seriously constrain the actions of officials of economic policy. As such, let's assume that economic agents have rational expectations. If the authorities announce an economic policy measure, economic agents will anticipate correctly whether officials will follow this policy to its conclusion or not. If economic agents anticipate that the authorities will not be able to ensure complete implementation of the announced measure, their behavior will reflect this anticipation. The result is that the economy finds itself exactly in the situation that authorities had wished to remedy by envisaging the implementation of the measure in the first place. One of the examples that the two authors F. E. Kydland and E. C. Prescott took in one of their articles, and which won them the Nobel Prize in Economics, refers to a public policy aimed at preventing the population from settling in dangerous areas where they are exposed to different risks, including a high risk of floods. This situation is rampant in several African countries. Let's assume that the authorities announce that it is forbidden to build in such areas and that defaulters will not be compensated in case of disasters. If economic agents anticipate that the authorities cannot avoid providing assistance to settlers in case of probable disaster, they will settle in these prohibited areas. We therefore have an example here of a case where the rational expectations of economic agents, coupled with the authorities' lack of credibility, leads to a result which is contrary to that sought by the authorities.

One of the domains of predilection where the rational expectations of economic agents have the highest impact on the capacity of the authorities to attain the goals of their policy is that of monetary policy. In fact, to the extent that a reduction of the inflation rate is most often accompanied by an increase in unemployment and vice versa, the authorities should generally seek a compromise between the two. Using the game theory model, economists succeeded in demonstrating that in the presence of rational expectations, if the authorities lack credibility, all attempts on their part to reduce inflation rate will end up in failure, even if they are very determined to achieve this result. The economy will settle into an equilibrium characterized by a high level of inflation and unemployment rates. This result occurs because, when authorities announce their intention to reduce the inflation rate to 2 per cent, for example, economic agents judge this performance to be beyond the scope of the authorities and consequently integrate a higher inflation rate, about 5 per cent, into their pricing decisions. The result is that the inflation rate will settle at 5 per cent instead of the 2 per cent targeted by the authorities. Concerning the unemployment rate, it will not be any lower. This example once more shows us the constraining role that the rational expectations of economic agents can play in the actions of public authorities.

Faced with these rational expectations and the constraint they represent to the conduct of economic policy, what should the authorities do? The goal here is not at all for them to prevent economic agents from formulating their expectations, which will obviously be impossible. The authorities should know how to orient the expectations of economic agents in a way which is favorable to the economic policy goals that they are pursuing. This is necessary for the success of the actions of public authorities. Ignoring the expectations of economic agents in the elaboration and conduct of economic policy is equivalent to a sailor attempting to sail without knowing the direction of the wind; it is like rowing against the current, and the consequences are easy to guess.

The means to influence the expectations of economic agents in a way which is favorable to the economic goals being pursued are varied and also dependent on the particular context of each country. As such, one of the most important roles of planning – as practiced with much success in capitalist economies, particularly in France, Japan,

Korea, and for close to five decades in countries like Tunisia – is to orient the expectations of economic agents. By placing coherent economic projections that reflect the ambitions of the public authorities at their disposal, planning also plays a non-negligible role in the orientation of economic agents' expectations. In fact, planning as practiced in capitalist countries is different from that which was practiced in countries with socialist economies before they abandoned their planning model in the 1990s. This is because, in the former, the information contained in the plans (particularly on economic growth and its sectoral distribution, prices, investment and consumption) was mostly comprised of projections destined to fix the expectations of economic agents, while in the latter it was mostly comprised of production targets and prices which the country should imperatively attain by the end of the plan. For example, from 1945 (that is, at the end of the Second World War) to 1980, France prepared seven plans.[17] Conducting an economic policy without seeking to know the expectations of economic agents is tantamount to heading directly for failure.

Managing expectations becomes much more difficult in the context of a globalizing economy. In fact, globalization diversifies the information resources of economic agents and consequently contributes to the greater sophistication of their decision-making models within the framework of rational expectations. It thus becomes more difficult for authorities responsible for economic policy to outplay the vigilance of economic agents. In other words, globalization reduces the degree of myopia of economic agents given that they have access to different information sources and behavioral patterns. This helps them to incessantly perfect their own models of elaborating expectation.

Limiting crowding out and encouraging crowding in

Another major constraint to be taken into consideration and attentively managed within the framework of the implementation of the economic policy outlined in this book is linked to what economists refer to as the effects of crowding out and the effects of crowding in. The effects of crowding out refer to the fact that the actions of some economic agents may have as their result a reduction of the effort or actions of other economic agents. Economists mostly analyze this phenomenon within the context of budgetary policy and have proved that it could be a factor of reduction of the effectiveness of budgetary policy. In fact, under certain assumptions – in particular that (i) economic agents have rational expectations, (ii) public expenditure finances goods and services needed by economic agents, (iii) budgetary policy is not sufficiently coordinated with other instruments, particularly monetary policy – public expenditure may not significantly contribute to demand directed to the economy to the extent that it simply replaces private sector expenditure. As such, an increase in public expenditure results in a drop in private expenditure, leaving the global level of demand directed to the economy unchanged.

In the first hypothesis, the fact that an increase in public expenditure is not expressed by an increase in global demand directed to the economy results from the functioning of a mechanism that economists call Ricardian equivalence. According to this mechanism, when public authorities increase government spending to stimulate demand directed to the economy, economic agents, whose expectations are rational by hypothesis, say public authorities will increase taxes in the near future to finance the increase in expenditures, and so react by increasing their savings. The result is a drop in public savings expressed by an increase in private savings; there is a crowding-out effect. In the second hypothesis, we are in the presence of what economists call windfall effects. Economic agents substitute public financing with expenditure that they may have undertaken anyway. Here again is the crowding-out effect. In the third hypothesis, the crowding-out effect is through an increase in interest rates, which reduces private demand.

This crowding-out effect may also thwart the efforts of authorities aimed at ensuring an adequate level of production of some goods and services in the economy, where public-sector production may lead to a price drop on the market and reduces private-sector supply. Public-sector production may also lead to an increase in the prices of factors of production used in the production of the goods in question, thereby reducing profitability in producing these goods by the private sector.

The effects of crowding in refer to the fact that the behavior of some economic agents may incite other economic agents to act in the same manner. This effect may be observed in the behavior of private economic agents faced with public regulations. As such, when public authorities take a measure to regulate an aspect of the behavior of economic agents, they generally wait until a certain number among them start applying the measure before launching its application. The crowding-in effect offers great opportunities to officials of economic policy to the extent that it suffices for them to incite a limited number of economic agents to implement a measure so that the rest of them follow. Officials of economic policy should know how to exploit the effects of crowding in, thereby limiting the effects of crowding out. Every day, this task is rendered more complicated by globalization. In fact, globalization builds the capacity of economic agents to be rational in their expectations, which, as we have seen, strengthens the effects of crowding out.

Effects of hysteresis

These effects refer to the fact that when a measure of economic policy produces an impact, it persists for a long time even if the measure is withdrawn later. This effect is not a problem when the measure produces the desired impact, but quickly becomes a constraint where the measure produces a contrary effect to that which was desired by the officials who implemented it; better still, the measure was mistaken from the outset and the authorities wish to withdraw it. This effect tells us that despite the withdrawal of the measure, the impact will remain for a long time. This effect was initially identified in an analysis of the effects of variations of exchange rate, where economists observed that if economic agents adjust prices following a variation of exchange rate, a return of the exchange rate to its initial level does not lead to readjustment of prices by economic agents. The validity of this hypothesis has been extended to several other areas of economic policy. The main implication of this constraint is that the authorities must guard against making mistakes in choosing economic policy measures because it may be difficult to wipe out the negative effects which have already been produced.

Constraints linked to our insufficient knowledge of the transmission mechanisms of economic policy

Transmission mechanisms are what economists call "models" of the economy. The manifestations of our insufficient knowledge of the transmission mechanisms of economic policy are twofold: first, there is our imperfect knowledge of the required time lags for economic policy initiatives to produce the full desired effects and, secondly, the fact that economic systems have become more complex, particularly with the importance of psychological factors. This increased complexity, which globalization further contributes to, reduces the capacity of officials of economic policy to correctly anticipate the effects of the economic policy measures or initiatives they undertake. In fact, despite the progress so far accomplished, economic research has not yet succeeded in fully clarifying the transmission channels and time lags of impulses coming from economic policy instruments. The fact that we do not know economic mechanisms very well should not surprise us to the extent that, as I have already mentioned in this book, economic policy aims first at making people act in the way that policymakers desire and mobilizing them for action. It is well known that the motives for human behaviors are still imperfectly understood.

Whether impulses from monetary policy, budgetary policy, increasing human capital, or even from actions aimed directly at influencing the behavior of economic agents by influencing their preferences, tastes and perceptions, we do not yet know precisely when they will have a significant and measurable effect on the supply capacity of the national economy or even on demand directed to it. In some developed countries, there are estimates as to delays of transmission of monetary policy actions, but in most African countries such estimates do not yet exist. This inaccuracy as to transmission delays introduces a divergence among the mandates of politicians and the impact of economic policy. In fact, due to this divergence, the positive effects of some good measures of economic policy may not be visible during the tenure of the politicians who started them. This divergence may be at the origin of a certain degree of instability in the conduct of economic policy to the extent that, in the absence of visible results, pressure mounts for a change of policy although current policies are perhaps the best. This instability can only make the task of economic policy officials more difficult and even contribute to reducing its efficiency. It is due to our imperfect knowledge of the transmission of economic mechanisms that economic policy finally becomes a real art that officials must know how to practice. Its outlines and success factors become specific to each country. It is for this reason that I consider analyses which consist only of recommending to countries measures which might have appeared successful in others lightweight, frivolous and baseless. Because of the complexity of relations between instruments and goals, and despite the immense progress to date, economists have not yet succeeded in perfectly elucidating all these relations; thus they speak of the "black box" in the economic model.

Constraints linked to political cycles

Economists have since demonstrated the influence that the political system of a country may have on the elaboration and conduct of economic policy. This observation has led to the theory of political cycles. According to this theory, politicians in general wish to stay in power and consequently are all too ready to carry out an economic policy which will immediately guarantee this, even if the long-term effects may not be optimal for the economy. For example, this tendency leads to investment choices guided more by political imperatives than by the desire to achieve lasting results on the final, intermediate and operating goals that I have enumerated in the foregoing chapters.

As we can see, the constraints which surround economic policy action are many, complicated and difficult to manage, so that even for a well-intentioned government to succeed in its economic policy is a daunting task. For a government to find its way through this labyrinth of constraints, and to identify and successfully implement measures which will produce the required results (i.e., companies which incessantly invest to modernize and build their production capacities on the one hand, and consumers who incessantly increase their demand for goods and services produced by the national economy on the other, all this with a view toward generating a strong growth capable of creating jobs, the ultimate goal of economic policy), is a task that requires not only skill and creativity, but also a good dose of voluntarism and determination, and a stable conception of what, in the end, characterizes the success of an economy.

The economic constraints that I have just examined function individually and collectively to mutually strengthen each other to reduce the scope of the effects of economic policy actions. As such, most often, the lack of credibility of economic policy officials couples with the rational expectations of economic agents to produce the effects described above. A situation characterized by credibility and favorable rational expectations offers economic policy officials opportunities to effectively and efficiently accomplish the goals of a particular measure of economic policy by influencing the behavior of economic agents in the manner required for the measure to succeed. Similarly, in the presence of the rational expectations of economic agents, if authorities set incompatible targets – considering the dilemma of the magic square, the impossible trinity and the prevailing economic circumstances – this will quickly put to question the credibility of the authorities and of the goals set.

What opportunities does globalization offer African economic policy?

Globalization therefore increases the constraints of economic policy and makes these constraints stronger. It also increases their scope. However, the more globalization limits the possibilities of economic policy action, the more it can also be a source of opportunity. If it results in an effective liberalization of trade in goods and services, and movements of capital and ideas at the global level, globalization will increase the positive effects of a good economic policy. For example, it will offer great possibilities to significantly increase demand directed to the national economy, which, I have said is one of the priority intermediate goals of economic policy.

The usual presentation of opportunities offered by globalization insists on an expansion of the possibilities of choice and a drop in prices, particularly of imported goods that it may offer consumers,[18] and opportunities to import ideas, technology and institutions for development. However, to import all these goods and institutions, we must first export. That is why a country's benefits from globalization stem first from the possibilities it offers to increase its exports, to sell more to the rest of the world, which helps to generate more economic activities, create more jobs and more income for its citizens. Where would the necessary income to benefit from the choices offered and to acquire cheap imported goods come from if exports do not increase? The real measure of a country's benefits linked to globalization, on which African economic policy officials should have insisted and to which they should have referred to first, then becomes its impact on the demand of goods and services directed to the national economy. It is due to this failure to fully consider the strategic reality that African countries (and other developing countries in general), have not, over time, successfully engaged in multilateral negotiations over the rules governing globalization, and have thus missed out on their integration into globalization.

As such, the principal opportunity that globalization would offer economic policy may be the expansion of foreign demand addressed to a country. On this note, I cannot avoid stating that globalization, as it operates presently, does not offer many opportunities to Africa. In fact, one of the key messages of this book is that world demand directed to Africa is still very low. It is even, in my opinion, the main explanatory factor of the low share of Africa in world trade. I am saying that if the difficulties of African supply can explain the fact that sub-Saharan Africa's share in world trade dropped from about four per cent in the 1960s to about two per cent[19] in 2007, as experts say, it is mostly in low demand addressed to Africa by the rest of the world that the fundamental determinants of this marginalization of Africa in world trade can be sought.[20] The reasons for this low demand are many, but two seem to play the greatest roles. First, there are trade measures implemented by the rest of the world, particularly the developed countries, which introduce distortions in world prices. For now, these distortions have the greatest effects in terms of agricultural products exported by Africa. Indeed, these measures most often lead to a rise in the prices of these products on domestic markets of developed countries and consequently reduce the demand for African agricultural products in these countries. This is particularly true for several categories of agricultural products exported by African countries. Thus, for example, when Ugandan president Yoweri Museveni indicated that the agricultural production of his country cannot be sold on world markets because of protective measures, he was right.

Beyond these price distortions, there are other factors which, in my opinion, have more important effects on demand addressed to Africa by the rest of the world. A study has indeed shown that there is a "country of origin effect" in the demand for goods and services by consumers worldwide. This effect plays more in favor of developed countries and to the detriment of developing countries: if a product comes from a developed country, it increases its power of attraction in the eyes of consumers worldwide, thereby encouraging its demand, while the idea of originating from a developing country is still associated with a set of negative perceptions which discourage its demand. This effect is so powerful that in some cases, experts have demonstrated that consumers are willing to purchase from a developed country a product that is 40 per cent more expensive than a product having the same functional characteristics but coming from a developing country. This "country of origin effect" is, in my opinion, a powerful factor of reducing demand addressed to developing countries in general and African countries in particular.[21] This very limited access to the rest of the world explains why Africa up to now has not been able to take full advantage of the process of globalization and has, on the contrary, recorded continuous inadequate economic growth. It should be noted that the fact that a country cannot draw an advantage from its participation in the process of globalization when it is cut off from the rest of the world was established by economist A. Vamvakidis in an article published in 1996. Indeed, studying the relationship between openness to trade and economic growth in a historical perspective going back to the 1870s, he said that

> the positive correlation between trade openness and growth in the 1970s and 1980s disappears in the 1950s and 1960s, and becomes negative in the 1920s and 1930s. The correlation seems to be negative even for earlier decades, starting in the 1870. [...] Openness in the rest of the world has a significant positive impact on the growth of an economy. Empirical estimations and theoretical foundations suggest that an economy should be open to international trade when the rest of the world is open, but openness becomes irrelevant if the rest of the world is closed.[22]

In fact, Africa, and particularly sub-Saharan Africa, is one of the regions whose exports encounter the greatest barriers to world markets. Let's take the example of agricultural products, an area where Africa could have significant trade interests, if only the international environment was favorable. Let's also take the example of tariff measures: the statistics of UNCTAD show that developed countries applied an average tariff of 13.6 per cent on imports from sub-Saharan Africa, while their imports from developing countries in America and Asia and economies in transition were levied only 10.2 per cent, 9.2 per cent and 13.4 per cent respectively (see Table 10.1 below). The tariffs imposed by

Table 10.1. Weighted average tariffs of the most recent year (in %)[23]

	Tariffs actually applied	Tariffs of the Most Favored Nation (MFN)
Tariffs applied by developed countries on imports of agricultural products from:		
Sub-Saharan Africa	13.6	18.1
Developing countries of the Americas	10.2	13.9
Developing countries in Asia	9.2	11
Countries in transition	13.4	19.4
Developed countries	14.8	16.2
Tariffs applied by developing countries on imports of agricultural products from:		
Sub-Saharan Africa	14.6	17.9
Developing countries of the Americas	12	15.2
Developing countries in Asia	17.2	19.1
Countries in transition	14	14.1
Developed countries	16.2	19.4

developing countries on their imports of agricultural products from sub-Saharan Africa were also among the highest. It attained an average of 14.6 per cent against 12 per cent on their imports from Latin American developing countries and 14 per cent on their imports from countries in transition. Given that the tariff measures are only a part of the trade barriers, we can imagine that the barriers actually encountered by Africa to other world markets would be highest if we also took into account nontariff measures.[24]

This discussion actually shows that, for globalization to offer Africa the immense opportunities that many claim it will, African countries must pursue their efforts with the aim of obtaining a real openness with markets of the rest of the world – that is, an openness which manifests itself by significantly increasing demand addressed to Africa from the rest of the world. In this perspective, the pursuit of present efforts within the framework of WTO negotiations is indispensable, but it should be supported particularly by efforts aimed at redressing unfavorable perceptions, which still slow down real development of demand addressed to Africa from the rest of the world. Efforts by developed countries leading to a drop in prices of products exported by Africa to the domestic markets of developed countries must also be pursued. The commitments in favor of an open global economy which the G20 member states reaffirmed during their summit of April 2, 2009 in London must also apply to trade with Africa.

Part Four

FOREIGN AID AND AFRICAN
ECONOMIC POLICY

Throughout this book, I have argued that having a good economic policy primarily determines the economic growth of countries. I have defined the conceptual outlines of this good economic policy and I have examined the manner in which globalization, an unavoidable phenomenon imposed on all today, affects economic policy. To complete the subject, it is now left for me to examine the role of foreign aid. Everybody today will admit that aid exerts, and will continue to exert for some time, considerable influence on the economic policy of African countries.

The debate posed by international aid is twofold: that of its priorities – that is, what it should seek to do, what problems it has to solve or what goals it must pursue – and that of its mode of delivery or how aid funds should be made available to recipient countries. I will attempt to answer these two questions in Part Four. We begin by examining the trends that stem from recent developments of foreign aid (Chapter 11). The following chapter, Chapter 12, opens the debate on what foreign aid must seek to do to be effective and contribute to economic policy, while Chapter 13 examines the modes of delivery.

Chapter Eleven

RECENT TRENDS OF FOREIGN
AID TO AFRICA

Introduction

The beginning of the twenty-first century particularly appeared to offer sub-Saharan African countries a favorable context in terms of foreign aid. Actually, we seem to be witnessing a renewal of the commitment of donors in favor of an increase of assistance to Africa. We have never witnessed a situation of such optimism in the economic history of Africa. The level of generosity expressed by rich countries in favor of Africa seemed to be stronger than ever. In this chapter I will examine some of the major initiatives on aid, but particularly, I will prove that what mostly characterizes aid is the gap between pronouncements by donor countries and effective delivery.

New Initiatives Seem to Indicate a New Level of Solidarity of Rich Countries

Initiatives of the United Nations System

In September 2000, world leaders met in the United Nations Millennium Summit in New York. Here they adopted the Millennium Declaration to try to put the fight against poverty at the center of the development agenda of the international community, as well as aid to developing countries to assist them in this fight. This declaration set a total of eight goals to be attained before 2015 to speed up poverty reduction in the world. These goals, better known today under the appellation Millennium Development Goals (MDGs), target substantial progress in developing countries in fields as varied as the proportion of the population living with less than a dollar per day, hunger, primary education, maternal and child health, the fight against the HIV/AIDS pandemic, gender equality, access to drinking water and the environment (Box 11.1 below describes these goals). Since their adoption in September 2000, the MDGs have greatly influenced economic policies and the sectoral allocation of resources implemented by developing countries with the support of their development partners. As asserted by François Bourguignon, the senior vice president and chief economist of the World Bank, "these goals were first adopted to mobilize the international community" in order that it should increase its aid to poor countries.[1] Typically, to many countries, the strategy to attain these goals consisted in seeking to allocate an increasing share of their resources to sectors viewed as priority sectors, like health, education, infrastructure and

Box 11.1. Millennium development goals[2]

(i) Eradicate extreme poverty and hunger
   - Reduce by half the proportion of the population whose income is less than 1 dollar per day
   - Reduce by half the proportion of the population suffering from hunger

(ii) Achieve universal primary education
   - Give all children, boys and girls, the opportunity to complete the entire primary school cycle

(iii) Promote gender equality and empower women
   - Eliminate gender inequality at all levels of education

(iv) Reduce child mortality
   - Reduce the mortality rate of children below five years by two-thirds

(v) Improve maternal health
   - Reduce the maternal mortality rate by three-quarters

(vi) Combat HIV/AIDS, malaria and other diseases
   - Stop the propagation of AIDS and reverse the trend

(vii) Ensure environmental sustainability
   - Integrate principles of sustainable development in national policies; reverse the present trend of loss of environmental resources
   - Reduce by half the percentage of the population which does not have access to potable water
   - Significantly improve the living conditions of at least one hundred million inhabitants of shanty towns

(viii) Global partnership for development
   - Increase official development assistance
   - Increase access to markets

access to potable water and sanitation. The Millennium Declaration contains a special recommendation on Africa, which requires the international community to increase the flow of resources to Africa.

In January 2005, a report prepared at the request of the secretary general of the United Nations, Kofi Annan, proposed a practical approach to achieving the MDGs.[3] This report aimed at filling an important gap in the strategy adopted in 2000. In fact, while adopting these goals, the world leaders who met in New York in September 2000 did not elaborate a real strategy to ensure their implementation. It was to fill in this gap that the UN Millennium Project, an organ of the council set up by the secretary general in July 2002, launched a vast research project aimed at identifying the best possible approach to attaining the MDGs by 2015. This research, the findings and recommendations of which are presented in the above-mentioned report, was carried out in 10 thematic working groups under the supervision of the economist Jeffrey Sach.[4] It also depended on an impressive network of contributions from the academic, political, scientific and developmental world. The main message from the 10 key recommendations of this report (see Box 11.2) emphasizes the necessity, for developing countries, to substantially and quickly increase public investments in order to promote rural and urban development, guarantee universal access to primary education and increase access to secondary and higher education, eliminate gender inequalities, improve environmental management, strengthen national capacities in the fields of science, technology and innovation, and strengthen good governance. These massive investments in the different sectors may

---

Box 11.2. The ten key recommendations of the UN Millennium Project[5]

(i)   Developing countries' governments should adopt development strategies bold enough to meet the Millennium Development Goal (MDG) targets by 2015. We term them MDG-based poverty reduction targets. To meet the 2015 deadline, we recommend that all countries have these strategies in place by 2006. Where Poverty Reduction Papers (PRSPs) already exist, those should be aligned with the MGDs.

(ii)   The MDG-based poverty reduction strategies should anchor the scaling-up of public investments, capacity building, domestic resource mobilization, and official development assistance. They should also provide a framework for strengthening governance, promoting human rights, engaging civil society, and promoting the private sector.

(iii)   Developing countries' governments should craft and implement the MDG-based poverty reduction strategies in transparent and inclusive processes, working closely with civil society organizations, the domestic private sector and international partners.

(iv)   International partners should identify at least a dozen MGD "fast-track" countries for a rapid scale-up of official development assistance (ODA) in 2005, recognizing that many countries are already in a position for a massive scale-up on the basis of their good governance and absorptive capacity.

(v)   Developed and developing countries should jointly launch, in 2005, a group of Quick Win actions to save and improve millions of lives and to promote economic growth. They should also launch a massive effort to build expertise at the community level.

(vi)   Developing countries' governments should align national strategies with such regional initiatives as the New Partnership for Africa's Development and the Caribbean Community (and Common Market) and regional groups should receive increased direct donor support for regional projects.

(vii)   High-income countries should increase official development assistance (ODA) from 0.25 percent of donor GNP in 2003 to around 0.44 per cent in 2006 and 0.54 per cent in 2015 to support the Millennium Development Goals, particularly in low-income countries, with improved ODA quality (including aid that is harmonized, predictable, and largely in the form of grant-based budget support). Each donor should reach 0.7 per cent no later than 2015 to support the Goals and other development assistance priorities. Debt relief should be more extensive and generous.

(viii) High-income countries should open their markets to developing country exports through the Doha trade round and help Least Developed Countries raise export competitiveness through investments in critical trade-related infrastructures, including electricity, roads and ports. The Doha Development Agenda should be fulfilled and the Doha Round completed no later than 2006.

(ix) International donors should mobilize support for global scientific research and development to address special needs of the poor in areas of health, agriculture, natural resources and environment management, energy and climate. We estimate the total needs to rise to approximately $7 billion a year by 2015.

(x) The UN Secretary General and the UN Development Group should strengthen the coordination of UN agencies, funds, and programs to support the MDGs, at Headquarters and country level. The UN country teams should be strengthened and should work closely with the international financial institutions to support the goals.

be financed thanks to an increase in the official development assistance of developed countries, whose terms of delivery would have been improved upon, particularly by a greater resort to budgetary aid to the detriment of project assistance.

As it appears, the essence of the recommendations of this report is summarized in massive public investments in various sectors, financed mainly by a rapid increase in official development assistance. There is no doubt that I would have loved to have seen concrete, original and wide-range propositions aimed at relaunching economic activity in developing countries with a view toward creating the jobs necessary for the fight against poverty; as I have already said throughout this book, employment and economic growth should be at the center of all strategies aimed at poverty reduction in all dimensions. Poverty reduction will be achieved by very strong economic growth accompanied by the sustainable expansion of jobs – or it will not be achieved.

Initiatives of the Group of Eight (G8)

Even the G8, the exclusive club of the world's richest countries, at one point relaxed its agenda – traditionally consecrated to serious international trade and financial problems such as multilateral trade liberalization, growth and perspectives of world economy, movements of exchange rates among major world currencies, world energy security, international macroeconomic problems, the fight against financing terrorism and international financial crime – to concentrate on the fight against poverty in Africa. Since 2001, representatives of African countries have been invited to participate in annual G8 meetings to present their visions of the development needs of their continent and what they expect of rich countries.[6] Also, under pressure from Great Britain during its summit in July 2005 at Gleneagles in Scotland, the G8 adopted an ambitious financial aid plan to Africa.

The results of the G8 Summit of 2005, held in Gleneagles in Scotland, were heavily anticipated by all those interested in the African situation. Obviously, most observers were particularly curious to know what the most developed countries of the world were to decide on the ambitious plan proposed by Great Britain in favor of Africa. I know that a great majority of those who were interested in what this summit would produce for Africa particularly studied its results from the point of view of what the G8 countries decided on debt relief, increasing official development assistance, access to markets of rich countries, farm subsidies and the creation of an International Financial Facility to immediately mobilize a more significant volume of resources to finance development. I also know that those who went far enough in their curiosity to obtain the press release issued by the G8 countries on Africa at the end of their deliberations were quickly referred to paragraphs 24 to 31 and Appendix II of this press release, which contain the G8's decisions on promises of financing in favor of Africa.

The discussions on Africa which were going to take place during the summit had been prepared for some time. In fact, in February 2004, then British prime minister Tony Blair had launched the Commission for Africa.[7] This commission was going to contribute once more toward placing foreign aid at the center of the debate on development in Africa. The announced goals of this commission had every reason to arouse the interest of all those working to restore hope to a marginalized continent. Indeed, the goals of the commission were five in number: (i) generate new ideas and actions to make Africa more powerful and prosperous, by using the British presidency of the G8 and of the European Union in 2005 as a springboard; (ii) support the best projects already in existence in Africa, particularly the New Partnership for African Development (NEPAD) and the African Union (AU), but particularly help to ensure that these projects attain their goals; (iii) help in the good implementation of present international commitments to Africa; (iv) offer a new positive perspective for Africa and its diverse cultures in the twenty-first century, a perspective to tackle unjust perceptions and bring changes; and (v) understand and respond to the aspirations of Africa for its future by listening to Africans. After about a year of work and consultations with stakeholders in Africa as well as outside Africa, the commission published its report in March 2005, entitled *Our Common Interest: Report of the Commission for Africa.*

In 2005, British prime minister Tony Blair wanted to make Africa one of the priorities of the British presidency of the G8 and the European Union. As such, in February, during the meeting of finance ministers and central bank governors of G8 member states which took place in London, and then in July, during the meeting of G8 leaders held in Gleneagles, Great Britain presented an aid plan to Africa that its then finance minister, chancellor of the exchequer Gordon Brown, qualified as the Marshall Plan. These proposals depended mostly on recommendations made by the Commission for Africa. By and large, the ambitious aid proposals made by Great Britain were not adopted during the G8 Summit in Gleneagles, only a few medium-range measures (see Box 11.3 below).

Box 11.3. Main measures adopted in favor of Africa by the G8 summit of July 2005 in Gleneagles

After two days of discussion, the G8 leaders reached an agreement on some aspects of the plan for Africa presented by the prime minister, Tony Blair. The points are summarized below:

Debt

Debts to the IMF, the International Development Association (the World Bank concession counter) and the African Development Fund of heavily indebted poor countries may be cancelled. G8 countries may supply the resources necessary so that the financial situations of the institutions concerned are not compromised. To reach this decision, G8 countries overcame French and Japanese opposition.

International Financial Facility

In all, we can say that G8 countries did not support the establishment of the International Financial Facility (IFF) as initially conceived by Great Britain – that is, financed by an international loan guaranteed by the G8 countries. Japan and Canada expressed a provisional opposition to this mechanism, while Germany, Italy and France rather preferred an IFF for the fight against HIV/AIDS and expressed conditional support to the general IFF if a small-scale pilot proved conclusive. France proposed a European tax on aircraft fuel to finance the international facility.

Trade

Concerning trade measures, the G8 recommended that this question be examined by the WTO Summit in Hong Kong in December 2005.

In a nutshell, then, most provisions which formed the originality and ambition of this plan – such as the setting up of the IFF to further mobilize resources to finance poverty reduction programs, cancel 100 per cent of the bilateral and multilateral debt owed by the poorest African countries, suppress before 2010 all subsidies to exports and all agricultural aid that cause distortions, and reduce, before 2015, customs duties and nontariff obstacles to African exports – did not receive strong support from other G8 countries. They were therefore practically abandoned, except for perhaps the measure on multilateral debt cancellation, which was adopted later.

Discussions on aid to Africa in the World Economic Forum of Davos

Africa's case was brought to the table of discussion of another exclusive rich club, the World Economic Forum, which toward January or February each year brings the business and political world together in the Swiss town of Davos to discuss major international problems. Thus, poverty reduction in Africa was one of the major themes of the fifth edition of this forum, held from January 26 to 30, 2005. On this occasion, a panel uniquely composed of the former American president Bill Clinton, British prime minister Tony Blair, French president Jacques Chirac, the German chancellor Gerhard Schröder, founder of Microsoft Bill Gates, president Thabo Mbeki of South Africa and president Olusegun Obasanjo of Nigeria animated a discussion on what the G8 could do and must do for Africa. The leaders were committed to acting promptly to reduce poverty, particularly in Africa. As such, Tony Blair declared that 2005 was a year to give great impetus to development efforts, and the billionaire Bill Gates said that 2005 was a year of challenges.[8] Blair in particular expressed the need to establish a plan which would bring together development aid, debt relief, the fight against illnesses, access to markets and good governance.

The American initiative: The Millennium Challenge Account

In a speech made in March 2002 at the Inter-American Development Bank in Washington DC, US president George W. Bush presented the broad outlines of a new plan that the United States was going to implement to help poor countries. According to the US president, the fight against poverty in the world required a serious mobilization of resources on the part of rich countries and the determined commitment of poor countries to ensure an effective use of resources placed at their disposal. It is within this context that the president announced that the US would increase its development aid budget by 50 per cent over the next three years (2003–06), thereby leading to an annual increase of 5 billion dollars. In order to ensure that these additional resources were used judiciously in the fight against poverty, they would be deposited in the Millennium Challenge Account (MCA), which would be used to finance poverty reduction projects in countries where the government rules equitably, invests in the population and encourages economic liberty. Among low-income countries (less than 1.435 dollars income per capita)[9] and those of the lower bracket of the middle-income group (less than 2.975 dollars income per capita), those who show proof of good governance were to be the main beneficiaries of these resources. During the meeting of finance ministers and central bank governors of G7 member countries held in February 2005 in London, John Taylor, then undersecretary of the United States Treasury in charge of international affairs, reaffirmed that, for the United States, the MCA was henceforth going to be the major instrument of increased US aid to low-income countries.

In order to determine countries eligible for MCA financing, a set of 16 indicators were developed to evaluate their performance in relation to good political governance, investment in human capital and economic liberties. Only countries whose evaluated performance is above the median in all three criteria are considered to have satisfactory performance (see Box 11.4). On May 6, 2004, the Board of Directors of the Millennium Challenge Corporation, the American body in charge of MCA, published the first list of 16 countries eligible to benefit from MCA financing in 2004. On November 8, 2004, the board published a list of 16 countries eligible to benefit from MCA financings in 2005.

Box 11.4. Millennium Challenge Account

Performance Indicators for Eligibility for MCA Financings

Political governance

- Civil liberties
- Political rights
- Voice and accountability
- Government effectiveness
- Primacy of the law
- Fight against corruption

Investing in human capital

- Share of public expenses consecrated to government primary education in GDP
- Primary education completion rate
- Share of public health spending in GDP
- Vaccination rate

Promotion of economic liberties

- Country's credit rating
- Inflation rate
- Budget deficit for three years
- Trade policy
- Quality of regulatory framework
- Number of days to start a company

The French initiative: An international tax to finance development

This initiative, which draws inspiration from the Tobin tax, after the name of the American economist James Tobin, who was the first to raise the idea of a tax on the speculative movement of international capital, revived the debate on modalities of financing development. This French initiative was welcome, particularly in an international context, where the performance of most rich countries in terms of development aid still struggles, despite commitments undertaken, to get close to the target of 0.7 per cent GNP set by the United Nations, and where resources consecrated to development aid finally prove to be insufficient. This insufficiency, which compromises the implementation of policies required to carry out the fight against poverty, is within a context where the threat of Africa's increased marginalization seems more and more real. It is for this reason that the ways and means that can help rally all stakeholders around this initiative must be sought. Taking advantage of an official visit to Senegal in February 2005, French president Jacques Chirac once more reiterated his proposal to implement this tax to finance the development efforts of poor countries.

Monterrey International Conference on Financing for Development

With a view to seeking better policies in order to promote development and poverty reduction, the International Conference on Financing Development was held in Monterrey, Mexico, from March 18 to 22, 2002. This conference, held under the auspices of the United Nations, was attended by fifty heads of state, and more than two hundred ministers and officials of the private sector, the civil society and most major international financial, trade, economic and monetary organizations, particularly the World Bank, the African Development Bank, the IMF and the Inter-American Development Bank. The conference, which brought together more than eight hundred participants, was the result of about four years of preparation (1999–2002). It led to the adoption of the "Monterrey Consensus" according to which rich, developing and countries in transition were committed to implementing important actions on political, domestic, international and systemic problems. This consensus was adopted by acclamation on March 22, 2002. New announcements in terms of official development assistance were made by the European Union and the United States. After this conference, the United Nations created a bureau in charge of financing development in the Department of Economic and Social Affairs, to monitor the implementation of the recommendations and discussions of the conference.

Launching a cycle of multilateral trade negotiations (a "development cycle") in Doha

Between 1947 and 1993, multilateral trade negotiations concluded eight cycles of multilateral trade negotiations under the auspices of GATT. Within the framework of the 8th cycle, the WTO created the Uruguay Round, which lasted from 1986 to 1993. During these successive cycles, progress recorded in terms of the liberalization of trade were on the reduction of customs duties and anti-dumping measures, the reduction of nontariff obstacles to trade, trade in services, intellectual property, dispute-settlement mechanisms, and trade in textile and agricultural products. When the Uruguay Agreement was signed in Marrakech in 1995, the dominant feeling in developing countries and even developed countries was that the developed countries benefited most from the cycles of multilateral trade negotiations concluded up to that point. Negotiations had been on the liberalization of products in which developed countries had major trade interests. To compensate this disequilibrium, developed countries accepted the launch of a new cycle of multilateral trade negotiations which might actually aim at being beneficial to developing countries.[10]

The Increasing Gap between Pronouncement and Execution

As we can observe, the initiatives of the international community in favor of aid are not lacking. However, what characterizes recent trends most in terms of aid is the fact that effective implementations do not always follow pronouncements. This further complicates aid and economic management in recipient countries. Thus, according to the *Global Monitoring Report* published by the World Bank in 2008, the commitments that the G8 countries and other donors undertook in Gleneagles to increase aid to developing countries before 2010 by 50 billion dollars – with half of this increase (that is, 25 billion dollars) directed to Africa – were probably not going to be upheld.[11] Figure 11.1 below illustrates this. Pure development aid in 2006 stood at about half the goals to be attained in 2010. Another report published by the OECD also sounded the warning.

Figure 11.1. DAC members' net ODA flows and prospects 1990–2010[12]

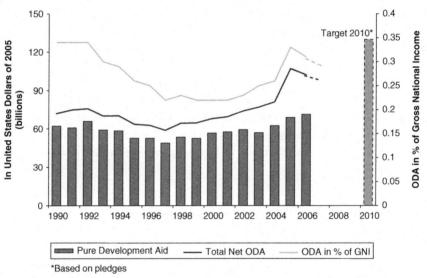

*Based on pledges

As I said at the beginning of this book, there is always a gap between pronouncements made by donor countries and effective delivery. According to information obtained by the London daily *Financial Times*, for example, during their 2008 summit, the G8 countries attempted to revise most of the pronouncements to increase aid which they had made during the 2005 summit. Such is the commitment undertaken by the G8 countries to increase aid to Africa by 25 billion dollars per annum. This commitment did not figure in the draft communiqué of the G8 meeting of July 2008 in Japan. They were also divided in the manner of implementing the commitment they undertook at the Heiligendamm Summit of 2008 to provide 60 billion dollars to fight against malaria, tuberculosis and AIDS and strengthen health systems in poor countries.[13]

The Doha Development Round also seems not to progress according to the rhythm desired by developing countries, although they are believed to be the highest beneficiaries.

The reasons for this delay seem to be linked particularly to the will of developed countries, either to include in the agenda of negotiations issues that developing countries do not consider priorities for their development (the Singapore Issues), or not to give in to measures of liberalization which may offer to developing countries real access to their markets, or not to include in the agenda of negotiations issues that developing countries consider priorities for their development.

Africa Remains the Continent that Receives the Least Foreign Aid

Another major trend of foreign aid is that, compared to other continents, Africa remains that which receives the least development aid, if we consider aid going through multilateral development banks. Statistics gathered by the World Bank show that, from 2000–2007 for example, Africa's share in the gross disbursement of multilateral development banks was very low. Figure 11.2 below describes the progress of total gross disbursements of the five biggest multilateral development banks, per region. These are the concessional and nonconcessional disbursements of multilateral development banks intervening in the region indicated. As such, disbursements to Africa are done by the World Bank and the African Development Bank. Disbursements to Asia are done by the World Bank and the Asian Development Bank. Disbursements to Latin America are done by the World Bank and the Inter-American Development Bank. And disbursements to Europe are done by the World Bank and the European Bank for Reconstruction and Development.

The fact that disbursements to Africa increased from 2006 to 2007 did not change this trend fundamentally, given that at the same time disbursements to developing countries in Asia increased even faster. This trend is also surprising particularly when we know that Africa is a continent whose needs are very important and that, consequently, donor countries very often reassert their wish to place Africa at the center of their efforts in

Figure 11.2. Gross disbursements of multilateral development banks per region[14]

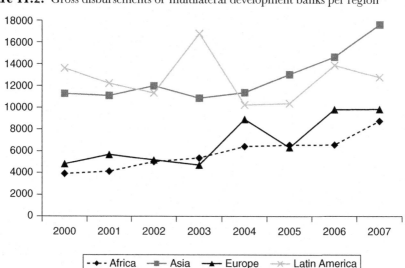

terms of aid. Once more, there is disparity between ambitions displayed and those effectively delivered.

Summary

To conclude, in recent years there has been a semblance of renewal in the commitment of rich countries to further help poor countries. On several occasions, Africa has been portrayed as one of the highest aid beneficiaries. Unfortunately, most of these announcements are not usually followed by actions, at least actions to the standard of the announcements made, thereby singularly complicating macroeconomic and economic management in countries benefiting from aid.

Chapter Twelve

WHAT GOALS FOR FOREIGN AID?

"To reinforce foreign aid beyond debt relief and humanitarian aid, we have to be very imaginative."

> Donald Kaberuka, president of the African Development Bank Group,
> *Financial Times*, November 14, 2005

Introduction

In this book, I have examined a good economic policy mainly by questioning the structure of the goals and instruments which define it. I will adopt the same approach in examining the role of foreign aid, as this approach appears so relevant and important to my purpose. Thus, the aim of this chapter is to examine the goals that foreign aid may pursue in order to support the implementation of the economic policy that I have defined in this book. Even if one of the operating goals of economic policy is the search for its independence and liberty to choose its own orientations, which is obtained through less dependence on foreign aid, I postulate that this search will be essentially a long-term task. This is due to the present financial situation of most aid-dependent countries, especially in the context of Africa. As a matter of fact, and in the medium term, African countries will continue to resort to foreign aid. In such a context, the question is to know how aid can best work to contribute positively to the implementation of economic policy. Answering this question entails, first and foremost, defining good goals for foreign aid – that is, what aid should aim at achieving. As with any venture, defining goals is a precondition for success. The goals define the results that we hope to obtain. They also help to assess if we have succeeded or not. Defining good goals for foreign aid will therefore be my concern in this chapter.

The Goal of Reducing Poverty under Debate

The idea that aid must seek to reduce the endemic poverty ravaging poor countries has generally been accepted by all. Since the 1970s, when the president of the World Bank drew the attention of the international community to the scourge of poverty and decided that the mission of this institution in developing countries would henceforth be the fight against poverty, this has been the major goal of foreign aid to poor countries. At the entrance of the main building of the World Bank Headquarters in Washington, DC, we find a noticeboard on which is inscribed "Our dream is a world free of poverty."

The economist William Easterly's book has relaunched the debate on what aid should do – what it should set up as goal. To him, if aid has not been effective up to this point, it is merely because poverty reduction as a goal may be too ambitious, distant, unrealistic and impossible to attain. He noted that the foreign-aid system has spent about 2.3 trillion US dollars during the last fifty years, with little to show for it.[1]

According to Easterly, foreign aid rests on a collective system of responsibility for a multitude of utopian goals, such as: (i) reduce poverty; (ii) change the behavior and policies of governments which themselves do not seek general interest, particularly through structural adjustment programs and the practice of conditionality;[2] and (iii) attempt to impose on recipient countries practices aimed at instituting a market economy which, even if working well in developed countries, does not take into account the local realities of the countries in which they are to be implanted. According to him, these overambitious goals, coupled with less efficient practices today, explain the failure of foreign-development aid.[3] To him, for aid to be effective, it must concentrate on small achievements which have a positive impact on the lives of the poor, such as providing them with drugs, vaccines, antibiotics, good quality roads, fertilizers, potable water and books. Aid should also ensure that those who have positive ideas that can contribute to improve the daily life of the poor have resources to implement them. To implement these orientations, he therefore suggests that aid renounces the ambitious goals that he judges unrealistic, such as poverty reduction. It should only aim at supporting those he calls "searchers," who contribute concrete solutions which improve the daily life of the poor, to the detriment of those he calls "planners," who elaborate great projects aiming at reducing poverty and changing the behaviors of governments, and whose efforts always remain short-lived.

If William Easterly's idea is seductive, according to which establishing ambitious goals is not effective and does not contribute to advance the fight against poverty, the effectiveness of the idea that foreign aid should simply renounce the setting up of goals and should somehow proceed by trial and error, by financing ideas which *a posteriori* turn out to work, is also debatable. Which human endeavor seriously wishing to succeed can overlook predefined goals? How can we identify success, or how can we distinguish it from failure, if it has not been previously defined? Without any vision concretized by clear and precise goals, human endeavors may only lead to confusion.

If some have criticized the goal of poverty reduction for its excessive ambition, others, on the contrary, have criticized the lack of ambition which may be, according to them, inherent in a goal simply targeting poverty reduction. The horizon must be a strong economic growth that creates decent jobs for all; such a goal would be more stimulating, impassioning and energizing, gathering all talents to the service of collective well-being. These are arguments that I often hear from African intellectuals. Previously, I noted that in most African countries, "poverty reduction and growth strategy papers," "economic development and growth strategies" or better still "growth and job creation strategies" now replace the "poverty reduction strategy papers" launched at the end of the 1990s. Does this change of language express adhesion to this second conception? It seems so. We should obviously reduce poverty, but we need strong economic growth which creates jobs to get to it. Concentrating on these two conditions therefore seems primordial to me. Moreover, it is what I have developed throughout this book.

I demonstrated in the first and second parts of this book that the well-being of citizens varies according to a multitude of factors, but in order to be efficient in its contribution to this improvement, economic policy should concentrate on obtaining concrete results on influential fundamental factors – that is, mainly economic growth and the level of employment in the economy. It is by further concentrating on these two final goals that economic policy could find the inspiration and legitimacy necessary for its success. To be effective, foreign aid must target the same goals as the national economic policy. Even if these two goals appear very distant from what aid can directly influence and, consequently, the responsibility for these two variables lies with the government, it seems to me that establishing the horizon of aid on these two variables may contribute much to positively reorient it toward greater efficiency.

Concentrating the Attention of Actors on Economic Growth and Job Creation in Recipient Countries as Final Goals of Foreign Aid

Careful examination reveals that the degree of mainstreaming of the key final goals of job creation and economic growth in donors' aid practices fits a pattern covering four distinct periods. The first period up to the mid-2000s reflects some neglect of the two key final goals of employment and economic growth in donors' aid programs. This is followed by the period from the mid-2000s up to about 2011, during which there was some discussion of these key issues, but not much action. Then there is the period which started with Arab Spring in 2011, which I expect to last well into the mid-2010s. This period has witnessed some attempts at better integrating these considerations into donors' aid programs, but which still need to be strengthened and consolidated. Finally, I expect to have the post–Arab Spring period from the mid-2010s onwards, during which the gains made in this area may come under serious pressure.

The period up to the mid-2000s: The marginalization of economic growth and employment

It is well understood that in previous years foreign aid has somehow neglected fields that contribute directly to the development of economic activity to concentrate more on purely social issues. Though there were some attempts at supporting the private sector, particularly by creating a department or entity dedicated to the private sector in every aid agency, it holds that these attempts were still very limited compared to the great needs that exist concerning what should be done, as well as the manner of doing it. Aid has been greatly tilted toward interventions aimed at compensating the insufficiency of social sectors (education, health, etc.), sometimes to the detriment of the development of companies which, finally, create resources that improve the standard of living and effectively contribute to the fight against poverty.

Contrary to what we may think, increasing the concentration of foreign aid on obtaining economic growth and creating jobs will not be an easy change. The change will even be a difficult one, because it is a structural change among development partners. Practices and policies should change. As surprising as it may appear, foreign-aid agencies do not yet really give a foreground role to economic growth and employment in their interventions. The fact that even the MDGs, as adopted in September 2000 by the entire international community meeting at the headquarters of the United Nations and which were supposed to be the convergence point for countries as well as development partners in terms of poverty reduction, did not contain explicit goals on economic growth and employment was quite emblematic of practices of the international community.

Also, the fact that the IMF (an influential and well-respected institution among the community of donors which has the power to mobilize the rest of the partners) in its discussions with African countries does not treat employment issues (though a foreground macroeconomic variable) with the level of commitment and concentration I may wish, either within the framework of programs under its lending facilities or within the framework of its surveillance activities, graphically illustrates how little is space accorded these concerns in international actions.[4] This practice is not limited to the IMF. Thus, up to this point, the World Bank has not really placed the search for high-level employment in African countries at the center of goals targeted by the programs that it finances. When project appraisal reports mention this variable, they perceive it as having resulted from its interventions in the fields of education and training, or better still within the framework of labor-intensive social projects or microcredit projects. Evaluations carried out to date have concluded that these types of programs are limited in their efficiency in terms of employment. An ambitious, full-fledged macroeconomic and voluntarist approach is needed.

Commenting in 2003 on the trade negotiations of the Doha Round devoted to development that had just been launched under the WTO, Dani Rodrik, a professor of economics at Harvard University in the US, asserted that

> there existed ways of expanding the scope of negotiations in a way that really targets development. Let's take a very clear example: developing countries may have much to gain in a domain [...] where the Doha Round does not undertake any commitment, like the liberalization of temporary labor flow at the international level. It may be difficult identifying another topic bearing a comparable potential to raise the level of income in poor countries. Even a relatively limited temporary work visa program, in rich countries, may have the capacity to generate, for workers of poor countries, an increase in income exceeding the predictions on all Doha propositions taken together![5]

What is interesting in this commentary is not so much the propositions on employment that it contains, but the fact that it draws attention on the little interest that the international community granted, within the framework of a cycle of multilateral trade negotiations deemed to be that of development, to actions aimed at increasing income through the promotion of employment to the benefit of poor countries. As we can see, for the three main organizations in charge of world economic governance, those that have more influence on the economic policy of African countries, employment has not yet been placed at the center of their intervention policies and programs in African countries.

Among the reasons which caused aid to concentrate insufficiently on economic growth and employment, there is first the fact that the countries themselves did not really place these concerns at the center of their economic policy. However, as we have seen, the situation is changing. There is also the weight of well-established misconceptions, especially concerning employment in developing countries. Thus, we hear that employment is not a problem in developing countries because most people work. The problem is rather with productivity, which is low. Another misconception is that employment may be a very difficult notion to manage in sub-Saharan Africa. Most of those who have jobs work in the informal sector, thereby making all assessments of the employment situation difficult, or even impossible, by resorting to traditionally used statistical tools in modern analyses of the labor market. By definition, the informal sector is that which escapes all regulations and where the major dynamics are least known. Also, employment may not be a variable directly under the control of authorities in charge of economic policy. Furthermore, we always hear that the level and progress of the employment situation may be the result of several factors, sometimes linked to the international environment. In such conditions, it may be difficult to concentrate on employment and set up goals on this issue. I am of the view that a variable as important as employment is difficult to manage, should have spurred action in this domain instead of discouraging it.

Besides this apparent difficulty, which may be linked to the slippery character of the statistical object that is employment, obviously, we also have a defect in the statistical tools themselves. I am thinking here particularly of definitions of the concept of unemployment, which very often result in the conclusion that it is not a problem in Africa. In fact, the different definitions of the concept of unemployment used to establish official statistics of the employment situation are so restrictive that they often result in a measure which has nothing to do with the reality. They describe a situation characterized by a satisfactory level of employment in the economy, while the reality is totally different (i.e., characterized by massive unemployment). As such, the International Labor Office (ILO), whom most of the international community use as a reference, define the unemployed as:

> all persons above a specified age who, during the reference period, were without work, currently available for work and seeking work. However, it should be recognized that national definitions and coverage of unemployment can vary with regard to factors such as age limits, criteria for seeking work, and treatment of, for example, persons temporarily laid off, discouraged about job prospects or seeking work for the first time.[6]

Another factor which caused aid to insufficiently consider improving levels of employment is linked to the fact that, up until recently, African countries were still less democratic. Thus, development programs did not place this variable at the center of their economic policy, even if it was a major preoccupation of citizens, and since aid depends on national policy it also gave insufficient attention to employment. However, this situation is also changing to the extent that an increasing number of African countries are attaining political democracy. As a matter of fact, in such a system, citizens will also request that their political leaders obtain concrete results in the unique field that matters to them: that of employment. Furthermore, the civil society, whose active role is more and more perceptible in several African countries, will have an increasing influence on decisions of national economic policy and will seek to include a specific consideration of employment concerns therein. Besides the role played by the insufficient development of a democratic system of governance in the marginalization of employment in aid policies, other external factors also played an important role.

The mid-2000s to 2011: Signs of positive evolution

Despite this environment which was less inclined to integrate economic growth and employment into the policies of the international community in terms of foreign aid, signs of change started appearing. Thus, in an important report published in 2004 (which somehow remained unperceived, but whose influence was increasing), the World Commission on the Social Dimension of Globalization (see Box 12.1 below) made the following recommendation: "Making decent work a key goal of economic policy, by giving priority to employment creation, protecting fundamental rights at work, strengthening social protection, and promoting social dialogue."[7]

According to me, though the work of this commission on the social dimension of globalization was not sufficiently publicized and valued, it seems that it represented an important step in the consecration process of employment as a fundamental goal in the policies of the international community.

In another development, the idea of focusing on growth and employment seemed to also be spreading throughout the community of development researchers as well as in the world of decision makers. As such, at the level of research, three economists based in the United States suggested that measures aimed at facilitating the international mobility of labor should occupy a more important place in multilateral trade negotiations. They estimated that insofar as the difference in wages between poor and rich countries is wide, to the tune of 500–1000 per cent, a tentative flow of labor between the North and South may generate high-income benefits for workers of poor countries who go to work in rich countries. According to them, these benefits may go directly to the workers themselves without passing through channels such as the exchange of goods and governments, with their inherent inefficiencies. Box 12.2 below describes the outline of this suggestion in greater detail.

The World Bank also spoke highly of the merits and opportunities offered for the development of their countries of origin by money transfers carried out by nationals of poor countries working in rich countries. In this context, it recommended that countries should set up mechanisms to facilitate these transfers. The fact that theoretical reflection and decision makers like the World Bank were finally reflecting on work as a means to fight against poverty is good thing and progress which should be recognized.

However, while we have to work to consolidate this orientation, we should also remember that it is in the poor countries themselves – that is, in their respective countries – that the poor need jobs, and not jobs created in Northern countries where they can work within the framework of temporary work visa programs. The collective challenge of poor countries and their development partners which we all face should therefore be to work to create jobs in poor countries where the need is highly felt. Independently of the fact that the positive impact of cash remittance on development has not been finally demonstrated,[8] a strategy to create jobs directly in poor countries may have the additional advantage of resolving part of the social integration problems that the presence of foreign labor would certainly create

Box 12.1. World Commission on the Social Dimension of Globalization February 2002–February 2004

The World Commission on the Social Dimension of Globalization was set up in February 2002 by the ILO with the aim of contributing to the search for a consensus on which national and international policies to implement so that more people benefit from globalization. In this perspective, the commission also had as its goal to help the international community to conceive more coherent policies in order that economic and social goals be attained simultaneously. Besides its composition and functioning, the commission was meant to combine the experiences, perceptions and aspirations of the key actors of globalization in their diversity of living standards, cultural contexts and social standings. As such, co-presided by two incumbent heads of state, the commission was made up of eminent personalities (one of whom was a Nobel Prize winner in economics) from different horizons, such as the political world, civil society, the labor community, the business community and the university milieu, and also representing the industrialized and developing countries. The commission started work at the beginning of 2002, and before publishing its final report in February 2004, held twenty-two national and regional dialogues – six of which were in Africa, four in Asia, five in Europe and seven in Latin America – and a subregional dialogue in Beirut. It also held six thematic dialogues, one with the civil society in Johannesburg, South Africa, one with Ibero-American employers in Santo Domingo, Dominican Republic, one with business leaders under the aegis of the OIE in Geneva, Switzerland, one with the ICFTU/CMT in Brussels, Belgium, one with the World Social Forum in Port Allegro, Brazil, and one with the World Economic Forum in Davos, Switzerland. The commission also held six coordination meetings in Geneva.

At the end of its work, the commission made policy recommendations, both at the national and international levels, aimed at achieving a fair globalization. Among national recommendations, policies aimed at promoting employment occupy a good position. The report also emphasized improving governance. At the international level, the report insisted that the rules and policies that govern world trade and finance must be flexible enough to enable developing countries to adopt and implement policies that better respond to their level of development and specificity. The other recommendations of the report were related to the necessity of improving regulations on international migrations and foreign direct investment flow, ensuring a better application of fundamental standards of work, as well as greater access for products of developing countries to world markets.

in host developed countries. I may not be complete in my efforts to place employment at the center of poverty reduction goals if I do not mention the remarkable job done in this field by the United Nations Economic Commission for Africa. In the foregoing chapter, I mentioned the fact that several meetings of African finance ministers also focused on the means to place employment at the center of poverty reduction policies. Finally, the

Box 12.2. Impact of a temporary work visa program in rich countries[9]

Let us take the example of a temporary work visa program on about three per cent of the work force in rich countries. Within the framework of this program, skilled and unskilled workers of poor countries may be authorized, by cohort, to work in rich countries for a period of three to five years. At the end of its period, each cohort may return to his or her country and may be replaced by another. Realizing the inherent difficulty in conceiving a temporary work contract program which is actually temporary, the authors suggested a set of incentive measures to encourage workers to return to their countries of origin when their contract expires. Among these measures were the retention of a percentage of income until the worker returns to his country and a penalty system – for example, reducing the quota of workers from countries whose nationals do not return. The authors estimate that a temporary work visa program of this type may easily generate income profit of about two hundred billion dollars per annum for citizens of poor countries. Also, the workers may return to their countries with more qualifications, team spirit, a greater work ethic and, particularly, resources to eventually invest.

Commission for Africa, created by then British prime minister Tony Blair to reflect on means to help Africa, also formulated the following recommendation: "Donors should help African governments to implement national action plans on employment."[10] Despite these policy statements it would not be an exaggeration to claim that much of this remained at the level of intentions. Concrete actions of the type I describe in this book were still lacking.

The Arab Spring effect, 2011 to the mid-2010s: Some attempts at better integrating the key final goals of employment and economic growth in donors' aid programs

At the beginning of the year 2011, popular discontent in Tunisia (which apparently had been brewing for some time) turned into a political revolution and led to the overthrowing of President Ben Ali. The Tunisian Revolution sent major shockwaves throughout the Arab World in which many countries witnessed a change of political regime. These revolutions became known as the Arab Spring. The international community interpreted these major political changes as a reflection of the citizens' demand for more political freedom, more economic inclusion (including more jobs) and increased well-being more generally. In most aid agencies, the Arab Spring therefore marked the starting point for stepping up efforts toward better integration of job creation and growth concerns in aid programs designed for developing countries. In developing countries, including those in Africa, economic policy officials also seized this opportunity to proclaim their desire to focus more on employment and economic growth as key final goals of economic policy. As a result of the Arab Spring, therefore, seeking increased impact on job creation and inclusive economic growth gained momentum in the policy discourses of economic policy officials and international development partners in developing countries. Starting in 2011, aid agencies and developing countries launched major employment programs and initiatives, mainly focused on youth employment.

The post–Arab Spring period: From the mid-2010s onward

It remains to be seen, however, whether the shift triggered by the Arab Spring in relation to donors' focus on the key goals of employment and economic growth will last. Two scenarios are possible: either the trend will continue or it will reverse. I discuss these two scenarios below:

Scenario 1: Continuation of the trend

Under this scenario, the significant shift triggered by the Arab Spring lasts and employment and economic growth continues to occupy a central role in donors' aid programs to Africa. Donors show more determination to achieve concrete results on the two key variables. This is the scenario most stakeholders in Africa would most probably like to see. Under this scenario, the following measures could further strengthen the links between donors' aid programs and employment creation in African countries.

(a) Adapting international indicators of employment to the context of developing countries

One of the major obstacles to a better integration of employment in the economic policies of African countries and intervention programs of donors seems to be linked to a very restrictive definition of the concept of unemployment, as practiced in the international scene. As a matter of fact, the application of the ILO definition stated above often results in a very low unemployment rate in African countries, whereas a significant fraction of the population is visibly not at work. Considering the African context, it may be desirable to re-examine this definition to adapt it so that it better expresses the employment situation in these countries and from there show the necessity of action that is beneficial to both African decision makers and donors.

(b) Instituting an employment test

The impact on employment should be the criterion for evaluating aid programs aimed at reducing poverty. Within this framework, priority should be given to programs having a clearly positive impact on employment – that is, those expressed through the creation of new jobs or safeguarding already existing jobs. The fact that this impact on employment is easily quantifiable and can present a more direct relationship with an aid program, compared to the more slippery goal of poverty reduction (often measured with the help of global indicators which are not always available in time, such as the proportion of persons living below one dollar per day), makes this variable particularly operational in terms of evaluating the impact of aid. As seen earlier, an increase in employment always has advantages for the national economy and our individual and collective well-being. A drop in the level of employment always results in negative consequences for the individual and national well-being and consequently for poverty reduction.

Scenario 2: A reversal of the Arab Spring effect

Under this scenario, donors will revert to previous practices of declaring poverty reduction as the final goal of their aid programs in Africa. In fact, despite its virtues, scenario 1 is not guaranteed. It is possible that the policy agenda of donors will experience major drifts, which will lead them to focus less on employment and growth as final goals of their aid programs. Already in early 2013, the World Bank, a major aid donor, announced that it was going to focus on two goals: (i) ending extreme poverty in a generation by decreasing the percentage of people living with less than one dollar and twenty-five cents a day to no more than 3 per cent by 2030 and (ii) to promote shared prosperity by promoting the income growth of the bottom 40 per cent of the population in each country. The two new World Bank goals appear well intentioned. But, as I have discussed at length in this book, poverty reduction is a poor guide as final goal of development policy because it has had the unintended consequence of leading countries and donors to lose focus, especially when the poverty concept is given a multidimensional meaning, as is often the case in international policy discussions. Considering the influence that the World Bank has in the donor community, it is therefore likely that the donor community may experience a shift back to poverty focus instead of employment and growth. My position is that development policy goals should target employment and growth directly to be effective.

What Contribution Can Aid Make to the Productive-Capacity Building of African Economies?

Support to companies and infrastructure at the center of aid priorities

As I have demonstrated at length in this book, it is thanks to its economic policy that a country can generate the economic growth necessary for job creation. I have also proven that productive-capacity building is one of the two critical intermediate goals that economic policy should target. Finally, I have realized that to attain these intermediate goals, economic policy must obtain concrete results at the level of confidence enjoyed by officials of economic policy with economic agents, good governance, social cohesion, macroeconomic stability, the business environment, the quality of infrastructure, the strengthening of human capital and the financing of the economy. These are the domains I referred to as the operating goals of economy policy.

The question now is which among these operating goals can lead to the effective contribution of development partners. It seems to me that apart from infrastructure and the financing of companies, the other operating goals are far too complex to be influenced from outside. In fact, whether it is social cohesion, governance, confidence of economic agents, or even macroeconomic stability (to the extent that it depends partially on the confidence of economic agents), they call for social and institutional settlements peculiar to each country, and as such, it may be extremely difficult for development partners to effectively intervene in these sectors. It is to this perspective that the economist William Easterly alluded in his assertion that the more institutions are necessary for the good functioning of the market, the more illusory it is to try to impose them from outside. It therefore seems that the only domain where aid can be really effective, and where it can afford its best contribution to the development of poor countries, may be to make up the chronic deficit in infrastructure which these countries suffer from. Aid could also play an important role in productive-capacity building in African countries if it concentrated more on financing companies.

Measures to strengthen the good governance of companies operating in Africa

Good governance is a fundamental element for the success of economic policy. As we have it, when governance is deteriorating, the links between instruments and goals of economic policy are ruptured, thereby rendering any action on the instruments ineffective. I think that if donor countries took measures to promote good governance in their companies operating in Africa, it may have a real sustainable impact on improving governance in African countries. Here, the problem is not that donor countries have done nothing at all. Great progress has even been achieved already in this light. I may cite the Convention on Combating Bribery of Foreign Public Officials in International Business Transactions[11] adopted in 1997 by the OECD and the Extractive Industries Transparency Initiative launched by Tony Blair during the World Summit on Sustainable Development held in Johannesburg in South Africa in 2002. The major problem here is to actually apply these already existing instruments. Indeed, their application is obstructed by what I may call insufficient will on the part of donor countries, which could contribute to strengthen the implementation of these conventions if they really had the will to do it. Reacting to the suspension by British authorities of an ongoing investigation on a major foreign corruption case, the secretary general of OECD, Angel Gurría, had the same feelings: "The political will of our members, collectively and individually, is of capital importance. [...] I am happy that the OECD created a forum where we can have a complete and sincere exchange of ideas on these questions."[12] The German engineering group Siemens has presently been involved in several corruption cases with officials of developing countries, including African countries. The company discovered about 1.3 billion euros in suspicious payments.[13] Many deals in the mining sector in several African countries have also often raised governance issues.[14] It is therefore important that donor countries which have signed and ratified the OECD Anti-bribery Convention should not impede its implementation. A good implementation of this convention may offer a great service to efforts aimed at promoting good governance and the fight against poverty in Africa.

Can Aid Contribute to Stimulating the Demand for Goods and Services Addressed to African Economies?

Developed countries must significantly reduce their level of protection of trade

It is often heard that industrialized countries are already doing much to stimulate demand addressed to African companies, particularly within the framework of different mechanisms of trade preferences set up for the benefit of developing countries, and particularly African countries. The fact that Africa's share in world exports has been in constant decline since these trade preferences were instituted more than three decades ago, particularly the Generalized System of Preferences,[15] shows clearly that they are not effective, at least in their present state of functioning. Whether it is that of the European Union, Japan or the United States, the different schemes of trade preferences set up by developed countries did not really contribute to their intended goal, that of stimulating demand addressed to African companies, either because they did not cover products presenting a sure trade interest to recipient countries, or the necessary procedures to benefit from them were often out of reach considering the limited capacities of these countries. However, it is much more the inherent uncertainty in the manner of functioning of these regimes (they are valid for short periods and renewed periodically; countries offering preferences can revoke them at any moment if they estimate that preferential imports threaten their local industries) which have, in my opinion, hindered the efficiency of trade preferences granted to date. In fact, faced with this uncertainty, the investment necessary to benefit from theoretically authorized preferences simply does not take place.

Some researchers question the scope of benefits that trade liberalization in developed countries could give poor countries. After all, countries like China, India or better still Vietnam developed their exports several decades ago and had fast growth without benefiting from trade preferences. To another extent, it is not certain that liberalization in Northern countries has a positive impact on poverty reduction in Southern countries. Taking agriculture as example, they say that liberalization in Northern countries may even upset some poor countries who are importers of agricultural products, if this is accompanied by a price increase. This effect may vary according to the poverty profile and structure of markets in the country. Moreover, the impact of this liberalization on prices may not even be significant. Thus, Nancy Birdsall, Dani Rodrik and Arvin Subramanian note that: "Most studies predict that the effect of such liberalization on world prices may be negligible. According to estimates of the International Monetary Fund, world prices of rice, sugar and corn will increase only by 2.8%, those of cotton by 4% and those of cow meat by 7%."[16] Isn't there proof that the hope of development in poor countries should not depend on opening markets of Northern countries?

To buttress this point of view, economist Dani Rodrik compares the economic performances of Mexico, which, according to him, is at an advanced integration stage with the world's biggest economy, the United States (Mexico has a long border of more than two thousand miles with the United States, and benefits from privileged access to the American market – that of goods and services as well as labor – and support from the American Treasury, which manifested itself particularly during the peso crisis of 1995). He also compares those of Vietnam (a country which was under American trade embargo up to 1994, whose exports to the United States up until recently did not benefit from the clause of the Most Favored Nation and, particularly, a country which is still not a member of the WTO). He demonstrates therefore that since the signing of the NAFTA Agreement in 1992, the Mexican economy recorded an annual growth of per capita income of less than 1 per cent, while Vietnam recorded an annual growth rate of its GDP per capita of more than 5.6 per cent between the beginning of its economic reforms in 1988 and the re-establishment of diplomatic relations with the United States in 1995, and continued from this date to grow at an annual rate of 4.5 per cent. In Africa, he estimates that the point of view which consists in attributing the economic success of Mauritius and Botswana to the existence of an export demand for their products (textiles and diamond respectively) does not go beyond this assertion. In Sierra Leone, diamond did not produce the same economic miracle as in Botswana. The conclusion he draws from these comparisons is that domestic efforts are more important than any other thing, including access to external markets.[17] What I can say here is that obviously it has never been an issue that access to external markets cannot replace the economic policy that a country may pursue to promote its development. The point of view I support in this book is that economic development depends on what economic policy does on the one hand to stimulate strong demand addressed to companies, and on the other hand to strengthen national productive capacities. Access to foreign markets can only help efforts aimed at creating that demand. Efforts to act on supply are also important. It is not therefore surprising that access to markets does not represent everything.

However, drawing the conclusion from the above analysis that poor countries should not give the liberalization of markets of developed countries an important place in their economic policy strategy may not be logical for at least two reasons: on the one hand, if it is clear that all hopes of development should not depend on access to Northern markets, an increased access to these markets may constitute a booster, increase the impact of a good economic policy, and may as such increase the rate of economic growth of African countries. Besides, the fact that some countries develop themselves without benefiting from trade preferences does not prove that these are not important. The rate of development of these countries might certainly have been faster if they benefited from a strong demand for their products.

What African countries need at the trade level is that industrialized countries should take strong measures to stimulate the demand of goods and services addressed to African companies. These measures must certainly include a substantial reduction of the level of protection, whether it is tariff or nontariff, on which the desire of expanding African exports hits, but they must go far beyond these simple measures at the border. Developed countries must take measures to really stimulate the demand that their economies direct to African economies. Actually, it is significantly increasing the content of their economic growth in export demand addressed to Africa. What is certain is that the African imports content of developed countries' growth is not presently at a satisfactory level. It is not left for Africans to identify measures that developed countries may take to increase it; it is their responsibility to identify these measures since they can better master their economies than any foreign observer. Developed countries have always shown proof of great creativity, and I am sure that if they really want it, they are capable of proposing a wide range of measures to increase and diversify their demand for African exports.

In this perspective, it seems to me that the Economic Partnership Agreements that Europe is still trying, by dint of much tension with the ACP countries, to make them accept, are far from delivering the goods. Most of the experts who were interested in these agreements and analyzed their content concluded that far from offering perspectives of a mutually beneficial true partnership between Europe and Africa, these agreements instead seem to express a short-term vision of a Europe that seeks to appropriate all trade advantages. Let's take for example one of the most important domains for Africa in these negotiations, the issue of access to markets. In their current formulation, Europe's proposal is limited to the suppression of tariffs on exports of African products and requests that, in the name of reciprocity, Africa should do same. From Africa's point of view, such measures may not contribute anything to improving the access of African products to the European market for at least two reasons. First, we just saw that measures aimed at improving the access of African products to markets should go far beyond simple border measures on customs duties. Actions are necessary beyond borders, particularly at the level of reducing subventions, opening internal distribution channels in Europe to further favor the entry and marketing of African products on the European market and improve the perception of African products.

I insisted at length on the negative impact suffered by African trade due to image deficit that African products suffer on world markets, including European markets. Europeans must help Africa to change these perceptions for the interest of a harmonious and mutually beneficial development of trade with Africa. It is left for them to seek and propose adequate measures in this light, insofar as they master the preferences of European consumers better than Africans. Another reason for which the European proposal on access to markets is insufficient is due to the fact that during the last five decades – that is, in fact, since it started practicing preferential agreements with ACP countries (Yaoundé, Lomé I and II, Everything but Arms), Europe would have already progressively eliminated tariffs on exports of African products and, according to available statistics, would have suppressed tariffs on almost 98 per cent of its imports from African countries. In such conditions, it is clear that any suppression of tariffs on the remaining 2 per cent may not constitute significant progress, given that the suppression of tariffs on the 98 per cent imports has not had a positive impact on the access of African products to European markets, since African exports destined for Europe have not stopped dropping during the period covered by these different agreements.

Other points of these agreements discussed lengthily by observers concern the transitional period to enable African economies to adjust to this program of free trade Europe may provide to African countries. On the issue of the transitional period, Europe proposes a period of about fifteen years, which is surprising to say the least, particularly when we know that Europe itself has already benefited from a period of almost fifty years to progressively adjust to the suppression of tariffs on its imports from ACP countries. We have just seen that today it has already suppressed tariffs on 98 per cent of these imports – this during the last fifty years within the framework of the progressive implementation of different preferential agreements with the ACP countries. Today, insisting on such a short adjustment period for these countries, whose economic structures are so fragile and unstable, seems anything but an economic partnership for development, as president Abdoulaye Wade of Senegal advocated. On the issue of adjustment aid, the European proposal seems to insist on the effects of the EPAs on tariff revenues.

The impact of the suppression of tariffs on public revenues is really an important issue, especially considering the fact that public revenues of several African countries still rely on customs duties, but more important considerations concern the impact on employment and economic growth. On these issues, no clear proposal has been made. I attended a conference where an EU commission expert asserted that these unknown effects are difficult to quantify. It is not obvious that this is necessarily the case. It suffices to give oneself the time and means to carry out detailed fieldwork, in consultation with the few production units on the continent, to have an estimate of the potential effects of these agreements on economic growth and employment on the continent. Besides, the EU itself does not take any economic policy decision without prior full understanding of possible consequences on economic growth and employment in its member states. In such conditions, I may ask whether taking time to better analyze the consequences of these agreements on economic growth and employment in African countries would have led to the same intransigence on the part of the European Union. The impacts on economic growth and employment must meet those on public finances at the center of trade negotiations of African countries, those ongoing with the European Union, but also and particularly any other future trade agreement. On these issues, the EPAs would not pass a development impact test.

Much has therefore been said about the EPAs, but it seems president Abdoulaye Wade of Senegal has fully summarized African fears on these agreements:

> To date, by some sort of parallelism of form, she [Europe] negotiated with the African Union; henceforth, she intends to negotiate separately with each of our five sub-regions. Summarily, from the outset, she intended setting up a disintegration system by asserting the wish to strengthen African integration [...] granting sums of money [talking about funds promised by the European Union to compensate the drop in tax revenues] does not compensate sustainable structural disequilibria. [...] Among measures to protect my economy from destructive competition and a sum of money, I prefer protection measures! Money is spent so fast, and later? [...] That is why most African countries, starting with those of West Africa, reject these new agreements. [...] It is a question of survival for our people and our economies, already tried and tested by farm subsidies practiced by industrialized countries, to the tune of 1 billion dollar/day, and which throws, for example, 12 to 15 million cotton producers into misery.[18]

The words of President Wade add to what I said earlier. The interest of wanting to concentrate adjustment aid measures on the sole question of consequences in terms of tariff revenues is questionable. This is more so because this negative impact is not always guaranteed. The net impact actually depends on the impact on economic growth. A well-conceived agreement, formulated better than EPAs in their current formulation, which can therefore strongly stimulate economic growth, in the final analysis can have an impact on tax revenues even if some tariff revenue losses may be recorded from the beginning. Also, even by accepting a drop in tax revenues, it is not certain that this constitutes a net loss for the national economy since part of this drop is actually expressed by a redistribution of revenues to the benefit of economic agents (this is what economists call an increase in consumer surplus). Moreover, the European Union itself, which insists on concentrating attention on the drop in tax revenues, created a fund to help its member states adjust to the consequences of globalization.[19] Consequences borne by this fund are those on employment and not on tax revenues, thereby showing clearly that consequences on employment and economic structures are far more important, as emphasized by President Wade.

More recently, Nigerian economist and former governor of the Nigerian Central Bank Charles Soludo also expressed skepticism about the proposed EPAs in these terms:

> Since 2002 the EU has been negotiating EPAs as reciprocal trade arrangements to replace the current non-reciprocal deals, whereby African countries receive preferential access to EU markets. […] To continue to have access to European markets, Africa is now being asked to end tariffs on at least 80 per cent of imports from the EU. It must also meet other intrusive conditions that prevent African governments from using the kinds of policies that all industrialised countries once employed to build their own economies. […] It is not clear what benefit Africa's poorest countries will receive. Furthermore, the issues the developing countries have rejected under the WTO, such as investment, competition and public procurement, are being smuggled into EPAs. Studies show that, on a net basis, EPAs will be harmful. They will wipe out industries and agriculture, and increase unemployment and poverty. Africa will become a dumping ground for Europe. […] The apparent sweetener in the form of a promise of "EU aid for trade" is also not credible. […] Trade ministers of the affected countries and the African Union have largely rejected the agreements offered by the EU. Africa and Europe need to talk to each other frankly and directly, now.[20]

However, I have always been surprised to see that, responding to criticism that the EPAs in their present state are not a foreign-aid tool, European officials in charge of negotiations responded that EPAs are a trade agreement and that Europe's development aid is negotiated and granted within the framework of periodic reconstitutions of the European Development Fund. My surprise stems from the fact that Europe has always joined the other members of the international community in asserting that trade is a greater tool for foreign aid and for the fight against poverty; why separate the two now?

I think that Europeans and Africans must look into the future and launch real negotiations to establish a new and mutually beneficial framework for their trade relationships. These negotiations, which may draw from the ideas already advanced in this book, would for example take place within the framework of a structure which may be set up to conduct a strategic economic and mutually beneficial dialogue for both parties. This structure would certainly regroup representatives of the public and private sectors of the two parties, African international organizations, representatives of Africans in the diaspora and the African civil society. This dialogue may examine far-reaching trade-reform measures, beyond reforms on border provisions, which Europe could implement to really open up the European markets to African products. As such, dialogue would cover the reforms required at the level of the European domestic market and means of increasing European demand for African products. A reform which, in my opinion, would have a great positive effect on trade between the two continents may be, for example, the setting up of a Small Economies Act[21] between Europe and Africa, in order to encourage European countries, or companies of developed countries in general, to reserve a certain proportion of their purchases for African companies (see Box 12.3 below).

Box 12.3. A Small Economies Act for Africa?

In the 1970s, within the framework of their efforts to increase their aid to poor countries, rich countries promised to reach the goal of devoting 0.7 per cent of their GNP to foreign aid. To date, several rich countries have not attained this goal, and even if they had attained it, it is not certain that with the present mechanisms to deliver aid, this would have had a significant impact on poverty reduction in the recipient countries. As I have already emphasized, visibly and significantly increasing demand for goods and services addressed to African economies may be a more effective means to stimulate economic growth in these countries. As such, if we take the side of demand, a Small Economies Act, conceived on the model of the US Small Business Act, may accomplish much in this perspective. Different concrete mechanisms may be imagined to implement this act to the benefit of the poorest countries, of which the majority is found in Africa. One of these mechanisms may consist in that governments of rich countries commit to reserve a certain proportion of their purchases for African companies. Rich countries can also implement mechanisms to encourage their private sector to reserve a certain proportion of their purchases for companies of the countries to be assisted. I anticipate legal difficulties that the implementation of these suggestions may pose; first, in rich countries themselves where the spirit and the letter of public procurement codes make equal treatment a principle to be respected; then, at the international level, there is need to pass a WTO test. A voluntary commitment of rich countries may suffice to successfully plead in Geneva for the WTO to ratify such a provision.

Such a measure may significantly boost demand addressed to African companies and really promote their development. If the principle of such a measure is achieved, Europe, the United States and Africa may work together to obtain the required backing from the WTO to implement it. Other reforms can be imagined. It suffices that political desire exists on both sides and that such a strategic dialogue takes place so that several ideas emerge.

Europe has always advised African countries not to worry about any adverse impacts of the EPAs because EU development aid would help compensate these potentially negative effects. This advice is not satisfactory for the following reasons: (i) a trade agreement ought to be assessed purely on its trade effects, and if these are not going to be positive, as is likely to be the case with the EPAs, then that agreement ought not to be entered into; (ii) the long-term availability of the aid promised by the EU to help cushion the negative impacts of the EPAs is not guaranteed as this aid will be financed by the European Development Fund, which is negotiated and reconstituted periodically, and the outcomes of these negotiations (amount, financial terms, other conditions, etc.) cannot be predicted over the long term.

Aid can also contribute to directly stimulate the demand of goods and services addressed to African economies

Besides contributing to financing infrastructure and companies, whose importance I previously raised, there exists a varied range of actions that aid can undertake to further contribute to stimulating demand addressed to African companies. Thus, aid has an important role to play in terms of effective information, whose role I analyzed at length in forming perceptions of economic agents, which in turn significantly determine demand directed to African countries within the context of globalization. Aid can also contribute usefully to the creation of trademarks, which also play an important role in demand. Finally, each time it is possible, donors should also seek possibilities to resort directly to goods, services and assets offered by African countries. The example of the African Development Bank, which launched a program of local currency of regional member states, better illustrates efforts which can be made to stimulate demand addressed to African countries. Before, when the African Development Bank granted financing to one of its regional member states, it placed hard currency at the disposal of this state, such as the US dollar, the Japanese yen, the euro, the French franc and the German mark (before entry into the euro). The introduction of loans in the currency of the regional member states should contribute to reduce currency risks supported by countries and develop local financial markets.

Also, in one of its projects, the African Development Bank recently sought to better inform consumers with the aim of creating demand for exports of a regional member state. It is particularly the case with the Export Marketing and Quality Awareness Project in Ghana. Details on this project are presented in the box below. The African Development Bank is not alone in making efforts to stimulate demand addressed to its developing member countries; the United Nations has just started doing same (see Box 12.4 below).

From the end of the 1990s, a literature developed around the concept of "original sin," which proved that the incapability of emerging countries to borrow in their own currency in international financial markets had negative macroeconomic consequences on their economy. Thus, this literature on original sin showed that the idea that emerging and developing countries in general are unable to borrow in their own currency on international financial markets was a factor of increased instability of their GDP, volatility of capital flows and less efficiency of monetary policy. The fact that debt is written in foreign currency could also influence foreign reserves, the choice of trade policy and the borrowing limit of countries on international financial markets, and increase risks of debt unsustainability.[22] It is partially to enable their borrower countries to alleviate these problems that multilateral development banks, which until then offered only loans in hard currencies, recently launched initiatives to develop financial products written in

Box 12.4. Existence and strengthening of donors' efforts to stimulate demand addressed to aid recipient countries

African Development Bank

Regional preference in contract award

For a long time now, the African Development Bank has given its borrowers the opportunity to give preference to national and regional bidders in contracts which fall under projects it finances. It is a good measure which contributes to productive-capacity building through demand stimulation.

Acting on consumer preferences: The Export Marketing and Quality Awareness Project in Ghana

This project, financed by the African Development Bank in Ghana, aims at increasing the incomes of flower producers and cassava exporters. The promotion of marketing at the level of export markets figures among the components of the project. The main expected effects of this component include developing marketing trademarks of Ghanaian products and their use by exporters, constructing and rehabilitating marketing and demonstration infrastructure, promoting marketing at the level of export markets, and searching and documenting consumer needs on international markets and major export markets of Ghanaian products in the European Union. The project equally finances a technical aid to identify international markets, study and document consumer preferences of Ghanaian horticultural products on these markets, and analyze the present and potential markets for diverse Ghanaian horticultural products in order to give priority to those offering the most promising perspectives on expansion. Studies on consumer preferences will supply useful information on their opinions on the different characteristics of Ghanaian products compared to those of competitors who are already present on the markets. This information will be later disseminated to farmers' associations. Being well informed, the actors of the sector will as such be in a better position to respond to changes in consumer preferences which are linked to changes in promotional campaigns of competitors. The aim of these efforts will be to create awareness on international markets that the new Ghanaian products are up to standards. Specific activities will include organizing consumers' meetings in selected markets, using international media and publicity firms to make adverts in newspapers and magazines, and participating in special events such as food and culinary trade fairs. The total cost of the project is 18 million units of account and the African Development Bank Group has contributed to the financing of this project to the tune of 17 million units.

The United Nations

In 2008, the United Nations World Food Program (WFP) announced that it would review in depth its buying policy of agricultural products that it distributes to populations suffering from famine in poor countries. In the past, its policy consisted in sourcing supplies from rich countries to distribute in poor countries. Henceforth, it will source supplies directly from local farmers. With this change in policy, the WFP expected to purchase about forty thousand tons of farm products in the years to come, from small farmers in Africa, Latin America and Asia. For 2008, the WFP expected to devote between five and six billion dollars to farm purchases. According to Josette Sheeran, executive director of the WFP, "It is a solution where everybody is winner. [...] We assist our beneficiaries, who have little or nothing to eat, and we assist local farmers who have only limited or non-existing access to markets where they can sell their harvests."[23] This summarizes all the advantages of the new policy and perhaps shows the way to the community of donors.

the local currency of the borrower country.[24] This is particularly the case of the African Development Bank, the Asian Development Bank or even the World Bank. The latter even created a fund of close to 5 billion dollars, which aims at supplying aid to developing countries to enable them to develop bond markets issued in their own currency. This literature of original sin therefore served as a base for efforts of multilateral development banks aiming at increasing demand in financial assets written in the currency of borrower countries.

Insofar as the incapacity of emerging countries, and developing countries in general, to borrow in their own currency on international markets expresses insufficient demand – to say things clearly, an empty demand of financial assets written in their currency on these markets – I can say that this literature has in like manner explained in theory the increased role that I foresee for foreign aid in the stimulation of demand for goods and services addressed to aid recipient countries. For, in the final analysis, I can also assert that the problem of original sin does not only concern financial assets issued by developing countries. It concerns all goods and services offered by these countries. Today, there exists a whole literature which tends to show that goods and services offered by these countries are perceived as of inferior quality compared to goods and services supplied by developed countries, thereby reducing their demand. It is well known that goods or services offered by a developed country will have a higher demand than the same goods and services with exactly the same characteristics and functions supplied by a developing country.[25] Therefore, there is a "real" original sin which is twinned with the "financial" original sin raised above. Given that debt, whose wordings in foreign currency pose problems may only be the result of accumulated current account deficits over time, "financial original sin" is only a mirror, the image of "real original sin." It is not only the demand for financial assets issued by developing countries and written in their own currency that should be stimulated by a voluntary effort, particularly on the part of international aid agencies, it is also the demand of goods and services supplied by these economies which should be stimulated.

Summary

In this chapter, I showed that for aid to produce results which really matter to recipient countries it must first concentrate clearly on the stimulation of economic growth and job creation in poor countries. By so doing, it will fully rally behind the economic policy approach whose main aspects have been presented at length in the previous chapters. To attain this final goal, it should also aim at clearly contributing to the two key intermediate goals of economic policy, which are: (i) productive-capacity building in African economies and (ii) stimulating demand for goods and services addressed to these economies. The evolution of employment must become a new criterion for measuring the effectiveness of aid. It is not only when a wave of clandestine immigrants fail in Europe that our attention should be drawn to the only thing which the poor really need – a job in their countries of origin. However, it does not suffice that aid identifies good priorities at the level of its final and intermediate goals for it to be effective and contribute to development. Conditions for its delivery, and its implementation, are also important. I am now going to concentrate on the appropriate channels for delivering aid in the next chapter.

Chapter Thirteen

HOW TO CHANNEL AID FOR IT TO BE EFFECTIVE

"Today at Accra, we are leading the way, united in a common objective: to unlock the full potential of aid in achieving lasting development results."
Accra Agenda for Action, Third High Level Forum on Aid Effectiveness, Accra, Ghana, September 3–4, 2008.

Introduction

The effectiveness of aid – that is, the importance of its contribution to the implementation of the economic policy of recipient countries – does not only depend on the fact that it targets good goals, but also on the manner in which it is channeled – that is, placed at the disposal of beneficiaries. Improving the effectiveness of aid is one of the domains where donors have deployed the greatest efforts, at least in terms of commitments aimed at changing their practices in recent years. Thus, whether in academic milieus or aid-providing international financial organizations, reflecting on conditions of effectiveness of foreign aid has developed considerably. In academic milieus, this discussion has developed mainly in two directions. The first has chosen recipient countries as the subject of the investigation, and as such, seeks to give an account of the conditions in which the political and institutional environment of these countries could be explanatory factors of the effectiveness of aid. It is in this perspective that research by two World Bank economists, David Dollar and Aart Kray, who proved the importance of institutions and policies pursued by recipient countries for the effectiveness of aid, is situated. A second side of economic research is particularly centered on policies of donors in terms of aid supply in order to examine in what ways these could be reformed such that their contribution to the effectiveness of foreign aid could be increased. The economist William Easterly identifies a certain number of measures to be taken to improve the effectiveness of aid. These measures are presented in Box 13.1 below.

In my opinion, beyond these general conclusions, improving the effectiveness of aid calls for appropriate responses to five major questions: predictability, the method of disbursing aid (that is, choosing between aid granted to finance specific projects and aid granted in the form of budgetary support and directly disbursed to the budget of the recipient country), the conditionality reform, the untying of aid and the role of new donors. This chapter is dedicated to examining responses to these questions. However, I will dwell on the commitments adopted by foreign-aid actors to improve upon the effectiveness of aid.

Box 13.1. How to channel aid for it to be effective: Proposals of economist William Easterly[1]

(1) Have aid agents individually accountable for individual, feasible areas for action that help poor people lift themselves up.
(2) Let those agents search for what works, based on past experience in their area.
(3) Experiment, based on the results of the search.
(4) Evaluate, based on feedback from the identified beneficiaries and scientific testing.
(5) Reward success and penalize failure. get more money to interventions that are working, and take money away from interventions that are not working. Each aid agent should explore and specialize further in the direction of what they prove good at doing.
(6) Make sure incentives in (5) are strong enough to do more of what works, then repeat step (4). if action fails, make sure incentives in (5) are strong enough to send the agent back to step (1). If the agent keeps failing, get a new one.

High Level Forums on Aid Effectiveness: The Paris Declaration and the Accra Action Plan, and the Busan High-Level Forum

From the point of view of efforts of the international community aimed at increasing the effectiveness of foreign aid, the second high-level forum on aid effectiveness, harmonization, alignment and management based on results which took place in Paris from February 28 to June 2, 2005 is probably one of the most important events of the process of reforming donors' policies relating to granting and managing foreign aid. This meeting, which grouped bilateral and multilateral representatives of donors to developing countries and civil society organizations, actually pursued and increased the scope of aid reforms initiated during the first high-level forum held in Rome in February 2003. The results of these conferences, which constitute a reference point in international efforts aimed at improving donor practices toward increasing the impact of aid on development, consist in a set of commitments undertaken by donors and aid-recipient countries to work together to ensure greater harmonization of policies and procedures of donors, align aid on national priorities of recipient countries, focus aid management on obtaining results, and promote greater ownership by developing countries of their development strategy. Today, they are better known in the world of development as the Paris Declaration on Aid Effectiveness, the Accra Agenda for Action, and the outcomes of the Busan High-Level Forum on Aid Effectiveness. Pursuant to the commitments of these aid forums, progress in their implementation was going to be monitored by means of a set of indicators.

Though it is necessary to pursue efforts aimed at improving aid modalities in order to make it more effective in the fight against poverty, I can say that the commitments undertaken in Paris and Accra, and more importantly Busan, constitute progress which should contribute to greater aid effectiveness. In fact, if they are effectively implemented, these commitments have the potential to contribute to reducing the transactions costs that aid-recipient countries pay indirectly and which stem particularly from the fact that these countries must often dedicate a greater part of their already insufficient resources to managing aid, including receiving several donor review missions, producing several follow-up reports and managing different policies and procedures peculiar to each donor, particularly at the level of procurement of goods and services and financial monitoring of the implementation of projects financed thanks to aid. Harmonizing donors' policies and procedures, which consists in ensuring that, if possible, donors have common policies and procedures and carry out joint missions, should contribute to reducing these transaction costs.

Another domain where the implementation of the commitments mentioned above could contribute to a greater impact of aid is that of aligning aid programs on development strategies and economic policies defined by recipient countries themselves. In fact, experience has finally demonstrated that because of their different historical origins and their institutional mandates and governance structure, donors each have a domain of predilection in which they wish to concentrate most of their activities. This diversity of mandates coupled with the desire of donors to intervene in certain specific domains has resulted in the fact that some interventions did not correspond to the priorities of the country. The positive impact of such interventions on the development of the recipient country could only be limited. In such a context, commitments undertaken by donors during the various aid forums to align their interventions to the defined priorities can only contribute to increasing the impact of aid.

Predictability of Aid

Among the domains where commitments undertaken by donors did not go far enough, at least not as far as aid recipient countries would have expected, is the predictability of aid. The absence of long-term predictability of aid is perhaps the factor which contributes most to the ineffectiveness of aid. In fact, long-term visibility of future aid flows is indispensable for the good planning of its use by public authorities within the framework of their budgetary management. Indeed, the instability of public expenditures has as its result a non-optimal allocation of public spending. Thus, when the government receives aid flows which are not projected in the budget, it is likely that this aid will be "squandered," in the sense that it will, in a hurried and unprepared manner, be allocated to financing expenses which were not the subject of studies or satisfactory preparation to establish their high profitability. A recent IMF report showed that a greater part of unexpected aid was often either saved or devoted to debt repayment, the implementation of which requires the least prior preparation of all public spending. As such, lack of predictability of aid flows reduces the effectiveness of aid by introducing distortions in the structure of public expenses.

Considering the high impact of unpredictability on aid effectiveness, the commitment undertaken by donors to reduce by half the proportion of aid which is not disbursed in the budgetary year during which it was programmed is real progress and should contribute to the greater predictability of aid, and therefore to its effectiveness in the fight against poverty. In fact, what is more important is giving longer-term visibility to recipient countries as far as the arrival of aid flow is concerned, particularly by giving them assurances on the availability of aid flow, over a long period of ten or fifteen years. Such assurances on the temporal horizon are necessary to giving recipient countries the assurance that they can count on future aid flow in order to plan a structure and an optimal level of their public expenses. We should also note that halving the proportion of aid which is not disbursed the year in which it is programmed may not constitute anything great in increasing the predictability of aid if it continues to be programmed annually, as is the present practice of several donors including international financial organizations. Current practices should therefore be reformed in order to give long-term assurances on the availability of aid flow.

As a New Privileged Instrument of Aid, Is Direct Budgetary Support Preferable to Targeted Project Aid?

From the outset, foreign aid was conceived to finance specific projects whose goal was to create physical infrastructure in recipient countries. As such, the World Bank statutes stipulate that the financing granted should, but for exceptional circumstances, finance specific projects?[2] Specific projects aim at achieving a clearly identified physical infrastructure in different sectors of the economy in aid recipient countries. These infrastructures may be, for example, important roads or bridges in the development of the country, or other physical and tangible assets in different domains, like energy, potable water or sanitation systems. Another sector where this approach has often been used is that of social infrastructures in the educational and public health sectors. This was the case with constructing and/or equipping health centers, in one or several regions of the national territory, and teaching establishments, to increase the reception capacity of the health system and/or the educational system of the country. Project aid is also used to finance infrastructure deemed necessary for the development of the agricultural sector, such as constructing irrigation systems or preservation and storage systems for products before their distribution and sale on markets, and training farmers in new farming techniques. In short, all infrastructures whose importance to economic development and poverty reduction can be proven are eligible for financing through project aid.

From the approach of project aid, the donor maintains quasi-total control on the implementation process of the project and disbursement of the aid resources. This control is exercised mainly at two levels: that of the process of procurement and contract awards and that of the disbursement of resources. Concerning procurement and contract awards, it should be noted that conditions of aid award often include: obliging the recipient country to respect the recipient's procedures in contract awards. As such, all the procedures for contract signing and award, from the studying of tender documents to the signing of the contract through the reception and evaluation of tenders, should take place under the donor's supervision. Their approval is required before the final conclusion of the contract between the government of the aid-recipient country and the contractor, even if the donor is not part of the contract, which, in itself, remains strictly a commitment linking the government and the contractor. Aid resources remain in the hands of the donor, who takes charge of carrying out disbursements to the benefit of the contractor, at the request of the government and after obtaining assurances from the recipient country that the contract has been appropriately executed and all the procedures respected. As such, project loans are characterized by the following: (i) specific expenses to be financed and award procedures to be used are identified during evaluation of the project and recorded in the loan agreement linking the recipient country and the donor; (ii) disbursements are made by donors at the request of the country, and as activities advance on the field and expenses are incurred; and (iii) disbursements follow the pace of implementation of the project, and can take place over a period of three to five years, or even more.

From the 1980s, when developing countries faced acute economic and financial crises and had urgent need for financial resources, the World Bank relied on the clause of exceptional circumstances contained in its statutes to begin granting loans which were not destined to finance specific investments. The use of these loans (which were called structural adjustment loans at their creation and, since the late 1990s, budget support loans)[3] has increased considerably. Whereas they represented only a negligible part of official development assistance in the 1980s, today they play a key role. According to the European Union, one of the largest providers of development aid, this form of aid represented about 25 per cent of its 13 billion euro external aid over the 2003–09 period. Statistics from other bilateral and multilateral agencies also show significant progression in the share of budgetary support. Thus, this budgetary aid represented about 31.3 per cent of the 11.3 billion units of account (UC)[4] operations in the nonconcessional window and 21.8 per cent of the 10.9 billion UC operations in the concessional window respectively at the African Development Bank Group over the period 1999–2009.

Despite this intensive use of budget support as a means of providing aid, the issue of its capacity to foster economic reforms, one of the primary goals which led to its creation, is re-emerging in the aid-effectiveness debate. Some experts and stakeholders argue that despite its positive contribution to some key determinants of aid effectiveness in general (such as harmonization, aid alignment, ownership by recipient countries, transparency, mutual accountability, and reduction of transaction costs), budgetary aid has not been effective in delivering on its promise of spurring reforms in recipient countries. Thus, with respect to public financial management – an area which has been the focus of increased donors' support, including mainly through budgetary aid – progress had been below expectations.[5]

It is in this context that donors have recently tried to improve their practices with respect to budgetary support. Thus, in 2010, the European Commission launched a consultation on *The Future Approach to EU Budget Support to Third Countries* leading to the formulation of a new budget support policy. After a long gestation period, the World Bank adopted a new instrument in 2012, namely the Program for Results Financing. In 2012 the African Development Bank also adopted a new policy on budgetary support or program aid.

In addition to actions being taken in aid agencies, means to reform budgetary aid to make it more effective also generated voluminous literature in the aid-effectiveness research circle. In this literature, fungibility and conditionality (I will discuss conditionality below) were often presented as key explanatory factors of the rather weak link between budgetary aid and economic reforms in developing countries. In an interesting article, two economists, Tito Cordella and Giovanni Dell'Ariccia, studied the respective merits of project aid and budgetary support in a theoretical model. Their model relies on three hypotheses. They assume that the capacity of donors to monitor the effective use of resources is imperfect in the case of budgetary support and that governments of recipient countries can have other goals than the effectiveness of aid supplied. They also rely on the fungibility of aid. With these two assumptions, they show that project aid is preferable if aid is more important than the country's own resources and that otherwise, budgetary aid is preferable. They also prove that project aid is preferable compared to budgetary support if donors' goals and those of governments are too divergent.[6]

My own assessment of where we stand is that more efforts are still needed on the part of donors, recipient countries and other stakeholders toward strengthening the contribution of budgetary support to the design and implementation of economic reforms by recipient countries, an area where this instrument was expected to make its greatest contribution to aid effectiveness. Although the World Bank's Program-for-Results aims at a greater use of budgetary support as a means of channeling aid, its current design does not, however, seem to suggest an enhanced role for this instrument in the advancement of reforms, which is the central objective of budgetary support as I have just said. Moreover, conditionality and fungibility of resources cannot adequately explain the lack of progress in reforms supported by budgetary support.[7]

In a recent paper, I outlined a new framework aimed at strengthening the linkages between budgetary aid and economic reforms in developing countries. Building on the definition of economic reform as an action by the government targeting the economic policy instruments discussed in this book, and designed to effect changes in the behaviors of public and/or private economic agents with a view toward either boosting their sustainable and noninflationary demand addressed to the national economy or increasing their productive investments to achieve national economic growth and employment creation targets, this approach advocates the following three requirements for strengthening the linkages between the provision of budgetary aid and the implementation of economic reforms by recipient countries: (i) devote budget support to the implementation of reforms whose cost involves an increase in either public transfers or public sector wages or public sector net lending or a fall in tax or nontax revenues or a combination of these; (ii) clearer identification of the changes in economic behaviors that the projected changes in public expenditures or public revenue incurred in (i) will generate. These behavioral changes are the reforms targeted by the budgetary aid; and (iii) align budgetary support financing with the estimated budgetary cost of the expenditures and revenue changes identified in (i), an approach which few donors have adopted today. Apart from enhancing transparency, this approach would afford the stakeholders the means of more fully guaranteeing accountability, thereby strengthening the link between budgetary support and implementation and, consequently, the outcomes of reforms. The challenges often mentioned in assessing the budgetary cost of reforms can be overcome.[8]

Untying Aid

Aid tying, which to some donors, particularly bilateral donors, consists in tying the granting of aid to its use in order to acquire goods and services from the donor country, has long been one of the most widespread practices in terms of aid. Several studies have proved that this practice reduces the value of aid. As long as the scope of competition is limited when aid is tied, the result obtained is that purchases often take place at a higher price than if they took place within the framework of an open competition.[9] Even if critics of tied aid have concentrated on the additional cost which results from it, this is not the only inconvenient aspect of tied aid. Another way through which the impact of tied aid on the development of recipient countries is reduced is owed to the fact that it does not contribute to the demand for goods and services addressed to the companies of the recipient country, which is, as I have seen, one of the key intermediate goals of economic policy. Every tied part of aid constitutes a reduction of potential demand that it could have generated to companies of recipient countries; and when we know that stimulating this demand is necessary for economic growth and job creation, we understand easily that the contribution of foreign aid is considerably reduced when tied. Despite this clear recognition of the low contribution of tied aid to the development of recipient countries, even though this contribution is its proclaimed goal, progress to eliminate, or at least reduce, the practice of tied aid has up to this point been too slow. Moreover, during the Paris forum on the effectiveness of aid, donors could do no better than to make a minimal commitment which consisted in saying they would make progress on this question, whereas they made concrete commitments on other problems. This difficulty is due to the fact that donors do not want to give up one of their crucial economic goals, which is to create and maintain demand for their companies. However, I think if donors declare the desire to contribute to the development of poor countries, we should stick to their commitment to the end and enable the aid they give to really contribute to development. It serves no purpose to take with one hand what one has given with the other. Donors should therefore take measures to put an end to the practice of tied aid.

Debt Relief

When the Mexican minister of finance announced in September 1982 that his country could no longer respect its commitments to repay its foreign debt, the international community fully realized that, far from contributing to their development, the foreign debt accumulated by poor countries had become a burden. Since then, much theoretical literature has not only helped to elucidate the means through which an excessive foreign debt slows down development efforts,[10] but has also spurred efforts undertaken by the international community to curb these negative effects. Earlier debt relief efforts based solely on rescheduling did not produce the expected results to the extent that they only consisted in displacing the problem of debt in time. What I can say today is that progress has now been accomplished since the launch, in the mid-1990s, of the Highly Indebted Poor Countries Initiative. According to available projections, this initiative contributed to a favorable evolution of African countries' foreign-debt indicators. Thus, projections carried out by the IMF and the World Bank in 2007 showed that, for the group of 25 African countries[11] which attained the decision point of this initiative, the debt service ratio would have moved from an average of 17 per cent exports in 2000 to 3.2 per cent exports in 2011.[12] The same projections showed that public expenditures contributing to poverty reduction increased in this group of countries, moving from an average of about 37 per cent of the central government revenues in 2000 to 60 per cent of these revenues in 2011. By canceling debt owed to the IMF, IDA and the African Development Fund by low-income African countries, the Multilateral Debt Relief Initiative (MDRI) that the G8 members approved in July 2005 during the Gleneagles Summit further contributed to reduce the debt burden of African countries and the constraints it imposes on economic policy.

By freeing resources that should have been transferred abroad as debt repayments and by putting them at the disposal of national treasuries to finance efforts of economic growth and job creation, debt relief accomplished much in terms of foreign aid. This aid modality is even more remarkable in that, for the moment, it is the only one to have passed the test which, to me, is the most important – that is, of predictability. As a matter of fact, debt cancellation commitments are irreversible and as such, give governments long-term visibility which is necessary to plan a good use of liberated resources. In fact, to most MDRI recipient countries, and according to the profile of their accumulated debt toward the institutions involved at the effectiveness date of the initiative, they will not repay the debts in question during the next four decades, given that the relief from the International Development Association (IDA), the World Bank concessionary window which grants financings to the poorest countries involved in the cancellation, for example, will run from 2007–44.[13] This is like unconditional budgetary support over a period long enough to enable informed planning.

Beyond debt relief, the challenge for the international community is now to contribute new resources, because, even if debt relief liberates resources, it does not bring new ones. This immediate need to contribute new resources is even more necessary as the benefits of debt relief will be spread over the next four decades. Thus, although international institutions have announced fabulous amounts of debt relief, very little of these amounts will be immediately available, even in the next five or ten years. Concretely, this means, from the point of view of available financings, current efforts at fighting against poverty will not receive the expected support. According to World Bank statistics, 3.2 per cent of the relief from which potentially MDRI-eligible African countries will benefit was going to be available during the period covered by the fourteenth reconstitution of the IDA (2007–08), 7.1 per cent will be available during the period covered by the fifteenth reconstitution (2009–11) and 10.2 per cent during the sixteenth reconstitution (2012–14). Table 13.1 below shows the schedule of debt relief granted by the IDA within the framework of the MDRI.

Thus, during the period separating us from the deadline to attain the MDGs – that is, when investments are most urgently needed toward attaining these goals – only 20.5 per cent of resources granted under this important initiative will be placed at the disposal of African countries, the rest coming in distant periods in time. Though we can raise problems of absorption capacity in some cases, the least I can say is that this rate

Table 13.1. Debt relief estimate within the framework of the MDRI[14]

Country	Year				
	2007–08	**2009–11**	**2012–14**	**2007–16**	**2007–44**
Benin	18	31	38	126	467
Burkina Faso	30	62	85	271	1,027
Burundi	1	3	3	7	13
Cameroon	4	14	42	109	587
Central African Republic	0	1	3	5	35
Chad	8	29	40	114	506
Comoros	0	0	1	1	17
Congo Republic	0	6	8	21	83
Côte d'Ivoire	0	17	65	131	744
Democratic Republic of Congo	7	19	38	88	660
Ethiopia	18	39	57	151	1,582
Gambia	7	18	38	88	660
Ghana	67	119	151	446	2,019
Guinea	14	50	61	179	744
Guinea Bissau	0	5	7	17	85
Liberia	0	0	1	1	3
Madagascar	42	81	103	296	1,197
Malawi	21	73	86	242	1,067
Mali	30	53	69	221	854
Mauritania	11	22	31	86	371
Mozambique	22	66	97	257	884
Niger	11	19	26	74	506
Rwanda	4	7	13	33	235
Sao Tome and Principe	0	1	2	4	25
Senegal	41	102	152	397	1,255
Sierra Leone	3	8	12	33	262
Somalia	0	1	2	4	13
Sudan	0	2	7	13	42
Tanzania	60	111	151	431	1,898
Togo	0	2	7	13	42
Uganda	62	116	160	451	1,882
Zambia	25	51	69	195	1,269
Total	**506**	**1,129**	**1,625**	**4,505**	**15,978,061**
% Total	**3.2**	**7.4**	**10.2**	**28.2**	**100**

seems a little bit slow. The temporal relief profile of the African Development Fund, the concessionary window of the African Development Bank, is similar.

Therefore, the British idea raised earlier to create an International Financial Facility to immediately mobilize the resources necessary for financing development, particularly during the years separating us from the maturity of the MDGs, takes on its full meaning due to this interval between debt relief and its benefits. I think it is necessary to revive the IFF initiative if rich countries really wish to supply more resources for financing development under satisfactory predictability conditions.

What Do We Do with Conditionality?

The practice of conditionality – that is, the idea of donors linking disbursements of aid to implementation – of a certain number of measures concerning their economic policy is an old characteristic of relations between aid donors and recipients. Economic policy measures of the conditionalities of the first generation generally sought to liberalize external trade, privatize public companies, reduce demand, devaluate exchange rates and other goals leading to stabilization and adjustment. Although I may trace the origin of conditionalities to the 1950s (even the Marshall Plan had conditions), it is with the advent of structural adjustment loans in the 1980s that the practice of conditionality in granting aid experienced considerable development. To the IMF, the body that contributed most to the development of the practice of conditionality, this always represented a critical element of its relationship with its borrowing countries. According to the IMF statutes, conditionality serves two important purposes. First, it reassures borrowing member countries that the IMF resources will be available when it has implemented the reform measures agreed upon with the IMF. Conditionalities also serve another important goal; they aim at reassuring the IMF that the member country borrowing its resources will be capable of reimbursing its debts insofar as this reimbursement also depends on the return of the borrowing member country to a sustainable external position, which is one of the goals of the economic reform programs supported by the IMF.

Since the mid-1990s, criticisms against conditionalities have become increasingly sharp. Criticism first targeted the IMF, one of the institutions which played a major role in the practice of conditionality. As such, increasing the number of conditions in programs that it supported, and the domains that these conditions covered, exposed the IMF to more and more criticisms from several observers. The criticisms indicated particularly that the extension of these conditions did not contribute to countries' ownership of their economic reform program, but also that the IMF did not usually have the necessary expertise in domains of reforms where it imposed conditions. The observers also criticized the IMF for not sufficiently consulting all stakeholders before establishing conditionalities.

The practice of conditionality does not only pose problems in terms of countries' ownership of their development policy. Criticisms also insisted on the fact that conditions can introduce distortions in the conduct of countries' economic policy, by focusing the attention of officials on specific actions required to fulfill conditions, whereas the success of economic policy is measured by progress on a set of results, particularly the final, intermediate and operating goals discussed in the foregoing chapters. When donors insist on specific conditions such as attaining a floor level in terms of foreign reserves or a ceiling level of the banking sector credit to the government, measures which are often part of IMF conditionalities, or even some specific structural conditions, governments have the impression that once these actions are accomplished, they will have accomplished their duty in terms of economic policy, but it is not the case. Economic policy is far more complex than that. I have amply demonstrated this in the preceding chapters.

Generally, summarizing the several criticisms that the practice of conditionalities raised, the British aid agency, the Department for International Development (DFID), said:

Concerns have been raised that some conditionality has promoted reforms that have made poor people worse off. [...] The spotlight has also fallen on privatisation and trade reforms. There is particular concern that in the 1980s and 1990s donors pushed for the introduction of reforms, regardless of whether these were in countries' best interests. [...] Evidence on the social impact of privatisation policies in the area of public services, particularly in the absence of effective competition and regulation, has been a subject of much debate. In some cases, developing country governments have limited capacity to regulate the private sector effectively. There are examples where privatisation has not benefited poor people, and therefore the use of conditionality in such cases has been criticized. [...] In many cases, either donors or developing countries have not kept to the conditions that they signed up to. Developing countries sometimes agreed conditions in areas of reform even though they were unconvinced of the case for change. Unsurprisingly, countries have largely ignored conditions set in such circumstances, or the reforms pursued have not been sustained. Put simply, conditionality which attempts to "buy" reform from an unwilling partner has rarely worked. Donors, too, have sometimes failed to fulfill their part of the bargain. Aid has been withdrawn in response to domestic financial pressures in donor countries or external political events, with limited notice or consultation. There are also frequent examples of donors continuing to provide assistance even when countries have not kept to their agreement.[15]

This increase in criticism led donors to re-examine their practices as far as conditionalities are concerned.

In response to this criticism, in 2002 the IMF elaborated new directives to guide its practices. These directives particularly emphasized the necessity to be henceforth more "parsimonious" in choosing conditions and even instituted a criticality test to ensure that only conditions really necessary to attain the goals of the program it supported were finally included in the program.

In an effort to re-examine its practices concerning the conditionalities that it undertook in consultation with different stakeholders, particularly government officials of its borrowing countries, representatives of civil society, parliamentarians, intellectuals and the World Bank itself also identified practices which should guide conditionality in its support of reforms. Among them, it cites the ownership of reforms by countries, the need to harmonize conditions with other development partners and ensure that conditions are well adapted to particular contexts of countries, that they are necessary to obtain the expected results, and finally that they contribute to promote transparency and accountability. This re-examination led the World Bank to realize that some domains such as trade liberalization, privatization and price adjustment of some public services had become very sensitive and that the conditions in these domains should therefore be implemented with precaution.

DFID also reviewed its practices concerning conditionality. As a result of this review, in March 2005, it published a new policy on conditionality.[16] This new policy was followed by the publication, in January 2006, of directives to orient its personnel in the implementation of the new policy.[17] In all, the new policy emphasized the following five principles: (i) contributing to countries' ownership of their development program, (ii) favoring a participative approach based on evidence in decision making on policies, (iii) promoting predictability, (iv) promoting harmonization with other development partners, and (v) promoting transparency and the responsibility of the British government and its partner countries. The new policy also clearly indicated that conditions should be based on the global program of the government and not on specific policies.

Despite these efforts, it should be noted that reforming the policies and practices of donors on conditionality in a satisfactory way to both donors and countries in need of financial assistance is not an easy task. How can we reconcile the legitimate desire of donors to ensure that their resources are used satisfactorily and the desire of aid-recipient countries not to have economic and social policies imposed on them? The above DFID report better illustrates the risk that exists in the practice of seeing conditionality move rapidly from the field of safeguarding the integrity of resources put at the disposal of states to that of interfering in their economic policy. I have visited several African countries to participate, with other aid agencies such as the World Bank and IMF and even some bilateral agencies, in negotiations with governments on the use of donors' resources to finance countries' economic reform programs. These experiences enabled me to realize to what extent countries sometimes express a feeling of impotence and resignation on the conditions that donors impose on the disbursement of resources, particularly when these have as a result made them take measures they would not have freely chosen.

The inherent difficulty in all attempts to reconcile donors' wishes to link disbursements of resources to the implementation of a certain number of measures (which implies that governments' responsibility is toward donors instead of their fellow citizens) and the legitimate desire of aid recipients to be independent may be illustrated by the ambiguity that I can infer from the directives to implement the new policy of conditionality that the DFID issued to its personnel. As a matter of fact, the new policy on conditionality aimed at making it such that conditions avoided seeking to impose policy choices on partner countries, but aimed at assessing the overall implementation of the program of poverty reduction. According to its real terms, it concerned governments concentrating on the outcomes or results, and not on specific measures (inputs). In order to guide its personnel in the implementation of the new policy of conditionality, the directives issued in January 2006 gave as a possible example the establishment of an anticorruption commission as a condition of disbursement.[18] It is obvious that establishing an anticorruption agency is only one means among many others to fight against corruption (and is therefore an input) and does not reflect the outcomes of an overall policy on the fight against corruption.

Despite accomplished efforts, even the IMF did not succeed in satisfactorily reforming its practices on conditionalities. In particular, its goals of parsimony and that of retaining only critical conditions were until recently still far from being attained. This is the outcome of an evaluation of its practices that its office of independent evaluation completed in 2007.[19] This evaluation, which reviewed 7,136 conditions contained in 216 programs approved between 1995 and 2004, revealed for example that about one-third of the conditions included in its programs were still out of its scope of expertise, whereas the 2002 directive aimed at making it such that conditions included in its programs were increasingly drawn from its core of expertise. This evaluation also showed that the average number of structural conditions per program per annum did not drop as expected, placing it at about seventeen, which was almost the same number as when the 2002 directive was elaborated. This evaluation also revealed that conditions contributed very little to fulfilling the roles they were assigned, namely (i) giving assurances to the IMF that it will be repaid and (ii) improving the predictability of disbursements by giving assurances to borrowing countries on what they should do to obtain disbursements of resources. Table 13.2 below summarizes information on the structural depth of conditions examined by the evaluation and the quality of implementation of conditions by countries.

Table 13.2. The IMF: Distribution of structural conditions per level of structural depth and rate of implementation according to the level of structural depth[20]

Sectors	Structural depth (%)*				Rate of implementation per level of structural depth (%)		
	Low	Limit	High	Average**	Low	Limit	High
Fiscal policy/tax administration	34	60	6	0.72	59	69	50
Management of public spending	36	62	3	0.67	58	51	33
Financial sector	53	44	4	0.51	58	48	13
Public company reforms	33	65	2	0.69	42	44	0
Privatization	64	25	11	0.47	30	33	17
Public service reforms	57	36	7	0.5	22	45	33
Social policies	59	35	6	0.47	44	50	0
Other domains of competence of the IMF	35	63	3	0.68	70	61	50
Other domains of competence of the World Bank	47	48	5	0.59	58	49	50
All sectors	43	53	4	0.62	53	56	32

*Low structural depth (conditions themselves not likely to induce significant change); limited (conditions that can themselves, if they are implemented, produce an immediate and perhaps significant change, but which are not followed by other measures necessary to make them sustainable) and high (conditions which, if implemented, will themselves produce a sustainable institutional change).
**Average structural depth calculated by assigning 0 to low, 1 to limited and 2 to high.

As it seems, only about 4 per cent of all the conditions had a high structural depth, 43 per cent had a low structural depth and 53 per cent had limited structural depth. If I state a hypothesis that only conditions having a high structural depth are likely to produce the economic effects necessary for the IMF to be reimbursed, I can therefore conclude that the conditions included in its programs did not fulfill this criterion. Yet the IMF was regularly reimbursed,[21] thereby showing that, contrary to the goal officially assigned to them, it is not the conditions that guarantee the reimbursement of loans. This conclusion is strengthened if I take into consideration the fact that only about one-third (32 per cent) of conditions having a high structural depth were effectively implemented. At the end of calculations, only 1 per cent of all the conditions guaranteed reimbursements assigned to conditions. Generally, the rates of implementation of conditions were weak enough, thereby showing that countries did not use conditions to improve upon the predictability of disbursements, which is also one of the goals assigned to conditions. Otherwise said, the IMF was regularly reimbursed even if conditions did not play any role there.

If, as the above statistics show, only a small proportion of conditions had a high structural depth – that is, were binding on the economic policy of aid recipient countries – why did the practice of conditionalities raise so much controversy and such debate in the world of development, and continue to do so? This debate may be due to the fact that the few binding conditions that donors attach to their aid are often found under domains considered by countries as very sensitive to their economic policy. It is mostly in fields such as the policy of liberalization of foreign trade, tariffs of public services or better still privatization of public companies. This hypothesis may be supported given that donors, including the Bretton Woods institutions themselves, henceforth recognize these domains as being sensitive and have become more careful when it concerns them.

Faced with these difficulties, it is not surprising that despite reform efforts, results obtained are still far from fully satisfying the expectations of all stakeholders. Commenting on the criticism that some advance that China does not impose conditions on its loans to African countries, a senior European official suggested that Western countries should study the hypothesis of abandonment of conditionalities in their loans. During the annual meetings of the IMF and the World Bank held in Singapore, the discussion between supporters and opponents of conditionalities was once more relaunched. To the US economist William Easterly, conditionalities should be abandoned because, as he says, conditions imposed by donors have never permanently changed the behavior of any government in the world.[22]

As it therefore appears, the use of conditionalities is evolving considerably. I have already noted that during the various recent high-level forums on aid, development partners themselves wanted this evolution. Moreover, in the context of the financial crisis, the IMF recently announced the creation of a new instrument to come to the aid of economically well-managed emerging economies, but which, despite all, was affected by the crisis. According to some IMF officials, very few conditions would be attached to this instrument and at times there may be no conditions; the IMF can even approve aid under this instrument without carrying out missions to the country to evaluate its management, and in some cases for a few days only. Several observers have already commented that the IMF loans granted to Greece, Hungary, Ukraine and Iceland after the financial and sovereign debt crisis contained fewer conditions than usual, presaging changes to come.

This trend toward less conditionalities is certainly a welcome development, but I doubt whether moving toward no conditions at all or abandoning conditionalities altogether, as some advocate, would contribute toward more effective aid. I think citizens in developing countries demand more accountability on the part of their governments on the use of resources. In this context, I think more efforts are needed toward further streamlining conditions while at the same time making them more supportive of countries' own economic policies.

Toward this end, it seems that the European Union has experimented with an approach which seems promising. It consists in seeking to set up conditions not on precise actions but on outcomes. Such an approach has the advantage of leaving the countries with the opportunity to choose policies which will help to achieve the expected results. It is an advantage because the traditional approach of imposing policies on countries has clearly shown its limits. However, traditional donors, particularly the IMF and the World Bank, seem hesitant in view of this change. Results are less verifiable, they say. The links between actions and results would be rather uncertain and less controlled, such that exercising accountability will be difficult, given that it will not be easy to tell whether it is because the country has not been able to meet its commitments, or because other factors beyond its control have intervened, that it has not obtained results. We think this difficulty can be resolved with the necessary voluntarism. A senior European politician promised full employment to his fellow citizens and repeated several times on camera that it was not a promise but a commitment. If it is possible to undertake commitments on such a global variable as employment in an economy as sophisticated as European economies are, then it should be possible to identify results on which conditionalities should be based, particularly in the context of developing countries' economies, where, due to their low level of sophistication, the major determinants of economic dynamics are more easily understood.

In an approach of conditionalities based on results, commitments may be selected among the final, intermediate and operating goals examined in this book, instead of establishing them only on the basis of instruments, as is the case in the present practice. In countries which have been able to establish a positive track record on their economic management capacity, conditionalities can be established on the basis of the final and intermediate goals – as such, leaving them some degree of independence in choosing their operating goals and instruments. These approaches will also require much more effort on the part of stakeholders to better understand the links in the chain of results, but also to improve upon the quality of instruments and indicators for measuring these results. In the end, this effort will be beneficial to the quality of aid in general; for it should be admitted that the present practice, which consists in basing conditionalities on economic policy instruments and not on results, is also explained by the facility offered by such an approach. In fact, if a good number of donors' conditionalities depend on economic policy instruments, and not on results, it is also because information on instruments are more rapidly and easily available, and not because instruments may be considered superior from the point of view of the results sought, which are very complex. This point is well known and analyzed in the literature, which often talks about processes substituting for substance.

Opening Up the Rest of the World to African Exports

I have already discussed at length in the preceding chapters the importance of opening up the rest of the world to African exports as a way to support African economic growth and job creation. This conduit is perhaps the most effective way to provide aid to the African continent.

The growth in strength of new donors

On September 17, 2006 in Singapore, during the Annual Meetings of the IMF and the World Bank, the first international act of recognition of the growing strength of Asia in world economy probably took place. On that occasion, the International Monetary and Financial Committee (the organ in charge of advising the IMF on its management of the international monetary and financial system) approved within the framework of the implementation of the first phase of a series of reforms aimed at improving IMF governance, an immediate increase of the quota of a certain number of countries, among which were two Asian countries, China and South Korea. According to the terms of the press release, this decision aimed at realigning the quotas of these countries on their relative importance in the world economy. This decision constituted a recognition by the international community of one of the major evolutions going on in the world economy – that is to say, the accession to the rank of world economic power of China and a number of other Asian economies.[23] During the last three decades, the Chinese economy experienced an average annual growth rate of its GDP of 9.4 per cent. According to a recent report of the International Comparison Program, a program run by the World Bank, China's GDP in purchasing power parity terms is poised to overtake the United States' in 2014, which would make China become the world biggest economy.[24] Presently, China is the country with the highest world foreign exchange reserves, passing the 3,000 billion dollar mark.

As for India, a 2007 study by Goldman Sachs investment bank showed that it will record an average growth rate of 8 per cent per annum up until 2020. According to the report, the Indian economy is going to exceed the US economy in terms of GDP and is going to be, by 2042, the second world economy after China. India's GDP was also projected to exceed that of Italy, France and Great Britain by 2017, that of Germany in 12 years and that of Japan in 18 years. The *Times of India*, a leading daily in India, asserted the following: "Combine our new found economic and political clout with our influential diaspora and our status of global soft power (from Bollywood and Indian art to yoga and spirituality) and brand India is on a roll like never before." A study carried out by the Chicago Council of Foreign Affairs concluded that Indians already consider themselves the most powerful people in the world after the United States.[25] All these developments testify the increasing economic role that Asian countries are playing in world economy. Some commentators have not hesitated to assert that the world economic center is gradually shifting toward Asia.

Partially due to this increasing economic importance, the attention of African economic officials and their development partners has recently tilted to the spectacular rise of China and what it implies to the development prospects of Africa. It should be said that it is not only in Europe, where the importation of Chinese textiles made headlines in the news,[26] or in the United States, where the exchange rate of the yuan is at the center of international economic policy (first under the administration of President Bush,[27] but also since the arrival of President Obama); the rapid economic growth of China and Asia has also been accompanied by an acceleration of its economic ties with Africa. According to a report published by the World Bank, Asia receives about 27 per cent of exports from Africa as opposed to only 14 per cent in 2000. Asian exports to Africa have also increased at a sustained rate, about 18 per cent per annum, a higher rate than exports to other regions. Direct investments between the two continents are also experiencing a rapid growth.

Europeans and Americans also criticize China's economic policy by asserting that it has as a result a very strong increase in exports and will cause the economic development of China to depend on exports rather than on domestic consumption. One of the goals of their economic policy dialogue with China is therefore for China to stimulate its domestic consumption more and reduce exports, which they call rebalancing Chinese economic growth. In its research, the Conference Board, a US think tank, has suggested that China should use its enormous foreign reserves to finance a national retirement plan, which, by strengthening China's social security system, would incite the Chinese to reduce their precautionary savings and consume more. This would then lead to domestic demand-led growth instead of export-led growth. I do not see why the idea of a developing country like China depending on exports to increase its economic growth would constitute disequilibrium or bad economic policy.[28]

I hear several criticisms, coming particularly from traditional donors, on the issue of economic relations between China and Africa.[29] Trade may be highly concentrated on raw materials. Concerning trade, the recent trend showed that African exports to China were highly concentrated on subsoil resources. Africa should not only be a source of raw material supply to satisfy the great energy needs generated by the rapid economic growth experienced by China. It is this feeling that Thabo Mbeki, then South African president, certainly wanted to express when he indicated at a students' congress in Cape Town that African countries may be condemned to underdevelopment if they are content in exporting raw materials to China and importing manufactured goods, a replica of former colonial relationships whose results on development we already know. We should think of solutions which can be implemented to increase and diversify Chinese imports from Africa. I also hear that the rise in strength of China as an aid provider risks provoking a reduction of the role of conditionality implemented by international financial institutions and bilateral donors. This conditionality could play a significant role in stimulating economic reforms in aid-recipient countries.

Other Western critics insist on the fact that, to them, China does not take into account human rights considerations in investment decisions and, as such, invests in countries that do not respect human rights. According to these critics, the idea of investing in these countries does not incite them to improve upon their practices. These concerns should be applied to all development partners, including traditional donors. As a matter of fact, traditional donors were not very vigilant on human rights in their investment decisions in Africa as well as in other parts of the world.

All this shows that the question Africa should have asked itself is not, as others try to insinuate, who between China and the traditional donors is more virtuous in its relations with Africa. Experience has shown that traditional donors and China today situate their relations with Africa within the framework of the search for their interests. Africa should rejoice over the competition among donors created by the arrival of China. We learn from economic theory that competition is a source of efficiency and produces the best results. This is actually what Donald Kaberuka, president of the African Development Bank Group, said when he asserted that if long-term and predictable resources for financing development were not available from other sources, it was natural for Africa to seek them where they were available, adding, "The traditional donors have to be a bit more modest than that because, frankly, after all these 40 years of trying to improve the quality of aid we are not yet there."[30]

Some also say that China's loans risk creating a new debt crisis in African countries. Even if the Chinese defend themselves by saying that their financing is most often either grants or loans with very concessional conditions, some observers estimate that the lack of transparency which characterizes some of these Chinese financial transactions with African countries does not help to know exactly what is happening, even the amounts borrowed or the financial conditions attached to these loans. Beyond this discussion on the comparative performances of Chinese and Western aid[31] it seems that, to Africa, the question to be asked is twofold: What type of partnership should be undertaken with China? What contribution can China offer to a successful implementation of the type of economic policy outlined in this book for African countries?

To answer these two questions, I should first bear in mind that in the context of its new economic strength, China is both a trade partner and an aid provider to Africa. As trade partner, the role China can play to contribute to the implementation of African economic policy is enormous. First, it seems that, for the newfound dynamism of economic relations to be mutually beneficial to the two parties, it is necessary for African exports to China to be considerably diversified and to not remain concentrated on raw materials, particularly oil and energy products. In this quest for diversification of African exports to China, I believe China itself has a big role to play, contrary to what we often hear, that all that is left for African countries is to diversify their exports if they want to benefit from their trade with China. I believe that China must study a number of measures, obviously including the reduction of tariff and nontariff barriers, but also going much further to diversify its demand for goods and services addressed to Africa. This is the type of mutually beneficial trade that I foresee between Africa and China.[32] Obviously, these efforts on the part of China should be complementary, with efforts of African countries aimed at strengthening their supply capacity by facilitating the trade and business atmosphere in Africa. This view of the Chinese role is all the more important because the present structure of its trade with Africa reflects the structure of its trade with the rest of the world, where China is mainly an exporter of manufactured products and an importer of raw materials, particularly energy products.

At the level of elaboration and implementation of economic policy, I also believe that China has a rich experience to share with African countries. How did a country which was so poor only about fifty years ago succeed – thanks to a real, heterodox economic policy, developed locally, based on principles and orientations sometimes far from those expressed by the international aid agency – in generating spectacular economic growth, reduce poverty and rise to the rank of world economic power in less than half a century? I think it is at this level that Africa may not so much copy measures implemented by China, because the contexts are certainly different, but may draw lessons for the process of elaboration and conduct of economic policy – in short, for the science and art of economic policymaking which I have lengthily discussed in this book.[33]

Part Five

SOME SUCCESSFUL EXPERIENCES OF ECONOMIC POLICY IN AFRICA AND BEYOND

After outlining throughout the previous chapters what seems to be the broad outlines of an economic policy capable of leading Africa toward economic development and social progress, a dream it has nursed for close to half a century, I will, in this fifth and last part of the book, examine some examples of what I can qualify as a successful economic policy. Here, I am interested in some cases of countries which recently experienced a remarkable economic development and to see which overall approach they followed to elaborate and implement their economic policy, and which orientations they gave their economic policy. This type of exercise is not new. Literature abounds with studies which attempt at drawing the attention of developing countries to the experiences of those among them which have experienced rapid development which took them close to the levels of developed countries. However, as shown throughout this book, these studies are more prominent through the exaggerated simplicity of their conclusions, generally of the type "Let's liberalize trade and maintain macroeconomic stability"[1] than through the richness of teachings that they contain about the fundamental orientations that economic policy officials should really give their everyday actions, so that they may produce, in all economic agents, the catalyst effect they are waiting for that will have them adopt the production and demand behaviors necessary for economic growth and job creation. The aim of my approach in Part Five is therefore to see to what extent the orientations outlined in the foregoing chapters are found in the economic policy implemented by countries that have succeeded in their economic development or are on the way to success.

As already indicated, for the past half century, African economic policy seems quite far from that described in this book, to the extent that finding examples of successful economic policy to describe is difficult. Insofar as the orientations outlined in the preceding chapters retain my interest here, and that these seem not to depend on context and that it is in the choice of measures to implement these orientations that the specificities of each country should be taken into account, the choice of countries to be examined no longer has much importance. In this perspective, and also considering, on the one hand, the fact that the few examples of successful economic policy on the continent (Mauritius, Botswana) are often the subject of analysis in literature,[2] and on the other hand, the necessity to diversify useful sources of experience in African countries, in Chapter 14, I will examine the rich experience of the Tunisian economic policy. Also, considering the economic policy challenges that it took up and the success recorded to date, post-apartheid South Africa also illustrates the conduct of an economic policy which is rich in lessons. Its experience will be examined in Chapter 15. I will conclude Part Five with Chapter 16, where I will examine some economic policy experiences in developed and in emerging countries in Asia.

In studying success in terms of the economic policy of countries like Tunisia and South Africa, the following chapters also provide new contributions to the discussion on comparative economic policy experiences and what these comparative experiences offer as lessons to developing countries. As a matter of fact, the literature on the comparative experiences of development policies is up to this point overconcentrated on the study of the experience of Asian countries. By offering an analysis of the experience of countries like Tunisia and South Africa – two scarcely studied experiences in literature and moreover two countries situated in Africa – this book enriches and diversifies the literature on comparative economic policy experiences.

Toward better situating this discussion in context, one clarification is in order: The claim I make here is not that the two countries discussed have solved all their economic problems. There are still very difficult challenges confronting them, which I clearly highlight, but my claim is two-pronged: firstly, over the period of study, the two countries recorded some successes that are not in dispute, and secondly, my aim is to try to identify the economic policy these two countries implemented to achieve their relative economic successes. I further find that those economic policies are in line with the framework discussed in the book. I also present facts to support my claims about the two countries.

Chapter Fourteen

A SUCCESSFUL ECONOMIC POLICY EXPERIENCE IN AFRICA: ECONOMIC POLICY IN TUNISIA

"Tunisia had long been portrayed as an economic success story in the region. [...] The social unrest and political turmoil that engulfed Tunisia in January [2011] indicated that despite the country's comparative economic success, key social and development challenges had not been addressed."

Towards a New Economic Model for Tunisia (joint report by the African Development Bank, the Millennium Challenge Corporation, the Tunisian government and USAID, 2012)[1]

"Promoting employment and improving upon revenue will be an absolute priority in conformity with the orientations of the 11th Plan. [...] Accelerating the growth rate will constitute a primordial goal of the next five-year development plan expressing the political wish to concretize the priority reserved for employment. [...] Tunisia aspires, with the favor of experiences acquired, to take up the challenges both internally and externally in order to meet the pack of developed countries. Among these challenges, employment will occupy the first position."

Republic of Tunisia, *11th Development Plan 2007–11*[2]

Introduction

On December 17, 2010, in Sidi Bouzid, a town of about forty thousand inhabitants, located 300 km south of Tunis, Mohammed Bouazizi, a young, 26-year-old Tunisian, selling fruit on the streets of this city usually known to be calm – an activity he performed, like many other young Tunisians, for lack of a better job – set himself on fire after a quarrel with the police. He died of his wounds on January 4, 2011 in a hospital near Tunis. His action marks the starting point of events that ended 23 years of rule by President Zine El Abidine Ben Ali, and to what is now referred to as the Tunisian Revolution.

This revolution was rightly interpreted by many as reflecting the profound despair of a population affected by unemployment, inequality and especially the absence of democracy. But there is also no doubt that Tunisia was, considered a model for many countries of the South, given its economic performance since independence. This chapter is out to show how the type of economic policy I have presented throughout this book describes the economic policy strategy implemented by Tunisia and which enabled it to record the remarkable economic success it was known for prior to the revolution, and which was often mentioned in literature. First, I will show that the search for the development of employment and strong economic growth appear to be fundamental final goals that Tunisian economic policy officials established. Second, I will also show that the development of a national productive tissue as well as the stimulation of strong demand addressed to the national economy – what I call intermediate goals – also appeared among the Tunisian economic policy goals. Third, I will show that most of the operating goals I have identified were also concerns of Tunisian economic policy officials. Finally, I will show how the instruments owned by the authorities were deployed to achieve the operating, intermediate and final goals.

In a nutshell, I will attempt in this chapter to reveal the preferences of Tunisian economic policy officials in choosing the goals to pursue, the aim being to show that it is the structure of the goals described in the conceptual framework presented in this book which underlie the economic policy measures implemented.[3]

Brief Overview of Tunisia

Tunisia is a North African country. It is part of the Maghreb region, which also comprises Algeria, Libya, Morocco and Mauritania. With a surface area of only 163,610 km², it is the smallest state of this group, but the third largest if we consider its population of about 10.1 million inhabitants. Cultivable land covers about forty per cent only of the total land surface of the country. The country has a long maritime front of about 1,300 km. Its subsoil contains natural resources such as oil, phosphate, iron ore, lead and zinc, but in moderate quantities, such that Tunisia is not classified among countries that are rich in subsoil natural resources. Despite this little favorable initial endowment, Tunisia is one of the rare Maghreb countries, and even in Africa in general, which was able throughout the last nearly six decades – that is, since her independence on March 20, 1956 – to achieve, thanks to a well-oriented economic policy, a level of economic development and social progress which placed it at the level of emerging countries. The medium-term goal of the authorities is to further increase the standard of living toward narrowing the gap with emerging countries of the OECD.

Some Characteristic Elements of Tunisian Economic Success

In line with what I have developed throughout Part Two, two outstanding facts seem to characterize the economic policy success by Tunisia since its independence: rapid and sustained growth and progress in terms of employment. At the level of economic growth, Tunisia experienced over a long period (1980–2010) sustained growth of its GDP at a rate higher than 4.3 per cent per annum.

Overall, Tunisian economic growth performance was comparable to the performance of other regions of the world. Thus, apart from the emerging markets and developing countries grouping, from 1980–2010, Tunisia recorded a higher average annual economic growth than the Middle East and North Africa and the sub-Saharan Africa country groupings (see Figure 14.1 below).

Figure 14.1. Average annual growth rate, 1980–2010[4]

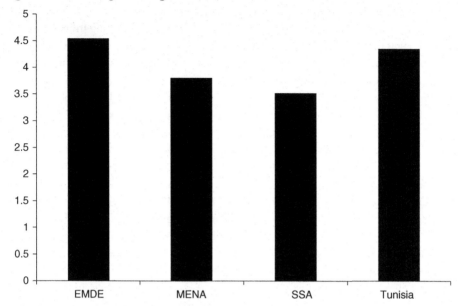

EMDE: Emerging markets and developing economies
MENA: Middle East and North Africa
SSA: Sub-Saharan Africa

Figure 14.2. Tunisia: Increase in gross national product per capita relative to other regions, 1980–2010[5]

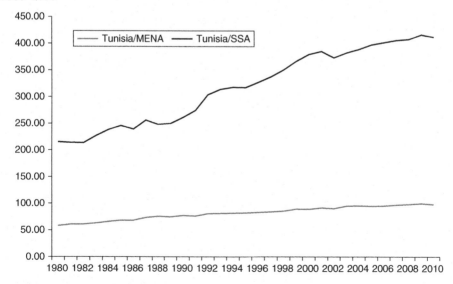

MENA: Middle East and North Africa
SSA: Sub-Saharan Africa

The growth performance also translated into steady growth of the GDP per capita, both in absolute terms and relative to other country groupings. Thus, in purchasing power parity terms, Tunisia GDP per capita increased close to fivefold, growing from 1.906 US dollars in 1980 to 9.356 US dollars in 2010. Figure 14.2 below retraces the evolution of Tunisian GNP per capita relative to the average in the MENA and sub-Saharan African regions. As it appears in this figure, the country improved its wealth per capita compared to the these regions. From 1980–2010, its GNP per capita increased from about 58 per cent and 215 per cent of the average of the group of countries represented by MENA and sub-Saharan Africa respectively to 98 per cent and 412 per cent.

This satisfactory growth was also accompanied by some job creation. Thus, Figure 14.3 below, which describes the evolution of the unemployment rate, shows that Tunisia's performance was broadly comparable to that of some comparators. As such, this unemployment rate dropped from about 16 per cent in 1995 to 13 per cent in 2010, but both the speed and the extent of this drop were not enough to catch up with the growing number of job seekers. Overall then, the one area of Tunisia's economic performance where major challenges remained was that of employment creation. The challenges to be taken up at the level of unemployment remained, therefore, considerable. Most observers believe that this unsatisfactory performance on employment creation was a key contributor to the revolution that country experienced in 2011.

Figure 14.3. Tunisia: Unemployment rate compared with other countries (percent of total labor force)[6]

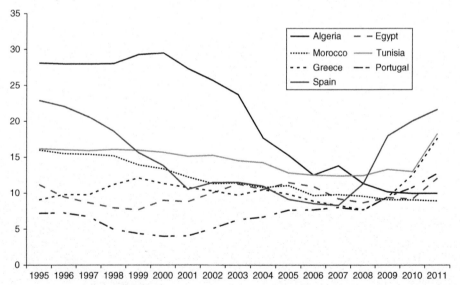

The Tunisian economic growth, which was also accompanied by continuous improvement of the level of income per capita and some improvement, albeit insufficient, in the unemployment rate, gave the economy the means to improve upon other important social indicators. Thus, the population living below the national poverty line experienced a considerable drop from 16.1 per cent over 1980–84 to 12.9 per cent in 1995 and

4.2 per cent in 2000.[7] The census published in 2012 showed a poverty rate of 4.6 per cent. Besides, as shown in Table 14.1 below, the good performance of the Tunisian economy was accompanied during this period by an improvement of other frequently used social indicators to measure the evolution of the quality of life.

Table 14.1. Evolution of social indicators of Tunisia, 1970–2012[8]

| Year | Life Expectancy | | | SFI | IMR | MMR | AIR | | |
	Total	Men	Women	Per woman	Per 1,000	Per 100,000	Total	Men	Women
1970	54.2	53.7	54.7	6.5	126.6		72.6	59.1	85.2
1975	58.1	57.3	59	5.9	100.2		63.8	50.6	77
1980	62.4	61.1	63.8	5.2	73.5	1000	55.1	41.6	68.8
1985	65.8	64.3	67.6	4.5	55		48	35	61.1
1990	68.8	67.1	70.8	3.5	40.1	74.8	40.9	28.4	53.5
1995	71.2	69.3	73.2	2.6	29.7		35.3	24	46.7
2000	72.6	70.7	74.8	2.1	24	54.8	29	18.6	39.4
2001	72.9	70.9	75	2.1	23.1		28	17.8	38.2
2002	73.1	71.1	75.3	2	22.2		26.9	16.9	37
2003	73.3	71.3	75.5	2	21.6	50	25.9	16.1	35.7
2004	73.5	71.5	75.7	1.9	21	47	24.8	15.2	34.5
2005	73.7	71.9	75.9	1.9	20.3		23.8	14.4	33.3
2012	75.6			2.0	15.7				

SFI: Synthetic fertility index
IMR: Infant mortality rate
MMR: Maternal mortality rate
AIR: Adult illiteracy rate

Thus, life expectancy at birth, which in 2012 was close to 76 years, whereas in 1970 it was only 52.2 years, resembled that of developed countries more than that of developing countries. The infant mortality rate, maternal mortality rate and the synthetic fertility index also experienced substantial improvements, thereby expressing remarkable progress in terms of standard of living, health, education, protection of women's rights and protection of the environment. The adult mortality rate also dropped considerably.

Five-Year Development Plans as Instrument of Formulation and Implementation of Economic Policy

In this book, I have defined economic policy as the conscious, systematic and voluntary action of public authorities aimed at influencing the economic performance of a country in a way that it leads to the improvement of the well-being of its citizens. In Tunisia's case, the five-year development plan was no doubt the clearest manifestation of the fact that the country had a real economic policy. The introduction of the plan as a major instrument of development and implementation of economic policy dates back to the beginning of the 1960s. The plan, elaborated every five years, set up economic goals to be attained by the country over the next five years, the policy which would be implemented to attain them and the anticipated public and private financial resources to be mobilized to finance its implementation toward attaining the set goals.

Institutionally, the preparation of the plan was controlled by a certain number of provisions which guaranteed credibility and conferred on it the authority to serve as a reference to the actions of all stakeholders. As such, the plan was part of a law voted by the Chamber of Deputies and the Chamber of Counselors, the two chambers of the Tunisian legislative power. I believe this process embodies a lesson which can really inspire most sub-Saharan African countries where the PRSP, which is presently the country's main economic policy document, is not examined by parliament and is not voted as law. This fact, in my opinion, not only deprives these countries of the rich and potentially productive debate which this examination in parliament would give rise to, but also of an opportunity to contribute to the credibility of this important policy document.

The process of elaboration of the five-year plan, which often lasted two to three years, was based on very close collaboration between public authorities and all the other national stakeholders, including civil society, the private sector and the administrative regions of the country. This process was coordinated by the Higher Council of the Plan, presided over by the president of the republic. The Ministry of Development and International Cooperation coordinated the elaboration of all documents necessary for the preparation of the plan and played the role of rapporteur before the Higher Council of Plan. Moreover, the president of the republic was himself involved in the implementation of the plan. He held regular meetings with stakeholders, including the prime minister and the ministers, civil society organizations and the private sector, to monitor its implementation.

Insofar as the plan covers a period of five years, the orientations contained therein are implemented annually with the help of economic budgets. Tunisia completed the execution of its 10th five-year plan in 2006 and the execution of the 11th Plan, which covered 2007–11, started in 2007. The execution of economic policy through the five-year plan has been practiced by most developed countries, including Japan, France and South Korea. As in these market economy countries, the Tunisian planning was indicative; that is, it aimed more at informing economic agents on the intentions of the state and orienting state economic policy action during the period covered by the plan, than authoritatively fixing quantities and price goals to be attained. The quest for goals and orientations of the plan was obligatory to the state, but the private sector remained free of its decisions.

Employment and Economic Growth at the Center of Final Goals of the Economic Policy Defined in the Five-Year Plans

The search for development of employment, and by extension the search for strong growth, were constant in the final goals established by successive five-year plans elaborated by Tunisia. Thus, the orientation note which defined the broad outlines guiding the preparation of the 10th Plan showed, for example, that the first goal consisted in winning the employment war. In the 10th Plan, which covered the period 2002–2006, I can read: "The major challenge of the 10th Plan consists in attaining the highest level of growth which helps to achieve the priority goal of employment, favoring the preservation of financial equilibriums and guaranteeing the bases of a sustainable development."[9] To concretize this goal, the 10th Plan aimed at creating 380,000 new jobs from 2002–06, thereby satisfying 95 per cent[10] of additional job applications planned during the same period. To attain this employment goal, the 10th Plan aimed at reaching a growth rate of 5.5 per cent against 5.3 per cent during the 9th Plan.

Revealed Intermediate Goals of Economic Policy: A High Concentration on the Development of Productive Sectors and Demand Addressed to the Economy

A high concentration on productive sectors

To attain growth and job creation goals, the strategy recommended by the five-year development plans rests on a clear identification of actions to be implemented and investments to be achieved to stimulate the productive sectors. Thus, the 10th Plan identified nine productive sectors, which were agriculture, manufacturing industries, energy and mines, transport, communication technologies, tourism and leisure, craft industry and computer sciences. For each sector, plan documents reviewed the previous plan achievements and showed the sectoral growth projections in volume for the ongoing plan, the program of investments necessary to attain the sectoral goals envisaged by the source of financing (administration, public companies and the private sector), as well as by activities. This high concentration on the productive sectors is expressed particularly by a voluntary approach, which places the company and its development at the center of economic policy concerns. Thus, this fundamental option is found in the 10th Plan, which says:

> The industrial enterprise constitutes a fundamental support of the national economy, by virtue of how much it provides, the perspectives it opens to employment, and the production and exports that it ensures for the well-being of the development dynamics of our country. It also represents a national achievement which is born and is developing in favor of the combined efforts of all the members of the entrepreneurial family: investors, administration officials, technicians, managers and workers. Each of them represents a determining factor which contributes, jointly with others, to the growth of the company, its stability and development.[11]

Stimulation of demand addressed to the economy

In all the economies of the world, demand addressed to the economy generally represents a preponderant source of activity for the productive system. Usually, consumption plays an essential role in this demand. This implies that an important share of resources produced in the economy is to satisfy consumption needs. This is then followed by investments – that is, the expenses of companies when modernizing and expanding their productive capacity – and finally exports. The Tunisian economy was not an exception to this rule. As such, consumption represented about 60 per cent of Tunisian economy in 2005, contributed 3.5 per cent to the GDP growth rate, which was 5 per cent, or a contribution of 70 per cent to growth.[12] The Tunisian planner took note of this reality and was bent on considering it. The five-year development plans also give particular importance to stimulating demand and domestic consumption as a driving force of economic growth.

Thus, examining the management of the Tunisian economy over the period 1960–2000, some authors note that

> since the sixties, the officials of Tunisian economic policy have manifested a real determination to stimulate demand addressed to the economy. To achieve this, multifaceted efforts were implemented. Hence, they developed and implemented the value chain concept in the sixties, which aimed at "giving priority to the establishment of businesses which can integrate in a supply/demand chain, leaning on each other, with their production complementing either upstream or downstream." It is this approach that inspired the voluntary efforts implemented to develop key sectors of the Tunisian economy such as manufacturing, food processing, tourism, and that of construction materials.[13]

The value chain approach has also over the years been supported by macroeconomic instruments, including monetary and fiscal policy, which I will examine below.

In this process of stimulating demand, the potential of domestic demand was not neglected, as is unfortunately the case in the policies of many African countries today. The same author thus notes:

> In addition to the rare programs to value domestic products destined for export – the main one being the enrichment of phosphate to produce phosphoric acid – most new businesses were of the SME dimension, created based on domestic demand that is hoped to be stimulated through a conservative Keynesian approach. [...] This approach of stimulating demand proved profitable faster than anyone anticipated.[14]

The orientations contained in the 11th Plan also clearly aimed at

> strengthening the consumer's arbitration role, considered as an essential element in a market economy and to confer on consumption an important role for economic growth. As a matter of fact, within the framework of the opening of the domestic market to foreign goods and services, it becomes indispensable to promote quality in order to orientate consumer preferences toward Tunisian products and services and to improve their competitiveness. On this count, actions will be during the period of the 10th Plan based on intensifying consumer information.[15]

I dwelt on this point earlier, when I indicated that one of the key intermediate goals of economic policy must be to stimulate demand addressed to the economy. Moreover, under the 10th Plan, emphasis was also placed on improving competitiveness and the quality of national products in order to orient the expansion of consumption toward domestic products and favor the growth of domestic supply compared to imports.

Revealed Operating Goals of Tunisian Economic Policy

The examination of successive five-year development plans elaborated and implemented by Tunisia shows that, in striving to mobilize the talents and energy of all national development actors to attain strategic goals, policies implemented by the successive plans aimed at strengthening infrastructural quality, improving the business atmosphere, ensuring adequate financing to the economy, winning the confidence of economic agents, promoting good governance and improving the quality of human resources, while recognizing the necessity of a successful and controlled integration into the world economy and also that of protecting macroeconomic stability and the main financial stability of the nation. At the level of macroeconomic equilibria, Figure 14.4 below shows that inflation was maintained at a lower level compared to various country groupings such as emerging markets and developing economies, the Middle East and North African countries, and sub-Saharan African countries.

Figure 14.4. Evolution of the inflation rate, 1990–2010 (average consumer prices, in %)[16]

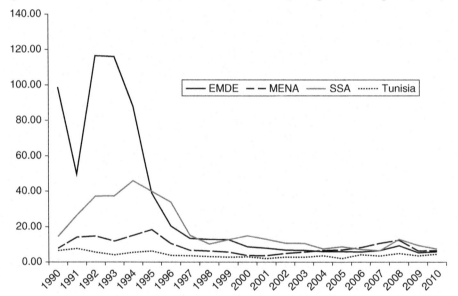

EMDE: Emerging markets and developing economies
MENA: Middle East and North Africa
SSA: Sub-Saharan Africa

At the level of infrastructure, the plan documents further contained infrastructural projections which were indispensable for productive-capacity building, and the means to finance the investments necessary for the desired improvement of infrastructure. Infrastructural domains retained in the 10th Plan were transport facilities, town planning, rural and urban development, protection of the environment, preservation of natural resources and the fight against desertification, land issues, rural electrification and potable water. The third and last part of the document on the sectoral content of the plan covers human resources and social and cultural development. In fact, as the results of in-depth analysis shows, the rationale of actions targeted by the five-year development plans was to give priority support to the development of productive sectors. The development of infrastructure and social sectors is targeted in their support role to this development. Earlier, I cited the 10th Plan, which clearly recognized and reaffirmed the fundamental role of national companies as a source of wealth and job creation.

I also believe here that this harmony and equilibrium between, on the one hand, the imperative to support the development of a competitive national productive tissue and, on the other hand, social development could have inspired several sub-Saharan African countries and their development partners, who, apparently, did not succeed in finding an equilibrium between these two concerns, thereby giving the impression that, for a long time, the company's interest had not yet been sufficiently elevated to the same level as the social development concerns at the center of economic policy.[17] I will now examine the key instruments of economic policy used by the successive five-year development plans and the manner in which they were used to attain the goals pursued.

Instruments of Economic Policy in Tunisia

The insights that can be gained by a study of the Tunisian economic policy are not only found in the lessons we can draw from it on the importance, on the one hand, of the process of its elaboration and implementation and, on the other hand, on the choice of goals and their broad outlines. It is also found in the manner in which different instruments were used in the pursuit of goals. It is not so much the instruments in themselves that constitute the originality of economic policy, given that those found here are practically the same as those found in other economies of the world and on which I dwelt in Part Two; it is the manner in which they were deployed and placed at the service of national economic policy goals as stated in the plan. Here also, the Tunisian experience seems full of lessons for several developing countries.

Although this presentation of instruments may give the impression of a return to a sectoral approach, the goal targeted here is more to show how the use of each instrument is clearly guided by the perspective to contribute to the final, intermediate and operating goals (creating a supply capacity and stimulating demand) established by the authorities within the framework of economic policy. Obviously, the levels targeted by the authorities for each instrument strongly depend on the Tunisian context. Beyond these levels, it is the manner in which the instruments contribute to goals that arouses interest.

Monetary policy

Monetary policy played an important role in maintaining macroeconomic stability, which is necessary for the pursuit of intermediate goals. Without compromising macroeconomic stability, supporting demand addressed to the economy through adequate development of credit to the economy, including well-calibrated consumer credit, is also a key objective of monetary policy. The Central Bank of Tunisia (CBT), which is in charge of defining and implementing monetary policy, was created in September 1958, and the national currency, the Tunisian dinar, in October 1956. Since then, the conduct of monetary policy has experienced profound changes. Thus, its goals moved from defending the value of the dinar and its stability, as defined in a 1988 law, to that of preserving price stability, following an amendment of the law on the creation of the CBT adopted in October 2006. Thus, during the 9th and 10th Plans, the major goal of monetary policy was the control of inflation and the optimization of the financing of the economy with the interest rate as the major intervention instrument. The October 2006 reform provided a course to a policy of targeting the inflation rate during the second stage of a process whose first stage was to continue to give priority to a quantitative approach based on actions on the monetary base, through the use of the open-market operations. Monetary policy results up to this point were satisfactory given that inflation remained low over a long period in Tunisia.

This satisfactory result in terms of price stability demanded much expertise in the conduct of monetary policy, for the evolution of the exchange rate was marked by depreciation, thereby mechanically exerting upward pressures on the price of tradable goods and, therefore, generating risks to price stability; monetary authorities therefore exercised vigilance on the prices of nontradable goods. According to the criteria usually used in literature, the CBT enjoys *de jure* independence in the definition and conduct of monetary policy.[18]

Budgetary policy

Budgetary policy also contributed to macroeconomic stability and to stimulating demand addressed to the economy. From this point of view, several outstanding facts characterized Tunisia's budgetary policy. Overall, the evolution during the last decades does not show excessive deficits. There were no budgetary pressures on macroeconomic stability. Concerning public expenditures, the policy consisted essentially in allocating sufficient resources to different public investment programs in the areas of infrastructure useful to the development of productive sectors, and in the other above-mentioned sectors. Public debt service also remained within bearable limits.

Concerning public revenues, one of the main challenges was to adjust to the drop in taxes on international trade due to the implementation of trade liberalization agreements signed by the country with its various trade partners. However, as shown in Figure 14.5 below, budgetary performance was good insofar as the overall budgetary deficit remained low and more stable than that of other emerging North African countries like Egypt and Morocco, for example. The two difficult episodes are 1986–88[19] and 1988–92, during which the country experienced macroeconomic difficulties leading to a recourse to a standby facility and an IMF extended facility respectively. Since then, the country had not resorted to IMF aid, though it had good cooperative relations with this institution within the framework of consultations under Article IV.

Tunisian budgetary policy also sought to contribute directly to demand addressed to national companies. A set of provisions particularly on granting national preferences within the framework of procedures of public procurement contributed to success in this domain.[20] Budgetary policy also pursued an important goal of contributing to

Figure 14.5. Evolution of overall budgetary deficit, 1980–2005[21]

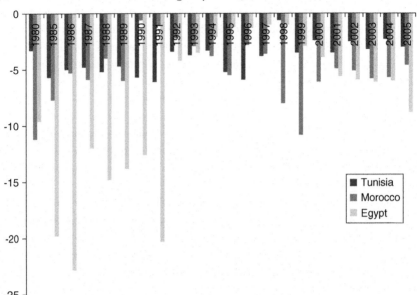

social cohesion thanks particularly to social transfers representing an important share of Tunisian public expenses.

Exchange rate policy

In a world where the increasing globalization of markets increases the probability of the unexpected occurrence of economic shocks and also increases their scale when they occur, it is necessary to have an exchange rate policy which enables the economy to adjust to them at the lowest cost. At its independence, Tunisia was a member of the Franc Zone, but in December 1958 the link between the Tunisian dinar and the French franc was ruptured and the dinar left the Franc Zone.[22] After that, Tunisia adopted a flexible exchange rate policy which aimed at promoting price competitiveness of the national economy.[23] This policy relied successively on the targeting of the real exchange rate and more recently on a managed floating of the exchange rate without prior announcement of its path. The exchange rate was as such determined on the interbank market, which is the market on which commercial banks carry out their transactions at freely negotiated rates. The exchange system permitted the convertibility of the dinar for current account operations since Tunisia had accepted the obligations of Article VIII, sections 2(a), 3 and 4 of the IMF in 1993. The ambition of the authorities within the framework of their program of reforms was to liberalize the capital account.[24] As we can see in Figure 14.6 below,[25] the contribution of the exchange rate policy to the strengthening of national economic competitiveness was aided by the downward trend of the real exchange rate of the dinar over the long term. Thus, since 1980, the evolution of the exchange rate of the dinar has shown a real downward trend. Insofar as the nominal depreciation is accompanied by an appropriate monetary and budgetary policy, it did not lead to a rise in inflation.

Figure 14.6. Tunisia: Evolution of real effective exchange rate index (base 100 = 2000)[26]

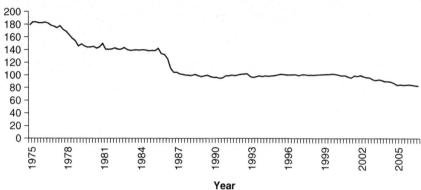

Trade policy

Tunisia is a member of the WTO. Conscious of the small size of its domestic market, Tunisian authorities made the progressive integration into the world economy a major pillar of their strategy of economic growth and job creation. What is interesting in the globalization strategy retained by the authorities is not so much the affirmation of this option, but their recognition that it is through the expansion of exports and not that of imports that the benefits of its integration into the world economy will accrue. It is this wise vision that inspired the conduct of the liberalization process of trade undertaken by the authorities. The goal of this liberalization process was therefore to first stimulate exports. Tunisia's trade policy is as such made of a careful blend of a strong commitment to the promotion of exports and to the development of a local industry substituting imports. It is therefore a growth strategy based on a mixture of the promotion of exports and the substitution of imports. This mixture enabled trade policy to be both a powerful instrument of stimulation of demand addressed to the economy and a contribution to the building of the national productive capacity, thanks to adequately calibrated competition from imports. Several countries, particularly in sub-Saharan Africa, are still unable to find this equilibrium between the two important contributions of trade policy and almost always give preeminence to the second (competition from imports) to the detriment of the first (stimulation of demand addressed to the economy).

At the level of liberalization of imports, an important stage in this process was the signing in 1995 of the Association Agreement with the European Union. Within the framework of this agreement, customs duties on products of List 1, composed of capital goods and inputs not produced locally, were to be cancelled starting in 1996. Those of products of List 2, comprised of intermediary consumptions and raw materials not produced locally, were also to be cancelled starting in 2001. The canceling of customs duties of products of List 3, comprised of locally made goods and goods likely to be exposed to competition, had to be spread over a period of 12 years, ending in 2007. Customs duties were also cancelled on products of List 4, which comprised of locally made industrial products. In exchange, all Tunisian industrial products were to enjoy duty-free access to the European Union market. Overall, this agreement did not concern

Table 14.2. Tunisia: Evolution of MFN Tariffs, 1994–2005[27]

	MFN tariff, 1994		MFN tariff, 2004		MFN tariff, 2005		EU preferential tariff, 2005	
	UITR	ITR	UITR	ITR	UITR	ITR	UITR	ITR
Total	30.7	0.43	32.7	0–200	31.7	0–150	18	0–150
Per WTO definition								
Agriculture	35	10–43	69.3	0–200	66.8	0–150	63.6	0–150
Living animals	38.5	10–43	97.4	20–180	91.8	20–150	91.8	20–150
Dairy products	23.5	15–43	92.1	15–180	95.3	15–150	94.2	0–150
Coffee, tea, cocoa, sugar, etc.	38	15–43	73.1	0–200	72.1	0–150	67.7	0–150
Flowers and plants	27.3	20–43	37.3	0–180	36.9	0–150	34.7	0–150
Fruits and vegetables	42.1	15–43	104.3	0–200	96.8	0–150	94.6	0–150
Cereals	29.0	15–43	45.3	0–100	45.3	0–100	45.1	0–100
Oleaginous grains and fatty products	30.6	15–43	45.2	10–200	42.6	10–150	38.0	0–150
Beverages and beers	41.1	20–43	52.2	20–100	51.7	20–100	47.9	6.6–100
Tobacco	36.0	25–43	27.1	22–43	27.1	22–43	19.0	0–43
Other agricultural products	27.4	17–43	29.8	0–150	28.0	0–150	21.8	0–150
Non-agricultural products (except petrol)	30.1	0–43	23.6	0–43	23.0	0–43	6.3	0–43
Fish and fishing products	40.2	17–43	40.2	0–43	40.1	0–43	40.0	0–43
Precious stones and metals, mineral products	29.9	0–43	25.7	0–43	25.6	0–43	5.3	0–14.2
Metals	28.0	0–43	20.4	0–43	20.4	0–43	40.0	0–14.2
Chemical products and photography equipment	24.7	0–43	15.5	0–43	15.5	0–43	2.1	0–27
Plastic leather shoes and traveling items	34.2	17–43	32.8	10–43	32.8	10–43	7.6	0–14.2
Paper and wood pulp furniture	35.0	0–43	31.4	0–43	31.6	0–43	8.2	0–14.2
Textiles and clothing	39.1	17–43	35.4	0–43	31.1	0–43	9.1	0–43
Transport equipment	27.2	0–43	18.3	0–43	18.3	0–43	4.1	0–14.2
Non-electric machines	19.9	0–43	12.4	0–43	12.5	0–43	2.7	0–14.2
Electric machines	31.2	10–43	23.9	0–43	24.0	0–43	5.1	0–14.2
Non-agricultural products	29.9	0–43	23.4	0–43	23.7	0–43	4.2	0–14.2
Per CITI sector								
Agriculture, hunting, forestry, fishing	34.1	10–43	66.3	0–200	61.9	0–150	60.5	0–150
Extractive industries	22.9	0–43	13.9	0–43	13.6	0–43	1.5	0–14.2
Manufacturing industries	30.7	0–43	30.8	0–200	30.0	0–150	15.5	0–150
Per degree of processing								
Raw materials	28.9	0–43	48.3	0–200	45.3	0–150	41.6	0–150
Semi-finished products	29.1	0–43	23.5	0–150	21.5	0–150	7.2	0–150
Finished products	31.9	0–43	33.5	0–180	33.3	0–150	17.9	0–150

MFN: Most Favored Nation
UITR: Unweighted import tariff rate
ITR: Import tariff rate

farm products, a sector considered by Tunisia as very important to its economy. In order to strengthen its integration in the world economy, Tunisia also signed a number of preferential trade agreements, among which I can mention the agreement creating the Greater Arab Free Trade Area (which became effective in 1998), the Arab–Mediterranean Free Trade Agreement (2004), the free trade agreement signed with the European Free Trade Association (2004) and the agreement of the Arab Maghreb Union (1989).[28]

Table 14.2 above describes the evolution of the structure of customs duties of the Most Favored Nation (MFN) applied by Tunisia. It shows that the successful liberalization strategy pursued by Tunisia may be qualified as heterodox, like those pursued by countries such as South Korea, Mauritius and several other countries which have recently achieved some remarkable economic successes. This is because, on the one hand, the level of tariffs appeared relatively high (above 15 per cent, which is considered the peak of tariffs), and on the other hand, customs duties on farm products were clearly higher than those of manufactured goods. I can also observe that even in the group of manufactured goods, customs duties on consumer goods were higher than those on intermediate and capital goods. Such a tariff structure gives the advantage of not penalizing investments by giving an acceptable level of protection to locally based industries.

In order to better prepare the economy to face foreign competition in the context of globalization, the authorities conceived and successfully implemented an upgrading program for the national economy. In its industrial sector,[29] reflecting once more the priority given to the development of the national productive tissue, this upgrading program, which started in 1996, aimed at preparing and adapting national companies and their environment to the demands of trade liberalization, by seeking to improve their performances and competitiveness in order that they should be able to face foreign competition with possibilities of succeeding. Within the framework of this program, the government financed, for industrial companies and those supplying services to industry, the costs linked to modernizing companies' productive capacities, organization and management methods, training and development efforts, quality compliance and certification, market research and the search for partners for industrial companies. According to the seventh survey carried out by the authorities, the upgrade program had a positive impact on the competitiveness of firms. In fact, 79 per cent, 73 per cent and 61 per cent of firms respectively believed that the upgrade program had a positive impact on product quality, productivity and human resources.

At the level of promoting exports, the Association Agreement of 1995 with the European Union offered Tunisia preference and contingent tariffs on some farm products, particularly olive oil, meat, spices and fruits and vegetables, wine, tinned fruits and vegetables, and tinned fish and shellfish. Concerning non-farm products, the agreement further facilitated the entry of Tunisian products into European Union markets. Besides negotiations leading to reducing tariff barriers which Tunisian products faced on foreign markets, there also existed a set of domestic mechanisms aimed at favoring exports. As such, depending on whether the company was "totally exporting" or "partially exporting," "resident" or "nonresident," the code of incentives to investments and the foreign exchange regulations provided specific advantages at the level of taxes, customs and access to foreign exchange. Table 14.3 below describes the advantages granted according to the statutes of the company. The authorities also set up a number of structures which offered services to exporting companies in the domains of financing, insurance, export guarantees, promotion of exports and support to exporters for marketing.[30]

Table 14.3. Tunisia: Advantages granted exporting companies according to their status, 2005[31]

Privileges	Nonresident totally exporting companies	Resident totally exporting companies	Resident partially exporting companies
Obligatory repatriation of export earnings	No	Yes	Yes
Exemption of taxes on benefits	100% (10 years), then 50% later	100% (10 years), then 50% later	Only on benefits from export revenue: 100% (10 years), then 50% later
Exoneration of customs duties on capital good and inputs	Yes	Yes	Yes
Exoneration of VAT and consumption levies on inputs and capital goods	Yes	Yes	Yes

Another trade policy measure which contributed much to Tunisia's economic performance, particularly by stimulating demand, is the compensation scheme. This scheme required foreign companies supplying the Tunisian market with vehicles to devote a percentage of their turnover in Tunisia to the buying of automobile parts made in Tunisia. Observers acknowledge that this measure played an important role in the development of the Tunisian mechanical industry.[32] Presently, this sector has about 553 companies and provides more than thirty thousand jobs. Among these companies, 90 are totally exporting companies. The production of this sector includes automobile parts (clutch discs, suspensions and brakes, transmission shafts), trailers and tractor-trailers, dumpsters and bodyworks, machine-made mechanical parts and prefabricated metallic constructions. This sector's exports, which go mainly to France, Italy, Germany and Spain, increased from 540 million dinars in 2002 to 1.4 billion dinars in 2006, an increase of 159 per cent.[33]

Competition and regulation policy

The set of economic policy measures implemented also contained measures aimed at promoting competition and imposing obligations on economic agents through regulation. Concerning regulation, one of the domains of intervention of the state was the regulation of prices: as such, a set of laws guaranteed the principle of price freedom – that is, prices are determined through a free game of competition on markets. However, the regulatory framework also excluded some vital commodities from the field of competition. For these commodities, prices were subsidized.[34] Commodities excluded from competition also included goods supplied by the monopolies controlled by the state and goods which are not naturally subjected to competition. In the Tunisian context, such a policy contributed to social cohesion, which was, as we have seen, an important operating goal of the Tunisian economic policy.

The use of price to regulate supply and demand with a view to supporting production was also remarkable in Tunisia. Thus, some analysts of the Tunisian economic policy also noted that "this complex agricultural/industrial/price circuit, which in Europe was set up in a century, worked in a few years in the young republic, illustrating the efficient manner in which things were carried out in terms of endogenous industrialization."[35]

Exhortation

Pleas to economic agents launched by authorities for them to adopt a favorable behavior in the pursuit of the economic goals of the nation were also a very useful instrument in the implementation of economic policy. This was the case, for example, with making consumers modify their behavior to favor local products. Thus, campaigns on the "consume Tunisian" theme were organized to inform consumers and sensitize them to the benefits which would accrue for the national economy from changing their behavior in favor of increased demand for local products.

Policy to improve the attractiveness of the territory

A policy of territorial attractiveness strengthens efforts aimed at influencing the preferences of economic agents (producers and consumers) for the national economy, which is, as we have seen, an important operating goal of economic policy. As such, Tunisia had a real policy of promoting the attractiveness of the territory among foreign investors. Thus, the foreign investment promotion agency FIPA-Tunisia, a public body created in 1995 under the trusteeship of the Ministry of Development and International Cooperation, played an important role in the implementation of this policy. It was particularly in charge of providing the necessary support, especially in terms of contacts, information, advice, accompaniment and support, to foreign investors and to promote foreign investment in Tunisia. To this effect, it had a vast network of representations in the world, in Paris, Cologne, Milan, Brussels, London and Montreal. It organized information seminars abroad on investment opportunities in Tunisia and also participated in exhibitions abroad. Within the framework of its activities, it informed foreign investors on these opportunities and the main reasons which make Tunisia a privileged site for foreign direct investments. It also provided, in abundant documentation elaborated in several languages, all useful information on the Tunisian economy, human resources, infrastructure and investment incentives.[36] These efforts aimed at increasing the attractiveness of the territory were not only for foreign investors. It also targeted nationals, whether residents or nonresidents. Different facilities were as such granted to Tunisians abroad with the aim of attracting their savings toward the country so that they should invest there.

Public–private partnerships

Tunisian economic policy also relied on important efforts to encourage public–private partnerships in the financing of different sectors of the national economy.

The Role of Foreign Aid in Tunisian Economic Policy

Tunisia resorted to foreign aid from different multilateral and bilateral sources. Her main multilateral partners are the African Development Bank and the World Bank. Her main bilateral partners are the European Union, France, Germany, Italy. Tunisia is also a model in terms of using possibilities that foreign aid can offer a country. Contrary to the experience of several countries, where foreign aid determines orientations and the implementation of national economic policy, in the case of Tunisia, foreign aid helped to finance the economic policy defined independently by the country within the framework of the five-year development plans I dwelt on earlier. That is, donors did not decide which economic policy the country should pursue in exchange for their aid, but the country, after choosing within the framework of an essentially domestic process which economic policy it intended to implement, later decided what type of external financing (amount, source, purely financial and not political conditions) it would need to implement it. I believe this type of partnership has several profound lessons for the rest of the continent.

Thus, I have demonstrated the broad orientations of economic policy which helped Tunisia to achieve the satisfactory economic performances it enjoyed prior to the revolution. The conclusion I draw from this analysis is that this economic policy showed extraordinary vision; first, at the level of strategic choices in terms of the various strategic goals to be pursued, but it also showed creativity, a capacity to adapt and an exemplary voluntarism in terms of using the different instruments of economic policy. This examination has enabled us to better realize that the ingredients necessary for a good economic policy are beyond the simple prescription of liberalization that many recommend to countries. Economic policy linkages are infinitely more complex than that. The most important is at two levels: first at the level of anchoring goals on employment and economic growth, followed by the implementation of a set of measures to strengthen the national productive capacity and stimulate demand addressed to national companies.

It is obvious that such a review cannot be exhaustive insofar as certain specificities peculiar to Tunisia will surely not fail to escape the foreign observer that I am. I have identified the fundamental orientations which inspired the economic policy in Tunisia, and the manner in which they were expressed in the actions that were implemented.

After this examination, two questions immediately come to mind: first, that of why other countries have not been able to identify and implement the same policies. In other words, what is peculiar to Tunisia that could as such have favored the emergence of a national consensus around an economic policy of such good quality? Second, that of whether other countries can adopt the same policies for their development. I will now try to answer these two questions.

Why Was Tunisia Able to Elaborate and Implement Such a Successful Economic Policy?

In fact, it is extremely difficult to answer the question of why some countries, and not others, succeed in defining a good economic policy and successfully implementing it. The research field interested in this question has already produced voluminous literature without really exhausting the subject. This literature seems to be satisfied with attributing the economic success of countries to the quality of their institutions, which it mainly defines as the existence of adequate checks and balances among powers, the practice of democracy in government and the respect of property rights.[37] As I have said earlier, this explanation is insufficient because these attributes cannot be the only ones to bring about economic growth and development. Even equipped with good institutions as defined in this literature, a country still needs to have a good economic policy strategy, particularly in the present context of globalization. However, it seems that by extending the reasoning contained in current literature a little bit further, we find a place for institutions among factors that finally explain why a country succeeds in choosing a good economic policy. In fact, if we admit that in the absence of good economic policies the economic situation of the country will deteriorate, citizens will be unhappy and consequently will seek to change the government during the next elections, then the existence of good institutions forces the government to define and implement good economic policies in order to satisfy its citizens and remain in power. If we follow this line of reasoning, the only way for a government to remain in power consists in satisfying citizens by contributing to the improvement of their standard of living, thanks to its economic policy. In fact, in this case, good institutions lead to the adoption of good economic policies and strategies. Equipped with the above line of reasoning, I can effectively explain the choice of good policies in Tunisia through the quality of institutions of economic management that the country enjoyed. In fact, most studies of the quality of institutions in developing countries usually ranked Tunisia high, especially in respect of the primacy of the law, political stability, the effectiveness of the government and the fight against corruption. However, these studies also showed that the areas where progress was still to be made in Tunisia concerned political inclusiveness and participation of stakeholders.

If good economic policies find their source in the quality of institutions, where do good institutions themselves come from? This is the question to be asked immediately after having answered the previous one. Researchers are mobilized in finding an adequate answer to this question. All attempts up to this moment have attributed the origin of good institutions to a combination of favorable historical factors and the perceptiveness of leaders who knew how to lead their country toward good institutions at particular moments in the history of their country. This is only a first response and needs to be developed further.

Future Challenges

As the 2011 revolution amply demonstrated, Tunisia had achieved much in terms of economic and social progress since independence, but much more still remained to be done.

Tunisia shall therefore continue to build on its past successes to tackle the daunting challenges which still lie ahead. Going still further to search for new opportunities of production and expansion of demand addressed to the economy, with a view toward further stimulating job creation and economic growth. This approach is necessary since many new jobs are needed, particularly for the increasing young graduates of higher education. Apparently, the progress achieved thus far was not sufficient, to the extent that unemployment, particularly among young graduates, is a serious problem today. The 11th five-year development plan and orientations for the 2007–16 decade has already anticipated these priorities well.

Concerning Tunisian supply, means should be sought to significantly increase the level of investment by companies for building the production capacity of the economy. A 2008 study of the World Bank showed that the level of domestic investment was still low compared to similar countries.[38] As a matter of fact, domestic investment did not follow the boom of foreign direct investments that the country had experienced.

As far as demand is concerned, and more specifically foreign demand, it seems that a particular effort must be made to further diversify its sources. In this context, it will be necessary to discover the means and the products to be sold to dynamic markets like those of Asian countries, which have been experiencing rapid economic growth. Other African countries offer an important source of trade relations which should be fully developed, particularly taking into consideration the strong economic growth that some among them have been experiencing for some years now. The message here is that, while consolidating the achievements of European demand, which currently represents more than eighty per cent of foreign demand addressed to Tunisia, and which also experiences a comparatively slower growth, efforts should be doubled in the years ahead toward searching and discovering new sources of demand. In this quest, partners outside the European Union should not only be seen as a source of demand. Opportunities to benefit from their technology should also be explored to strengthen Tunisian supply.

Summary

In this chapter, I dwelt on one of the most successful experiences of economic policy on the continent, the case of Tunisia. This country was able to quickly move to the rank of emerging country thanks to a coherent, creative and voluntary economic policy, whose main orientations conform to the conceptual framework developed in this book. Despite past achievements, the road ahead is still bumpy. Tunisia has to also give an economic content to the political revolution achieved in early 2011.

Chapter Fifteen

POST-APARTHEID SOUTH AFRICA'S ECONOMIC POLICY: LESSONS FROM A SUCCESSFUL EXPERIENCE

"Because development brings great structural change that affects different interests in different ways, the achievement of our goals requires of us the capacity to mobilise a highly complex society in pursuit of broad national objectives. It means building a broad partnership of major social forces."

Nelson Mandela, address to the World Economic Forum,
Davos, January 29, 1999

"[…] I thought it right to mention this experience as it puts a proper context to the debates we must conduct on our use of public money. As we address the necessary questions of deficits, interest and exchange rates, inflation, labour market flexibility, the affordability of social welfare systems and many others, we dare not forget that the purpose of it all, and the mandate which brings us to this house, is the continued and sustained improvement in the lives of each and every South African […]"

Nelson Mandela, opening of the President's Budget Debate,
Cape Town, March 2, 1999

"This year opened with the inspiring news that our people were highly optimistic about their future and the future of our country, ranking eighth in the world on the optimism index. Gallup International, which issued this report, said we have three times more optimists than pessimists, and that the optimism figure had doubled even since 2002. […] The results obtained by Gallup International have been confirmed by a recent domestic poll conducted by Markinor. According to this poll, 65% of our people believe that the country is going in the right direction. 84% think that our country holds out a happy future for all racial groups. 71% believe that government is performing well. […] With regard to the economy, late last month the Grant Thornton International Business Owners Survey reported that 80% of South Africa's business owners are optimistic about the year ahead, making them the third most optimistic internationally. Again last month, the First National Bank and the Bureau for Economic Research reported that the consumer confidence index is at its highest in 25 years. […] What all these figures signify is that our people are firmly convinced that our country has entered its Age of Hope. They are convinced that we have created the conditions to achieve more rapid progress towards the realisation of their dreams. They are certain that we are indeed a winning nation. While we must indeed celebrate the high levels of optimism that inspire our people, who are convinced that our country has entered its Age of Hope, we must also focus on and pay particular attention to the implications of those high levels of optimism with regard to what we must do together to achieve the objective of a better life for all our people. We have to respond to the hopes of the people by doing everything possible to meet their expectations."[1]

Thabo Mbeki, president of South Africa, State of the
Nation Address, Pretoria, February 3, 2006

By the time the government headed by President Nelson Mandela got to power in South Africa, in April 1994, after the first democratic elections in the history of the country, the South African economy was already in a process of decline. Income per capita had dropped every year since 1982. Dominated by mineral exploitation[2] and gold production in particular, the primary sector had experienced great difficulties partially due to a drop in yields, a drop in the price of gold and in its international status, resulting from a long process which stemmed from the demonetization of gold following the abandonment of the gold exchange standard in the international monetary system, and some structural adjustments taking place in the subregion which contributed to the increase in the price of labor of black workers in the mines.[3] The manufacturing sector, which existed then thanks to very high protection, had also started a decline, which expressed the impact of the increasing isolation of the South African economy from the world economy. Thus, between 1983 and 1993, the gross investment rate had dropped from about 26 per cent of GDP to about 15 per cent of GDP. With a deficit of more than 9 per cent of GDP in 1993, public finances had also deteriorated considerably, expressing an expansion of different programs that the apartheid government, under the effect of domestic and foreign pressures, had attempted to implement to better resist change. The unemployment rate was high and could have been close to 45 per cent of the working population.[4] The apartheid policy had also created one of the most inegalitarian societies of the world in South Africa.

Since its return to democracy in April 1994, South Africa has made significant economic progress, which some observers have not hesitated to qualify as a real miracle. The different aspects of this progress are beginning to be amply documented in literature.[5] However, though current literature illustrates this progress, particularly that achieved at the level of economic growth, employment, public finance management, foreign trade liberalization, monetary policy and inflation control, exchange regime management, attraction of foreign direct investments, provision of basic social services to the population, and challenges left particularly at the level of employment, this literature is still scanty in terms of a systematic analysis of the economic policy underlying this remarkable success.[6]

My goal in this chapter is, therefore, to contribute to a better understanding of the economic performance of post-Apartheid South Africa by revealing the major orientations which underlie the economic policy elaborated and implemented. Therefore, my aim here is not so much to come back to a presentation of the economic results of post-Apartheid South Africa, or to attempt a prospective analysis of major challenges of the future,[7] but particularly to trace the outline of the economic policy which was implemented by South African government to attain the impressive results that the country obtained up to this point. I will therefore see that this economic policy is a perfect illustration of what I have described throughout this book.

Brief Outline of Post-apartheid South Africa's Economic Performance

As I said earlier, South Africa has made significant progress since the end of apartheid and its accession to democracy. At the level of growth, the country more than doubled its annual average growth rate. Though the annual average growth rate of the real GDP was about 1.25 per cent between 1980 and 1994, it attained about 3 per cent between 1995 and 2003, 4.9 per cent in 2006 and 4.8 per cent in 2007. Despite a difficult year in 2012 (marked by some of the most challenging industrial actions in the mining sector), the economy grew by 2.5 per cent in 2012, and is expected to reach 2.7 per cent in 2013 and 3.8 per cent in 2015. The South African economy has expanded by about 83 per cent since 1994. In terms of GDP per capita, its growth attained 3.4 per cent in 2004, 3.7 per cent in 2005 and 3.6 per cent in 2006, whereas it registered a drop until the mid-1990s. Income per capita increased from 3,000 US dollars in 1994 to 4,500 US dollars in 2012, which represents about a 40 per cent increase. Generally, since 2000, South Africa's economic growth is very much aligned with the trend in other emerging economies, except China and India, which have grown significantly faster, as shown in Figure 15.1 below.[8]

Public finances were rehabilitated to the extent that the budget is now on a more stable footing. This rehabilitation of public finances also contributed to a relaxation of interest rates. Inflation was successfully curbed. Though it was in two digits, at about 10–15 per cent at the beginning of the 1980s, it dropped to about 3.4 per cent in 2005. The fiscal deficit for 2012/13 was 5.2 per cent of GDP, and is projected to fall to 3.1 per cent of GDP

Figure 15.1. Growth rate of South Africa and some emerging economies[9]

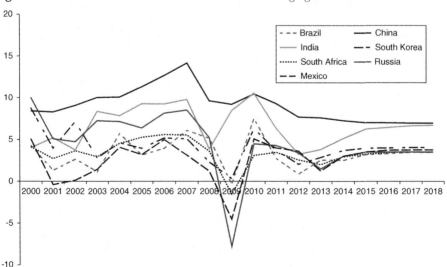

in 2015/16. The sovereign risk of South Africa was also reduced considerably, which had positive effects on the country's borrowing cost. This evolution was favored by the implementation of a careful debt policy which made public debt drop from 43.5 per cent of the GDP in 1994 to 31.3 per cent of the GDP in 2007 and, according to projections, would stabilize around the prudent range of 40 per cent of the GDP over the medium term. There was also a modest employment growth which increased from about 1.5 per cent per annum from 1980–93 to about 1.75 per cent from 1995–2003. Between 2000 and 2004, about 280,000 new jobs were created. This performance improved given that the number of new jobs created reached 500,000 in 2006. Despite this performance, the unemployment rate did not change much, standing at 26.4 per cent in 2006, and 24.7 per cent in the third quarter of 2013.[10] This high unemployment rate continues to be a challenge to the country.

All these successes were obtained at the same time the country was increasing its integration into the world economy thanks to the implementation of important measures of trade liberalization.[11] On the eve of the ANC presidential elections, which took place during the 52nd National Conference of the party in December 2007, the London daily *Financial Times*, particularly known for its conservatism when it concerns Africa, described South Africa's economy in recent years in the following terms:

> The country's economy continues to shine after eight years of growth under Mr. Mbeki's stewardship. [...] Even as the US and UK cut interest rates, South Africa is trying to tame a boom that is evident as much in rising consumer prices and unchecked credit growth as in a surging stock market. The South African Reserve Bank last week raised its benchmark interest rate for the fourth time this year to 11 per cent, marking a cumulative 400 basis point rise in the past 18 months. [...] Ahead of the 2010 Football World Cup, the government is spending an estimated $70bn (€48bn, £33bn) on infrastructure improvements. Contracts for highways, rail lines, power plants, fibre optic networks, and stadiums are pouring forth from Pretoria, and are, in turn, leading to unprecedented corporate capital expenditure programmes. [...] The Johannesburg Stock Exchange has outperformed most exchanges this year, rising 25 per cent in the past 12 months to 29,388.65.[12]

An important constituent of progress concerns poverty reduction and impressive progress in terms of access to social services of a previously disadvantaged population. As a matter of fact, in domains such as water supply, sanitation, housing, electricity, communications, education and health, progress has been remarkable. For example, the proportion of South African households having access to electricity increased from 32 per cent in 1994 to more than 73 per cent at the beginning of the 2000s and stood at 85.3 per cent in 2013. 90.8 per cent of households had access to potable water and 76.9 per cent had access to improved sanitation in 2013. The government also set up a social security system ensuring cover to all South Africans. The adult literacy rate increased from 69.6 per cent in 1995 to 74.2 per cent in 2005. Also, although reducing inequality remains a challenge, progress is being made in this area. Thus, the number of black people and women in senior management has increased from less than 10 per cent in the 1990s to over 40 per cent in 2013.[13] Between 2000 and 2005, the number of blacks earning a monthly wage of between 4,000 and 12,000 rands experienced an increase of about 1.1 million.[14]

Another important result is the increase in credibility. In fact, as we will see below, the quest for credibility appears to have been one of the specific goals of economic policy set by the government. And efforts in this domain seem to have been rewarded. South Africa today has a respected democracy in Africa and the world. The signs of this increase in credibility are numerous. The country was given the organization of the 2010 FIFA World Cup, one of the major sporting events of the planet. South Africa was also part of the group of five major emerging powers, including Brazil, China, India and Mexico, which regularly participated in the G8 meetings at the invitation of the member states of the G8. With a view toward increasing the representativity of the G8, at one point the idea was discussed to expand it to include these five countries and transform the G8 into a G13. This idea was superseded when the G20 gained prominence in the wake of the financial crisis which started in 2007. The OECD, which regroups developed and democratic countries, also announced that it had launched the process of a strengthened partnership with South Africa, which may lead to the admission of the country as member of the OECD. A further sign of the increased credibility of South African economic policy is the admission of the country to the BRICS group, the powerful grouping of the world's leading emerging economies, namely Brazil, Russia, India, China and South Africa. Its first summit took place in Yekaterinburg, Russia in 2008, where the leaders of the first four countries formally declared the membership of the BRIC economic bloc. South Africa joined the bloc in 2010, resulting in BRICS. BRICS aims to promote peace, security, development and cooperation, and a more equitable and fair world. BRICS represents about 43 per cent of the world's population, roughly 20 per cent of global GDP, and combined foreign reserves estimated at 4.4 trillion US dollars. South Africa's BRICS membership is expected to contribute to increased foreign direct investments in the country and in Africa, and also promote regional integration in the continent. At the Fifth BRICS Summit, which South Africa hosted in Durban in March 2013, important decisions were made by the BRICS leaders, including strengthening engagement with the African continent and the establishment of a BRICS development bank to support infrastructure development in the developing world.

Also, despite a very challenging year in 2012, the country managed to achieve some good economic results. In addition to the positive growth outcome (see above), many other events reaffirmed the maturity and credibility of the country's economic system. Thus, the country ended the year with about eighty thousand more jobs created than it started. In his 2013 budget speech, Pravin Gordhan, finance minister of South Africa, announced plans by businesses to invest about 71.5 billion rands in 2013 and in the medium term, in spite of the difficult events in the mining sector which the country had experienced in 2012. The number of tourists arrivals in South Africa also registered a substantial increase in 2012 of more than 10 per cent, with more than nine million tourists visiting the country, while the global tourism market increased only by about half.

Post-apartheid South Africa's Economic Policy

The role of the state in the economy

Before examining the broad outlines of the economic policy itself, a bit of deviation is necessary to clarify one of the fundamental options of economic policy. As such, the South African government acknowledged that the state has an important role to play in the economy. The state must work in harmony with the private sector to improve upon the well-being of the population. The state always practiced great transparency on this option. Even President Mandela, when he addressed the World Economic Forum in Davos in 1991, though the ANC was not yet in power, asserted that when he took over, the economic policy of the ANC government would be founded on the principles of a mixed economy in which the state and the private sector would work together, hand in hand. This option was maintained by his successors, Thabo Mbeki, Kgalema Motlanthe and Jacob Zuma.

Formulation and implementation of economic policy

The process of formulation and implementation of economic policy in South Africa reveals a high level of sophistication, characterized particularly by a high mastery of major economic issues, a high level of transparency and a well-established participative approach. This participative approach relies on a close collaboration between the state, the business community, trade union representatives and civil society. The National Economic Development and Labour Council is the place par excellence where these different actors gather to exchange ideas in order to contribute to the formulation of the national economic policy. This participative approach and the quality of economic policy which results from it are facilitated by the fact that the ANC, the party in power, had a long tradition of internal discussions on issues of economic policy, even before its accession to power.[15] The ANC has a Department of Economic Planning, which is effective in terms of economic reflection. Its goal is to inform and train ANC officials on economic issues, promote the effective participation of ANC members in the formulation of the national economic policy, as well as to collect and treat economic intelligence. Trevor Manuel, whose success as minister of finance in managing the South African economy is recognized, was for long the head of this department. The formulation and implementation of economic policy in South Africa also benefited from the expertise of different structures. Thus, different institutions in the trade union world, such as COSATU, the most important and powerful confederation of trade unions, and the National Union of Mineworkers, the ally of the ANC, all developed a real interest in economic policy issues. Organizations of the business community, universities and diverse structures of the state such as the central bank also developed formidable capacities in terms of reflection on issues of economic policy.

The national economic policy which results from consultations among all stakeholders is often contained in a succession of economic programs adopted by the government and made public. Thus, apart from the Ready to Govern program which was elaborated by the ANC in 1992, five other programs have been successively adopted since 1994: the Reconstruction and Development Program (RDP; 1994–96), Growth, Employment and Redistribution (GEAR; 1996–2000), the Accelerated and Shared Growth Initiative for

South Africa (ASGISA; since 2000), and more recently the New Growth Path and the National Development Plan adopted in 2012.

Goals targeted by economic policy in South Africa

Throughout this book, I have demonstrated the importance of a conceptual framework clearly articulating the final, intermediate and operating goals for the success of economic policy. Examination of the South African economic policy reveals that it established a set of three fundamental goals: eradicate poverty, create employment and reduce inequality. As such, a goal linked to the reduction of inequality is added to the usual final goals of job creation and growth,[16] which I have identified in this book as key fundamental final goals of any effective economic policy. This seems logical, considering the specific situation of South Africa characterized by an unusually high inequality of income. In my opinion, these goals are at the basis of all South African economic policy. Concerning employment, President Mbeki said, "One will not be exaggerating to say that, given its impact on every thing else we do as a nation, including crime prevention, reconciliation and the very survival of our democracy, the jobs summit is perhaps the most important event since our first democratic elections; an important launching pad for a determined national drive as we move into the 21st century."[17]

The concentration on these three fundamental goals is clearly visible in the economic programs that the country has elaborated and implemented up to now. GEAR, for example, contained quantified projections on the real annual growth of the GDP, employment and on the number of new jobs which would be created every year during the period of its implementation. Concerning employment, GEAR projected that the number of new jobs created each year increased from 126,000 in 1996 to 252,000 in 1997, 246,000 in 1998, 320,000 in 1999 and 409,000 in 2000. The idea of establishing quantified goals in this manner is already an important step toward realism and the concreteness of the government's intentions in terms of economic policy. In the national development plan Vision 2030, the goal of job creation is viewed as being inextricably linked to that of promoting strong economic growth.

To attain this triple goal, economic policy seems to rest on an optimal combination of efforts targeting, on the one hand, the strengthening of the national productive capacity and the productivity of national companies and, on the other hand, the stimulation of the demand addressed to the economy. This double concern is actually clear in elaborated and implemented concrete measures of economic policy. In the rest of this chapter, I will attempt to reveal the major economic policy orientations that the authorities established in order to attain this double goal, whose achievement appears to be the stepping stone toward economic growth, job creation and the reduction of inequality and poverty.

South Africa's Major Economic Policy Operating Orientations

The search for credibility and sustainability

This is perhaps the most important of the operating orientations, and seems to have constantly inspired the definition and conduct of the economic policy of South Africa since the end of apartheid. My examination of this economic policy actually reveals that, from the point of view of South African leaders, the impact on credibility and sustainability is one of the most important criteria for appreciating economic policy measures. Thus, the influence of this search for credibility appears evident in the manner in which different instruments are used, whether it is budgetary policy, monetary policy, trade policy, industrial policy or even tax policy, to mention just a few examples.

Let us take the example of budgetary policy. When the ANC government was installed in 1994 following the victory of the party in the first democratic elections, it had several calls in favor of an expansionary budgetary policy. The argument advanced was that such an orientation was necessary to boost the economy and improve access to basic social services of the population, which were previously disadvantaged under the apartheid regime. At the same time, the supply of foreign resources was also abundant, as many international lenders were ready to lend to South Africa at that time. However, conscious of the negative consequences that weak control of public finances may have on the credibility of all its economic policies, the government opted for a policy of drastic reduction of the budgetary deficit. To the government, the immediate risk which would have resulted from the inadequate control of public finances was linked to the intervention of international lenders, with the consequence being loss of credibility and sovereignty over national economic policy. It is to remedy this risk that *Ready to Govern*, an ANC economic policy document, asserted in 1992 that relations with international financial institutions will be conducted so as to "protect the integrity of domestic policy formulation and promote the interests of the South African population and the economy."[18]

Besides the restrictive orientation that it gave budgetary policy, the pursuit of the goal of credibility influenced the conduct of budgetary policy in three other ways. The rate of reduction of the deficit was ambitious. Though the budgetary deficit reached 9.5 per cent of the GDP during the 1992/1993 fiscal year and 8 per cent of the GDP during the 1993/1994 fiscal year, the RDP aimed at bringing it down to 4.5 per cent of the GDP in five years despite the state of the economy at that time. However, upon his appointment to the post of minister of finance, Trevor Manuel, who had occupied the post of head of the Department of Economic Planning of the ANC, established more ambitious goals under GEAR – that is, 4 per cent of the GDP for the 1996/1997 fiscal year, 3.5 per cent for the 1997/1998 fiscal year, 3 per cent of the GDP for the 1998/1999 fiscal year and 3 per cent of the GDP for the 1999/2000 fiscal year. Credibility also influenced the composition of deficit reduction. The government also decided to obtain the desired reduction of budgetary deficit by depending solely on improving the management of public spending – that is, without increasing the level of taxes. This improvement of public spending management included a recollection and reduction of certain expenditures. Thus, defense, economic services and the general administration saw their expenses reduced.[19] In fact, economic research carried out to date concludes that public finance rehabilitation is more credible in the eyes of economic agents, and is therefore more sustainable when it depends on measures aimed at improving the management of public expenditures than on measures aimed at increasing public revenues, particularly through increasing taxes.

Finally, the government also counted on the composition of the team in charge of managing public finances to strengthen the credibility of its action. Thus, although the ANC had several competent managers, it was to Derek Keys, once minister of economic affairs and later minister of finance in the previous government, that President Mandela chose to entrust the Ministry of Finance of the first post-apartheid government. When he resigned a few months later in September 1994 for personal reasons, Chris Liebenberg, a respected banker in the business community (he was chief executive officer of Nedcor, one of the biggest South African banks), was chosen by President Mandela to succeed him. Despite the presence of these personalities in the National Party, the party which ruled South Africa during the apartheid period, their experience and competence were well established. Their appointments to the important post of minister of finance enabled the government to credit its economic policy and win the confidence of economic agents. In 1996, when Chris Liebenberg resigned,[20] President Mandela appointed Trevor Manuel as minister of finance. Today, he is considered one of the best finance ministers that post-apartheid South Africa has had, due to his very successful management of the country's economy (see the economic performance of South Africa above). These examples really show how the South African authorities used all the means at their disposal to credit their economic policy.

Another domain where the search for credibility appears to be one of the major goals which underlay government action is that of the monetary policy. As already emphasized in this book, I consider that, from the point of view of monetary policy, the credibility of authorities is strengthened if monetary authorities – that is, mainly the central bank – enjoy a certain level of independence in the conduct of monetary policy. Conscious of this reality, which economic research and general experience tend to confirm, the constitution of 1996, in its Article 224, reasserted the independence of the South African Reserve Bank, the central bank, in these terms:

(1) The primary object of the South African Reserve Bank is to protect the value of the currency in the interest of balanced and sustainable growth in the Republic.
(2) The South African Reserve Bank, in pursuit of its primary object, must perform its functions independently and without fear, favour or prejudice, but there must be regular consultation between the Bank and the Cabinet member responsible for national financial matters.

The lesson I can draw from South Africa's experience with economic policymaking since the coming to power of the democratic government is that the independence of the central bank is a reality. In fact, a number of episodes put to test the capacity of the central bank to exercise its independence and that of the authorities to respect this independence: for example in 1998,[21] during the implementation of the GEAR program, the rand recorded rapid depreciation, which reached between April and August 1998 about 28 per cent in nominal terms compared to the US dollar. Foreseeing the risk to price stability, the central bank implemented a restrictive monetary policy which led to an increase in interest rates. Some observers estimated that by leading to an increase in interest rates and therefore to slowing down investment, such a policy did not contribute to the GEAR goals in terms of growth and job creation. However, it seems to me that we should see therein an exercise of the central bank's independence and not a problem of coordination and lack of cooperation of monetary policy as was suggested by some observers.[22]

The political sphere also contributed to the search for credibility, particularly with the ANC giving much predictability, stability and sustainability in its management of political power. Political transitions between President Mandela and his successor Thabo Mbeki on the one hand, and between President Mbeki and his successor Kgalema Motlanthe and then Jacob Zuma on the other hand, were carried out with much predictability and respect of democratic principles, with measures also being taken to reassure economic agents on the stability of the economic policy of the government.

The search for social cohesion and stability

Under the apartheid regime, the participation of blacks in economic activities was suppressed and discouraged by a set of legislative measures established by the apartheid government in the eighteenth century,[23] with the result being that the majority of blacks were excluded from economic activities and were assigned residences in poverty-stricken areas. There resulted a high inequality in the distribution of the country's resources, which, even after the end of apartheid, continued to constitute a serious threat to social cohesion and stability, the new democratic system and, consequently, the future economic growth of the country and the creation of jobs that the country would need. It is for this reason that one of the great goals established by the democratic government on its accession to power in April 1994 was to reduce these inequalities.

Thus, considering the specific context of South Africa, where inequalities are such that they threaten the country's economic and social tissue, the search for social cohesion appears to have been one of the major operating orientations which underlay the conduct of economic policy. The influence of this goal of social cohesion and stability is expressed, for example, in the use of instruments such as budgetary policy and regulation, as well as most of the instruments at the disposal of the authorities, and where it is possible to consider this goal.

As such, at the level of budgetary policy, this goal is implemented by the three major channels, which are (i) the importance of social transfers;[24] (ii) the search for an increase in the public spending share allocated to the development of sectors such as education, health, housing, access to electricity, water and sanitation, and aiming more specifically at redressing the inequalities created by the apartheid regime; and (iii) budgetary policy, which also aims at contributing to social cohesion. Therefore, the budget is one of the first instruments used to pursue the goal of social cohesion and stability.

Another major instrument used by the government to promote this same goal is the Black Economic Empowerment (BEE) program. BEE consists in a set of well-structured, coherent and analytically sound legislative and regulatory measures which aim at reducing social inequalities and promoting economic growth. To ensure that the positive effects of BEE as initially conceived effectively reach all the classes of the population and do not benefit only certain elites, the authorities strengthened the program and baptized

---

Box 15.1. Results targeted by BBBEE[25]

The principal results targeted by the BBBEE program are as follows:

(i) a substantial increase of the number of blacks who own and exercise control in existing and newly created companies;

(ii) a substantial increase of the number of blacks who own and exercise control in existing and newly created companies in priority sectors identified by the government in its macroeconomic reform strategy;

(iii) a significant increase of the number of new companies owned by blacks, companies that have benefited from this program aimed at promoting black entrepreneurship and the number of companies created by blacks;

(iv) a significant increase of the number of blacks in high management positions in companies;

(v) an increasing proportion of ownership and management of economic activities is reserved for community and broad-based companies (such as trade unions, employment funds or other forms of collective companies) and cooperatives;

(vi) increasing ownership of land and other productive assets, improvement of access to infrastructure, accrued acquisition of increasing competences and participation in productive economic activities in underdeveloped zones, including the 13 nodal zones identified in the urban renewal program and the sustainable integrated rural development program;

(vii) accelerated and shared economic growth;

(viii) increase in the income of blacks and reduction of income inequalities between and in racial groups.

---

the new version of the program *Broad-Based Black Economic Empowerment* (BBBEE). The main results targeted by this important dimension of South African economic policy are enumerated in Box 15.1 above.

To attain these results, legislative and regulatory measures of the BBBEE affect public procurement and contracts, the restructuring of public companies, the representation of the interests of blacks in institutional structures of the state, and government partnership with the private sector. Mechanisms are also provided to ensure adequate and sustainable financing of the BBBEE – that is, which are compatible with macroeconomic stability, economic growth imperatives of the country, and a certain diversification of national companies while leaving commercial risks to the private sector.[26, 27] The BBBEE has also been revised to further improve it. The country also has a system of social grants which contributes to poverty reduction and social cohesion, a key operational objective of economic policy, and also strengthens demand addressed to the economy. The number of beneficiaries grew from 2.7 million people in 1994 to 16 million in 2013.

Other major sectoral goals

These include the development of infrastructure, education and skills development, rural development, human settlements, and the fight against crime and corruption. As I have already indicated, infrastructural development – particularly in domains such as education, health, transport, energy, urban development and communications – also constitutes one of the major goals of South African economic policy. In his 2013 Freedom Day celebrations speech, President Zuma indicated that the total value of infrastructure projects currently underway and in planning in South Africa amounts to over 3.6 trillion rands (about 412 billion US dollars).[28] In 2012 for example, 675 km of electricity transmission lines, the largest amount in more than 20 years, were laid. In 2012, about 7,000 km of new fiber-optic cables were also laid. The objective is to achieve 100 per cent broadband Internet penetration by 2020. About 95 per cent of the population has access to the potable water infrastructure and 85 per cent have access to electricity. These infrastructure investments have also increasingly taken into account climate change concerns:

> A total of $5.5 bn was invested in renewable energy in 2012, up from a few tens of millions in 2011. [...] That means that South Africa had the biggest annual clean energy investment growth rate in the world in 2012, outstripping China, Japan, South Korea and a host of other economies. [...] With crisis-hit Europe cutting subsidies for green power, South Africa has become an unlikely bright spot in the global renewables energies.[29]

The government views infrastructure as a key enabler of growth and job creation.

Orienting demand toward locally produced goods and services

The examination of post-apartheid South Africa's economic policy clearly shows that efforts aimed at fully exploiting all the contributions of demand to economic growth and job creation are at the center of economic policy. These efforts aim at orienting domestic and foreign demand toward goods and services produced in South Africa. At the level of domestic demand, macroeconomic policy, particularly budgetary policy, it is firmly oriented toward maintaining macroeconomic stability while at the same time contributing positively toward orienting public demand toward locally produced goods and services. Monetary policy is firmly anchored on price stability. Exhortation, which plays an important role in stimulating demand addressed to the national economy, is also used. Thus, one of the measures which emerged from the Employment Summit of 1998 was the elaboration of Proudly South African, a program to orient demand toward locally produced goods (see Box 15.2 below).

The authorities also seized the opportunities that came up to support demand addressed to South African companies. For example, when the national currency, the rand, experienced rapid depreciation in 1996 and 2001,[30] the authorities saw a threat to price stability,[31] but also wanted to benefit from the new price competitiveness that this

Box 15.2. The proudly South African initiative

The aim of the Proudly South African campaign, an initiative launched in 2001 by the National Economic Development and Labour Council with the support of the South African government, the business community, trade unions and community organizations, was to promote South African companies and their products and services, create jobs and promote the country's economic growth. In fact, the idea of such an initiative was launched during the Employment Summit which took place in 1998. It aims at attaining the aforementioned goals by encouraging economic actors to buy South African products and services, thereby stimulating demand in South African companies and economic growth, and helping to protect jobs. Participation in this initiative is open to all types of companies, so long as they respect a certain number of criteria, particularly: (i) at least 50 per cent of the cost of production of its goods or services, including labor, must be incurred in South Africa (companies whose activities consist in importing and reconditioning their products are not eligible to participate in this initiative); (ii) company goods or services must respect the highest quality standards; (iii) the company must commit to respect equitable work standards; and (iv) the company must commit to respect environmental norms. Companies participating in the program may place a logo on their goods and services which identifies them and attests to their participation in this initiative. They also receive assistance in the preparation of their bids within the framework of contracts, are exhibited on the website of the program, participate at reduced rates in written and audiovisual advertising campaigns, and also receive information beforehand on contract opportunities and can participate freely in business seminars and meetings. Companies also pay a membership contribution, which stands at 0.1 per cent of turnovers on goods and services carrying the logo of the campaign. The chief executive of the campaign, Martin Feinstein, said: "We want to create a culture where buyers in government, provinces, local authorities and the private sector better understand the implications of their buying decisions on job creation in the country. [...] We think that South African companies of all sizes should buy their raw materials and equipment from other South African companies, if they provide the value of their money." Barely six months after its launch, more than one hundred and sixty South African companies, including big companies such as South African Airways, the Old Mutual financial services group, the M-Net media group and the Pick n Pay group, one of the greatest chains of supermarkets in Africa, were participating in the campaign, and varied South African products like fruits, leather products and foodstuffs were already displaying logos. Some time later, a survey showed that about 92 per cent of South Africans were ready to support South African trademarks and 77 per cent sought local products. When we know that the annual economic growth of more than 5 per cent experienced by South Africa during the early 2000s was mainly drawn from consumption, we understand once more the importance of initiatives aimed at attaining the goals of this type of program.

Addressing the launch of the Proudly South African "Buy Local" summit in November 2012, deputy president Kgalema Motlanthe said:

Proudly South African has since its inception sought to wet the appetite of both domestic and international consumers for our locally produced goods. No doubt this has contributed directly to building national pride, patriotism and social cohesion. [...] All of us, as business leaders, organised labour and civil society, also carry the responsibility to cultivate a taste for South African manufactured products. [...] In this way the Proudly South African brand will thrive through all our actions as individuals and organisations [...] the campaign to promote South African manufactured goods is a critical part of our growth and development strategy.

depreciation offered the economy. Thus, one of the responses of depreciation in 1996 was the reduction in customs duties in order to support this increase in competitiveness (it was particularly the case within the framework of the GEAR plan). Figure 15.2 below describes the evolution of the exchange rate of the rand. It appears it depreciated, thereby giving a competitive advantage to local producers. Overall, the South African rand has been very flexible, and the economy has so far absorbed this flexibility quite well, with exchange rate movements having a low pass-through to inflation and a limited impact on domestic economic agents' balance sheets. These outcomes also reflect the underlying strengths of the economy.

Figure 15.2. Evolution of the South African rand exchange rate[32]

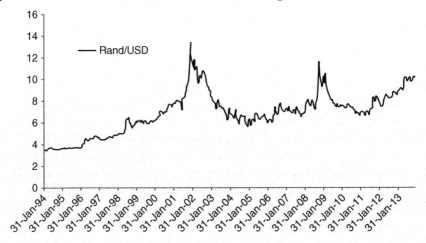

Also, the 2013/14 fiscal year budget made provisions for personal income tax relief of 7 billion rand. Besides these measures, BBBEE is no doubt, beyond its role in the domain of social cohesion, one of the most important instruments of stimulation of domestic demand toward supporting economic growth. In fact, according to South African economic policy officials, BBBEE should also significantly contribute to stimulating demand by contributing to increase the purchasing power of a greater number of South Africans.

At the level of foreign demand, the authorities first went for it on regional markets through an increased participation in regional economic integration efforts, particularly within the framework of the Southern Africa Development Community (SADC) and Southern Africa Customs Union (SACU). I have often visited member countries of these organizations and have seen that South African products are highly present. For example, many South African chains of supermarkets were somehow present everywhere in these countries, and had several South African products on their shelves. Friends who have also visited member countries of the SADC report the same presence of South African products. These regional integration efforts have paid off. About one hundred and eleven thousand direct jobs and more than three hundred and twenty thousand indirect jobs in South Africa are supported from trade with other African countries.[33]

Besides regional integration efforts, South African economic policy officials have fetched demand for South African products on other world markets, particularly by actively participating in multilateral trade negotiations and negotiating bilateral trade agreements with trade partners, particularly the European Union. As result of all these efforts, it is well known that effective demand-management efforts have contributed to the economic growth that South Africa has experienced recently.

Procurement

National procurement is also a tool used to strengthen demand addressed to the national economy. In 2011, a procurement accord was signed to achieve this objective. The country's minister for economic development describes this accord in these terms: "The local procurement Accord signed with business and labor, established a common national commitment to strengthening local supply chains, creating more jobs and improving the competitiveness of South African factories."[34] The Local Procurement Accord in effect committed business, labor, government and communities to a partnership to increase domestic procurement toward boosting local manufacturing capacity. The designation of certain products or sectors for local public sector procurement is also aimed at further stimulating domestic demand addressed to the economy. Toward this end, the following products/sectors have so far been designated: rail stock, power pylons, bus bodies, canned/processed vegetables, certain pharmaceutical products, furniture products, textiles, clothing, leather and footwear, valves, manual and pneumatic actuators, electrical and telecommunication cables, and components of solar water heaters. Other procurement related instruments to further stimulate domestic demand addressed to the economy include provisions governing the procurement by state-owned companies and the National Industrial Participation Programme. All these provisions are governed by the Preferential Procurement Policy Framework Act.

National productive capacity

The major operating orientations of the economic policy I have just seen – particularly the search for greater credibility of economic policy and of authorities responsible for it, social cohesion and stability, infrastructural development, and the stimulation of demand addressed to economy – tend to create an environment which is favorable to the development of the national productive capacity insofar as they contribute to greater confidence of investors. Besides these orientations, the development of the productive capacity is also a specific goal of South Africa's economic policy. Several instruments

---

Box 15.3. Some initiatives of industrial policy

Besides the broad outlines of its economic policy, which are generally very favorable to investments aimed at increasing the country's productive capacity, the government, on its accession to power, quickly understood the need for an effective and well-targeted industrial policy to consolidate the country's productive base. As such, several programs were set up. Among them we have the strategic investment program, which was set up to support important investments; the critical infrastructure program, which grants aid to public and private companies which invest to develop infrastructure necessary for private investments; the spatial development program; the special program for industrial innovation; the technological and human resources program for the industry, which aims at strengthening partnerships between training institutions and industry; and the industrial development regional program. The Industrial Development Corporation, a very influential government structure, supports industrial projects financially by providing financing in the form of loans, participation and guarantees. The small- and medium-size sector also draws the attention of the government. Thus, considering that one of the means to reduce inequalities may be to contribute to the rapid development of small- and medium- size companies, the government also launched a number of initiatives and institutions to provide selective aid to these companies. Among these, I can mention the Ntsika agency for the promotion of companies, which grants financial aid to small companies, as well as Khula Finance, which grants loans and guarantees to small- and medium-size enterprises. The merger of Khula and of the small business activities of the Industrial Development Corporation resulted in the establishment, in 2012, of the Small Enterprise Finance Agency (SEFA). The mandate of SEFA is to foster the establishment, survival and growth of small- and medium-size enterprises and contribute toward poverty alleviation and job creation.

There also exist supports to stimulate productions for exports, particularly the Export Marketing and Investment Assistance scheme, which aims at partially compensating exporters for costs incurred in activities aimed at developing export markets for South African products and services and at encouraging new foreign direct investment flows in South Africa.

State-owned companies are also a key instrument in the government's industrial policy drive. Thus, on the occasion of the 2013 budget vote, minister of public enterprises Malusi Gigaba said:

Our portfolio of State-Owned Companies (SOC) have aggressively been accelerating investment to maintain aggregate demand precisely when there is a downturn globally and the private sector is too apprehensive to invest. [...] Three years ago, our portfolio of SOC invested R53 billion; but in the next financial year, we will be investing over R113 billion. [...] The Department of Public Enterprises held the Supplier Development Summit attended by SOC's suppliers, customers and other key stakeholders. At the summit, the SOC communicated their next generation supplier development, localisation and transformation plans and further explored how they and large companies in strategic sectors can collaborate around supplier development to create a truly national effort around achieving our objectives. [...] Over the coming year, we will be mobilising our entire SOC portfolio, along with their customers and suppliers, to give added momentum to a comprehensive industrialisation and transformation programme in our economy. [...] As part of this we will be exploring set-asides and other mechanisms radically to accelerate the promotion of black industrialists and the entrance of youth and women owned businesses into the mainstream economy.[35]

and measures are at the service of this goal. I can cite different programs aimed at implementing a real and effective industrial policy[36] and a controlled liberalization of trade to stimulate increases in productivity where increased foreign competition appears necessary for their achievement. Box 15.3 below presents some industrial policy initiatives set up by the authorities to act positively on the productive capacities of the economy.

Like any other country in the world, South Africa was also affected by the financial crisis which started in the United States from the summer of 2007 and which quickly became an economic crisis. Thanks to appropriate banking and exchange regulations, South Africa was less exposed to the toxic financial products which caused the financial crisis. However, like other emerging countries, it suffered some effects of the financial crisis, particularly when, in order to re-establish their financial health in their country of origin, foreign investors proceeded to withdraw their capital from most emerging economies. This crisis also had an impact on foreign demand addressed to South Africa. Consequently, growth slowed down, particularly during the third quarter of 2008, bringing down the growth rate in the whole of 2008 to 3.1 per cent against 5.1 per cent in 2007.

Significant increases in credibility procured by the overall good economic management of the economy before the crisis, and particularly a sustainable budgetary policy, gave the country resources to better manage the crisis. Thus, South Africa was among the first African countries to come out of it from 2010. This rapid exit was helped by the government's recovery plan. The crisis exit plan announced by President Motlanthe included investments of 787 billion rands (about 60 billion euros / 77 billion US dollars) to improve upon infrastructure toward supporting growth, accelerating the implementation of the extended program of public works, strengthening institutions financing development, supporting industrial and agricultural restructuring, and implementing social assistance programs to reach more than thirteen million citizens without counting educational and health resources.[37] Besides the crisis exit plan, the recovery was also to be boosted by the successful organization, in 2010, of the FIFA World Cup, and the drop in interest rates.

The Challenges Ahead

Since the end of apartheid in 1994, South Africa has undoubtedly made significant progress on many important fronts. Despite this, the country faces many challenges going forward. The recent report by Goldman Sachs has clearly identified some of them. These include the need to boost economic growth, tackle the high unemployment and inequality, and stabilize industrial relations. The Twenty Year Review report recently released by the South African Government has further elaborated on the remaining challenges.[38] As discussed in this book, the country has a sound, well-oriented and credible economic policy framework to address the challenges going forward. It should now focus on consistent implementation.

Summary

As conclusion, I can say that the economic policy implemented by South Africa since the beginning of the post-apartheid era seems to be well oriented. Economic policy priorities – particularly economic growth, job creation, reduction of inequality and poverty, social cohesion, credibility, the sustainability of policy choices and the independence of economic policy with regard to foreign influences – were well-anticipated, and concrete measures to enliven these priorities were correctly identified and implemented. The energy crisis showed that the success of this economic policy was such that it took many by surprise, including its own architects. In fact, the economic boom was so rapid that it generated an energy demand which exceeded the capacities installed. In response to the crisis, the government elaborated and implemented a development plan for the energy sector, which involved both efforts to save energy and important investments to increase the national production of energy. More than forty billion dollars of investments were committed to the energy sector. For the period to come, economic policy shall maintain its course with respect to the defined national priorities and continue to give confidence to economic agents.

Chapter Sixteen

SOME ECONOMIC POLICY EXPERIENCES IN DEVELOPED AND EMERGING COUNTRIES

"The Union shall establish an internal market. It shall work for the sustainable development of Europe based on balanced economic growth and price stability, a highly competitive social market economy, aiming at full employment and social progress, and a high level of protection and improvement of the quality of the environment. It shall promote scientific and technological advance."

Treaty on European Union (2008), Title 1, Article 3[1]

Introduction

Be they developed countries or countries that have recently attained remarkable economic development levels, like those in Asia, their experiences show that they pursued the final, intermediate and operating goals described in detail in Part Two of this book in a voluntary and determined manner. Even if contemporary literature on these experiences does not structure the presentation of policies carried out and measures taken by these countries on the different goals that I just described, a careful reading of this literature enables us to realize that the specific measures of economic policy that it describes are guided and inspired by the firm wish to attain these goals. In this chapter, I will briefly present the pertinent points of these experiences.

Asian Emerging Countries

In his study on possible lessons to be drawn from the experience of East Asian countries, the Nobel laureate in economics Joseph E. Stiglitz notes that all these countries demonstrated a genuine wish to develop a national capacity to produce a varied range of manufactured goods,[2] which corresponds to a commitment to the intermediate goal of building national productive capacities that I have identified in this book. He also notes the voluntary efforts in these countries to improve upon the reputation and image of their products on foreign markets, which corresponds to the intermediate goal of stimulating demand addressed to the national economy. He also notices in these countries specific measures to reduce income inequalities and promote a fruitful partnership between the state and the private sector, which corresponds to some of the operating goals which I have identified.[3]

Concerning specific measures of economic policy implemented toward attaining these goals, they present a great variability, which is normal considering the diversity of contexts. As already emphasized, detailed examination of these measures as such does not present an interest in itself if it is not for illustrative purposes only, because economic policy measures are always context specific and cannot be replicated *tel quel* in another context. Let us take the example of China. The measure on the establishment of community enterprises and the responsibility system of households contributed much to the productive-capacity building of the Chinese economy and, indirectly, to economic growth and job creation, by creating the confidence that economic agents needed in an environment still influenced by insufficient recognition of private property rights and the guarantees that it procures.[4] Concerning the stimulation of demand addressed to the economy, it is also one of the major successes of Chinese economic policy. As such, independently of macroeconomic instruments such as exchange rate policy and monetary policy, efforts were also made to orient consumer preferences toward Chinese trademarks and products. Thus, a survey by McKinsey concluded that Chinese consumers had confidence in homemade products. What is interesting is that this feeling was not changed by polemics in the United States and Europe on the quality of Chinese products. Thus, according to this McKinsey survey, only 11 per cent of respondents indicated having strong or moderate confidence in foreign products and about half of them also added that they may change to a local product if they are offered a product of the same quality. About 53 per cent clearly indicated that they would prefer Chinese trademarks.[5] I am sure these figures will make several economic officials of African countries envious; the preference in these countries for foreign products is so developed that it constitutes one of the major obstacles to their development. I have already dwelt on the case of Nigeria.

Japan, South Korea and other East Asian countries also implemented specific measures adapted to their contexts and aimed at attaining the final, intermediate and operating goals that I highlighted at length in Part Two of this book.[6] The search for social stability was and remains one of the great orientations of the economic policy of Malaysia. Thus, since the end of the 1970s, one of the important goals of the new economic policy has been to reduce income gaps among its different ethnic groups.[7]

Developed Countries

The same observation may be made concerning the economic policy implemented by countries that are today developed. An examination of the orientations of the economic policy implemented by these countries shows that these broad orientations always followed the structure of the conceptual framework that I present in this book. Thus, it will be easy enough to realize that the economic policy implemented always expressed voluntarism in the pursuit of these various goals.

I have dwelt on how economic growth and the promotion of employment are at the center of goals targeted by US economic policy and how the law, particularly the Federal Reserve Act (one of the most important laws of the country given that it governs the functioning of its central bank), obliges it to pursue two goals: one, price stability; the other, job creation. What is important to be noted here is that the law does not establish a hierarchy between these two goals, to the extent that we can say that US legislators consider these two goals equally important. The Federal Reserve should ensure that its actions, at any moment, are part of the pursuit of these two goals. As such, it always justifies its monetary policy decisions on the basis of their consequences in terms of employment (and its main driver, economic growth) and price stability. This law also obliges the governor of the Federal Reserve to testify on the state of the US economy twice a year in Congress. This testimony is always oriented toward perspectives on economic growth and employment, the fundamental variables on which congressmen evaluate the performance of the governor of the Federal Reserve. This does not mean that the control of inflation is not a goal. Inflation control is an important goal, but the Federal Reserve always strives to control it without compromising the perspectives of growth and job creation.

When we study US economic policy deeply, we also realize that the stimulation of demand addressed to the economy and the development of the productive capacity of the US economy are also variables whose evolution the authorities monitor closely. As a matter of fact, decisions to modify or to leave interest rates unchanged, which media often solemnly announce, are always taken with the aim of stimulating demand[8] addressed to the economy (if projections show that growth will slow down) or, on the contrary, to slow down increase in demand (if projections show that growth is accelerating and that the economy is moving toward overheating). Also, efforts presently deployed by the United States and Europe to influence China's exchange rate policy toward greater appreciation of the Chinese currency aim at strongly stimulating foreign demand addressed to the US economy.[9]

In the United States, the adoption of the Small Business Act, for example, was a measure clearly aimed at contributing to the development of small- and medium-size enterprises and indirectly to the development of the entire productive capacity of the US economy by acting on demand addressed to small- and medium-size enterprises (see Box 16.1 below). This concentration on the need to develop the productive capacity was so strong and established in the US economic policy model that it found itself in the Marshall Plan set up to help reconstruct Europe after the Second World War. Thus, the operational mechanisms of the Marshall aid included the following facts: (i) grants by the United States to European countries should be used by European governments solely to give loans to companies with the aim of rehabilitating and developing their productive capacity; (ii) amounts reimbursed should serve in financing essential infrastructure to develop business and increase production.[10] Emphasis was therefore clearly placed on the development of productive capacities of European economies.

The economic policy of the European Union, and that of its member states, also follows the same orientations as those I have discussed. Thus, despite the multitude of goals it is pursuing, the European Union made the promotion of strong economic growth and job creation into a fundamental goal of its economic policy. Therefore, as quoted at the beginning of this chapter, Article 3 of the Treaty on the European Union and the Treaty on the Functioning of the European Union strongly emphasizes balanced economic growth and full employment among the key objectives of the union. A careful observation also shows that the European Union also consciously pursues what I call

Box 16.1. Small Business Act of the United States

The Small Business Act was adopted by the US Congress on June 30, 1953 to "aid, advise, assist and protect" small enterprises. This law also created the Small Business Administration (SBA), an organ of the US government, whose mission was to ensure the implementation of this law. This law enabled the US government to implement a number of provisions (such as loans, guarantees and a variety of other aid instruments) to aid small American companies to modernize their production tools, but it provided particular mechanisms to guarantee them a satisfactory demand for their production. Among these mechanisms aimed at stimulating demand addressed to small- and medium-size enterprises within the framework of the SBA, is the obligation of the Federal Government to award 23 per cent of its contracts to these enterprises. For big contracts, those which due to their size cannot be directly awarded to small- and medium-size enterprises, the SBA negotiates with big contractors their subcontracting plan with smaller ones. Drawing inspiration from the US model, other countries like Canada, South Korea, France and Japan have adopted this measure. Besides obliging the Federal Government to award a quota of its contracts to small- and medium-size American enterprises, the Small Business Act also restricts access to Federal Government procurement contracts by non-American small- and medium-size enterprises. It is estimated that the SBA strongly contributes to the development of American companies. In fact, the public contracts they win under the SBA often constitute, to some of them, their first contracts, and their first contract with important buyers. Besides the income procured by these contracts, which enables them to modernize their production tools and make a more competitive offer later, the reference established as such serves as a launch pad for more important contracts. It is estimated that thanks to this law, American companies have increased their workforce by about 60 per cent on average, seven years after their creation.

intermediate and operating goals. To cite just one example, the Common Agricultural Policy, which today has transformed Europe into one of the greatest world agricultural powers, was set up primarily to assure Europe of a great production capacity in the agricultural sector.[11]

During the European Council held in Brussels in June 2007 to reach an agreement on streamlining the European constitutional treaty (after the victory of the "no" camp in the French and Dutch referenda), European leaders debated the question of whether the promotion of competition should be a fundamental goal of the union or simply a means to attain the fundamental goals of economic growth and employment. Finally, after serious discussion, Europeans agreed to retain the promotion of competition as a means and not as an end in itself of economic policy.[12] This meant giving the promotion of competition in the EU single market an operating goal role, as indicated in the economic policy model developed in this book. The fact that European leaders lengthily discussed this question shows the importance they attach to a clear vision of the different goals pursued and the importance given each of them for the success of their economic policy.

Summary

What this last part of the book has empirically demonstrated with the aid of some real world examples is that the economic growth sought by developing countries, particularly those of Africa, essentially originates from a good economic policy. This is characterized by ingenious, creative and imaginative efforts that economic policymakers implement to ensure that, on the one hand, the main driving forces of growth (demand addressed to the economy and the strengthening of its productive capacities) remain permanently stimulated, and on the other hand, other variables which determine demand and productive capacities (particularly those I referred to as operating goals in the second part of this book) are well oriented. Finally, there are several passing points to be crossed simultaneously and several levers to be activated at the same time for growth to be adequately stimulated. Therefore, growth does not result from fragmented efforts which search for the "binding constraints" and try to resolve them one after the other as they present themselves, as recent literature on growth diagnostics has tried to suggest, but from joint and simultaneous efforts on several fronts guided by a systemic vision of the economy and the society, as discussed in this book.

CONCLUSION

The reality is that Africa is becoming a remarkable success story. [...] Africa's consumer sectors – goods, telecom and banking, amongst others – present the largest opportunity and are already growing two to three times faster than those countries belonging to the Organization for Economic Cooperation and Development (OECD). [...] The rate of return on foreign investment in Africa is higher than in any other region in the world. This is not surprising given the competitive edge of the continent. [...] Estimates from the African Development Bank suggest that companies participating in infrastructure investments in Africa can earn commercial rates of return from 5 to 10 percent in the water sector, 17 to 25 percent in the power sector and 25 to 30 percent in telecoms. Across sectors, infrastructure investments average returns of between 15 and 20 per cent.

Jacob Zuma, president of the Republic of South Africa,
"An Opinion Piece on Africa," January 27, 2013

"We chose to focus on growth because we think that it is a necessary condition for the achievement of a wide range of objectives that people and societies care about. One of them is obviously poverty reduction, but there are even deeper ones. Health, productive employment, the opportunity to be creative, all kinds of things that really matter to people seem to depend heavily on the availability of resources and income, so that they don't spend most of their time desperately trying to keep their families alive."

Michael Spence, chair of the Commission on Growth and Development[1]

Africa in a Process of Revival

I can say without risk of deceiving ourselves that the beginning of the twenty-first century, which we are experiencing now, appears to mark a new beginning in the partnership between rich and developing countries to eradicate poverty. During the 1990s, a number of factors which progressively transformed the domestic and external environment of the African continent combined their effects to once more focus attention on the economic problems of Africa.

Internally, three key factors came into play. First, there is the emergence of democratic demands in several countries which, in hindsight, expressed the aspirations of the African people to a better life, free of poverty. Second, on the continental scene, two great African countries, South Africa and Nigeria, staged a remarkable comeback.

By acceding to what now appears to be a sustainable internal democracy after many years of military rule, Nigeria – which had always displayed responsible behavior on the African scene, particularly within the framework of its efforts to maintain subregional peace and security and to defend West African democracy – has given a new dimension to its international respectability as well as a new credibility to its commitment to democracy and the economic development of the African continent.[2]

The end, in 1994, of its apartheid regime enabled the total reintegration of South Africa into the political and economic chessboard of the continent. This great African country is playing a lead role as one of the major driving forces of the new African consensus for peace, political democracy and poverty eradication on the continent, and reversing the marginalization of Africa in the globalization process. One of the pillars of South Africa's diplomatic efforts is "A Better Africa in A Better World."

Finally, we also witnessed the emergence of some champions of the political and economic renewal of the African continent, such as President Thabo Mbeki of South Africa. On his accession to power in 1999, following in the footsteps of Nelson Mandela, and relying on both the enormous potential of his country and the immense political experience of the powerful political party to which he belongs, the African National Congress, he intended to make an important contribution to the African renaissance.[3] The launch of the New Partnership for Africa's Development (NEPAD) marked one of the highest points of this renewal process.

New Partnership for Africa's Development

During the African Union Summit held in July 2001 in Lusaka, Zambia, African heads of state adopted the New Initiative for Africa (NIA), which became, in October of the same year, NEPAD.[4] The leaders gathered in Lusaka were aware that it was not the first time that a plan for economic development and poverty reduction for Africa had been adopted at the continental level, but this time they intended to capitalize on the renewed political will to ensure the success of NEPAD.

NEPAD realized that despite the immense resources of its subsoil and its rich environmental, historical and cultural heritage, Africa was still the poorest continent on earth. More than half of the African population lives below the poverty line on less than a dollar a day and most social indicators describe pervasive poverty. According to NEPAD, colonialism, the Cold War, the wheels of world economy and the lack of African political and economic leadership contributed to the process of impoverishment in the continent and its marginalization in the world economy. In fact, Africa's role in the world economy up to this moment was limited to that of supplier of raw materials and cheap labor. While noting that the process of globalization had increased the costs for Africa of its inability to compete, NEPAD also acknowledged that globalization, if well managed, may offer good perspectives for economic prosperity and poverty reduction on the continent.

What justifies the approach initiated by NEPAD for Africa's development strategy, and which also distinguishes it from former plans,[5] is that its authors from the start conceived it as a partnership framework between African countries and developed countries. As in any partnership, NEPAD wants that every party, both African and developed countries, should assume a number of commitments in order to attain the goals together. Thus, NEPAD set up as long-term goals to (i) eradicate poverty, (ii) place African Countries, both individually and collectively, on a path of sustainable growth and development, (iii) halt the marginalization of Africa in the globalization process, (iv) accelerate the empowerment of women, and (v) fully integrate Africa into the global economy. NEPAD subscribes to the Millennium Development Goals adopted by the international community in September 2000. To achieve the goals it set up, NEPAD aims at increasing the annual growth rate of the GDP of African countries to 7 per cent and at contributing to the achievement of the MDGs.

To attain its goals, NEPAD targets actions at two levels: (i) contributing to the achievement of conditions necessary to ensure sustainable development – peace, security, democracy and political good governance – and the improvement of economic and corporate governance; and (ii) thanks to massive investments, fill the gap that presently exists between Africa and developed countries in a number of priority sectors in order to improve the continent's competitiveness and enable Africa to participate in the process of globalization. Priority sectors retained by NEPAD are infrastructure (information and communication technologies, energy, transport, water and sanitation), human resources development (fill the gap in the domain of education, reverse the trend of brain drain, reduce poverty, improve health), agriculture, environment, culture, and science and technology. In order to establish priorities in the implementation of sectoral programs, NEPAD identified four programs whose implementation would start as soon as possible: programs on the fight against transmissible diseases (HIV/AIDS, malaria and tuberculosis), information and communication technologies, debt reduction and access to markets. Projects whose implementation was recommended were also identified in the agricultural sectors, the promotion of the private sector and infrastructure, thereby contributing to regional integration. For the financing of all sectoral programs it identified, NEPAD planned improving the mobilization of domestic resources, but also to seek (i) an increase in capital flows, particularly through a substantial debt relief, an increase in the size and quality of official development assistance, and actions aimed at reducing the perception of risk in Africa and encourage public–private partnerships in order to increase Africa's ability to further attract private capital; and (ii) an increase in the access of African products to international markets.

To attain the goals it set, the framework of partnership defined by NEPAD attributes responsibilities to African and developed countries. Thus, African countries undertook to (i) consolidate mechanisms of prevention, management and resolution of conflicts toward restoring and maintaining peace on the continent; (ii) promote political democracy and respect for human rights, the transparency of legal and regulatory institutions, and the role of women in development; (iii) strengthen macroeconomic stability; and (iv) promote national-capacity building for the respect of law and the maintenance of public order. Concerning developed countries, they would take measures to (i) substantially increase the volume of foreign aid to Africa and improve the mechanisms for its delivery; (ii) facilitate the access of African products to their markets; (iii) encourage private-sector investments in Africa; (iii) support governance reforms of international financial institutions in order that they better consider priorities of African countries; (iv) strengthen the fight against corruption, including the facilitation of the repatriation of gains from such practices to Africa; (v) facilitate access to appropriate medicines; and (vi) extend the consumer protection norms in force on their domestic markets to African countries.

In October 2002, during the final examination of the NEPAD, the United Nations General Assembly decided to approve the recommendation of the secretary general to recognize NEPAD as the new framework for the support of the international community to the development of Africa. In 2001 and 2002, the group of eight most developed countries of the world, the G8, meeting in its annual summit, gave its support to the NEPAD process. During the G8 Summit held in Kananaskis, G8 leaders even adopted the Africa Action Plan, which aimed at supporting the implementation of NEPAD.

Since the adoption of NEPAD, remarkable progress has been made, though much is still left to be done. Globally, progress has been made in practically all the domains where African countries have undertaken commitments within the framework of NEPAD, but this progress has certainly been more distinct in the domains of the maintenance of peace, the promotion of political democracy, respect for human rights and the maintenance of macroeconomic stability. At the level of the maintenance of peace and the promotion of political democracy, the setting up of the African Peer Review Mechanism (APRM) was an important step in the long route to democracy in Africa. The APRM is an autoevaluation mechanism in which each country voluntarily participates and which aims at ensuring that the practices of participating countries in terms of political and economic governance are in conformity with norms established by NEPAD in these domains. Presently, 23 countries have voluntarily signed the memorandum of understanding to participate in this mechanism.[6] The first evaluations show the interest countries give this process and the contribution they may make to their efforts toward promoting democracy and good governance in their internal affairs. The several reforms introduced at the functional level of the African Union, particularly the creation of a Peace and Security Council and the close frequency of summits of heads of state (twice a year instead of once a year during the era of the Organization of African Unity), contributed to greater involvement of African institutions in the promotion of peace and democracy as well as the search for solutions to the numerous conflicts ravaging the continent. This involvement certainly contributed to progress in conflict resolution in many countries of the continent. African countries have also made progress on the maintenance of macroeconomic stability in recent years.

An Exhortation to Hope

I started this book with the hypothesis that even though current concerns relating to an increase in the volume and effectiveness of foreign aid may be justified, it is high time African countries gave great attention to the improvement of their economic policy. For, in the final analysis, the much-expected economic growth and prosperity stems from a good economic policy and not from an increase in aid, even if this is accompanied by a considerable acceleration of donors' efforts to improve the conditions of its delivery. The G8 countries noted this in July 2005, when they were taking unprecedented measures to increase aid to Africa. On that occasion, they also chose to remind African countries of the need for them to "decide, plan and organize their economic policy in accordance to their own development strategies and shall be accountable to their citizens."[7]

In this light, this book is an exhortation to hope in the future of the African continent. I have shown that, with a new economic policy – that is, an economic policy guided by the imperative of promoting job creation and strong economic growth, and relying on the double imperatives of (i) stimulating strong and sustainable demand for goods and services produced by African economies, and (ii) strengthening the national productive tissue – Africa is capable of coming out of the present situation of extreme poverty to join, within record time, the club of rich countries which produce a high level of well-being for their citizens. In order to achieve that, it suffices to adopt and implement the renewed and effective economic policy I have discussed at length in this book.

Stimulating National Supply and Demand Addressed to the Economy to Promote Growth and Create Jobs: First Goals of Economic Policy

One of the major themes I have developed in this book is that economic policy is at the same time a science and an art, but more of an art than a science, and one which calls for imagination, creativity, determination and a desire on the part of the authorities. Authorities are responsible for, on the one hand, stimulating, in a noninflationary manner, demand for goods and services addressed to the national economy (expressed by domestic and foreign economic agents), and on the other hand, facilitating the emergence of a national productive tissue capable of responding satisfactorily to this demand. In my opinion, these are the two fundamental guideposts of any economic policy which seriously strives at attaining final goals like strong economic growth, job creation, and the reduction of social inequalities and poverty, which are much cherished by all political and economic policy officials throughout the world. I find here the two fundamental concepts on which any economic activity or progress made by economic sciences since the creation of this discipline are based, and which also guided the economic policy implemented with much success by countries which today enjoy economic prosperity and social progress.

All economic battles fought by states internationally, at least for countries which have mastered the art of economic policy, whether in multilateral or bilateral frameworks, finally have as their goal either to acquire an important share of the world demand for goods and services, or to attract to their territory an important part of the world productive capacity. All a government can do to stimulate the demand for goods and services addressed to national companies, in a noninflationary manner, as I said earlier, is good economic policy. Also, all a government can do to successfully stimulate national companies to expand and modernize their production process and tools, as well as to stimulate foreign companies to localize their production activities on the national territory, is good economic policy. An economy where demand addressed to the economy is strong and constantly strengthening, and in which companies modernize and expand their production tools, is an economy in good health. As we have seen throughout this book, it is for this reason that stimulating demand in the national economy and building its supply capacity constitute what I refer to as intermediate goals of economic policy. They are intermediate because they help to attain the fundamental final goals of economic growth and job creation.

These two developments will actually contribute to an increase in the wealth produced and number of jobs created, factors which will create a favorable environment for the pursuit of all the other goals that economic policy officials may wish to pursue, such as the redistribution of wealth and the reduction in regional disparities toward fostering social cohesion. It is the materialization of this virtuous circle which is at the center of an economic policy's success in generating strong, inclusive and sustained economic growth and job creation.

To be effectively implemented, such policy orientations demand that indicators be developed to monitor different aspects of private demand's attitudes toward goods and services produced on the continent, but also to follow different aspects of producers' behaviors toward investment in the country. Even if much is still left to be done to perfect the monitoring efforts of producers' attitudes, I cannot help admitting that some progress has already been made at this level. Contrarily, it is not the same with monitoring and influencing private demand's attitudes toward goods and services produced in different African countries. Today, very few African countries have developed indicators enabling them to monitor the level and trend of consumers' attitudes toward national productions. Such insufficiency heavily penalizes growth perspectives, given that, beyond some factors recently identified in the literature and the current debates on economic growth in Africa, it is the anticipation of a strong and sustainable demand which constitutes, to an investor, the first determinant of his decision to invest in order to develop its productive capacity, and also his decision to recruit.

The Search for Credibility and Confidence of Economic Agents: Indispensable for the Success of Any Economic Policy

Theoretical analysis has highlighted the important role of credibility and of the expectations of economic agents in the success of any economic policy approach. As earlier seen in this book, credibility is an invaluable asset for economic policy officials. The search for credibility must be a prerequisite for any economic policy official striving to obtain even minimum success in the conduct of his or her economic policy.

It is for this reason that one of the messages I have aimed at in this book is that economic policy officials must seek a high level of credibility from economic agents. The current approach, which simply consists in "manipulating" economic policy instruments with the aim of attaining predetermined levels of variables linked particularly to macroeconomic balances, without a real economic strategy embedded in the expectations of economic agents and without demonstrating a real effort to gain credibility, has a necessarily limited scope in terms of stimulating economic growth and creating jobs, which are indisputable factors of social well-being. One of the themes sustained in this book is that what is important for economic policy is not so much to attain a particular level for a given economic policy instrument, or better still to succeed in the implementation of a specific measure, but the manner in which the action of the public authorities, positively interpreted by economic agents, catalyzes their behaviors and induces them either to increase their investments aimed at developing national productive capacities, or to increase their demand of goods and services produced by the national economy. It is the size of this catalytic effect on economic agents' confidence and action which becomes, in my opinion, the essential measure of the success of economic policy.

Thus, the success of economic policy is measured by its ability to mobilize economic agents around economic growth and job creation, which are the primary goals of economic policy. As already seen throughout this book, this capacity does not only depend on the level attained by the instruments, which are under the direct control of the authorities, but also and particularly on the manner in which economic agents – that is, consumers and investors – perceive the actions of economic policy officials. This does not mean that it is not important whether the budgetary balance (if we are interested in this variable, for example) is in surplus or in deficit or even that the deficit, if it exists, is at one level rather than another. It also does not mean that it is not important if the rate of a customs duty in force in a country, to go by an example at the center of the globalization process, is at 10 per cent or 100 per cent, or if the country applies quantitative restriction measures of trade. It is simply that it is the adhesion of economic agents to what public authorities do that will finally determine the scope of the effects and impacts of a given level of the budgetary balance or of a given level of trade liberalization with the rest of the world. All experts are now unanimous that today's developed countries built their development, and moreover continue in this vein, on skillful use of various measures to protect their markets,[8] while the benefits of the progress made so far by most African countries in liberalizing trade with the rest of the world are still to set in. It is also well known that Asian countries which experienced serious financial and economic crisis toward the end of the 1990s all had a satisfactory budgetary balance.

This book maintains that in failing to pay enough attention to all the final, intermediate and operating goals developed in this book, the process of elaborating and implementing economic policy in Africa lacked one of the essential dimensions of economic policy, which explains its failure to stimulate sustainable, inclusive and job-creating economic growth.

Within the context of globalizing economies, which are also characterized by more progress toward democratic societies in which economic agents enjoy some degree of freedom in their economic behavior, the search for credibility appears more of an art than a science, insofar as it consists not only in depending on objective indicators to decide on measures to be taken, but also, and more and more so, in resorting to subjective information to analyze, understand and finally try to influence the behaviors of economic agents, particularly producers and consumers. Economic policy therefore become a constant quest, whose goal is to win the confidence of consumers and producers, and to stimulate an increase in consumers' demand for goods and services produced by the national economy and an increase in producers' investments in the country to produce goods and services demanded by national and foreign economic agents.

NOTES

Introduction

1 G8 Statement on Africa, Gleneagles, July 2005. http://www.g8.utoronto.ca/summit/2005gleneagles/africa.pdf (accessed June 25, 2014), paragraph 31.

2 See for example, Jean-Yves Capul, ed., *Découverte de l'économie 3: Les politiques économiques*, Cahiers Français 284 (Paris: La documentation française, 1998); Benoit Ferrandon, ed., *La politique économique et ses instruments*, Les notices de la documentation française (Paris: La documentation française, 2004). See also: N. Acocella, *Economic Policy in the Age of Globalisation* (Cambridge: Cambridge University Press, 2005); A. Bénassy-Quéré et al., *Politique économique* (Brussels: de Boeck, 2004); or Darreau Philippe, *Croissance et politique économique* (Bruxelles: de Boeck, 2003).

3 J. Saint-Geours, *La politique économique des principaux pays industriels de l'Occident*, 2nd edition (Paris: Sirey, 1973), 2, quoted in Christian de Boissieu, *Principes de politique économique*, 2nd edition (Paris: Economica, 1980), vii (my translation).

4 Ibid.

5 Ahmed Silem et Jean-Marie Albertini, eds, *Lexique d'économie*, 8th edition (Paris: Dalloz, 2004).

6 Although some policy reforms might have contributed, it is often argued that the high growth rates mostly reflect natural resources exploitation, favorable weather conditions and foreign aid, and have not been transformative. For a recent discussion of the persisting structural weaknesses of African growth, see Dani Rodrick, "La fragile croissance africaine," *La Tribune*, December 17, 2013. Online: http://www.latribune.fr/opinions/tribunes/20131217trib000801484/la-fragile-croissance-africaine.html (accessed April 29, 2014).

7 See C. Burnside, D. Dollar, "Aid, Policies, and Growth," *American Economic Review* 90, no. 4 (September 2000): 847–68.

8 In 2008, an OECD report drew attention to the fact that, at the pace at that time, rich countries were not going to be able to keep their promises of doubling aid to Africa by 2010. See OECD, *Development Cooperation Report*, available at: http://www.oecd.org/document/38/0,2340,en_2649_201185_38144422_1_1_1_1,00.html (accessed April 29, 2014). Also, during a summit held from June 6 to 8, 2007 in Heiligendamm, Germany, the G8 countries discussed the issue of whether they should reiterate the commitments made in 2005. For some G8 members, there was no need to refer once more to the 2005 Gleneagles commitments in the final press release of their 2007 summit because these commitments could not be respected (see Hugh Williamson, "G8 Split over Africa Aid Pledges," *Financial Times*, June 5, 2007). Under pressure from public opinion, the G8 countries simply chose to reaffirm their commitment to honor their 2005 pledges, without saying how. This posed the question of the future of the Gleneagles commitments, given that the projections made at the time, based on achievements so far, showed that those commitments were not going to be met. See *Growth and Responsibility in Africa*, G8 Summit Declaration, Heiligendamm, June 8, 2007. Online: http://www.g-8.de/Content/DE/Artikel/G8Gipfel/Anlage/Abschlusserkl_C3_A4rungen/WV-afrika-en,property=publicationFile.pdf (accessed April 29, 2014).

9 Barney Jopson, "Policy: Turning Back to the IMF," *G20: Africa and the World* (*Financial Times* Special Report), April 2, 2009, 4.

10 This expression appeared in the literature in the late 1980s in the writings of the American economist John Williamson. In the initial version of the Washington Consensus, Williamson spoke of liberalization of interest rates, but due to objections of economists, including that of Joseph Stiglitz, who had expressed doubts about the place and role of the liberalization of interest rates as envisaged in the original formulation, he later clarified his thoughts by stating he wanted to say financial liberalization. On this point, see John Williamson, "What Should the World Bank Think about the Washington Consensus?" *World Bank Research Observer* 15, no. 2 (August 2000): 251–64.

11 Commission on Growth and Development, *The Growth Report: Strategies for Sustained Growth and Inclusive Development* (Washington, DC, 2009). Available on the website of the commission: http://siteresources.worldbank.org/EXTPREMNET/Resources/489960-1338997241035/Growth_Commission_Final_Report.pdf (accessed April 29, 2014). The works of the commission were funded by the governments of Australia, the Netherlands, Sweden and the United Kingdom, the William and Flora Hewlett Foundation and the World Bank.

12 The commission was comprised of 21 members, including the governors of the central banks of China and Indonesia, the former president of Mexico, the chairman of the Monetary Authority of Singapore and two Nobel Prize winners in economics.

13 In the context of developing countries, it has often been argued that demand is not a problem because they face infinite demand in world markets. But, as we shall see, this result is based on a hypothesis that is increasingly questionable; that is, the existence of perfect substitutability between the goods and services offered by these countries and those available in world markets.

14 See William Easterly, "Trust the Development Experts – All 7bn of Them," *Financial Times*, May 29, 2008.

15 For example, according to figures from the World Bank (World Development Indicators), gross income per capita of Switzerland is twice that of Greece and the gross income per capita of the Netherlands is higher than that of France by about eighteen per cent. These differences are significant.

16 This annual conference is organized by the African Development Bank in collaboration with the United Nations' Economic Commission for Africa (ECA) to encourage and promote research on economic issues related to the development of African economies. It equally aimed at stimulating dialogue and exchange among development actors such as economists, policymakers, researchers, the private sector and civil society.

Chapter One: The Sectoral Approach to Economic Policy and Its Limits

1 Justin Yifu Lin, *The Quest for Prosperity: How Developing Economies Can Take Off* (Princeton, NJ: Princeton University Press, 2012), 6, 103.

2 In fact, the areas covered by this sectoral analysis are often determined by what the international community views as important for these countries at that moment. One might well add labor market policies to the previous list, and issues such as environment, gender and public sector performance, to name just a few of the many areas studied. For an interesting discussion on these different priorities, see William Easterly, *The Elusive Quest for Growth: Economists' Adventures and Misadventures in the Tropics* (Cambridge, MA: MIT Press, 2001).

3 See, for example, A. Bénassy-Quéré et al. *Politique économique* (Brussels: de Boeck, 2004).

4 Dani Rodrik, "Introduction: What Do We Learn from Country Narratives," in *In Search of Prosperity: Analytic Narratives on Economic Growth*, ed. Dani Rodrik (Princeton, NJ: Princeton University Press, 2003).

5 These authors speak of "the binding constraint." See R. Hausmann et al., "Getting the Diagnosis Right: A New Approach to Economic Reform," *Finance et développement* 43, no. 1 (March 2006), 12–15.

6 Ibid.

7 For a detailed analysis of this succession of panaceas, all of which have been unable to produce the growth and economic development expected, see Easterly, *The Elusive Quest*.

Chapter Two: Conceptual Framework of a Systemic Economic Policy for Africa's Revival

1 Bill and Melinda Gates Foundation, "Bill Gates – 2007 Harvard Commencement," June 6, 2007. Online: http://www.gatesfoundation.org/Media-Center/Speeches/2007/06/Bill-Gates-Harvard-Commencement (accessed May 4, 2014).

2 Joseph Tchundjang Pouemi, *Monnaie, servitude et liberté, la répression monétaire de l'Afrique* (Yaoundé: MENAIBUC, 1979), 29 (my translation).

3 For a detailed analysis of this risk, see UNCTAD, *Trade and Development Report: Global Partnership and National Policies for Development* (New York: United Nations, 2006), 135.

4 For a complete and accessible summary of theories of economic growth, see Elhanan Helpman, *The Mystery of Economic Growth* (Cambridge, MA: Belknap Press of Harvard University Press, 2004). In this concise book, the author structures the discussion of the factors affecting economic growth according to the following themes: accumulation of physical and human capital, technology and innovation and their role in the productivity of accumulated capital, the role of political and economic institutions in economic growth, interdependence of the growth rates of different countries, and the role of income inequality in growth.

5 See J. M. Keynes, *Théorie générale de l'emploi, de l'intérêt et de la monnaie* (Paris: Payot & Rivages 2005).

6 De Boissieu, *Principes de politique économique*.

7 See Laurence H. Meyer, *A Term at the FED: An Insider's View; The People and Policies of the World's Most Powerful Institution* (New York: Collins, 2004), chap. 7, "Irrational Exuberance" for an illustration of the importance of subjective factors in relation to economic policy, namely monetary policy. Also see Lorenzo Bini Smaghi (member of the Executive Board of the ECB), "Three Questions on Monetary Tightening," speech at the Nomura Conference, Tokyo, October 26–7, 2006, for an interesting illustration of the art of economic policy as applied to monetary policy, notably as concerns the choosing of the moment and the extent of an action on an instrument.

8 See Amihai Glazer and Lawrence S. Rothenberg, *Why Government Succeeds and Why It Fails* (Cambridge, MA: Harvard University Press, 2001) for an interesting illustration of the manner in which credibility, rational expectations, crowding-out effects and multiple equilibria can affect economic policy. See also F. E. Kydland and E. C. Prescott, "Rules Rather than Discretion: The Inconsistency of Optimal Plans," *Journal of Political Economy* 85, no. 3 (June 1977): 473–92, for a theoretical analysis of the role played by credibility and rational anticipation. Also see Kungliga Vetenskapsakademien (Royal Swedish Academy of Sciences), *Finn Kydland and Edward Prescott's Contribution to Dynamic Macroeconomics: The Time Consistency of Economic Policy and the Driving Forces Behind Business Cycles*, Advanced Information on the Bank of Sweden Prize in Economic Sciences in Memory of Alfred Nobel (Stockholm: KVA Information Department, 2004). Online: http://www.nobelprize.org/nobel_prizes/economic-sciences/laureates/2004/advanced-economicsciences2004.pdf (accessed April 29, 2014).

9 In the United States for example, the short-term interest rates, which the Federal Reserve (the US central bank) tries to influence is known as the "federal funds rate." In fact, it is the rate at which banks exchange their excess liquidity among themselves for short periods of time, often for a day. The FED sets a target for the federal funds rate and tries to ensure that this target prevails for these exchanges between banks. In the eurozone, this short-term rate is referred to as the minimum open-market rate and the operating principle is the same; that is, make sure that the target for this rate prevails in interbank exchange of liquidity.

10 For an enriching analysis showing the inability of the ideas contained in the Washington Consensus to promote growth in developing countries, see J. Stiglitz, *La grande désillusion* (Paris: Fayard, 2002). See also Moisés Naim, "Washington Consensus: A Damaged Brand," *Financial Times*, October 28, 2002. For a defense without conviction of this concept, see John Williamson, "What Should the World Bank Think about the Washington Consensus?" *World Bank Research Observer* 15, no. 2 (August 2000), 251–64.

Chapter Three: Final Goals for a Systemic Economic Policy

1 Joseph E. Stiglitz, *The Roaring Nineties: A New History of the World's Most Prosperous Decade* (New York: W. W. Norton, 2003), 297.

2 The World Bank calls this type of document a "Country Assistance Strategy." The IMF does not really prepare a document of this type, but the report of its services on the economic and financial program that it supports in a country can be considered the closest thing to an assistance strategy.

3 It was only in 2006 that the Millennium Development Goals were revised to include a subgoal on the promotion of employment.

4 Moreover, the IMF had suspended its disbursements for lack of sufficient control over public expenditures and, as is always the case, other donors fell in behind the IMF and suspended their budgetary aid – that is, the part of their aid paid in directly to the state budget.

5 The Annual Meetings regroup the governors of the World Bank, who are generally finance ministers or governors of the central banks of member states. They are opportunities for these governors to jointly examine the progress made by the World Bank in accomplishing its mission and to decide orientations for future action.

6 For more detailed discussion of implicit choices in any definition of poverty, see S. Bouquerel and Pierre-Alain de Mallerey, "L'Europe et la pauvreté: Quelles réalités?" *Notes de la Fondation Robert Schuman* 31 (March 2006). For a discussion of international practices in terms of poverty measures, see Patrick Festy and Lidia Prokofiegtyva, "Mesures, formes et facteurs de la pauvreté: Approches comparatives" (INED Documents de travail no. 151, 2008).

7 As we will see later, available studies show that these other elements of the standard of living are closely related to the level of income.

8 These minimum nutritional needs are defined in minimum caloric needs and may afterwards be adjusted to take into account other non-nutritional needs.

9 The European Union has also adopted a multidimensional conception of poverty. However, by recognizing the importance of monetary poverty in determining the status of a person or household, the European Union gives a preponderant role to monetary poverty in its definition. Thus, among the 21 indicators that European leaders approved in December 2001, 10 refer to monetary poverty. We can also assert that by recognizing the role of employment in poverty, European indicators place importance on curbing the unemployment situation (7 indicators out of 21); this is not the case with the Millennium Development Goals, which at first did not make any reference to employment. I think that not setting a goal on employment constituted one of the major shortcomings of the Millennium Development Goals when they were first designed in 2000.

10 Although the approach of the European Union in terms of measuring poverty is based fundamentally on an objective approach, we can therein detect elements of a subjective approach. Thus, besides measures based on the objective appreciation of income, the 21 indicators retained by the European Union to measure poverty include an indicator which depends on a subjective approach to the poverty measure. It concerns the proportion of the working population from 16 years and above belonging to the first and fifth quintile of income and which declare a state of bad or very bad health.

11 In the European Union, France is part of the small number of countries which slightly differ from this standard of 60 per cent. The National Institute of Statistics and Economic Studies,

the French organ in charge of collecting information, uses the line of 50 per cent of average income.

12 Thus, for a long time, the World Bank arbitrarily fixed the poverty line at one dollar per day. By using this rate, it estimated that about 1.2 billion people in the world were poor – that is, live below the absolute poverty line. Some countries also calculate the national absolute poverty line based on a national definition of the level of resources necessary to procure the minimum consumer basket. These are in general different from the line of one US dollar per day retained by the World Bank.

13 See UNDP, *Human Development Report* (New York: United Nations). This report has been published every year since 1990.

14 Quoted in: "Dialogue with Angus Deaton: When Numbers Don't Tell the Full Story about Poverty in India and the World," *IMF Survey* 31, no. 13 (July 8, 2002): 215.

15 Ibid.

16 The questionnaires were not conceived to collect this information.

17 For a discussion of Emile Durkheim's thought on work, see Edward A. Tiryakian, "Le travail chez Emile Durkheim," in *Le travail dans l'histoire de la pensée occidentale*, ed. Daniel Mercure and Jan Spurk (Quebec: Laval University Press, 2003).

18 For a more detailed examination of the place occupied by work in Max Weber's thought, see Hans-Peter Müller, "Travail, Profession et 'Vocation': Le concept de travail chez Max Weber," in *Le travail dans l'histoire*.

19 Max Weber, *L'éthique protestante et l'esprit du capitalism*, quoted in Müller, ibid.

20 For detailed examination of the place occupied by work in Adam Smith's economic thought, see Daniel Mercure, "Adam Smith: Les assises de la modernité," in *Le travail dans l'histoire*.

21 For an analysis of the role of labor in a philosophical perspective, see Léopold Migeotte, "Les philosophes grecs et le travail dans l'antiquité," in *Le travail dans l'histoire*.

22 Beyond these beneficial effects of work, it should be noted that with the advent of modern societies, work has also become a source of suffering linked to stress, fear, fatigue, pressures exerted by management and the competition, and the development of new technologies which compete in a reduction of time and space and, finally, in a continuous pressure on all categories of personnel, from laborers to senior managers. Thus, several pathologies can be linked to work.

23 Robert Castel, *Guide FNAC des questions d'aujourd'hui* (Paris: FNAC, 2001).

24 In developed countries, the importance of social transfers contributes to reduce the link between income/employment and poverty. Thus, a recent study of poverty in the European Union showed that social transfers made the poverty rate to drop from 40 per cent before social transfers to 16 per cent after social transfers. See Sarah Bouquerel and Pierre-Alain de Mallerey, "L'Europe et la pauvreté: Quelles réalités?" *Notes de la Fondation Robert Schuman* 31 (March 2006).

25 African Development Bank, *Evaluation Report of the Support Project to the Sectoral Program of Health* (Tunis, October 2004).

26 Ibid.

27 The American economist Paul Krugman used the expressions "growth through inspiration" to characterize the first case and "growth through perspiration" to characterize the second. Studying the rapid growth of South East Asian countries, he drew the conclusion that this growth was more the result of perspiration than inspiration. Paul Krugman, *Pop Internationalism* (Cambridge, MA: MIT Press, 1997), 167–87.

28 Quoted in N. Gregory Mankiw, *Macroeconomics*, 3rd edition (New York: Worth, 1997), 362. The Employment Act was signed by US president Truman on February 20, 1946. In a speech made on October 26, 2005, at the Truman Medal Award and Economics Conference on the occasion of the reception of the Truman Medal for Economic Policy, Alan Greenspan, then president of the US Federal Reserve, traced the origin of this important law to two major developments of the time: on the one hand, fear that the problem of unemployment had not really been solved and, on the other hand, the influence of Keynesian thought, according to

which the insufficiency of global demand may stimulate the economy toward an equilibrium of underemployment necessitating an increase in public expenses to attain a better equilibrium.

29 For a detailed discussion of the South Korean experience, see Ji Hong Kim, "Lessons from Asia: The Experience of Korea," paper presented at the African Economic Conference on "Accelerating Africa's Development Five Years into the Twenty-First Century," Tunis, November 22–4, 2006.

Chapter Four: Intermediate Goals for a Systemic Economic Policy

1 South African Government Online: http://www.gov.za/speeches/view.php?sid=34999 (accessed April 29, 2014).

2 I prefer here the reference to the concept of world demand, which in the current context of economic globalization seems more relevant. Indeed, even if some analysts support the idea of a certain inertia of local behaviors, there is growing recognition that, in the context of globalization, economic agents, be they local or foreign, operate in the same economic space (i.e., deal with the same sources of demand expressed by domestic and foreign economic agents). For an interesting discussion of the effects of globalization on consumers' behavior, see Jagdish Bhagwati, *In Defense of Globalization* (New York: Oxford University Press, 2005).

3 I will dwell in greater detail on the negative effects of inflation in the subsequent chapters.

4 In this discussion and throughout this book, when I speak of demand for and supply of goods and services, I will mainly mean demand for, and supply of, tradable goods and services, unless otherwise specified. Economists make a distinction between tradable goods and services and nontradable goods and services. Tradable goods and services can be defined as those which are either importable or exportable – that is, which enter international trade. In comparison with the nontradable variety, tradable goods and services have the two distinct characteristics: (i) they are vital for our individual and collective well-being and even survival, and (ii) they offer virtually unlimited opportunities for growth and job creation since their demand goes beyond the national economy and can be generated everywhere in the world economy. Tradable goods and services include primary-sector products such as agricultural products, forestry, fishing and livestock products, secondary-sector products such as manufacturing, subsoil resources, and some highly sophisticated tertiary-sector products such as financial services, legal services, engineering services, advisory services, and tourism. Nontradable services mainly include other tertiary-sector services such government services, retail and other low-productivity and low-value-added services. Nontradable goods and services only offer limited possibilities for growth because growth in this sector can only come at the expense of growth in another sector of the economy, unless that growth is the result of strong productivity gains, which is rare in the nontradable sector. One of the key structural weaknesses of African economies is the outsized nontradable sector, which continues to weigh on their growth prospects. The economic policy framework I propose in this book aims to correct this.

5 As I shall observe, there are several other variables on which it is possible to act in order to influence demand.

6 Many efforts have been made to demonstrate the invalidity of the assumption of perfect substitutability; see for example the article by Donald R. Davis and Prachi Mishra, "Stolper-Samuelson Is Dead: And Other Crimes of Both Theory and Data," in *Globalization and Poverty*, ed. Ann Harrison (Chicago: University of Chicago Press, 2007). Despite these efforts, it often happens that some authors continue to refer to it; see for example Michael Spence, "Wealth of Nations: What Drives High Growth Rates?" *Wall Street Journal*, January 24, 2007. In this article, the author recognizes the fundamental role of demand as an engine of growth, but the assumption of perfect substitutability is implicit in his reasoning when he states that the global economy offers developing countries an unlimited global demand. We have just seen that this is not the case.

7 I should also say in passing that exports do not have a monopoly over foreign-exchange generation. When the share of domestic demand that is addressed to the economy increases at the expense

of one directed to the rest of the world (resulting in relatively lower unproductive or unnecessary imports), the demand for foreign exchange in the economy declines. This corresponds to an economy of foreign exchange, and also a gain in foreign exchange. Thus, proper management of demand may also contribute to gains in foreign exchange. Economists often recognize the virtues of imports when they incorporate technological progress and thus contribute to economic productivity; for this reason I have spoken here of unproductive imports – that is to say, those which do not incorporate technological progress. These kinds of unproductive imports often represent an important share of total imports in many African countries.

8 For a more detailed discussion of the weak demand prospects in developed countries and what it implies for demand management strategies and growth in developing countries see UNCTAD, *Trade and Development Report 2013* (New York: United Nations, 2013).

9 See Marcos Aguiar et al., *The New Global Challengers: How 100 Top Companies from Rapidly Developing Economies Are Changing the World* (Boston: Boston Consulting Group, May 2006). The study involved 100 companies including 44 Chinese, 21 Indian, 12 Brazilian, 7 Russian, 6 Mexican and 10 other countries including Egypt, Indonesia, Malaysia, Thailand and Turkey. These companies operate in sectors as diverse as industrial equipment, durable consumer goods, food and cosmetic products and extraction of natural resources. They had a combined turnover of 715 billion US dollars in 2004 (the combined GDP of Mexico and Russia), an annual growth of 24 per cent between 2000 and 2004 (ten times faster than the US economy), and had recorded profits of 145 billion US dollars, representing a relative margin in relation to sales of 20 per cent.

10 World Bank, *Malawi: Country Economic Memorandum; Policies for Accelerating Growth*, report no. 25293-MAI, Poverty Reduction and Economic Management 1, Africa Region (Washington, DC, January 2004).

11 Benn, Gelb and Ramachandran (2005), in Jorge Saba Arbache, "African Development Indicators 2006," presentation at the African Development Bank, Tunis, March 8, 2007.

12 See Alan Gelb, "Cost and Competitiveness in Africa," PowerPoint presentation to the PSD Forum, June 2006, in the session on "Taping Africa's Export Potential beyond Commodities: What is the Mix of Economy-Wide and Industry-Specific Reforms?" Development Economics Department, World Bank.

13 For a more detailed discussion of the measures implemented by low-income countries, including African countries, throughout the 1980s and 1990s, see "The ESAF at Ten Years: Economic Adjustment and Reform in Low-Income Countries," (IMF Occasional Paper no. 156, Washington, DC, 1997).

14 For an overview of this controversy see for example Paul Krugman, *End This Depression Now!* (New York: W. W. Norton, 2012) and J. Sachs, "Today's Challenges Go beyond Keynes," *Financial Times*, December 17, 2012.

Chapter Five: Operating Goals for a Systemic Economic Policy

1 To obtain this result, these two economists based their arguments on the rational expectations of economic agents, formulated for the first time in 1972 and 1973 by the American economist R. Lucas Jr. For more details, see Finn E. Kydland and Edward C. Prescott, "Rules Rather than Discretion: The Inconsistency of Optimal Plans," *Journal of Political Economy* 85, no. 3 (June 1977): 473–92. Also see Kungliga Vetenskapsakademien (Royal Swedish Academy of Sciences), *Finn Kydland and Edward Prescott's Contribution to Dynamic Macroeconomics: The Time Consistency of Economic Policy and the Driving Forces Behind Business Cycles*, Advanced Information on the Bank of Sweden Prize in Economic Sciences in Memory of Alfred Nobel (Stockholm: KVA Information Department, 2004). Online: http://www.nobelprize.org/nobel_prizes/economic-sciences/laureates/2004/advanced-economicsciences2004.pdf (accessed April 29, 2014).

2 It should be noted that in 2007, approximately eighty per cent of the cellphone market in Africa experienced some form of competition. All statistics cited here are from International

Telecommunication Union, *African Telecommunication / ICT Indicators: At a Crossroads* (Geneva: ITU Telecom Africa, 2008). If, in a bid to be rigorous in the comparison, we take the monthly gross national income instead of annual gross national income, the percentages for sub-Saharan countries will still be much higher.

3 For a more detailed analysis of these arguments and how they affect development, see P. Collier's article presented at the African Economic Conference of the African Development Bank in November 2006: "Africa's Economic Growth: Opportunities and Constraints," Centre for the Study of African Economies, Department of Economics, Oxford University.

4 For a discussion on the challenges of social cohesion in developed countries, see Ha-Joon Chang, "Economic History of the Developed World: Lessons for Africa," lecture at the Eminent Speakers Program of the African Development Bank, February 26, 2009.

5 This process is one in which the national economy creates jobs. When it reaches its maximum supply capacity, it also attains its full potential of job creation. The goal of economic policymakers on economic growth is to try to attain the point of maximum supply capacity of the economy.

6 The extent to which the authorities responsible for economic policy act too soon or too late usually depends on their comparative aversion to unemployment and inflation, respectively. The American economist Laurence H. Meyer, governor of the Federal Reserve from 1996 to 2002, calls "hawks" those officials of economic policy who have an extreme aversion to inflation and are ready to stop, even prematurely, increases in demand, in order to prevent the risk inflation. He calls "doves" those officials who, on the contrary, have an extreme aversion to unemployment and who are willing to wait until the risks of inflation become obvious before taking action to stop the expansion of demand.

7 This analytical framework is thanks to the work of the English economist William Phillips, who in 1950 noted while studying the trend of inflation in Great Britain that it was linked to the level of unemployment, which was rife in the economy.

8 This difficulty arises because changes in relative prices take place at the same time as changes in the general price level, thus contributing to less transparency in current economic developments. Economists call the opposite phenomenon of inflation deflation – that is to say, the decline in the general price level. It introduces into the economic system the same distortions as inflation.

9 Source: European Central Bank, *The Monetary Policy of the ECB* (Frankfurt: ECB, 2004), 41–3. Online: http://www.ecb.europa.eu/pub/pdf/other/monetarypolicy2004en.pdf (accessed April 29, 2014).

10 For more on this episode of Argentina and resentment toward external influences, especially that of the IMF, see Jude Webber and Richard Lapper "It Won't Be Easy… No Tears for the IMF as a Feisty Argentina Awaits Its Next Evita," *Financial Times*, October 26, 2007.

11 For a reminder of the thought of Keynes on this issue, see Jacques Sapir, "L'économie politique internationale de la crise et de la question du 'nouveau Bretton Woods': Lecons pour les temps de crise" (2008). Online: http://www.lhivic.org/travaux/articles/sapir_brettonWoods2.pdf (accessed April 29, 2014).

12 To be rigorous, I should also add the general price level, which is calculated as the average of prices of goods and services consumed in the economy.

13 High prices and inflation should not be confused. Inflation refers to a rapid variation with time of price levels. Prices can be high, but remain stable. In this case, there is no inflation.

14 In fact, the earnings of a bank come from three sources: these are the commissions earned on the services (such as transfers, account maintenance fees, etc.) they provide to their customers. There is also income from financial intermediation, which normally consists of the difference between interest earned on loans and interest paid on deposits. Finally, there are gains or losses on the financial assets they hold. In a well-functioning financial system, it is the income from financial intermediation that makes up the largest share of income of banks. But this is not the case in many African countries where the income from commissions has overtaken other

sources of income, a symptom of banks abandoning their core business. A proactive effort is necessary for banks to regain their core mandate.

15 Another key aspect of sustainability which is increasingly being recognized and discussed in policy circles relates to environmental sustainability and resilience to climate change. In this area, I think developed countries should do far more than they are currently doing to ensure the sustainability of global growth. For more discussions on climate change issues, see for example the outcomes of the various United Nations Climate Change Conferences. The most recent conference took place in Durban, South Africa, from November 28 to December 9, 2011.

16 See Ferdinand Bakoup and David Tarr, "How Integration into the Central African Economic and Monetary Community Affects Cameroon's Economy: General Equilibrium Estimates," World Bank Development Research Group, policy research working paper no. 187 (Washington, DC, 1998).

17 In economics, the notion of residence is distinct from that of nationality, even if the temptation of confusing the two is often high. Resident economic agents are economic agents who stay relatively long enough in a country.

18 For a presentation of the absorption approach, which has underpinned the macroeconomic framework in African countries, see International Monetary Fund, *Theoretical Aspects of the Design of Fund-Supported Adjustment Programs* (IMF Occasional Paper no. 55, September 1987).

19 See Stefania Fabrizio, Denis Igan and Ashoka Mody, "The Dynamics of Product Quality and International Competitiveness" (IMF Working Paper no. WP/07/97, 2007).

20 See, for example, Brice Pedroletti, "Les attaques contre les marques étrangères se multiplient en Chine," *Le Monde,* June 7, 2007, 16. Also see Mure Dickie, "Shanghai Finds Top Brand Names Wanting," *Financial Times,* January 20/21, 2007.

21 Allan Beattie "Manufacturing: Dying to Keep Up with Competition from the Chinese," *Financial Times Special Report,* Nigeria, Thursday July 12, 2007, 13.

22 For example, Dani Rodrik emphasizes social cohesion (see *The New Global Economy and Developing Countries: Making Openness Work* [Policy Essay no. 24, Overseas Development Council, Washington, DC, 1999]), the freedom to choose the economic policies that the international system should give to poor countries (see *One Economics, Many Recipes: Globalization, Institutions and Economic Growth* [Princeton, NJ: Princeton University Press, 2007]), and quality of institutions, which corresponds here to what I call governance (see ibid.; or D. Rodrik, A. Subramanian and F. Trebbi, "Institutions Rule: The Primacy of Institutions over Integration and Geography in Economic Development" [IMF Working Paper no. 02/189, 2002]). Dollar emphasizes opening up to the outside world (see, for example, David Dollar, "Globalization, Poverty and Inequality," in *Globalization: What's New?*, ed. Michael M. Weinstein [New York: Columbia University Press 2005]). Arvind Subramanian and Devesh Roy insist on exports (see, for example, "Who Can Explain the Mauritian Miracle? Meade, Romer, Sachs, or Rodrik?" in *In Search of Prosperity Analytic Narratives on Economic Growth,* ed. Dani Rodrik [Princeton, NJ: Princeton University Press, 2003]), ch. 8. Eugène Nyambal insists on institutional quality, education and the existence of a social contract (see *Créer la prospérité en Afrique: Dix clés pour sortir de la pauvreté,* L'esprit économique [Paris: L'Harmattan, 2006]). Obviously, none of these authors gives a complete overview of how a good economic policy must be defined, structured and implemented, as I do in this book.

Chapter Six: Instruments for a Systemic Economic Policy

1 Remarks by US Federal Reserve chairman Alan Greenspan at the receipt of the Truman Medal for Economic Policy before the Truman Medal Award and Economics Conference, Kansas City, Missouri October 26, 2005. Online: http://www.federalreserve.gov/boarddocs/speeches/2005/20051026/default.htm (accessed April 29, 2014).

2 For a detailed and insightful discussion of the links between the financial effects and the effectiveness of reforms measures, see F. Bakoup, "Promoting Economic Reforms in Developing Countries: Rethinking Budgetary Aid?" (African Development Bank, Working Paper, no. 167, 2013).

3 Among the several instruments used to attain this goal is the interest rate. It constitutes the price to pay for keeping a sum of money for a well-defined period of time. Thus, I will say "the interest rate is 5 per cent," which means if you borrow 100 dollars, at the end of the year you will reimburse 105 dollars – 5 dollars representing the interest or the price you will pay to whoever lent you this money for the year. There exist several interest rates in an economy according to the duration of the loan, the quality of the signature of the borrower and the level of risk run by the lender. However, the most important rate, that which determines all the other rates, is the interest rate determined on the money market and which is directly influenced by the central bank. Tomas J. T. Balino and Lorena M. Zamalloa present a comprehensive review of different instruments that the Central Bank can use to implement monetary policy toward controlling the quantity of means of payment in circulation: *Instruments of Monetary Management: Issues and Country Experiences* (Washington, DC: IMF, 1997). Despite the key role of the interest rate in monetary policy, the recent financial crisis also led to a significant shift in monetary policy instruments in developed countries toward what is now known as "unconventional or nonstandard monetary policy measures." These unconventional measures seek to directly influence the quantity of liquidity to be supplied to the economy instead of trying to achieve this the traditional way, which is to rely on the policy interest rate. For more details on central banks' unconventional monetary policy measures, see C. Borio and P. Disyatat, "Unconventional Monetary Policies: An Appraisal" (BIS Working Paper, no. 292, November, 2009). See also P. Cour-Thimann and B. Winker, "The ECB's Non-Standard Monetary Policy Measures: The Role of Institutional Factors and Financial Structure" (ECB Working Paper Series, no. 152B, April 2013).

4 Source: IMF, "World Economic Outlook Database, October 2013," consumer price at the end of the period. Online: http://www.imf.org/external/pubs/ft/weo/2013/02/weodata/index. aspx (accessed April 29, 2014).

5 See Joseph E. Stiglitz and Bruce Greenwald, *Towards a New Paradigm in Monetary Economics*, Raffaele Mattioli Lectures (Cambridge: Cambridge University Press, 2003).

6 The Cameroonian economist Joseph Tchundjang Pouemi insisted much during his time on the role of credit and money in economic activity. See Pouemi, *Monnaie, servitude et liberté*.

7 For a detailed and very enriching analysis of difficulties posed by access to bank credit in sub-Saharan Africa, see Emilio Sacerdoti, "Access to Bank Credit in Sub-Saharan Africa: Key Issues and Reform Strategies" (Washington, DC: IMF Working Paper, no. WP/05/166, 2005).

8 For a mathematical formulation and a discussion of Taylor's rule, see Michel Aglietta, *Macroéconomie financière*, 5th edition (Paris: La Découverte, 2008), 215.

9 See Kossi Tenou, "La règle de Taylor: Un exemple de règle de politique monétaire appliquée au cas de la BCEAO" (Documents d'études et de recherche de la BCEAO no. 523, Dakar, March 2002).

10 See Jean-Claude Trichet, "Some Lessons from the Financial Market Correction," speech delivered at the European Banker of the Year 2007 award ceremony, Frankfurt, September 30, 2008. Online: http://www.ecb.int/press/key/date/2008/html/sp080930_1.en.html (accessed April 11, 2014).

11 Ibid.

12 See Hassanali Mehran et al., "Financial Sector Development in Sub-Saharan African Countries" (Washington, DC: IMF Occasional Paper, no. 169, 1998).

13 For an interesting analysis of how budget deficits in developing countries are most often the primary source of excessive monetary creation, leading to inflationary pressures and macroeconomic imbalances, see Jean-Claude Nachéga, "Fiscal Dominance and Inflation in the Democratic Republic of Congo" (Washington, DC: IMF Working Paper, no. WP/05/22, 2005).

14 The concept of sustainability in budgetary policy seeks to account for the medium-term solvency of the state resulting from the dynamics of public debt generated by the budgetary

policy which is presently implemented. If this dynamics leads to a situation of insolvency, we say that budgetary policy is unsustainable. Sustainability is, therefore, an extremely important concept in budgetary policy, for the credibility of budgetary policy and, by ripple effect, of the economic policy in its entirety depends on it, considering the role of budgetary policy in the overall economic policy. For an in-depth discussion of this concept, see Agnès Bénassy-Quéré et al., *Politique économique*, 1st edition (Brussels: Editions de Boeck, 2004), 168–78.

15 Member states of WAEMU are Benin, Burkina Faso, Côte d'Ivoire, Guinea-Bissau, Mali, Niger, Senegal and Togo. CEMAC member states are Cameroon, Gabon, Equatorial Guinea, Congo Republic, Central African Republic and Chad.

16 For a discussion of this experience and use of budgetary rules, see Bénassy-Quéré, et al., *Politique économique*. Georges Kopits, "Fiscal Rules: Useful Policy Framework or Unnecessary Ornament?" (Washington, DC: IMF Working Paper, no. WP/01/145, 2001) also contains an interesting discussion of the conception and implementation of budgetary rules.

17 Kopits and Symansky, "Fiscal Policy Rules" (Washington, DC: IMF Occasional Paper, no. 162, 1998), in Bénassy-Quéré et al., *Politique économique*.

18 See Union économique et monétaire ouest-africaine, La Commission, "Rapport semestriel d'exécution de la surveillance multilatérale" (June 2008). Online: http://www.uemoa.int/ Documents/Publications/Surv_Multilaterale/2008/rsmjuin2008.pdf (accessed May 1, 2014).

19 I will study the example of South Africa in detail and hence show that the quality of fiscal policy carried out by this country has greatly contributed to the credibility enjoyed by the authorities and the economic management of this country in general. In fact, fiscal policy in this country has been carried out with the aim of credibility and sustainability at the forefront.

20 In economic policy, this coefficient is better known by the Keynesian multiplier appellation and indicates the proportion in which the GDP increases after a budgetary stimulation of *1*. In this coefficient, c designates the marginal propensity to consume and m the marginal propensity to import.

21 We may expect the different socioeconomic groups to have different behaviors of demand of goods and services produced by the national economy. This is expressed by the great variability of m. In these conditions, the goal must be that budget stimulation results in a proportionally higher increase of the incomes of economic agents, who have the lowest m.

22 Estimated losses of fiscal revenue are carried to foreign aid projections for 2008. "Republic of Senegal Joint IDA–IMF Staff Advisory Note of the Second Poverty Reduction Strategy Paper" (World Bank, report no. 38131-SN, December 20, 2006). Online: http://www-wds.worldbank. org/external/default/WDSContentServer/WDSP/IB/2007/06/15/000112742_200706 15155946/Rendered/PDF/381310File0replacement0IDA1SecM200710010.pdf (accessed April 10, 2014).

23 Generally, most fiscal revenues increase during boom and drop during recession. Literature often cites unemployment benefits as being the type of public spending which drops when the economic situation improves. But this type of transfer does not practically exist in African countries.

24 To see estimates of the effect of automatic stabilizers on the eurozone, see the interesting book by Jean Claude Prager and François Villeroy de Galhau, *18 leçons sur la politique économique* (Paris: Editions du Seuil, 2006), 464.

25 The American economist Arthur B. Laffer showed that there is a concave relationship between tax rates and tax revenues, with the tax revenue increasing first with the tax rate to a certain threshold and then decreasing. According to this relationship, the negative economic effects on the incentive to work, and therefore on production and tax revenues, end up outweighing the positive effects on tax revenues associated with the increase in the tax rate.

26 See Tax Justice Network – Africa and Action Aid International, *Tax Competition in East Africa: A Race to the Bottom?* (Nairobi/Johannesburg, April 2012). Online: http://www.taxjusticeafrica. net/sites/default/files/Tax%20competition%20in%20East%20Africa.pdf (accessed May 1, 2014).

27 In fact, very high import tariffs coupled with weak administrative capacity to enforce them had in many cases led to serious governance problems in the form of corruption, which as we have seen also seriously undermines the effectiveness of economic policy.

28 Some countries are currently aiming at strengthening the local content of public demand through reforms of public procurement. These efforts should continue and even strengthened. But this alone will certainly not do. These efforts on public demand need to be complemented with equally important efforts aimed at private demand. This is a challenging but necessary task for policymakers.

29 For an analysis of the debt overhang hypothesis, see Pierre-Richard Agénor and Peter Montiel, *Development Macroeconomics* (Princeton, NJ: Princeton University Press, 1999).

30 For a more detailed discussion of this episode of American economic policy, see chapter 7 of Lawrence H. Meyer, *A Term at the Fed: An Insider's View; The People and Policies of the World's Most Powerful Institution* (New York: Collins, 2004). See also: Alan Greenspan, *Le temps des turbulences* (Paris: J. C. Lattès, 2007).

31 For presentation of this point of view, see particularly Joseph E. Stiglitz and Jason Furman, "Economic Crises: Evidence and Insights from East Asia," *Brookings Papers on Economic Activity*, no. 2 (1998). Also see Jagdish Bhagwati, *In Defense of Globalization.*

32 For example, for a clear and easy to understand summary of the positive results for monetary policy of the European Central Bank's good communication with economic agents, see Jean-Claude Trichet, "Central Banks and the Public: The Importance of Communication," Lord Roll Memorial Lecture, London, 18 November 2008. Online: http://www.ecb.europa.eu/press/key/date/2008/html/sp081118_2.en.html (accessed April 29, 2014). In this communication, the governor of the ECB proves that by communicating better and efficiently on its monetary policy goals and strategy, the ECB succeeded in durably anchoring inflation expectations in the eurozone between 1.7 per cent and 2 per cent since the introduction of the euro. When we know that the objective of the ECB is a low inflation rate, but close to 2 per cent, we easily understand the positive role that good communication may play. Besides, the persistence of inflation, defined as the tendency of the inflation rate to deviate from its average after a shock, disappeared from the eurozone, still the result of a good communication effort. To accomplish all these is not unique to the ECB. Economic policy in Africa can also use information with the same efficiency and effectiveness. It suffices for policymakers to want it and to work for it.

33 Interview with by Bernard Njonga, president of Association citoyenne de défense des intérêts collectifs, in *Le Monde*, Economie supplement, January 16, 2007, Dossier Economie III (my translation).

34 For more detailed account of this exhortation effort, see Bernard Njonga, *Le poulet de la discorde: Plaidoyer et lobbying* (Yaoundé: Editions Clé, 2008).

35 For illustration of this approach, see Bruce Greenwald and Joseph E. Stiglitz, "Helping Infant Economies Grow: Foundations of Trade Policies for Developing Countries," *AEA Papers and Proceedings* (2006): 141–6.

36 These partnerships correspond to what J. Stiglitz called "cooperation" when he studied the development experience of East Asian countries. See "Some Lessons from the East Asian Miracle," *World Bank Research Observer* 11, no. 2 (August 1996): 151–77.

37 See Dani Rodrik, "Industrial Policy for the Twenty-First Century," New Thinking on Growth and Development Policy (Harvard University training program, 2004). The ideas developed in this article were repeated and intensified in Dani Rodrik, *One Economics, Many Recipes: Globalization, Institutions and Economic Growth* (Princeton, NJ: Princeton University Press, 2007).

38 Interview with Eric Woerth (French minister of the budget, public accounts and public service), in *Les cahiers de la compétitivité*, no. 1 (April 2008).

39 Dani Rodrik, "Industrial Policy."

40 Justin Yifu Lin, *The Quest for Prosperity: How Developing Economies Can Take Off* (Princeton, NJ: Princeton University Press, 2012).

41 If trade policy acts first on demand and not on supply, it is not surprising that attempts to link trade policy and productivity in the economy – a concept which by essence refers to characteristics of processes linked to supply – have not been conclusive or have generated much controversy in the literature. For a preview of this controversy, see for example Joseph E. Stiglitz and Andrew Charlton, *Pour un commerce mondial plus juste* (Paris: Fayard, 2007). Also see World Bank, *Economic Growth in the 1990s: Learning from a Decade of Reform* (Washington, DC: World Bank, 2005), ch. 5: "Trade Liberalization: Why So Much Controversy?" 135.

42 See Ferdinand Bakoup et al., "Regional Integration in Eastern and Southern Africa: The Cross-Border Initiative and its Fiscal Implications" (Washington, DC: IMF Working Paper, no. WP/95/23, 1995).

43 See Amihai Glazer and Lawrence S. Rothenberg, *Why Government Succeeds and Why it Fails* (Cambridge, MA: Harvard University Press, 2001).

44 This manner of defining the exchange rate corresponds to what economists call indirect quotation. It is in this manner that the exchange rate is expressed the world over, except in Great Britain, where it is expressed as the price of the national currency in a foreign currency. There, it is said a pound is worth so many euros or so many dollars. This manner of expressing the exchange rate, which economists also refer to as direct quotation, surely rose when Great Britain was the first world economic power, and saying that a pound is worth so much in this or that currency instead of saying a unit of this or that currency is worth so much pounds showed the desire to affirm this economic supremacy. Indirect quotation seems preferable because it helps to show that foreign currency is an economic good and consequently has a price to pay if we want to have it.

45 Extract from "Taux de change indicatif de la BCT pour les opérations en compte," website of the Central Bank of Tunisia: http://www.bct.gov.tn/bct/siteprod/cours_fixe.jsp (accessed May 1, 2014).

46 From the website of the Bank of France. Euro against the dollar: https://www.banque-france.fr/fileadmin/user_upload/banque_de_france/Economie_et_Statistiques/Changes_et_Taux/uc.d.usd.eur.sp00.a.csv (accessed May 1, 2014). Euro against the pound: https://www.banque-france.fr/fileadmin/user_upload/banque_de_france/Economie_et_Statistiques/Changes_et_Taux/uc.d.gbp.eur.sp00.a.csv (accessed May 1, 2014).

47 See Dominique Gallois, "Aéronautique: Charles Edelstenne, le président de Dassault Aviation, s'alarme des conséquences de l'euro fort," *Le Monde*, December 3, 2007. Also see Peggy Hollinger, "Low Dollar 'Threatens the Life' of Airbus," *Financial Times*, November 23, 2007.

48 In fact, the possibility of accelerating inflation is not inherent in the depreciation of exchange rate. If the rate of depreciation of the exchange rate (hence the creation of demand addressed to the economy that it generates) durably exceeds that of productive-capacity building, a policy of depreciation of exchange rate may lead to inflation. Depreciating the exchange rate discretely and profoundly does not bring much. If the depreciation of the exchange rate and efforts aiming at developing the productive tissue are concomitant, there will be no inflation. Such an association will be beneficial to the economy. Therefore, there is some fine-tuning to be carried out between these two processes. Apparently, Asian countries succeeded in this fine-tuning. Several observers think today that the depreciation of the exchange rate has been an important element of their strategy for building the productive capacity of their economies. If there is a domain where African countries could usefully study the experience of Asian countries and learn lessons for themselves, it is undoubtedly the management of the exchange rate.

49 See Nicolas Sarkozy, speech in Washington, DC, November 7, 2007. Online: http://www.elysee.fr/edito/index.php?id=23.

50 See the IMF, "Methodology for CGER Exchange Rate Assessments" (IMF research paper, November 8, 2006). Online: http://www.imf.org/external/np/pp/eng/2006/110806.pdf (accessed April 11, 2014). See also: "IMF Strengthening Framework for Exchange Rate

Surveillance," press release no. 06/266, November 29, 2006. Online: http://www.imf.org/external/np/sec/pr/2006/pr06266.htm (accessed May 1, 2014).

51 See Andrea Bubula and Inci Ötker-Robe, "The Evolution of Exchange Rate Regimes Since 1990: Evidence from De Facto Policies" (Washington, DC: IMF Working Paper, no. WP/02/155, 2002).

52 In the group of developed countries, the proportion of countries practicing a fixed exchange rate also increased. This is explained by the fact that a great number of European countries adopted a common currency: the euro. In fact, in this study, the member countries of a monetary union are classified in the category of countries with fixed exchange.

53 This category comprises various options, which range from a purely floating exchange rate to an exchange rate periodically adjusted according to a certain number of indicators to the currency board.

54 One of the major arguments of defenders of the fixed exchange rate, that a volatile exchange rate, induced by a rate that is not fixed, increases the incertitude which economic agents face and, as such, may have a negative impact on trade, is put to question more and more. In fact, three researchers put to question the empirical validity of this hypothesis. They prove that there actually exists a threshold effect in this relation and that the impact of volatility on the volume of trade varies according to the degree of volatility. Beneath a certain threshold the impact is not significant, and above it the impact of volatility is generally significant and positive (see Yanhong Zhang et al., "The Threshold Effect of Exchange Rate Volatility on Trade Volume: Evidence from G-7 Countries," *International Economic Journal* 20, no. 4 (December 2006): 461–76.

55 Babula and Ötker-Robe, "The Evolution of Exchange Rate Regimes."

56 Oxfam, "Starbucks Opposes Ethiopia's Plan to Trademark Speciality Coffee Names that Could Earn Farmers an Estimated £47 Million Annually; Oxfam Urges Company to Review Strategy and Sign Licensing Agreement," press release, October 26, 2006; "Starbucks CEO Meets with Ethiopian Government about Ownership of Coffee Names; Oxfam Calls on Starbucks to Make Progress on Trademark Issue," press release November 29, 2006; "Oxfam Calls on Starbucks to Stop Bullying the Poor; Starbucks Must Respect Ethiopia's Right to Choose Its Own Path to Development," press release, November 3, 2006. Starbucks, "Starbucks and the Ethiopian Government Agree to Work Together Toward a Solution that Supports the Ethiopian Coffee Farmers," press release, November 28, 2006. Online: http://news.starbucks.com/news/starbucks-and-the-ethiopian-government-agree-to-work-together-toward-a-solu (accessed May 1, 2014).

57 The International Association for Social Security provides a rich and in-depth analysis on possible approaches in the report entitled *Une sécurité sociale dynamique pour l'Afrique: Une stratégie pour le développement* (Geneva: Association internationale de sécurité sociale, 2008).

58 For an interesting illustration of these considerations within the context of the implementation of monetary policy, see "Three Questions on Monetary Tightening," speech by Lorenzo Bini Smaghi, member of the Executive Board of the ECB, Nomura Conference, Tokyo, October 26–7, 2006.

Chapter Seven: Means of Implementing a Systemic Economic Policy

1 For a discussion of the Laffer Curve, see Arthur B. Laffer, "The Laffer Curve, Past, Present, and Future," *Backgrounder* 1765 (June 1, 2004), published by the Heritage Foundation.

2 I identified earlier the free and independent choice of economic policy as an important operating goal.

3 It could also be called the law of economic policy planning.

4 Once elaborated by a country, these documents are subject to an assessment by the Bretton Woods institutions (the World Bank and IMF), which determine if they are of a sufficiently high standard to serve as a base for financial aid. This evaluation is presented in a joint staff advisory note.

5 See the World Bank and IMF, *2005 Review of the PRS Approach: Balancing Accountabilities and Scaling Up Results* (World Bank/IMF, August 19, 2005).

6 Ibid., 55.

7 The Employment Act was signed by President Truman on February 20, 1946.

Chapter Eight: Economic Policy in Particular Contexts: Economic Crises and Natural Resources–Based Economies

1 To learn more about the subprime crisis, see Patrick Arthur, et al., "The Subprime Crisis," report available at the site of the Council of Economic Analysis: http://www.cae-eco.fr/IMG/pdf/078.pdf (accessed May 1, 2014). Also see Frédéric Lordon, *Jusqu'à quand? Pour en finir avec les crises financières* (Paris: Editions Raison d'agir, 2008). Jacques Attali, *La crise, et après?* (2008), also contains an analysis of the current financial crisis.

2 It is true that several other factors, such as loose monetary policy implementation by the US central bank, a falling real estate market and an overall unstable macroeconomic framework despite appearances are often presented as being the origins of this crisis. But the trigger was certainly the loss of confidence. If economic agents had been able to live with almost all these factors since the 1980s, it was because they had confidence in the system. Reversal of trust ultimately triggered and aggravated the crisis. For an interesting discussion of the role of trust in triggering this crisis, see for example Sushil Wadhwani, "How Trust in Efficient Markets Helped Lead to the Crisis," *Financial Times*, December 17, 2008. Wadhwani is a former member of the Monetary Policy Committee of the Bank of England and manager of Wadhwani Asset Management based in England.

3 In 1994 in Mexico, the assassination of a candidate in a presidential election was enough to change the expectations of economic agents and to plunge the country into a severe financial and economic crisis.

4 In the absence of mechanisms to finance trade, part of foreign demand is in fact considered as insolvent and is not satisfied.

5 For a discussion on the transmission of the present economic crises to African countries, see for example Louis Kasekende, "On Shaky Ground," BBC News, *Focus on Africa* (2008). Also see Shantayanan Devarajan, then the World Bank chief economist for Africa, interview in *Le Monde*, Economie supplement, May 6, 2009, 13.

6 See Ricardo Haussmann, "Stop Behaving as Whiner of First Resort," *Financial Times*, January 31, 2008, 9.

7 The American Recovery and Reinvestment Act, which President Obama signed into law on February 17, 2009, provided financing to support American families' incomes, infrastructure development, education, health and energy. Online: http://www.treasury.gov/initiatives/recovery/Pages/recovery-act.aspx (accessed May 1, 2014). The Emergency Economic Stabilization Act of 2008, which was signed into law by President Bush, also provided financing which supported key parts of the American productive base and households incomes. For details on these two legislations, see http://www.treasury.gov/initiatives/financial-stability/Pages/default.aspx (accessed May 1, 2014).

8 For a detailed discussion of priorities for a better management of natural resources for development, see African Development Bank, *African Development Report 2007: Natural Resources for Sustainable Development in Africa* (Paris: Economica, 2008).

9 A suggestion recently made in the literature is that to reduce poverty African countries with natural resources may simply transfer a portion of the government revenues earned from their natural resources directly to the population. This would increase private consumption and the provision of public goods. See Shantayanan Devarajan et al., "The Case for Direct Transfers of Resource Revenues in Africa" (Center for Global Development Working Paper, no. 333, July

2013). Although this idea is being proposed as a development policy, its attractiveness still needs to be demonstrated. How would such a policy strengthen demand addressed to the economy and/or contribute toward productive-capacity building, the two key channels through which growth with job creation happen? This important question does not yet appear to have been satisfactorily answered in this literature.

10 One can mention Kenya, whose poverty reduction strategy prepared in 2004 aimed at creating jobs and wealth.

Chapter Nine: Globalization: A Variable Geometry Process

1 UNCTAD, *Development and Globalization: Facts and Figures* (Geneva: UNCTAD, 2008). Online: http://unctad.org/es/Docs/gdscsir20071_en.pdf (accessed May 1, 2014).

2 WTO, *International Trade Statistics* (Geneva: WTO, 2008). http://www.wto.org/english/res_e/statis_e/its2008_e/its2008_e.pdf (accessed May 1, 2014).

3 See Ayhan Kose, Christopher Otrok and Eswar S. Prasad, "Global Business Cycles: Convergence or Decoupling?" (Washington, DC: IMF Working Paper, no. WP/08/143, 2008). Chapter 4 of the IMF *World Economic Outlook* (Washington, DC: IMF, 2007) also contains an interesting discussion on the concept of decoupling. Online: http://www.imf.org/external/pubs/ft/weo/2007/01/pdf/text.pdf (accessed May 1, 2014).

4 For a comprehensive overview of a set of other globalization indicators, see UNCTAD, "Development and Globalization."

5 World Gross Domestic Product represents the value of goods and services produced by all world economies.

6 Household final consumption declined in China, but still represented a substantial share of GDP at about one-third.

7 UNCTAD, *Trade and Development Report 2013* (New York: United Nations, 2013), Table 1.7, 24.

8 See the IMF statutes adopted at the United Nations Monetary and Financial Conference held in July 1944 at Bretton Woods, New Hampshire, and modified successively on July 28, 1969, April 1, 1978 and November 11, 1992.

9 This surveillance is authorized by Article IV of its statute.

10 It should be said, and I will bring up this point again later, that IMF influence today is more on the economic policies of poor countries than on those of developed countries.

11 Indeed, reports elaborated by the IMF on developing countries, particularly African countries, be they reports under Article IV or reports related to its loan operations, show that the employment situation and the impact of policies supported by the IMF on employment are rarely treated in them. In fact, these reports most often treat the monetary conditions and countries' policies, taxes, exchange rate, monetary conditions, foreign-trade policy and perspectives on growth. Moreover, commenting on Stiglitz's book on *Globalization and its Discontent*, which criticized the IMF for not attaching any importance on employment, Kenneth Rogoff, then economic adviser and director of the research department of IMF, just responded that the IMF was preoccupied by employment, without giving any details to explain how (See "Rogoff's Discontent with Stiglitz," *IMF Survey* 31, no. 13 (July 2002).

12 Pro-cyclical fiscal austerity policies restrain demand addressed to economy during economic recessions instead of stimulating it and consequently increase the recession instead of curbing it.

13 Although most of these criticisms existed long ago, it is particularly the policies recommended by the IMF to Asian countries affected by the financial crisis of 1997–98 that revived and strengthened them.

14 For example, sub-Saharan Africa, which makes up about a quarter of the member states of the institution (45 members out of 184), was represented by only 2 administrators on the Board of Directors of the IMF.

15 The question whether financial institutions impose policies on developing countries which resort to their financial assistance constitutes a lively debate. Some, like the economist Jagdish Bhagwati, estimate that it is not the case (see Bhagwati, *In Defense of Globalization*). The Cameroonian economist Célestin Monga also shares this point of view, arguing that the staff of these institutions (he uses the case of the World Bank, which he masters well since he works there) come from diverse horizons, making it unlikely that they share the same point of view (i.e., that the institution may impose on countries); see Célestin Monga, *Un bantou à Washington* (Paris: PUF, 2008). However, it seems to me that basing the non-existence of policy ideologies peculiar to international financial institutions simply on the diversity of the personnel of these institutions is not convincing. All, or almost everybody, will admit today that institutions have, during their evolution, developed ideologies which support the interventions that they have imposed on countries. The Washington Consensus is an example.

16 See World Bank, *Global Monitoring Report 2008: MDGs and the Environment; Agenda for Inclusive and Sustainable Development* (Washington, DC: International Bank for Reconstruction and Development / World Bank, 2008). Online: http://siteresources.worldbank.org/INTPROSPECTS/Resources/334934-1327948020811/8401693-1327957281774/8402501-1328643991240/8944_Web_PDF.pdf (accessed May 1, 2014).

17 A study by Julien Reynaud and Julien Vauday tried to empirically test this hypothesis: see "IMF Lending and Geopolitics" (ECB Working Paper Series no. 965, November 2008). In this study, the authors resorted to econometric techniques to show that geopolitical considerations also influence IMF loan decisions, particularly concerning non-concessional loans. They also conclude that this result is less robust when it comes to concessional loans.

18 See interview with Ridrigo de Rato, then IMF managing director, *Financial Times*, April 6, 2006.

19 If the creation of the IEO was a good initiative (albeit overdue), the closure of this division, which was in charge of analyzing the socioeconomic effects of IMF programs, was not a right step in the right direction. Before the creation of the IEO, the IMF was one of the few major international institutions that did not have an independent retrospective evaluation office. This situation did not work toward good governance.

20 Satisfactory levels of inflation and foreign reserves retained which served as a reference for decision making, stood at an inflation rate of between 5 and 7 per cent and a level of foreign reserve representing two to three months of imports. For more details on this study, see "Le FMI et l'aide à l'Afrique sub-saharienne" (IMF evaluation report, 2007). Online: http://www.imf.org/External/NP/ieo/2007/ssa/fra/pdf/031207f.pdf (accessed May 1, 2014).

21 It is the developed countries that benefited most in these reductions.

22 WTO, *10 Benefits of the WTO Trading System* (2003).

23 For a presentation of this analysis, see Bhagwati, *In Defense of Globalization*.

24 Source: BBC News, http://newsvote.bbc.co.uk/mpapps/pagetools.

25 For a more detailed analysis of this asymmetry in the liberalization of trade the world over, see Joseph E. Stiglitz, *La grande désillusion* (Paris: Fayard, 2002); or Joseph E. Stiglitz and Andrew Charlton, *Pour un commerce mondial plus juste* (Paris: Fayard, 2007).

26 Source: BBC News, http://newsvote.bbc.co.uk/mpapps/pagetools.

27 See "South Africa Calls for a Political Guidance on the Development of a Post-Bali Work Programme," South Africa Government Online, Speeches and Statements, December 4, 2013. Online: http://www.gov.za/speeches/view.php?sid=42443 (accessed April 11, 2014).

28 See "Asian Countries Move to Protect Exports," *Financial Times*, October 24, 2008, 2.

29 See press release of the meeting of African finance and planning ministers and governors of African central banks.

30 See Martin Wolf, "Un nouveau Bretton Woods? Un impératif vital," *Le Monde*, Supplément Economie, November 11, 2008.

31 The debate on the governance of international financial institutions aims first at giving more weight to great emerging countries. Even if the representation of Africa in these institutions

improves at the end of this debate, this improvement cannot realistically give Africa the means to influence the economic policies advocated by these institutions.

32 For a more detailed analysis of the role of nongovernmental organizations, see Lys Vital, *Les organisations non gouvernementales dans la régulation de l'économie mondiale* (Paris: L'Harmattan, 2008).

33 Asian countries have particularly benefited from this transfer of manufacturing activities. African countries have once more been marginalized in this process.

34 See, for example, Philippe Bernard, "Coup de torchon à la bananeraie," *Le Monde*, June 10, 2008. There were also differences between Argentina and the electricity company. The latter wanted to increase tariffs, the IMF supported this demand, while the late Argentinian president Nestor Kirchner was opposed to it.

35 For defending the action of multilateral firms in developing countries, see Bhagwati, *In Defense of Globalization*.

36 Although this form of contract is widespread today, there exist others, particularly joint ventures in which an oil company and a domestic company together contribute the resources necessary for investment, and a system based on the award of licenses in which an oil company obtains an exploitation license and pays taxes on income obtained from the exploitation. If the division of production is the most widespread form in developing countries, a system based on fiscal measures is the most practiced in developed countries. This is particularly the case with the United States and the oil of the North Sea.

37 Robert Mabro, founder and president emeritus of the Oxford Institute for Energy Studies, interview in *Le Monde*, September 21, 2006, 16 (my translation).

38 Source: *Financial Times*, December 12 and 22, 2006.

39 See David White, "Oil Companies Urged to Soften Import Blow to Africa," *Financial Times*, November 14, 2005.

40 Source: IMF, *World Economic Outlook*, May 1997, 46.

41 Eric Chinje, paper presented at the International Media Summit on "Re-branding Africa," Accra, Ghana, September 18–20, 2006.

42 For more details on this study, see IMF, *World Economic Outlook* (Washington, DC: IMF, October 1997).

43 Pierre-Richard Agénor, "Does Globalization Hurt the Poor?" (Washington, DC: World Bank Policy Research Working Paper, no. 2922, October 2002).

44 We find here a hypothesis which should be familiar to all those interested in development to the extent that it is very widespread in the literature, and is even at the basis of some interventions financed by donors. This hypothesis is that the asset owned by the poor is their labor force.

45 For a detailed analysis of the effects of globalization on poor countries and recommendations aimed at improving its functioning, see Joseph E. Stiglitz, *La grande désillusion* (Paris: Fayard, 2002). Also see Bhagwati, *In Defense of Globalization*.

46 See Ann Harrison, ed., *Globalization and Poverty* (Chicago: University of Chicago Press, 2007).

47 Due certainly to these criticisms, the IMF has revised their position on capital account liberalization and now admits that countries can implement some capital flow management measures when needed.

48 For a more detailed discussion on the reforms necessary to enable poor countries to benefit from globalization, see Stiglitz, *La grande désillusion*.

Chapter Ten: Globalization: A Factor of Worsening Economic Policy Constraints, but also a Source of Opportunities?

1 It is true that the G8 has long demonstrated that the commitments it makes concern only those who want to believe in them. But, a popular adage says, hope enlivens life.

2 Joseph E. Stiglitz, "Some Lessons from the East Asian Miracle," *World Bank Research Observer* 11, no. 2 (August 1996): 151–77.

3 In choosing its orientation, the government has to decide whether to put its monetary policy at the service of demand or at the service of external equilibrium.

4 For more details on the experiences of countries in the management of challenges presented by financial globalization from the point of view of the use of the monetary policy instrument, see Charles F. Kramer et al., "Challenges to Monetary Policy from Financial Globalization: The Case of India" (Washington, DC: IMF Working Paper, no. WP/08/131, May 2008).

5 This point of view is articulated in particular by S. Mansoob Murshed, "Globalization and Development Policy," in *Handbook on Development Policy and Management*, ed. Colin Kirkpatrick et al. (Edward Elgar: Northampton, MA, 2002). Dani Rodrik, *One Economics, Many Recipes: Globalization, Institutions, and Economic Growth* (Princeton, NJ: Princeton University Press, 2007), part C: "Globalization" contains a more recent presentation of this point of view.

6 For a more extensive discussion and illustration of this hypothesis, see Ha-Joon Chang, *Kicking Away the Ladder: Development Strategy in Historical Perspective* (London: Anthem Press, 2002).

7 For more details on this experience, see Alan Beattie, "Malawi Cultivates Cash Gains for Its Farmers" and "Knowledge of Local Market Reaps Rewards," *Financial Times*, June 10, 2008, 3.

8 See School of Oriental and African Studies, Wadonda Consult, Michigan State University and Overseas Development Institute, *Evaluation of the 2006/2007 Agricultural Input Subsidy Programme, Malawi* (report conducted for the Ministry of Agriculture and Food Security, Lilongwe, Malawi, 2008).

9 For an interesting discussion of the respective roles of economic policy officials and the impact of policies themselves in the determination of credibility, see A. Drazen and P. Masson, "Credibility of Policies Versus Credibility of Policymakers," *Quarterly Journal of Economics* 109, no. 3 (August 1994), 735–54.

10 For example, by registering them in the constitution of the country.

11 The idea was, therefore, that the signing of an agreement with the European Union may act as a technology to strengthen the credibility of commitments of ACP signatory countries to trade liberalization and openness to the rest of the world.

12 Previously, I illustrated this trend by raising the case of Latin America, particularly Argentina. For another illustration of this reversal of perception of international financial institutions and the henceforth widespread feeling that developing countries must avoid their programs, see for example, Eugène Nyambal, *Creating Prosperity in Africa*. In this concise book on the means of creating prosperity in Africa, the author thinks that African countries must come out of programs with the IMF and the World Bank. For an analysis of the loss of influence of the Bretton Woods institutions before the crisis, see Laurence Caramel, "Les pays émergents ont de moins en moins recours aux financements du FMI et de la Banque mondiale," in "Perte d'influence pour les jumelles de Bretton-Woods," *Le Monde*, Economie supplement, September 19, 2006, 2. Also see: Michel Aglietta, interview in *Le Monde*, Economie supplement, September 19, 2006. In this interview, he confirms that the IMF runs the risk of becoming an extra technical body whose role will be reduced to monitoring the international financial system. Also see "Aide au développement: L'après Bretton-Woods a commencé," *Le Monde*, Economie supplement, May 22, 2007.

13 For more discussion of the difficult relationships between Greece and the troika composed of the European Commission, the ECB and the IMF, which monitors its economic policies, see Kerlin Hope, "Athens Adopts More Assertive Approach to Bailout Troika," *Financial Times*, December 9, 2013.

14 See Martin Wolf, "IMF's Ancien Régime Must Give Up Privileges," *Financial Times*, September 19, 2006.

15 See Simon Burall et al., *Assessing Key Stakeholder Perceptions of the Effectiveness of Multilateral Organisations: Final Report* (Centre for Aid and Public Expenditure, Overseas Development Institute, 2007). This study aimed at finding out the opinions of stakeholders on the performance of key international organizations intervening in their country, as well as the international organization they would prefer to see disburse a given amount of additional assistance to their

country. For example, this second part of the investigation asked the following question to stakeholders: "If a given amount of foreign assistance should be disbursed in favor of your country, from which international organization will you prefer such disbursement to come?" The study was on seven international organizations (the African Development Bank, the Asian Development Bank, the European Commission, Global Fund for the Fight against HIV/AIDS, Tuberculosis and Malaria, the United Nations Children Fund, the United Nations Development Program and the World Bank) and was carried out in six countries, among which were four African countries (South Africa, Ghana, Tanzania and Zambia). In each country, the study questioned a sample of government officials, parliamentarians and businesspersons. It was concluded from this study that in terms of the questions posed, the preferences of the countries under study were not correlated to the performance of organizations.

16 Without going into detail, the reasons often advanced in the literature revolve around the arrogance of international financial organizations, their steadfastness not to admit their mistakes, even when their advice does not produce the expected results, the low representation of developing countries in their decision-making proceedings and, particularly, the fact that these countries are not experiencing economic growth after more than three decades of applying policies advocated by these institutions. See Stiglitz, *La grande désillusion*, for an interesting discussion of some factors responsible for the break between the IMF and developing countries.

17 For more details on the contribution of planning to the economic success of France, see for example B. Ferrandon, "La politique économique en France depuis 1945," in *La politique économique et ses instruments* (Paris: Les notices de la Documentation française, 2004). For a concise and rich discussion of the theory and practice of planning worldwide, see J. C. Brada and S. Estrin, "Advances in the Theory and Practice of Indicative Planning," *Journal of Comparative Economics* 14 (1990): 523–30.

18 See Box 9.1: 'The 10 Advantages of the Trade System Promoted by the WTO', in the previous chapter.

19 IMF, *Perspectives économiques régionales: Afrique sub-saharienne* (Washington, DC: IMF, October 2007), 24. Online: http://www.imf.org/external/pubs/ft/reo/2007/AFR/ENG/sreo1007. pdf (accessed May 1, 2014).

20 Among these difficulties, experts often cite the quality of infrastructure, capacity weakness and even at times insufficient liberalization of the trade regimes by African countries. Without minimizing the scope of these factors, we should admit that experts recognize more and more the recent progress made by African countries on a certain number of these factors, including the liberalization of their trade policy vis-à-vis the rest of the world. See for example, the study completed by the World Bank Independent Evaluation Group entitled *Assessing World Bank Support for Trade, 1987–2004*, IEG Evaluation Report no. 35921 (Washington, DC: World Bank, 2006). Online: http://www-wds.worldbank.org/external/default/WDSContentServer/ WDSP/IB/2006/04/20/000012009_20060420132512/Rendered/PDF/359210PAPER0As 101OFFICIAL0USE0ONLY1.pdf (accessed May 1, 2014).

21 For a detailed discussion to this effect, see for example S. Anholt, *Brand New Justice: How Branding Places and Products Can Help the Developing World* (Amsterdam: Elsevier Butterworth Heinemann, 2003). This author proves that even if we witness a progressive improvement of the branding image of developing countries in the eyes of Western consumers, for now this improvement concerns only Asian countries and to a lesser extent Latin American countries. This seems to show that Africa still has a long way to go to lift up this barrier to increasing demand addressed to it within the context of globalization.

22 See A. Vamvakidis, "Trade Openness and Economic Growth Reconsidered" (Mimeo Harvard University, Department of Economics, 1996).

23 Source: UNCTAD, "Development and Globalization."

24 Nontariff measures whose effects are actually much more restrictive are not taken into consideration in this discussion.

Chapter Eleven: Recent Trends of Foreign Aid to Africa

1 See François Bourguignon, interview in *Le Monde*, Supplement Economie, April 2006.

2 World Bank, *World Development Report 2004* (Washington, DC: World Bank/Oxford University Press, 2003), 2.

3 See *UN Millennium Project: Investing in Development. A Practical Plan to Achieve the Millennium Development Goals* (London: Earthscan, 2005). Online: http://www.unmillenniumproject.org/documents/MainReportChapter0Frontmatter-lowres.pdf (accessed May 1, 2014).

4 The 10 themes on which the research groups worked were hunger, education and gender equality, maternal and child health, HIV/AIDS, malaria, tuberculosis and access to essential drugs, sustainable management of the environment, access to drinking water and sanitation, improving life in shanty towns, trade, science, technology and innovation. The 10 research groups produced 13 reports covering different aspects of the abovementioned themes.

5 See *UN Millennium Project*.

6 Presidents Olusegun Obasanjo of Nigeria and Thabo Mbeki of South Africa participated as observers at the G8 Summit of July 2005 in Gleneagles, Scotland.

7 The commission was presided over by Tony Blair and comprised: F. Adeola (former Nigerian banker and founder of a charity organization), K. Y. Amoako (then executive secretary of the United Nations Economic Commission for Africa), N. Baker (former American Senate member), H. Benn (secretary of state for international development in Tony Blair's government), G. Brown (chancellor of the exchequer in Tony Blair's government), M. Camdessus (former IMF managing director and personal representative of French president Jacques Chirac for Africa), B. Geldof (musician, particularly known for his commitment to the cancellation of third-world debt and his humanitarian actions), R. Goodale (then Canadian finance minister), W. S. Kalema (president of the Board of Directors of the Ugandan Investment Authority), T. Manuel (South African finance minister), B. W. Mkapa (president of the Republic of Tanzania), L. K. Mohohlo (governor of the Central Bank of Botswana), Ji Peiding (vice president of the Commission of Foreign Affairs in the Chinese parliament), T. Thiam (director of development and strategy of Aviva Assurance Group), A. K. Tibaijuka (assistant secretary general and executive director of UN Habitat, Tanzania), M. Zenawi (then Ethiopian prime minister).

8 See *Le Monde*, January 29, 2005.

9 This is the threshold of income used by the International Development Association.

10 For a discussion of the results of the preceding multilateral trade negotiations and the Doha Development Round, see Joseph E. Stiglitz and Andrew Charlton, *Pour un commerce mondial plus juste* (Paris: Fayard, 2007).

11 See World Bank, *Global Monitoring Report 2008: MDGs and the Environment; Agenda for Inclusive and Sustainable Development* (Washington, DC, 2008).

12 Ibid.

13 For more detailed discussion of the commitments agreed by the G8, but which may never be transformed into concrete actions, see Hugh Williamson, "G8 Heads Put $25bn Africa Aid in Doubt," *Financial Times*, June 30, 2008.

14 Source: World Bank: *Global Monitoring Report 2008*.

Chapter Twelve: What Goals for Foreign Aid?

1 See William Easterly, *The White Man's Burden: Why the West's Efforts to Aid the Rest Have Done So Much Ill and So Little Good* (New York: Penguin, 2006). Many other authors also share this view. See, for example, Dambisa Moyo, *Dead Aid: Why Aid Is Not Working and How There Is a Better Way for Africa* (London: Allen Lane, 2009). Some other assessments are, however, less pessimistic and believe that aid can improve lives in aid recipient countries. See, for example, Jeffrey Sachs, *The End of Poverty: Economic Possibilities for Our Time* (New York: Penguin, 2005). See also *UN Millennium Project*.

2 According to Easterly, conditionalities are inefficient and must be abandoned. No government
   has ever changed behavior in response to aid incentives. Governments always obtain resources
   and do not change.

3 Ibid. Easterly also identifies other reasons for aid failure such as the absence of mechanisms
   permitting (i) the accountability of donors to aid beneficiaries, (ii) beneficiaries to give their
   opinions on aid, and the lack of adequate incentive mechanisms.

4 However, it should be noted that the IMF almost always analyzes the evolution of employment
   and the consequences for employment of policies that it advocates when it concerns developed
   countries. Take the report of its services under consultations of Article IV for any developed
   country and one will find therein a discussion of the evolution of employment. But it is not
   always the case with reports on developing countries. In these countries, the discussion is very
   often limited to fiscal and monetary policy, the liberalization of trade, the exchange rate and
   other macroeconomic variables. For an overview of these reports, see the IMF website: http://
   www.imf.org/external/country/index.htm (accessed May 1, 2014). For another discussion of
   this fact, also see Gerald Epstein et al., *Employment, Poverty and Economic Development in Madagascar:
   A Macroeconomic Framework* (Amherst, MA: Political Economy Research Institute (PERI),
   University of Massachusetts, December 2008).

5 Dani Rodrik, professor of economics, Harvard University, interview in *Le Monde*, September
   9, 2003 (my translation). Since then, negotiations in the WTO on the aspects of trade
   liberalization which could have significant positive effects on the employment of workers of
   developing countries have not really progressed. These negotiations concern particularly Mode
   4 of the General Agreement on Trade in Services.

6 ILO, *Guide to Understanding the KILM* (Geneva: ILO, 2014). Online: http://kilm.ilo.org/2011/
   download/GuidEN.pdf (accessed May 4, 2014).

7 World Commission on the Social Dimension of Globalization, *A Fair Globalization: Creating
   Opportunities for All* (Geneva: ILO, 2004), 142. Online: http://www.ilo.org/public/english/
   wcsdg/docs/report.pdf (accessed May 2, 2014).

8 It seems as if in some cases, the negative impact on countries of origin, linked particularly to
   the departure of the most dynamic members of the society, who are also the main catalysts of
   the complex social changes which these countries need most to spur their development process,
   outweigh the positive effects linked to simple cash remittances from abroad.

9 See Nancy Birdsall et al., "How to Help Poor Countries," *Foreign Affairs* 84, no. 4 (July/August
   2005).

10 See Commission for Africa, *Our Common Interest*.

11 See OECD, *Convention on Combating Bribery of Foreign Public Officials in International Business
   Transactions and Related Documents* (OECD, 2011). Online: http://www.oecd.org/daf/anti-
   bribery/ConvCombatBribery_ENG.pdf (accessed April 11, 2014).

12 "OECD Secretary-General Stresses Governments' Role in Anti-Corruption Drive," OECD website.
   Online: http://www.oecd.org/document/43/0,2340,en_2649_201185_37948971_1_1_1_1,00.
   html (accessed April 11, 2014). The investigation targeted British company BAE Systems PLC,
   and concerned a contract on the sales of ammunitions to Saudi Arabia. An OECD working
   group sought to know whether this interruption conformed to the convention.

13 See Richard Mile, "Scandal Puts Siemens to the Test," *Financial Times*, January 21, 2008,
   Companies and Markets, 18.

14 See for example Tom Burgis, "Guinea's Mine Riches Stuck in Web of Intrigue," *Financial
   Times*, October 22, 2013.

15 The generalized system of preferences, which is today the framework within which developed
   countries grant trade preferences to developing countries, was created during the second
   session of UNCTAD held in 1968 in New Delhi, India. In 1979, contracting parties of
   GATT, predecessor of the WTO, adopted an enabling clause which instituted a permanent
   waiver to the clause of the Most Favored Nation in order to allow developed countries which
   wanted to grant a preferential tariff treatment under their respective preference schemes

to do so. Presently, there exist 16 preference schemes notified in the WTO Secretariat, particularly those of the European Union (whose first implementation dates back to 1971), the United States, Japan, Canada, Russia, Switzerland, Turkey, the Czech Republic, Norway, New Zealand, Poland, the Slovak Republic, Bulgaria and Byelorussia. Under these schemes, each country grants tariff preferences to developing countries on products, period, rules of origin and according to procedures chosen by itself. In March 2005, the European Union under its preference scheme launched the initiative "Everything but Arms," which aimed at offering all exports of less developed countries, except weapons, a limitless and customs duty–free access to the union's market. This initiative would have had a great influence if it was not limited only to less developed countries and if it was not subjected to the same restrictions as the SGP in its entirety, particularly the fact that it is valid only for a well-defined period and must therefore be renewed periodically. Also, it is subjected to the same rules of origin.

16 See particularly Birdsall et al., "How to Help Poor Countries."

17 For more details, see Dani Rodrik, "Trade Cannot Be a Substitute for Good Economic Planning," *Kenya Daily Nation*, August 9, 2005.

18 Abdoulaye Wade, "Europe-Afrique: La coopération en panne; Les nouveaux accords commerciaux proposés par l'Union européenne sont inacceptables et ne favorisent pas un vrai partenariat," *Le Monde*, November 16, 2007.

19 France was the first country to benefit from this fund.

20 See Chukwuma Charles Soludo, "Africa Needs Honesty over EU Trade Deals," *Financial Times*, April 10, 2012.

21 This Small Economies Act may be conceived following the model of the Small Business Act of the United States. I will come back to the Small Business Act later when examining economic policy in developed countries.

22 For a complete analysis of the consequences of original sin, see contributions in Barry Eichengreen and Ricardo Hausmann, eds, *Other Peoples' Money: Debt Denomination and Financial Instability in Emerging Market Economies* (Chicago: University of Chicago Press, 2005).

23 See Jean-Pierre Tuquoi, "Les Nations Unies réorientent leur politique d'achat des produits agricoles vers les pays pauvres," *Le Monde*, October 16, 2008.

24 Before these initiatives, loans granted by multilateral banks were in hard currency; that is, banks carried out disbursements in hard currency and the country should also reimburse in hard currency. Currency risks and other difficulties linked to original sin were managed by the country.

25 For a clarification of this effect, see for example the excellent work of Anholt, *Brand New Justice*.

Chapter Thirteen: How to Channel Aid for It to Be Effective?

1 William Easterly, *The White Man's Burden: Why the West's Efforts to Aid the Rest Have Done So Much Ill and So Little Good* (New York: New York, 2006), 382.

2 Article III, Section (4) (vii) of the International Bank for Reconstruction and Development and Article V, Section (1) (b) of the International Development Association. In spite of the fact that since 1946, the board of directors of this institution interpreted Article III of the IBRD statutes, particularly the concept of exceptional circumstances, as offering the possibility of granting financing not destined to specific projects, and that the first loans of the IBRD were granted to Denmark, France, Luxemburg and the Netherlands to finance programs of reconstruction and economic recovery, loans to finance specific projects remained the principal mode of financing of the World Bank until the 1980s.

3 After its creation in the 1980s, this method of providing aid became know under various appellations: structural adjustment loans, balance of payments supports/loans or policy reforms loans. All these appellations reflected donors' reluctance to use the term "budget support loans" under the pretext that aid-recipient governments' budgets did not offer enough

fiduciary guarantees. It is toward the 1990s that, under the impetus of the UK government's Department for International Development, donors ended up being more honest with themselves, accepting that funds disbursed under a loan not destined to finance a specific project (whether it is called a structural adjustment loan, balance of payment support/loan or policy reform loan) went into the budget of the recipient government. This is how the term budgetary support loan came into the jargon of donors. This explicit recognition of budgetary support was accompanied by donors' increased efforts to assess and strengthen the fiduciary framework of recipient countries.

4   1 UC = 1 special drawing right of the IMF.

5   See Matt Andrews, "How Far Have Public Financial Management Reforms Come in Africa?" (Harvard Kennedy School of Government, Faculty Research Working Paper Series, RWP10-018, May 2010).

6   For more details on this interesting discussion, see Tito Cordella and Giovanni Dell'Ariccia, "Budget Support Versus Project Aid: A Theoretical Appraisal," *Economic Journal* 117 (October 2007): 1260–79.

7   For discussion of this point, see F. Bakoup, "Promoting Economic Reforms in Developing Countries: Rethinking Budgetary Aid?" (African Development Bank Working Paper, no. 167, 2013).

8   For a more detailed presentation of this framework, see Bakoup, "Promoting Economic Reforms."

9   For a careful examination of the impact of the fact that aid is tied, see B. Osei, "How Aid Tying Can Impose Additional Cost on Aid Recipients: Evidence on Ghana," *African Development Review* 17, no. 3 (December 2005): 348–65.

10 For a clear and concise synthesis of this literature, see P. R. Agénor and P. Montiel, *Development Macroeconomics* (Princeton, NJ: Princeton University Press, 1999).

11 These countries are Burundi, Cameroon, Ethiopia, Gambia, Ghana, Guinea, Guinea Bissau, Madagascar, Malawi, Mali, Mauritania, Mozambique, Niger, the Democratic Republic of the Congo, the Congo Republic, Rwanda, Sao Tome and Principe, Senegal, Sierra Leone, Tanzania, Chad, Uganda and Zambia.

12 The averages are the author's calculations from data per country made available by the IMF and the World Bank. For statistics per country, see IDA and IMF, *Heavily Indebted Poor Countries (HIPC) Initiative and Multilateral Debt Relief Initiative (MDRI): Status of Implementation* (IDA/IMF, 2007). Online: http://www.imf.org/external/np/pp/2007/eng/082807.pdf (accessed April 11, 2014).

13 For the African Development Fund, the relief will be issued from 2007–54.

14 World Bank, *IDA's Implementation of the Multilateral Debt Relief Initiative* (Resource Mobilization Department, FRM, March 14, 2006). Online: http://www-wds.worldbank.org/external/default/WDSContentServer/WDSP/IB/2006/04/10/000160016_20060410165034/Rendered/PDF/3576810vol011IDA1R20061004215.pdf (accessed May 2, 2014). Numbers in SDR millions.

15 DFID, *Partnership for Poverty Reduction: Rethinking Conditionality* (UK policy paper, HM Treasury, 2005).

16 Ibid.

17 DFID, *Implementing DFID's Conditionality Policy* (draft how-to note, HM Treasury, 2006).

18 Ibid., 10.

19 See IEO (IMF), *Evaluation of Structural Conditionality in IMF-Supported Programs* (IMF, 2007). Online: http://www.ieo-imf.org/ieo/files/completedevaluations/01032008SC_main_report.pdf (accessed May 2, 2014).

20 Ibid.

21 Arrear rates on loans granted by the IMF are generally low. The institution has a set of policies and procedures to treat cases of arrears on loans.

22 William Easterly, *The White Man's Burden: Why the West's Efforts to Aid the Rest Have Done So Much Ill and So Little Good* (New York: Penguin, 2006), 368.

23 The other countries were Mexico and Turkey. See IMF, "Communiqué of the International Monetary and Financial Committee of the Board of Governors of the International Monetary Fund," (September 17, 2006). Online: http://www.imf.org/external/np/cm/2006/091706. htm (accessed April 11, 2014).

24 See Jamil Anderlini and David Pilling, "China Fought against Data Showing Economy to Take Top Spot This Year," *Financial Times*, May 2, 2014.

25 Jo Johnson, "India on Track to Be Global Economic Power," *Financial Times*, January 25, 2007, 4.

26 On December 31, 2004, the end of the Multifiber Agreement, which for close to thirty years fixed quotas for textile products in world trade, coincided with a rapid increase in Chinese textile exports toward the European Union. As such, Chinese exports of some products experienced an increase of more than five hundred per cent. Citing reasons of protecting their industry, particularly following pressure from producers who were afraid of job loss in the European textile industry, Europeans concluded an agreement with China in June 2005 aimed at limiting, until 2008, Chinese exports of certain textile products to Europe. Among the products concerned were pullovers, men's pants, blouses, T-shirts, gowns and suits, threads, cotton products, beddings, table linen and kitchen towels. Under this agreement, the increase in these exports was limited to 8–12.5 per cent per annum in 2005, 2006 and 2007.

27 According to economic theory, any country that lives above its means, like the United States, must take measures to put its economy in order. However, the United States has always looked at things otherwise. Each time their deficits reach frightening levels, no one knows by which analysis Americans end up concluding that it is the fault of their economic partners – either they sell too much to them or they do not buy enough from them. They therefore decide that it is left to their trading partners to take measures to adjust their economies. As such, in the 1970s, Japan was compelled by pressure from the United States to sign voluntary agreements restricting their exports to the latter, which estimated that Japan was too competitive on the US market, whereas they themselves were not competitive enough on the Japanese market. This time, the Americans consider China guilty of their trade deficit and think that it may manipulate the exchange rate of its currency, the yuan, with the aim of winning market shares in the United States and protecting its domestic market from American products. Americans are so determined on this issue of the Chinese exchange regime that they have succeeded on two fronts. On the one hand, I may say that the decision taken in June 2005 by the Chinese authorities to leave the yuan to float – which, in fact, put an end to the fixed exchange rate which for close to ten years existed between the yuan and the US dollar – was driving toward the flexibility demanded by the Americans. Furthermore, I cannot help seeing American influence in the decision taken in 2006 by the IMF to further concentrate on the monitoring of its member states' practices on exchange rates. However, the game is not yet won by the Americans. In fact, during the "strategic US–China economic dialogue" which took place in December 2006 in Beijing between the Chinese authorities and a strong US delegation comprising the secretary to the treasury Henri Paulson, Federal Reserve chairman Ben S. Bernanke and the trade representative Susan Schwab, China made clear they would not go far in terms of US demands on their exchange rate. Chinese vice premier Wu Yi coldly declared: "We have had the genuine feeling that some American friends are not only having limited knowledge of, but harboring much misunderstanding about the reality in China. [...] This is not conducive to the sound development of our bilateral relations." "China–US Economic Summit Begins," BBC News, December 14, 2006. Online: http://news.bbc.co.uk/2/hi/business/6176593.stm (accessed April 11, 2014).

28 For a discussion of this point, see Mure Dickie, "China Currency 'Not Main Cause' of Trade Surplus," *Financial Times*, December 3, 2007.

29 See for example, Victor Mallet, "The Ugly Face of China's Presence in Africa," *Financial Times*, September 14, 2006.
30 William Wallis, "Donor Bank for Africa to Meet in Shanghai," *Financial Times*, February 1, 2007.
31 In my opinion, this discussion coming from the West has no meaning because those in the West criticizing China saying that its trade with Africa is concentrated on raw materials and that the Chinese help to maintain dictators in power perhaps easily forget that, make no mistake, the same criticisms could be leveled at Western presence in Africa today. Africans should not allow themselves to be influenced by this discussion, but on the contrary, find means to prolong the prevailing competition among donors, for competition is the guarantor of the efficiency and effectiveness of aid to Africa, which may as such obtain more funds.
32 For a rather more optimistic analysis of China's presence in Africa, see for example Alice Sindzingre, "La Chine en Afrique: Le pire n'est pas sûr," *Le Monde*, Economie supplement, December 12, 2006. A World Bank report, "The Silk Road," prepared for the Annual Meetings of the Bretton Woods institutions, held in Singapore in September 2006, also contains an optimistic vision for Africa to accelerate China–Africa relations.
33 For an interesting analysis of some aspects of Chinese economic policy, read Yingyi Qian's article in Rodrik, *In Search of Prosperity: Narratives on Economic Growth*. Also see Stiglitz, "Qui a perdu la Russie?" in *La grande désillusion*. In this book, the author makes a comparative analysis of Chinese and Russian experiences of economic reforms in the 1990s.

Part Five: Some Successful Experiences of Economic Policy in Africa and Beyond

1 Readers who have read the foregoing chapters will easily understand why I qualify these conclusions as simplistic.
2 For a study of the economic success of Mauritius, see Arvind Subramanian and Devesh Roy, "Who Can Explain the Mauritian Miracle? Meade, Romer, Sachs, or Rodrik?" in *In Search of Prosperity: Analytic Narratives on Economic Growth*, ed. Dani Rodrik (Princeton, NJ: Princeton University Press, 2003), ch. 8. For an interesting attempt to explain the economic success of Botswana, see Daron Acemoglu et al., "An African Success Story: Botswana," in *In Search of Prosperity*, ch. 4. The study on the island of Mauritius attributes the economic success of this country to the combined effort of the trade liberalization strategy that it adopted and the preferential access of its sugar and textiles exports to European and US markets under the Multifiber Agreement on textiles and the GSP for sugar. This evidence seems insufficient as an explanation. Concerning the study on Botswana, it attributes the success of this country to the quality of its institutions. The quality of institutions can play an effective role in the economic performances of a country, but it must be accompanied by good and well-oriented economic policies. Insofar as this study says almost nothing on the economic policies that Botswana implemented, and which good institutions surely favored, we consider that it also does not give a satisfactory explanation of the economic performance of the country and that this still requires a thorough examination.

Chapter Fourteen: A Successful Economic Policy Experience in Africa: Economic Policy in Tunisia

1 African Development Bank, Tunisian government, US government, *Towards a New Economic Model for Tunisia: Identifying Tunisia's Binding Constraints to Broad-Based Growth* (Washington, DC: Millennium Challenge Corporation, 2012).
2 République Tunisienne, *XIème Plan de développement 2007–11*, vol. 1, *Contentu global*, ch. 1, "Schéma de développement du XIème plan" (Tunis, 2005) (my translation).

3 According to economic policy, beyond examining the published official documents and discussions with various economic policy officials, two other methods can be used to reveal preferences on economic policy. One consists in directly optimizing a function of subjective preferences under the constraint of objective data of the economy which economic policy officials face. This method is called the direct optimum. Another method called inverse optimum has two variants: one consists in determining the policy marginal rate of substitution (PMRS) among various economic policy goals from the technical marginal rate of substitution (TMRS), which is calculated from a specified model of the economy and the hypothesis of equality between the PMRS and TMRS to optimum. The PMRS is intended to show the policy preferences of economic policy officials. Another variant consists in determining the PMRS from a reaction function of policy officials in a given domain. For an in-depth discussion of these methods followed by an interesting synthesis of the results of their application, including within the framework of the fifth and sixth French plans, see de Boissieu, *Principes de politique économique*. The necessity to have a specified model of the economy makes the two methods presented above, which are based on the economic calculus, heavy and consequently considerably limits their use in the context of developing countries. In this chapter, the revelation of preferences within the framework of the Tunisian economic policy is based on examining published official documents.

4 IMF, World Economic Outlook Database, October 2013. Online: http://www.imf.org/external/pubs/ft/weo/2013/02/weodata/index.aspx (accessed May 2, 2014).

5 Ibid.

6 Ibid.

7 If we retain as the poverty line the proportion of the population living on less than two US dollars per day, the drop will be from 16.1 per cent over 1985–89 to 6.6 per cent in 2000. These statistics are from: African Development Bank, *Gender, Poverty and Environmental Indicators on African Countries*, vol. 7 (Tunis: Statistics Division, Development Research Department, African Development Bank, 2006). Online: http://www.afdb.org/fileadmin/uploads/afdb/Documents/Publications/Gender%20Poverty%20and%20Environmental%20Indicators%20on%20African%20Countries%202006.PDF (accessed May 2, 2014).

8 Ibid.

9 République Tunisienne, *Le Dixième Plan de développement, 2002–2006* (Tunis, 2000), vol. 1, *Contenu global*, part 2, ch. 2, "Les objectifs globaux et les équilibres généraux du Xe Plan," 41 (my translation).

10 République Tunisienne, *Le Dixième Plan de développement*.

11 Preface to the *Le Dixième Plan de développement* (my translation).

12 Ministry of Development and International Cooperation, *2005 Economic Budget* (Republic of Tunisia, November 2004), 28. In 2005, the contribution of investment and foreign trade stood at 2 and -0.5 per cents respectively.

13 For a more detailed discussion of some of the efforts of the Tunisian economic policy to stimulate demand addressed to the economy, see André Wilmots, *De Bourguiba à Ben Ali: L'étonnant parcours économique de la Tunisie, 1960–2000* (Paris: L'harmattan, 2004) (my translation).

14 Ibid.

15 Ministry of Development and International Cooperation, *2005 Economic Budget*, part 3, ch. 3, "Les politiques économiques et financières," 126 (my translation).

16 IMF, World Economic Outlook Database, October 2013.

17 The fact that development partners granted a preponderant place to social sectors in their aid programs, at times to the detriment of aid to productive sectors, is today the subject of a very heated debate. It would appear things have started changing.

18 These criteria include the process of appointment of officials and the degree of liberty they enjoy in defining monetary policy goals and their implementation. For a more complete discussion of the independence of the CBT, as well as other challenges of monetary policy which Tunisia has faced, particularly those posed by the implementation of a policy of targeting inflation (an objective the authorities set for themselves), see for example Pierre-Richard Agénor and

Ndiamé Diop, *Capital Account Liberalization, Exchange Rate Flexibility, and Monetary Policy in Tunisia: Issues, Progress, and Challenges* (World Bank, Tunisia Development Policy Review, Background Paper, 2008).

19 Uncertainties created by President Bourguiba's succession actually led to a certain slackening of financial discipline. This was expressed particularly by budgetary slippages, particularly at the level of public spending. However, the country quickly regained control of its public finances as soon as the uncertainties were cleared.

20 According to decree no. 2002-3158 of December 17, 2002, regulating public procurement, modified by decree no. 2003-1638 of August 4, 2003 and decree no. 2004-2551 of November 2, 2004, Tunisian products must be given priority in public contracts except where their price is above that of foreign products by 10 per cent (this margin was 20 per cent before 2002). Moreover, bidders are called upon to subcontract if possible with Tunisian companies. Dividing public procurement is obligatory if it will favor the participation of national companies. Invitations to tender must include a national subcontracting clause and studies must be carried out together with a Tunisian consulting firm. Source: WTO Trade Policy Review Body, *Trade Policy Review: Report of the Secretariat; Tunisia* (WTO, WT/TPR/S/152/Rev.1, September 7, 2005), 52.

21 African Development Bank, 2006.

22 The Franc Zone is the monetary arrangement which existed between France and its colonies, and which was maintained after the accession to independence of the former colonies. Today, it regroups France, the fourteen francophone countries of central and west africa, the island of Comoros and Guinea Bissau. Critics argue that the provisions of the Franc Zone arrangement undermine the economic competitiveness of its African member countries and also allow France to exercise some political control over them. Supporters argue that the Franc Zone helps those countries maintain macroeconomic stability.

23 Choosing a flexible exchange rate policy fits well with the fact that some prices are still insufficiently flexible, particularly due to the fact that some prices are still controlled and the labor market is relatively rigid. From 1970 to 1999, the average of a rigidity indicator calculated by the IMF stood at 0.39 (the higher the indicator, the more rigid the labor market). The value of this indicator for Egypt and Morocco stood at 0.39 and 0.24 respectively. Source: Abdelji Jbili and Vitali Kramarenko, *Choosing Exchange Regimes in the Middle East and North Africa* (IMF, 2003).

24 For a discussion of the progress achieved on the process of liberalization of capital account and potential benefits, see the IMF, *Tunisia: Selected Issues* (IMF Country Report no. 06/208, June 2006).

25 The real exchange rate index evaluates the nominal exchange rate (price of US dollars in dinar) deflated by the relative evolution of prices between Tunisia and its trading partners.

26 IMF, International Financial Statistics, May 2007.

27 WTO, *Trade Policy Review*.

28 For a succinct and concise analysis of provisions stipulated in these various agreements aimed at liberalizing trade and progress in their implementation, see the WTO, *Trade Policy Review*.

29 We see resemblance with the development policy implemented by South Korea, which had as one of its fundamental principles the idea that development would rely on industrialization. For an interesting discussion of South Korea's experience on economic policy, see "Korean Development Experience," paper prepared for the African Development Bank Economic Conference, Tunis, November 2006.

30 Among these structures, I can cite the Companie tunisienne pour l'assurance du commerce extérieur (Tunisian company for the insurance of foreign trade), which offered cover against the risk of nonpayment by the foreign client and even financing in the form of operating capital; the Centre de promotion des exportations (Centre for the promotion of exports), which provided aid in terms of training; the Agence de promotion de l'industrie (Agency for the promotion of industry); and the Fonds de promotion des exportations (Fund for the promotion of exports), which grants subsidies and loans to exporters, contributes to studies of international markets and offers other trade services to exporting firms.

31 WTO Trade Policy Review Body, *Trade Policy Review*.

32 For detailed analysis of this measure, see Mahmoud Ben Romdhane, "Commerce et stratégies de développement: Le cas tunisien" (African Center for Trade Policy, United Nations Economic Commission for Africa, ongoing work no. 53, 2007).

33 FIPA-Tunisia, "Presentation." Online: http://www.investintunisia.tn/site/fr/article.php?id_article=202 (accessed April 11, 2014). For more details on trade policy measures implemented by Tunisia, see the World Bank, *Intégration mondiale de la Tunisie: Une nouvelle génération de réformes pour booster la croissance et l'emploi* (Washington, DC, 2008).

34 Decree no. 95-1142 of June 28, 1995 establishes the list of products whose prices were subjected to homologation at all stages, including homologation at the stage of production, and the control of distribution margins.

35 See Wilmots, *De Bourguiba à Ben Ali* (my translation).

36 Information from FIPA-Tunisia, "Organisation." Online: http://www.investintunisia.tn/site/fr/article.php?id_article=134 (accessed April 11, 2014).

37 See, for example, Dani Rodrik et al., "Institutions Rule: The Primacy of Institutions over Integration and Geography in Economic Development" (Washington, DC: IMF Working Paper, no. 02/189, 2002).

38 See World Bank, "Intégration mondiale de la Tunisie." According to this study, the economic growth that Tunisia has experienced since the mid-1960s was particularly pulled, from the side of supply, by an increase of the total factor productivity, and to a lesser extent, by an increase in the stock of factors. This productivity has contributed to about 43 per cent of this increase.

Chapter Fifteen: Post-apartheid South Africa's Economic Policy: Lessons from a Successful Experience

1 South African government information website.
Online: http://www.info.gov.za/speeches/2006/06020610531001.htm (accessed June 30, 2006).

2 Due to some climatic conditions, agricultural contribution to the South African economy is traditionally low.

3 In fact, when Mozambique gained independence under a socialist regime, afraid that socialist ideas would spread, mine owners reduced their resort to labor from this country, thereby resulting in a relative increase of labor costs.

4 This assumes that we stick to the extended definition of unemployment which includes discouraged persons who are no longer looking for work. According to the official definition, the unemployment rate was about 26 per cent.

5 For an analysis of these economic successes and the challenges to come, see the report by Goldman Sachs, *Two Decades of Freedom: What South Africa Is Doing with It And What Now Needs to Be Done* (Goldman Sachs, 2013). See also the an earlier collective book written by a group of IMF economists and edited by Michael Nowak and Luca Antonio Ricci, *Post-apartheid South Africa: The First Ten Years* (IMF, 2005). See also the South African government report, "The Twenty Year Review" (2013).

6 An attempt in this perspective is, however, the very interesting and very rich work of Alan Hirsh, *Season of Hope: Economic Reform under Mandela and Mbeki* (Pietermaritzburg: University of KwaZulu-Natal Press and International Development Research Centre, 2005).

7 For such a presentation, see the report by Goldman Sachs, *Two Decades of Freedom*. See also South African government, "The Twenty Year Review."

8 Despite these positive trends, a recent monetary policy statement from the South African Reserve Bank pointed to a challenging outlook on account of the still-difficult labor relations in key sectors of the economy, which is impacting on confidence, high-wage demands in the mining sector, electricity supply constraints, the current-account deficit, and the slow pace of global economic recovery. For more details on these challenges see Governor Gill Marcus, "Statement of the Monetary Policy Committee," September 19, 2013. Online: http://www.gov.za/speeches/view.php?sid=39886&tid=122400 (accessed May 5, 2014).

9 IMF, World Economic Outlook Database, October 2013. Online: http://www.imf.org/external/pubs/ft/weo/2013/02/weodata/index.aspx (accessed May 2, 2014).

10 This resilience to the drop in unemployment rate, even in a context where the creation of new jobs accelerated, is explained by the fact that newcomers into the labor market were increasing more and more.

11 These measures involved suppressing quantitative restrictions to trade, reducing customs duties and simplifying the structure of tariffs.

12 See William McNamara, "ANC Likely to Make Mbeki Pay Despite Boom," *Financial Times*, December 14, 2007, 7.

13 Address by President Zuma at the Freedom Day celebrations, Union Buildings, Pretoria, April 27, 2013. Online: http://www.gov.za/speeches/view.php?sid=36059 (accessed May 5, 2014).

14 Michael Bleby, "South Africa on Tightrope as Key Rate Rises to Five-Year High," *Financial Times*, June 13, 2008, 3.

15 These discussions take place within the framework of policy conferences organized by the party regularly. The organization of these conferences is often facilitated by the Department of Economic Planning in the ANC. In fact, internal discussions on issues of economic policy in the ANC date back to the 1950s. The two previous conferences took place in June 2007 in Johannesburg and in December 2012 in Polokwane, respectively.

16 The apartheid system, which ended in 1994, had resulted in a high degree of inequality in South Africa, making a reversal of this trend a necessary condition for sustainable and inclusive growth. In his Freedom Day speech, President Zuma reported that although progress toward reduction of inequality had been achieved since 1994 (for example, the number of black people and women in senior management had increased from less than 10 per cent in the 1990s to over 40 per cent today; also, a recent study by the University of Cape Town showed that the black middle class in South Africa had more than doubled in the last five years, rising from 1.7 million people in 2004 to 4.2 million in 2012), further progress was still needed (at the management level whites are still 72.6 per cent and blacks are 12.3 per cent).

17 See Thabo Mbeki, State of the Nation Address, February 2006.

18 ANC, *Ready to Govern: ANC Policy Guidelines for a Democratic South Africa* (Johannesburg: ANC Policy Unit, 1992), in Hirsh, *Season of Hope*, 34.

19 Some specific measures of public spending reduction involved reducing the payment of parliamentarians, members of government and the president, reducing and redeploying civil servants (particularly by implementing a voluntary separation program), privatizing some public companies and reorganizing the framework of transfer of resources between the central government and the provinces.

20 Some observers believe that this resignation followed an agreement he concluded with President Mandela at the time of his appointment.

21 For an interesting discussion of factor surrounding the depreciation 1998, see Ashok Jayantilal Bhundia and Luca Antonio Ricci, "The Rand Crises of 1998 and 2001: What Have We Learned?" in *Post-apartheid South Africa: The First Ten Years*, ed. Michael Nowak and Luca Antonio Ricci (Washington, DC: IMF, 2005).

22 On this issue, see the interesting analysis of Hirsh, *Season of Hope*, 60–62.

23 Among these measures, I can cite the Mines and Works Act of 1911, the Natives Land Act (1913), the Apprenticeship Act (1922), the Industrial Conciliation Act (1924) and a set of other laws adopted after 1948. For a discussion of the provisions of these different measures and discriminatory effects of these measures, see the interesting book of Leonard Thompson *A History of South Africa* (New Haven, CT: Yale Nota Bene, 2001).

24 The coverage of the social grants system expanded from 2.7 million people in 1994 to 16 million in 2013, contributing significantly to the reduction in the proportion of people living below the poverty line. Concerning social transfers, the government asserted its wish to use social transfers as a means of attaining social cohesion goals, but also acknowledged the necessity to avoid creating a society of dependence.

25 South African Department of Trade and Industry, *South Africa's Economic Transformation: A Strategy for Broad-Based Black Economic Empowerment* (Pretoria: DTI, 2003), 12–13. Online: http://www.thedti.gov.za/economic_empowerment/bee-strategy.pdf (accessed May 5, 2014).

26 For a complete presentation of the financing mechanisms of BBBEE, see ibid.

27 Over six hundred billion rands of black economic-empowerment transactions (about sixty nine billion US dollars) have been implemented since 1995 (President Zuma, 2013 Freedom Day speech).

28 President Zuma, 2013 Freedom Day speech.

29 See Pilita Clark and Andrew England, "South Africa: A New Power Generation," *Financial Times*, May 7, 2013.

30 In hindsight, it seems today that it is not the fundamentals of the economy that explain the depreciation of 1996. In fact, it seems it was much more fed by baseless rumors on the health of President Mandela and perhaps by perceptions of some actors that there was a certain uncertainty in the government's economic policy. However, when the markets realized that the fundamentals of South African economy did not justify this depreciation, and particularly that the reaction of the authorities was appropriate, the rand gained stability before depreciation crossed the level where it would have constituted a risk to price stability. For more detailed analysis of the 1996 depreciation, see *Growth, Employment and Redistribution: A Macroeconomic Strategy* (Pretoria: Republic of South Africa, Department of Finance, 1996). Also see Bhundia and Ricci, "The Rand Crises."

31 Insofar as monetary policy is independent, it took measures necessary to protect price stability.

32 IMF, Exchange Rates Archives. Online: http://www.imf.org/external/np/fin/ert/GUI/Pages/Report.aspx?CT='ZAF','TUN'&EX=REP&P=DateRange&Fr=628929792000000000&To=635364864000000000&CF=Compressed&CUF=Period&DS=Ascending&DT=Blank.

33 Comments by economic development minister Ebrahim Patel in debate on the State of the Nation Address, available at: http://www.info.gov.za/speech/DynamicAction?pageid=461&sid=34358&tid=99116

34 Under the local procurement accord, the government has committed itself to achieving 75 per cent of its procurement locally over the medium term. "Media Statement on Local Procurement Accord," South Africa Government Online, October 31, 2011. Online: http://www.gov.za/speeches/view.php?sid=22829&tid=47666 (accessed May 5, 2014).

35 For more details on plans to strengthen the contribution of SOCs to the government's industrial policy objectives, see "Address by the Minister of Public Enterprises, Malusi Gigaba MP, on the Occasion of Budget Vote 11 at the Extended Public Committee on Public Enterprises in Cape Town," South Africa Government Online, May 14, 2013. Online: http://www.gov.za/speeches/2009/09021114561001.htm (accessed May 5, 2014).

36 For a presentation of these different programs, see South African Department of Trade and Industry, online: http://www.thedti.gov.za/publications.jsp?year=&subthemeid= (accessed May 5, 2014).

37 See "Budget Speech 2009 by the Minister of Finance, Trevor A Manuel," South Africa Government Online, February 11, 2009. Online: http://www.gov.za/speeches/2009/09021114561001.htm (accessed May 5, 2014).

38 See South African Government "Twenty Year Review" (2013). Online: http://www.gov.za/documents/detail.php?cid=400604 (accessed June 18, 2014).

Chapter Sixteen: Some Economic Policy Experiences in Developed and Emerging Countries

1 "Consolidated Versions of the Treaty on the European Union and the Treaty on the Functioning of the European Union," Title 1, Article 3 (2012/C 326/01). Online: http://eur-lex.europa.eu/legal-content/EN/TXT/?uri=uriserv:OJ.C_.2012.326.01.0001.01.ENG (accessed May 4, 2014).

2 On this subject, see J. E. Stiglitz, "Some Lessons from the East Asian Miracle," *World Bank Research Observer* 11, no. 2 (1996), 151–77.

3 Joseph E. Stiglitz, "Some Lessons from the East Asian Miracle," *World Bank Research Observer* 11, no. 2 (August 1996): 151–77.

4 For an in-depth study of this measure and many others which enabled China to make progress on the economic policy goals identified in this book, see Y. Qian, "How Reform Worked in China," in *In Search of Prosperity: Analytic Narratives on Economic Growth*, ed. Dani Rodrik (Princeton, NJ: Princeton University Press, 2003).

5 For more detailed commentary of these results, see Geoff Dyer, "Chinese Prefer Domestic Products to Foreign," *Financial Times*, October 29, 2007.

6 For a discussion of some of these measures, accompanied by a presentation of the economic theory which supports each of them, see Stiglitz, "Some Lessons from the East Asian Miracle."

7 Malaysia is a country made up of several ethnic groups. About 55 per cent of the population is made up of Muslim Malays, 25 per cent Chinese and 8 per cent Indians. Some provisions of this new economic policy aimed for example at making it such that Malays hold at least 30 per cent of private capital. This law contributed much to social appeasement, which was necessary for the economic miracle that the country experienced.

8 Household consumer demand and companies' investment demand.

9 If we move back in history, we realize that this approach has always been a constant of the economic policy of developed countries. For example, the Plaza Agreements in the mid-1980s, which resulted in a substantial appreciation of the yen from 240 yen to the dollar to about 120 yen to the dollar in less than two years, also participated in the efforts of the great powers aimed at readjusting shares of world demand in their favor (for an interesting analysis of this point, see David Pilling, "Weak Yen Gives Lift to Dynamic Exports," *Financial Times*, June 6, 2007. The same holds for the Louvre Agreements as well as the voluntary exports restraints agreements that the United States imposed on Japan in the 1980s.

10 For an interesting discussion of the functioning of the Marshall Aid compared with the present system of foreign aid, see Glenn Hubbard and William Duggan, "Why Africa Needs a Marshall Plan," *Financial Times*, June 5, 2007.

11 In fact, as stipulated in Articles 39 and 40 of the Treaty of Rome, which is in a way the founding treaty of the European process, the goals of the Common Agricultural Policy (CAP) were to: (i) increase production in the agricultural sector, (ii) guarantee a satisfactory standard of living for the agricultural world, (iii) stabilize markets of agricultural products, (iv) guarantee food security, and (v) guarantee reasonable prices for consumers. These goals were pursued by means of a set of sophisticated mechanisms to govern competition, manage prices and trade of agricultural products in the union, and provide aid to farmers with the aim of supporting production, marketing and storage. For a presentation of the operational mechanisms of the CAP as conceived at the beginning, see for example Julius Rosenblatt et al., "The Common Agricultural Policy of the European Community: Principles and Consequences" (IMF Occasional Paper no. 62, Washington, DC, November 1988). Also see the recent study of Nicolas-Jean Brehon, *L'agriculture européenne à l'heure des choix: Pourquoi croire à la PAC? Contribution au bilan de santé de la PAC* (Paris: Robert Schuman Foundation, 2008).

12 For more details on the discussions which took place during the European Council of Brussels of June 2007 on the role of competition in European economic policy, see George Parker et al., "Key Clause Dropped from Draft EU Treaty," *Financial Times*, June 22, 2007.

Conclusion

1 World Bank website. Online: http://web.worldbank.org/WBSITE/EXTERNAL/EXT ABOUTUS/ORGANIZATION/EXTPREMNET/0,,contentMDK:23225680~pagePK:64 159605~piPK:64157667~theSitePK:489961,00.html (accessed June 26, 2014).

2 Since Nigeria's independence, the country has always been ready to contribute to the economic and social progress of African countries. One of the first manifestations of this desire was the creation, in 1973, of the Nigerian Trust Fund. This fund, managed by the African Development Bank Group, has as its goal to contribute to the economic and social progress of the poorest countries of the continent by granting them financing at concessionary rates for the implementation of their economic and social development projects.

3 For an interesting discussion of the concept of African renaissance, see Ivan Crouzel, "La 'renaissance africaine' un discours Sud-africain?" *Politique africaine*, no. 77 (March 2000).

4 The NIA was born from the merging of two complementary plans presented practically at the same time, each aimed at serving as a strategic framework for efforts to promote African development. One was the Millennium Partnership Program for the Renaissance of Africa presented by presidents Thabo Mbeki of South Africa, Abdelaziz Bouteflika of Algeria and Olusegun Obasanjo of Nigeria. The other was the Omega Plan presented by President Abdoulaye Wade of Senegal. After the approval of the NIA by the African Union Summit (then the Organization of African Unity), the Committee of Heads of State and Government in charge of its implementation met in October 2001 in Abuja, Nigeria, and according to the mandate bestowed on it by the Summit of Heads of State and Government of the African Union proceeded to a rereading of the document to make necessary editorial amendments. It is on this occasion that the NIA was renamed NEPAD. For more information on NEPAD, see: http://www.nepad.org/nepad/frequently-asked-questions (accessed May 4, 2014).

5 In fact, history abounds in a number of development plans adopted at the level of the African continent. Among these plans, I can mention the Lagos Plan adopted in 1979, but whose implementation has not been up to expectations.

6 African countries which have already signed the memorandum of understanding of the APRM are Algeria, Burkina Faso, the Republic of Congo, Ethiopia, Ghana, Kenya (March 9, 2003), Cameroon (April 3, 2003), Gabon (April 14, 2003), Mali (May 28, 2003), Mauritius, Mozambique, Nigeria (May 9, 2004), Rwanda, Senegal, the Republic of South Africa, Uganda, Egypt (March 9, 2004), Benin (March 31, 2004), Malawi, Lesotho, Tanzania, Angola and Sierra Leone (8 July 2004).

7 *Growth and Responsibility in Africa*, G8 Summit Declaration, Heiligendamm, June 8, 2007. Online: http://www.g-8.de/Content/DE/Artikel/G8Gipfel/Anlage/Abschlusserkl_C3_A4rungen/WV-afrika-en,property=publicationFile.pdf (accessed May 1, 2014).

8 For example, see Ha-Joon Chang, "Economic History of the Developed World: Lessons for Africa," lecture delivered at the Eminent Speakers Program, African Development Bank, Tunis, February 26, 2009.

BIBLIOGRAPHY

Abed, George T., and Hamid R. Davoodi. *Challenges of Growth and Globalization in the Middle East and North Africa*. Washington, DC: IMF, 2003.

Acemoglu, Daron, Simon Johnson and James A. Robinson. "An African Success Story: Botswana." In *In Search of Prosperity: Analytic Narratives on Economic Growth*, edited by Dani Rodrik, ch. 4. Princeton, NJ: Princeton University Press, 2003.

Acocella, N. *Economic Policy in the Age of Globalisation*. Cambridge: Cambridge University Press, 2005.

Africa South of the Sahara 2008. New York: Routledge, 2008.

African Development Bank. *African Development Report 2007: Natural Resources for Sustainable Development in Africa*. Paris: Economica, 2008.

_____. *Evaluation Report of the Support Project to the Sectoral Program of Health*. Tunis, October 2004.

_____. *Republic of South Africa: Private Sector Country Profile, Final Report*. Tunis: African Development Bank, 2006.

African Development Bank, Tunisian government, US government. *Towards a New Economic Model for Tunisia: Identifying Tunisia's Binding Constraints to Broad-Based Growth*. Washington, DC: Millennium Challenge Corporation, 2012.

African National Conference. Policy discussion documents for the ANC National Policy Conference in June 2007 and the ANC 52nd National Conference in December 2007. Online: http://www.anc.org.za/ancdocs/policy/2007/discussion/contents.html (accessed July 30, 2007).

_____. *Ready to Govern: ANC Policy Guidelines for a Democratic South Africa*. Johannesburg: ANC Policy Unit, 1992.

Agénor, Pierre-Richard. "Does Globalization Hurt the Poor?" Washington, DC: World Bank Policy Research Working Paper, no. 2922, 2002.

Agénor, Pierre-Richard, and Ndiamé Diop. "Capital Account Liberalization, Exchange Rate Flexibility, and Monetary Policy in Tunisia: Issues, Progress, and Challenges." Washington, DC: World Bank, Tunisia Development Policy Review, Background Paper, 2008.

Agénor, Pierre-Richard. *The Economics of Adjustment and Growth*, 2nd edition. Cambridge, MA: Harvard University Press, 2004.

Agénor, Pierre-Richard, and P. J. Montiel. *Development Macroeconomics*, 2nd edition. Princeton, NJ: Princeton University Press, 1999.

Aglietta, Michel. Interview in *Le Monde*, Economie supplement, September 19, 2006.

_____. *La Crise: Pourquoi en est-on arrive là? Comment en sortir?* Paris: Michalon, 2008.

_____. *Macroéconomie financière*, 5th edition. Paris: La découverte, 2008.

Aguiar, Marcos, Arindam Bhattacharia, Thomas Bradtke, Pascal Cotte, Stephan Derting, Michael Meyer, David C. Michael and Harold L. Sirkin. *The New Global Challengers: How 100 Top Companies from Rapidly Developing Economies Are Changing the World*. Boston: Boston Consulting Group, May 2006.

Ahluwalia, Montek Singh. "Fiscal Targets Are Useless without Growth." Interview, *O Estado de S. Paulo*, September 4, 2006, Economy section, B3.

Algan, Yann, and Pierre Cahuc. *La société de défiance: Comment le modèle social français s'autodétruit*. Paris: Editions rue d'Ulm, 2008.

Anholt, S. *Brand New Justice: How Branding Places and Products Can Help the Developing World*. Amsterdam: Elsevier Butterworth Heinemann, 2003.

Arbache, Jorge Saba. "African Development Indicators 2006." Presentation at the African Development Bank, Tunis, March 8, 2007.

Association citoyenne de défense d'intérêts collectifs. *Campagne souveraineté alimentaire: Aidons-les à nous nourrir*. Yaoundé: ACDIC, 2006.

_____. *Poulets congelés: Comprendre le phénomène au Cameroun*. Yaoundé: ACDIC, 2004.

Association internationale de sécurité sociale. *Une sécurité sociale dynamique pour l'Afrique: Une stratégie pour le développement*. Geneva: Association internationale de sécurité sociale, 2008.

Babissakana, Abissama Onana. *Les débats économiques du Cameroun et d'Afrique centrale*. Les cahiers des notes d'analyse technique, no. 1. Yaoundé: Prescriptor, 2003.

_____. *Les débats économiques du Cameroun et d'Afrique centrale*. Les cahiers des notes d'analyse technique, no. 2. Yaoundé: Prescriptor, 2005.

Bakoup, Ferdinand. "Promoting Economic Reforms in Developing Countries: Rethinking Budgetary Aid?" Tunis: African Development Bank Working Paper Series, no. 167, January 2013.

Bakoup, Ferdinand, Abdelrahmi Bessaha and Luca Errico. "Regional Integration in Eastern and Southern Africa: The Cross-Border Initiative and Its Fiscal Implications." Washington, DC: IMF Working Paper, no. WP/95/23, 1995.

Bakoup, Ferdinand, and David Tarr. "How Integration into the Central African Economic and Monetary Community Affects Cameroon's Economy: General Equilibrium Estimates." Washington, DC: World Bank, Development Research Group, Policy Research Working Paper, no. 1872, 1998.

Balino, Tomas J. T., and Lorena M. Zamalloa. *Instruments of Monetary Management: Issues and Country Experiences*. Washington, DC: International Monetary Fund, 1997.

Banque africaine de développement. *Les ressources naturelles au service du développement durable de l'Afrique*. Rapport sur le développement en Afrique. Paris: Economica, 2007.

Banque centrale de Tunisie. "Taux de change indicatif de la BCT pour les opérations en compte." Online: http://www.bct.gov.tn/bct/siteprod/cours_fixe.jsp (accessed May 1, 2014.

Banque centrale européenne. *La politique monétaire de la BCE*. Frankfurt: BCE, 2004.

Banque de France. "Liquidité." *Revue de la stabilité financière*, Numéro Spécial 11, February 2008.

Banque mondiale. *Intégration mondiale de la Tunisie: Une nouvelle génération de réformes pour booster la croissance et l'emploi*. Washington, DC: Banque mondiale, 2008.

Bartik, Timothy J. *Jobs for the Poor: Can Labor Demand Policies Help?* New York: Russell Sage Foundation, W. E. Upjohn Institute for Employment Research, 2001.

Beattie, Alan. "Knowledge of Local Market Reaps Rewards." *Financial Times*, June 10, 2008, 3.

_____. "Malawi Cultivates Cash Gains for Its Farmers." *Financial Times*, June 10, 2008, 3.

_____. "Manufacturing: Dying to Keep Up with Competition from the Chinese." *Financial Times*, Special Report: Nigeria, July 12, 2007, 13.

_____. "Pile-It-High Advocates Set to Reap Gains." *Financial Times*, October 9, 2007.

Bekolo Ebe, Bruno. "Les contraintes à l'efficacité des politiques budgétaires dans les économies africaines." In *Budget et politique économique en Afrique*, edited by Roger Tsafack Nanfosso, 17–44. Yaoundé: Editions Clé, 2007.

Ben Ali, Zine El Abidine. Preface to *Dixième Plan développement 2002–2006*, vol. 1. Carthage, February 22, 2001.

Ben Romdhane, Mahmoud. "Commerce et stratégies de développement: Le cas tunisien." Centre africain de politique commerciale, Commission économique des nations unies pour l'Afrique, Travail en cours, no. 53, 2007.

Bénassy-Quéré, Agnès, Benoît Cœuré, Pierre Jacquet and Jean Pisani-Ferry. *Politique économique*. Brussels: de Boeck, 2004.

Benkimoun, Paul. "Polémique sur les brevets de médicaments: La Haute Cour de justice indienne déboute Novartis." *Le Monde*, August 8, 2007.

Bernard, Philippe. "Coup de torchon à la bananeraie." *Le Monde,* June 10, 2008.

Bertoncini, Yves, and Vanessa Wisnia-Weill. *La stratégie de Lisbonne: Une voie européenne dans la mondialisation.* Paris: Centre d'analyse stratégiques et Fondation Robert Schuman, 2007.

Betbèze, Jean-Paul. *Crise: Une chance pour la France?* Paris: PUF, 2009.

Bhagwati, Jagdish. *In Defense of Globalization.* New York: Oxford University Press, 2005.

Bini Smaghi, Lorenzo. "Three Questions on Monetary Tightening." Speech at the Nomura Conference, Tokyo, October 26–7, 2006.

Birdsall, Nancy, Dani Rodrik and Arvin Subramanian. "How to Help Poor Countries." *Foreign Affairs* 84, no. 4 (July/August 2005).

Blackwood, D. L., and R. G. Lynch. "The Measurement of Inequality and Poverty: A Policy Maker's Guide to the Literature." *World Development* 22, no. 4: 567–78.

Bleby, Michael. "South Africa on Tightrope as Key Rate Rises to Five-Year High." *Financial Times,* June 13, 2008, 3.

Boissieu, Christian de. *Principes de politique économique,* 2nd edition. Paris: Economica, 1980.

Borio, C., and P. Disyatat. "Unconventional Monetary Policies: An Appraisal." BIS Working Paper, no. 292, November 2009.

Bouayad, Anis. *Stratégie pour la France.* Paris: Economica, 2003.

Bouquerel, Sarah, and Pierre-Alain de Mallerey. "L'Europe et la Pauvreté: Quelles Réalités?" *Notes de la Fondation Robert Schuman* 31 (March 2006).

Bourguignon, François. Interview in *Le Monde,* Economie supplement, April 2006.

Brada, J. C., and S. Estrin. "Advances in the Theory and Practice of Indicative Planning." *Journal of Comparative Economics* 14 (1990): 523–30.

Brée, Joël. *Le comportement du consommateur.* Paris: Dunod, 2004.

Brehon, Nicolas-Jean. *L'agriculture européenne à l'heure du choix: Pourquoi croire à la PAC? Contribution au bilan de santé de la PC.* Paris: Fondation Robert Schuman, 2008.

Brémond, Janine, J.-F. Couet and M.-M. Salort. *Dictionnaire de l'essentiel en économie.* Paris: Liris, 2004.

Bubula, Andrea, and Inci Ötker-Robe. "The Evolution of Exchange Rate Regimes Since 1990: Evidence from De Facto Policies." Washington, DC: IMF Working Paper, no. WP/02/155, 2002.

Buck, Tobias. "Brussels Wants Fewer Private Sector Subsidies." *Financial Times,* June 8, 2005.

Burall, Simon, Ken Mease, Pooja Mall and Ajoy Datta, with Ndanga Kamau. "Assessing Key Stakeholder Perceptions of the Effectiveness of Multilateral Organisations." Final Report, Centre for Aid and Public Expenditure, Overseas Development Institute, 2007.

Burda, Michael. "Economic Truths behind Germany's Recovery." *Financial Times,* July 25, 2007.

Burgess, Kate. "Private Equity Explores the Sub-Sahara." *Financial Times,* Companies and Markets, August 10, 2007, 13.

Burgess, Kate, and William Wallis. "Africa Becomes Sunny Proposition for Funds." *Financial Times,* Companies and Markets, August, 10, 2007, 13.

Burnside, C., and D. Dollar. "Aid, Policies, and Growth." *American Economic Review* 90, no. 4 (September 2000): 847–68.

Capul, Jean-Yves, ed. *Découverte de l'économie 3: Les politiques économiques.* Cahiers Français 284. Paris: La documentation française, 1998.

Caramel, Laurence. "Perte d'influence pour les jumelles de Bretton-Woods." *Le Monde,* Economie supplement, September 19, 2006, 2.

Casale, Daniela, Colette Muller and Dorrit Posel. "Two Million Net New Jobs: A Reconsideration of the Rise in Employment in South Africa, 1995–2003." Paper presented at the conference on "African Development and Poverty Reduction: The Macro–Micro Linkage," Cape Town, South Africa, 2004.

Castel, Robert. *Guide FNAC des questions d'aujourd'hui.* Paris: FNAC, 2001.

———. "Travailler plus, pour gagner quoi? La multiplication accélérée des formes dévaluées d'emplois conduit à la dégradation du statut de travailleur, donc de citoyen." *Le Monde,* July 9, 2008, 17.

Center for Global Development. *Building Africa's Development Bank: Six Recommendations for the AfDB and its Shareholders.* Report of the AfDB Working Group, Center for Global Development, August 2006.

Chang, Ha-Joon. "Economic History of the Developed World: Lessons for Africa." Lecture at the Eminent Speakers Program of the African Development Bank, Tunis, February 26, 2009.

———. *Kicking Away the Ladder: Development Strategy in Historical Perspective.* London: Anthem Press, 2002.

Chelbi, Afif. Presentation at the workshop on "La compétitivité de l'économie tunisienne: Enjeux, Perspectives et stratégies," organized by the African Development Bank and the Tunisian government, Tunis, November 28, 2006.

Chinje, Eric. Paper presented at the International Media Summit on "Re-Branding Africa," Accra, Ghana, September 18–20, 2006.

Cohen-Tanugi, Laurent. *EuroMonde 2015: Une stratégie européenne pour la mondialisation.* Report for the French Presidency of the Council of the European Union. 2008. Online: http://www.euromonde2015.eu.

Collier, Paul. *Africa's Economic Growth: Opportunities and Constraints.* Paper prepared for the African Development Bank. Centre for the Study of African Economies, Department of Economics, Oxford University, Oxford, October 2006.

Commission des communautés européennes. "Commerce et développement, comment aider les pays en développement à tirer parti du commerce?" Communication de la Commission au Conseil et au Parlement européen. COM (2002), 513 final.

———. "Les règles d'origine dans les régimes commerciaux préférentiels: Orientations pour l'avenir." Communication de la Commission au Conseil, au Parlement européen et au Comité économique et social europée. COM (2005), 100 final.

———. "Sur le 'commerce équitable.'" Communication de la Commission au Conseil. COM (1999), 619 final.

Commission on Growth and Development. *The Growth Report: Strategies for Sustained Growth and Inclusive Development.* Washington, DC: World Bank, 2008. Online: http://siteresources.worldbank.org/EXTPREMNET/Resources/489960-1338997241035/Growth_Commission_Final_Report.pdf (accessed April 29, 2014).

Commission pour l'Afrique. *Notre intérêt commun: Rapport de la Commission pour l'Afrique.* Addis Ababa, May 2005.

Commission pour la libération de la croissance française présidée par Jacques Attali. *300 décisions pour changer la France.* La documentation française, XO Editions, January 2008.

Commission union économique et monétaire ouest-africaine. *Rapport semestriel d'exécution de la surveillance multilatérale.* June 2008. Online: http://www.uemoa.int/Documents/Publications/Surv_Multilaterale/2008/rsmjuin2008.pdf (accessed May 1, 2014).

Concialdi, Pierre, Jean-Pierre Guenanten and Sylvette Uzan-Chomat. "Chiffres du chômage: Le vrai débat; Face aux soupçons, il est urgent de construire un nouvel indicateur du marché du travail." *Le Monde débats,* October 10, 2007, 19.

Cordella, Tito, and Giovanni Dell'Ariccia. "Budget Support Versus Project Aid: A Theoretical Appraisal." *Economic Journal* 117 (October 2007): 1260–79.

Cour-Thimann, P., and B. Winker. "The ECB's Non-standard Monetary Policy Measures: The Role of Institutional Factors and Financial Structure." ECB Working Paper Series, no. 152B, April 2013.

Darreau, Philippe. *Croissance et politique économique.* Brussels: de Boeck, 2003.

Davis, Donald R., and Prachi Mishra. "Stolper–Samuelson Is Dead: And Other Crimes of Both Theory and Data." In *Globalization and Poverty,* edited by Ann Harrison, 87–108. Chicago: University of Chicago Press, 2007.

Demirgüç-Kunt, Asli, and Luis Servén. *Are All the Sacred Cows Dead?* Washington, DC: World Bank Policy Research Working Paper, no. 4807, 2009.

Denis, R. "Time-Inconsistent Monetary Policies: Recent Research." *FRBSF Economic Letter,* no. 2003–10 (April 11, 2003).

Devarajan, Shantayanan. Interview in *Le Monde,* May 6, 2009.

Devarajan, Shantayanan, and Marcelo Giugale, with Hélène Ehrhart, Tuan Minh and Huong Mai Nguyenet. "The Case for Direct Transfers of Resource Revenues in Africa." Center for Global Development Working Paper, no. 333, July 2013.

Department for International Development. "Implementing DFID's Conditionality Policy." Draft how-to note, HM Treasury, 2006.

Department for International Development. *Partnership for Poverty Reduction: Rethinking Conditionality.* UK policy paper, HM Treasury, 2005.

Di Bella, Gabriel, Mark Lewis and Aurélie Martin. "Assessing Competitiveness and Real Exchange Rate Misalignment in Low-Income Countries." Washington, DC: IMF Working Paper, no. WP/07/201, 2007.

Dickie, Mure. "China Currency 'Not Main Cause' of Trade Surplus." *Financial Times,* December 3, 2007.

_____."Shanghai Finds Top Brand Names Wanting." *Financial Times,* January 20/21, 2007.

Dollar, David. "Globalization, Poverty and Inequality." In *Globalization: What's New?*, edited by Michael M. Weinstein, 96–128. New York: Columbia University Press, 2005.

Drazen, A., and P. Masson. "Credibility of Policies Versus Credibility of Policymakers." *Quarterly Journal of Economics* 109, no. 3 (August 1994): 735–54.

Easterly, William. *The Elusive Quest for Growth: Economists Adventures and Misadventures in the Tropics.* Cambridge, MA: MIT Press, 2001.

_____. "Trust the Development Experts – All 7bn of Them." *Financial Times,* May 29, 2008, 11.

Eastwood, David B. *The Economics of Consumer Behavior.* Boston: Allyn and Bacon, 1985.

Economist. "African Banks on the Frontier of Finance." November 17, 2007, 77–78.

_____. "On the Poverty Line." Economics Focus, May 24, 2008, 92.

Eichengreen, Barry, and Ricardo Hausmann, eds. *Other People's Money: Debt Denomination and Financial Instability in Emerging Market Economies.* Chicago: University of Chicago Press, 2005.

Epstein, Gerald, James Heintz, Leonce Ndikumana, Grace Chang. *Employment, Poverty and Economic Development in Madagascar: A Macroeconomic Framework.* Amherst, MA: Political Economy Research Institute (PERI), University of Massachusetts, December 2008.

European Central Bank. *The Monetary Policy of the ECB.* Frankfurt: ECB, 2004. Online: http://www.ecb.europa.eu/pub/pdf/other/monetarypolicy2004en.pdf (accessed April 29, 2014)

European Union. "Règlement (CE) No 980/2005 du Conseil du 27 juin 2005 portant application d'un schéma de préférences tarifaires généralisées." *Journal officiel de l'Union européenne,* L 169/1 (June 30, 2005).

Felipe, Jesus. "Is Export-Led Growth Passé? Implications for Developing Asia." Asian Development Bank, ERD Working Paper Series, no. 48, 2003.

Ferrandon, B., ed. *La politique économique et ses instruments.* Les notices de La documentation française. Paris: La documentation française, 2004.

Festy, Patrick, and Lidia Prokofieva. "Mesures, formes et facteurs de la pauvreté: Approches comparatives." INED Documents de travail, no. 151, 2008.

Fielding, David, ed. *Macroeconomic Policy in the Franc Zone.* Studies in Development Economics and Policy. New York: Palgrave Macmillan, 2005.

Financial Times. "Asian Countries Move to Protect Exports." October 24, 2008, 2.

Fonds monétaire international. *La FASR à dix ans: L'ajustement et la réforme économiques dans les pays à faible revenu.* Etude spéciale du FMI, no. 156, 1997.

_____. "Le FMI et l'aide à l'Afrique sub-saharienne." Rapport d'évaluation. 2007. Online: http://www.imf.org/External/NP/ieo/2007/ssa/fra/pdf/031207f.pdf (accessed May 1, 2014).

_____. *Perspectives économiques régionales: Afrique sub-saharienne.* Washington, DC: IMF, October 2007.

FIPA-Tunisia. "Organisation." FIPA-Tunisia website. Online: http://www.investintunisia.tn/site/fr/article.php?id_article=134 (accessed April 11, 2014).

_____. "Presentation." FIPA-Tunisia website. Online: http://www.investintunisia.tn/site/fr/article.php?id_article=202 (accessed April 11, 2014).

Fouda, Séraphin Magloire. "Pour une efficacité de la politique budgétaire dans les unions monétaires africaines." In *Budget et politique économique en Afrique*, edited by Roger Tsafack Nanfosso, 77–108. Yaoundé: Editions Clé, 2007.

French, Howard W., and Lydia Polgreen. "China Brings Its Deep Pockets to Africa." *International Herald Tribune*, August 13, 2007, 1.

French Republic. "Divers documents sur la loi pour le travail, l'emploi et le pouvoir d'achat." Website of the Ministère des finances et des comptes publics. June 20, 2007. Online: http://www.economie. gouv.fr/Projet-de-loi-en-faveur-du-travail-de-l-emploi-et- (accessed May 4, 2014).

G8 Summit. *Growth and Responsibility in Africa*. Summit declaration, Heiligendamm, June 8, 2007. Online: http://www.g-8.de/Content/DE/Artikel/G8Gipfel/Anlage/Abschlusserkl_C3_A4run gen/WV-afrika-en,property=publicationFile.pdf (accessed April 11, 2014).

Gadrey, Jean, and Florence Jany-Catrice. *Les nouveaux indicateurs de richesses*. Paris: La Découverte, 2005.

Gallois, Dominique. "Aéronautique: Charles Edelstenne, le président de Dassualt Aviation, s'alarme des conséquences de l'euro fort." *Le Monde*, December 3, 2007.

Gardner, Edward. *Creating Employment in the Middle East and North Africa*. Washington, DC: IMF, 2003.

Gelb, Alan. "Cost and Competitiveness in Africa." PowerPoint presentation to the PSD Forum, in the session on "Taping Africa's Export Potential Beyond Commodities, What Is the Mix of Economy-Wide and Industry-Specific Reforms?" Development Economics Department, World Bank, June 2006.

Généreux, Jacques. *Introduction à la politique économique*. Paris: Editions du Seuil, 1999.

Ghali, Sofiane, and Pierre Mohnen. "The Tunisian Path to Development: 1961–2001." Case study from "Reducing Poverty, Sustaining Growth: What Works, What Doesn't, and Why a Global Exchange for Scaling Up Success, Scaling Up Poverty Reduction; A Global Learning Process and Conference," Shanghai, May 25–7, 2004.

Glazer, Amihai, and Lawrence S. Rothenberg. *Why Government Succeeds and Why It Fails*. Cambridge, MA: Harvard University Press, 2001.

Goldstein, Morris, and Philip Turner. *Controlling Currency Mismatches in Emerging Markets*. Washington, DC: Institute of International Economics, 2004.

Grant, Jeremy. "World Bank Boosts 'Local' Bonds." *Financial Times*, October 5, 2007.

Greenspan, Alan. *Le temps des turbulences*. Paris: J. C. Lattès, 2007.

Greenwald, Bruce, and Joseph E. Stiglitz. "Helping Infant Economies Grow: Foundations of Trade Policies for Developing Countries." *AEA Papers and Proceedings* (2006).

Guillaumont, Patrick. "La vulnérabilité économique, défi persistant à la croissance africaine." Paper presented at the African Economic Conference, organized by the African Development Bank, Tunis, November 22–4, 2006.

Hanmer, Lucia C., Graham Pyatt and Howard White. *What Do the World Bank's Poverty Assessments Teach Us about Poverty in Sub-Saharan Africa?* Summary of a report prepared for the SPA Working Group on Poverty and Social Policy. 1997.

Harel, Xavier. *Afrique pillage à huis clos: Comment une poignée d'initiés siphonne le pétrole africains*. Paris: Fayard, 2006.

Harrison, Ann, ed. *Globalization and Poverty*. Chicago: University of Chicago Press, 2006.

Hausmann, Ricardo. "Stop Behaving as Whiner of First Resort." *Financial Times*, January 31, 2008.

Hausmann, R., D. Rodrik and A. Velasco. "Getting the Diagnosis Right: A New Approach to Economic Reform." *Finance et développement* 43, no. 1 (March 2006): 12–15.

Helpman, Elhanan. *The Mystery of Economic Growth*. Cambridge, MA: Belknap Press of Harvard University Press, 2004.

Hirsch, Alan. *Season of Hope: Economic Reform under Mandela and Mbeki*. Durban: University of Kwazulu-Natal Press, Private Bag X01, 2005.

Hollinger, Peggy. "Low Dollar 'Threatens the Life' of Airbus." *Financial Times*, November 23, 2007.

Hubbard, Glenn, and William Duggan. "Why Africa Needs a Marshall Plan." *Financial Times*, June 5, 2007.

Independent Evaluation Office of the International Monetary Fund (IEO). *Evaluation of Structural Conditionality in IMF-Supported Programs.* New York: IMF, 2007. Online: http://www.ieo-imf.org/ ieo/files/completedevaluations/01032008SC_main_report.pdf (accessed May 2, 2014).

Institut national de la statistique. *Enquête nationale sur l'emploi en 1997.* Tunis: INS, 1999.

Institute of Development Studies. *Stepping Up to the Future: An Independent Evaluation of African Development Fund VII, VIII and IX.* Sussex: IDS, June 2004.

_____. "The Global Financial Crisis, Developing Countries and Policy Responses." *IDS In Focus Policy Briefing* 7.1 (March 2009).

_____. *Voices from the South: The Impact of the Financial Crisis on Developing Countries.* Sussex: IDS, November 12, 2008. Online: http://www.ids.ac.uk/go/financial-crisis-impact (accessed April 11, 2014).

International Development Association and International Monetary Fund. *Heavily Indebted Poor Countries (HIPC) Initiative and Multilateral Debt Relief Initiative (MDRI): Status of Implementation.* IDA/ IMF, August 28, 2007. Online: http://www.imf.org/external/np/pp/2007/eng/082807.pdf (accessed April 11, 2014).

International Labour Organization. *Guide to Understanding the KILM.* Geneva: ILO, 2014. Online: http://kilm.ilo.org/2011/download/GuidEN.pdf (accessed May 4, 2014).

International Monetary Fund. "Communiqué of the International Monetary and Financial Committee of the Board of Governors of the International Monetary Fund." September 17, 2006. Online: http://www.imf.org/external/np/cm/2006/091706.htm (accessed April 11, 2014).

_____. "Dialogue with Angus Deaton: When Numbers Don't Tell the Full Story about Poverty in India and the World." *IMF Survey* 31, no. 13 (July 8, 2002).

_____. *Post-Apartheid South Africa: The First Ten Years.* Washington, DC: IMF, 2005.

_____. *Tunisia: Selected Issues.* Washington, DC: IMF Country Report, no. 06/208, June 2006.

_____. *Tunisia: 2006 Article IV Consultation; Staff Report; Staff Statement; Public Information Notice on the Executive Board Discussion; and statement by the Executive Director for Tunisia.* Washington, DC: IMF Country Report no. 06/207, June 2006.

_____. *Methodology for CGER Exchange Rate Assessments.* IMF Research Department paper, November 8, 2006. Online: http://www.imf.org/external/np/pp/eng/2006/110806.pdf (accessed April 11, 2014).

_____. "IMF Strengthening Framework for Exchange Rate Surveillance." Press release no. 06/266, November 29, 2006.

_____. *Perspectives économiques régionales: Afrique sub-saharienne.* Washington, DC: IMF, October 2007. Online: http://www.imf.org/external/pubs/ft/reo/2007/AFR/ENG/sreo1007.pdf (accessed May 1, 2014).

_____. "World Economic Outlook Databases." Online: http://www.imf.org/external/ns/ cs.aspx?id=28 (accessed April, 11 2014).

International Telecommunication Union. *African Telecommunication / ICT Indicators: At a Crossroads.* Geneva: ITU Telecom Africa, 2008.

Jayantilal Bhundia, Ashok, and Luca Antonio Ricci. "The Rand Crises of 1998 and 2001: What Have We Learned?" In *Post-Apartheid South Africa: The First Ten Years,* edited by Michael Nowak and Luca Antonio Ricci, 156–73. Washington, DC: IMF, 2005.

Jbili, Abdelji, and Vitali Kramarenko. *Choosing Exchange Regimes in the Middle East and North Africa.* Washington, DC: IMF, 2003.

Ji Hong Kim. "Lessons from Asia: The Experience of Korea." Paper presented at the African Economic Conference on "Accelerating Africa's Development Five Years into the Twenty-First Century," Tunis, November 22–4, 2006.

Jonsson, Gunnar, and Arvind Subramanian. "Dynamic Gains from Trade: Evidence from South Africa." *IMF Staff Papers* 48, no. 1 (2001).

Kasekende, Louis. "On Shaky Ground." *Focus on Africa.* BBC World News. 2008.

Keynes, J. M. *Théorie générale de l'emploi, de l'intérêt et de la monnaie.* Paris: Payot & Rivages, 2005.

Khan, Mohsin S. "Current Issues in the Design and Conduct of Monetary Policy." Washington, DC: IMF Working Paper, no. WP/03/56, 2003.

Kopits, George. "Fiscal Rules: Useful Policy Framework or Unnecessary Ornament?" Washington, DC: IMF Working Paper, no. WP/01/145, 2001.

Kopits, George, and Steven A. Symansky. "Fiscal Policy Rules." Washington, DC: IMF Occasional Paper, no. 162, 1998.

Kose, Ayhan, Christopher Otrok and Eswar S. Prasad. "Global Business Cycles: Convergence or Decoupling?" Washington, DC: IMF Working Paper, no. WP/08/143, 2008.

Kramer, Charles F., Hélène K. Poirson and A. Prasad. "Challenges to Monetary Policy from Financial Globalization: The Case of India." Washington, DC: IMF Working Paper, no. WP/08/131, May 2008.

Krugman, P. *End This Depression Now!* New York: W. W. Norton, 2012.

Kungliga Vetenskapsakademien (Royal Swedish Academy of Sciences). *Finn Kydland and Edward Prescott's Contribution to Dynamic Macroeconomics: The Time Consistency of Economic Policy and the Driving Forces behind Business Cycles.* Advanced Information on the Bank of Sweden Prize in Economic Sciences in Memory of Alfred Nobel. Stockholm: KVA Information Department, 2004. Online: http://www.nobelprize.org/nobel_prizes/economic-sciences/laureates/2004/advanced-economicsciences2004.pdf (accessed April 29, 2014).

Kuznets, Simon. "Modern Economic Growth: Findings and Reflections." Prize lecture, Sveriges Riksbank Prize in Economic Sciences in Memory of Alfred Nobel, December 11, 1971.

Kydland, Finn E., and Edward C. Prescott. "Rules Rather than Discretion: The Inconsistency of Optimal Plans." *Journal of Political Economy* 85, no. 3 (June 1977): 473–92.

La voix du paysan, nos 192, 193, 194, 195, 196.

Laffer, Arthur B. "The Laffer Curve: Past, Present, and Future." *Backgrounder* 1765 (June 1, 2004).

Lardy, Nicholas, R. *Integrating China into the Global Economy*. Washington, DC: Brookings Institution Press, 2004.

Le Monde. "Chiffrage et déontologie: La réponse des experts de l'institut de l'entreprise au manifeste de l'Observatoire français des conjonctures économiques." March 6, 2007.

_____. Economie supplement. "Aide au développement: L'après Bretton-Woods a commencé." May 22, 2007.

_____. Economie supplement. "Chiffrage des programmes: Et si tout cela ne voulait rien dire." February 20, 2007.

_____. Economie supplement. "Le bonheur peut-il être un indicateur économique?" January 29, 2008.

_____. Economie supplement. "Neuroéconomie: Les émotions dictent-elles nos décisions?" January 15, 2008.

Legrand, Christine. "Sept pays d'Amérique latine lancent la Banque du Sud." *Le Monde*, December 12, 2007.

Lemaître, Frédéric. "L'économie rattrape Nicolas Sarkozy." *Le Monde*, August 16, 2007.

Lin, J. Y. *The Quest for Prosperity: How Developing Economies Can Take Off*. Princeton, NJ: Princeton University Press, 2012.

Mabro, Robert. Interview in *Le Monde*, September 21, 2006, 16.

Malawi Ministry of Health / Japan International Cooperation Agency. *Health Facility Survey Report*. Malawi, 2002.

Mallet, Victor. "The Ugly Face of China's Presence in Africa." *Financial Times*, September 14, 2006.

Mankiw, N. Gregory. *Macroeconomics*, 3rd edition. New York: Worth, 1997.

Manuel, Trevor A. "Medium Term Budget Policy Statement 2008 speech by Trevor A. Manuel, MP, Minister of Finance." South Africa Government Online. October 21, 2008. Online: http://www.gov.za/speeches/2008/08102114261001.htm (accessed May 6, 2014).

_____. "The World Economy in Crisis." Ministry of Finance, Republic of South Africa. November 18, 2008. Online: http://www.treasury.gov.za/comm_media/speeches/2008/2008111802.pdf

———. "Opening Comments to the Meeting of the Committee of 10 (C10)." Ministry of Finance, Republic of South Africa. January 16, 2009. Online: http://www.treasury.gov.za/comm_media/speeches/2009/2009011601.pdf (accessed May 6, 2014).

———. "Budget Speech 2009 by the Minister of Finance, Trevor A Manuel." South Africa Government Online. February 11, 2009. Online: http://www.gov.za/speeches/2009/09021114561001.htm (accessed May 6, 2014).

Marais, Hein. South Africa: Limits to Change; The Political Economy of Transition. New York: Zed Books, 1998.

Masson, Paul. "Globalization: Facts and Figures." Washington, DC: IMF Policy Discussion Paper, no. PDP/01/4, 2001.

Maxwell, Simon. "The Meaning and Measurement of Poverty." ODI Poverty Briefing, February 1999.

Mbeki, Thabo. "Radio and Television Address to the Nation by the President of South Africa, Thabo Mbeki, on the Occasion of Africa Day." South Africa Government Online. May 25, 2008. Online: http://www.gov.za/speeches/2008/08052608451001.htm (accessed May 6, 2014).

———. "State of the Nation Address of the President of South Africa, Thabo Mbeki: Joint Sitting of Parliament." South Africa Government Online. February 3, 2006. Online: http://www.gov.za/speeches/2006/06020310531001.htm (accessed May 6, 2014).

McGregor, Richard. "China Attacks GE Turbine Standards." Financial Times, August 10, 2007.

McNamara, William. "ANC Likely to Make Mbeki Pay Despite Boom." Financial Times, December 14, 2007, 7.

Mercure, Daniel. "Adam Smith: Les assises de la modernité." In Le travail dans l'histoire de la pensée occidentale, edited by Daniel Mercure and Jan Spurk, 119–42. Quebec: Les Presses de l'Université Laval, 2003.

Mercure, Daniel, and Jan Spurk. Le travail dans l'histoire de la pensée occidentale. Quebec: Les Presses de l'Université Laval, 2003.

Meyer, Laurence H. A Term at the FED: An Insider's View; The People and Policies of the World's Most Powerful Institution. New York: Collins, 2004.

Migeotte, Léopold. "Les philosophes grecs et le travail dans l'antiquité." In Le travail dans l'histoire de la pensée occidentale, edited by Daniel Mercure and Jan Spurk, 11–32. Quebec: Les Presses de l'Université Laval, 2003.

Mile, Richard. "Scandal Puts Siemens to the Test." Financial Times, Companies and Markets, January 21, 2008.

Millennium Project. Innovation: Applying Knowledge in Development. London: Earthscan, 2005.

Monga, Célestin. Un bantou à Washington. Paris: PUF, 2008.

Müller, Hans-Peter. "Travail, Profession et 'Vocation': Le concept de travail chez Max Weber." In Le travail dans l'histoire de la pensée occidentale, edited by Daniel Mercure and Jan Spurk, 251–77. Quebec: Les Presses de l'Université Laval, 2003.

Nachéga, Jean-Claude. "Fiscal Dominance and Inflation in the Democratic Republic of Congo." Washington, DC: IMF Working Paper, no. WP/05/221, 2005.

Naim, Moisés. "Washington Consensus: A Damaged Brand." Financial Times, October 28, 2002.

Nana-Sinkam, Samuel C. Le Cameroun dans la globalisation: Conditions et prémisses pour un développement durable et equitable. Yaoundé: Editions Clé, 1999.

Naudé, Wim, and Augustin Kwasi Fosu. "Marshall Plan Is the Wrong Analogy for Economic Development of Africa." Financial Times, Letters, June 7, 2007.

Nellor, David. "Africa's Aspiring Second-Generation Emerging Markets." IMF Survey 2008.

Njonga, Bernard. Interview in Le Monde, Economie supplement, January 16, 2007.

———. Le poulet de la discorde: Plaidoyer et lobbying. Yaoundé: Editions Clé, 2008.

Noël, Pierre. "How Oil Majors Can Thrive in an Age of State Monopolies." Financial Times, August 10, 2007.

Nowak, Michael, and Luca Antonio Ricci, eds. Post-Apartheid South Africa: The First Ten Years. Washington, DC: IMF, 2005.

Nyambal, Eugène. *Créer la prospérité en Afrique: Dix clés pour sortir de la pauvreté*. L'esprit économique. Paris: L'Harmattan, 2006.

Organisation international du travail. *Une mondialisation juste: Créer des opportunités pour tous*. Report, Commission mondiale sur la dimension sociale de la mondialisation, February 2004.

Organisation mondiale du commerce. *Examen des politiques commerciales: République sud-africaine; Rapport du secrétariat*. WT/TPR/S/34, April 6, 1998.

_____. *Examen des politiques commerciales: Tunisie; Rapport du secrétariat, Révision*. WT/TPR/S/152/ Rev.1, 2005, 52.

Osei, B. "How Aid Tying Can Impose Additional Cost on Aid Recipients: Evidence on Ghana." *African Development Review* 17, no. 3 (December 2005): 348–65.

Oxfam. "Oxfam Calls on Starbucks to Stop Bullying the Poor; Starbucks Must Respect Ethiopia's Right to Choose Its Own Path to Development." Press release, November 3, 2006. Online: http://www.oxfam.org.uk/press/releases.

_____. "Starbucks CEO Meets with Ethiopian Government about Ownership of Coffee Names; Oxfam Calls on Starbucks to Make Progress on Trademark Issue." Press release, November 29, 2006. Online: http://www.oxfam.org.uk/press/releases.

_____. "Starbucks Opposes Ethiopia's Plan to Trademark Speciality Coffee Names that Could Bring Farmers an Estimated £47 Million Annually; Oxfam Urges Company to Review Strategy and *Sign Licensing Agreement*." Press release, October 26, 2006. Online: http://www.oxfam.org.uk/press/releases.

Parker, George, Tobias Buck and Bertrand Benoit. "Key Clause Dropped from Draft EU Treaty." *Financial Times*, June 22, 2007.

Patat, Jean-Pierre. "Le mauvais procès fait à la Banque centrale européenne." *Le Monde*, Economie supplement, June 20, 2007, 6.

Patel, Ibrahim. "Address by Economic Development Minister Ebrahim Patel at Supplier Development Summit." South African Government Online. 14 Mar 2013. http://www.gov.za/ speeches/view.php?sid=34999 (accessed April 29, 2014).

Pedroletti, Brice. "Les attaques contre les marques étrangères se multiplient en Chine." *Le Monde*, June 7, 2007, 16.

Perez, Romain, and Stephen Njuguna Karingi. "How to Balance the Outcomes of the Economic Partnership Agreements for Sub-Saharan African Economies?" *World Economy* 30, no. 12 (2007): 1877–99.

Pilling, David. "Zoellick Charts Bank's New Direction." *Financial Times*, August 10, 2007.

Pisani-Ferry, J. *Politique économique*. Brussels: Editions de Boeck University, 2005.

Prager, Jean-Claude, and François Villeroy de Galhau. *18 leçons sur la politique économique*. Paris: Editions du Seuil, 2006.

Programme des Nations Unies pour le développement. *Rapport mondial sur le développement humain*. New York: PNUD.

Qian, Yingyi. "How Reform Worked in China." In *In Search of Prosperity: Analytic Narratives on Economic Growth*, edited by Dani Rodrik. Princeton, NJ: Princeton University Press, 2003.

Republic of South Africa. "National Electricity Emergency Programme." South Africa Government Online. 2008. Online: http://www.gov.za/aboutgovt/programmes/energy/ index.html (accessed May 6, 2014).

_____. "National Response to South Africa's Electricity Shortage." South Africa Government Online. January 2008. Online: http://www.gov.za/aboutgovt/programmes/energy/response_ cabinet.pdf (accessed May 6, 2014).

_____. "South Africa Calls for a Political Guidance on the Development of a Post-Bali Work Programme." South Africa Government Online, Speeches and Statements, December 4, 2013. Online: http://www.gov.za/speeches/view.php?sid=42443 (accessed April 11, 2014).

Republic of South Africa. *Growth, Employment and Redistribution: A Macroeconomic Strategy*. Pretoria: Republic of South Africa, Department of Finance, 1996.

Reynaud, Julien, and Julien Vauday. "IMF Lending and Geopolitics." ECB Working Paper Series, no. 965/November 2008.

Rodrik, Dani. "Feasible Globalizations." In *Globalization: What's New?*, edited by Michael M. Weinstein, 196–213. New York: Columbia University Press, 2005.

_____. *Has Globalization Gone Too Far?* Washington, DC: Institute of International Economics, 1997.

_____. "Industrial Policy for the Twenty-First Century." New Thinking on Growth and Development Policy, Harvard University training program, 2004.

_____. Interview in *Le Monde*, September 9, 2003.

_____. *The New Global Economy and Developing Countries: Making Openness Work*. Washington, DC: Overseas Development Council, Policy Essay, no. 24, 1999.

_____. *One Economics, Many Recipes: Globalization, Institutions, and Economic Growth*. Princeton, NJ: Princeton University Press, 2007.

_____. "Trade Cannot Be a Substitute for Good Economic Planning." *Kenya Daily Nation*, August 9, 2005.

Rodrik, Dani, Arvind Subramanian and Francesco Trebbi. "Institutions Rule: The Primacy of Institutions over Integration and Geography in Economic Development." Washington, DC: IMF Working Paper, no. 02/189, 2002.

Rogoff, Kenneth. "Rogoff's Discontent with Stiglitz." *IMF Survey* 31, no. 13 (July 8, 2002).

Rosenblatt, Julius, Thomas Mayer, Kasper Bartholy, Dimitrios Demekas, Sanjev Gupta and Leslie Lipchitz. "The Common Agricultural Policy of the European Community: Principles and Consequences." Washington, DC: IMF Occasional Paper, no. 62, November 1988.

Royal Swedish Academy of Sciences. "Edmund's Phelps's Contributions to Macroeconomics." Advanced Information on Sveriges Riksbank Prize in Economic Sciences in Memory of Alfred Nobel, 2006.

Russell, Alec, and Rebecca Bream. "Upheaval at Anglo American as Patricians Leave the Stage." *Financial Times*, August 10, 2007.

Sacerdoti, Emilio. "Access to Bank Credit in Sub-Saharan Africa: Key Issues and Reform Strategies." Washington, DC: IMF Working Paper, no. WP/05/166, 2005.

Sachs, J. "Today's Challenges Go Beyond Keynes." *Financial Times*, December 17, 2012.

Sachs, Jeffrey D. *The End of Poverty: Economic Possibilities for Our Time*. New York: Penguin, 2005.

Sadiq, Ahmed. "Global Food Price Inflation: Implications for South Asia, Policy Reactions, and Future Challenges." Washington, DC: World Bank Policy Research Working Paper, no. 4796, 2008.

Saint-Etienne, Christian. *La France est-elle en faillite?* Paris: Bourin editeur, 2008.

Sapir, Jacques. "L'économie politique internationale de la crise et la question du 'nouveau Bretton Woods': Leçons pour des temps de crise." 2008. Online: http://www.lhivic.org/travaux/articles/sapir_brettonWoods2.pdf (accessed April 29, 2014).

Sarkozy, Nicolas. "Discours devant le Congrès des Etats-Unis d'Amérique." Washington, DC: November 7, 2007.

School of Oriental and African Studies, Wadonda Consult, Michigan State University and Overseas Development Institute. *Evaluation of the 2006/07 Agricultural Input Subsidy Programme, Malawi: Final Report*. 2008.

Sen, Amartya. *L'économie est une science morale*. Paris: La découverte, 2003.

Silem, Ahmed, and Jean-Marie Albertini, eds. *Lexique d'économie*, 8th edition. Paris: Dalloz, 2004.

Sindzingre, Alice. "La Chine en Afrique: Le pire n'est pas sûr." *Le Monde*, Economie supplement, December 12, 2006.

Smith, Adam. *Recherches sur la nature et les causes de la richesse des nations*. Paris: Flammarion, [1776] 1991.

Soludo, C. C. "Africa Needs Honesty Over EU Trade Deals." *Financial Times*, April 10, 2012.

South African Department of Minerals and Energy. "Joint Announcement by Government, Eskom and Mining Industry on Energy Emergency Plan." South Africa Government Online.

January 26, 2008. Online: http://www.gov.za/speeches/2008/08012809151001.htm (accessed May 6, 2014).

South African Department of Trade and Industry. *South Africa's Economic Transformation: A Strategy for Broad-Based Black Economic Empowerment.* Pretoria: DTI, 2003. Online: http://www.thedti.gov.za/economic_empowerment/bee-strategy.pdf (accessed May 5, 2014).

Spence, Michael. "Wealth of Nations: Why China Grows So Fast." *Wall Street Journal,* January 23, 2007.

————. "What Drives High Growth Rates." *Wall Street Journal,* January 24, 2007.

Starbucks. "Starbucks and the Ethiopian Government Agree to Work Together Toward a Solution that Supports the Ethiopian Coffee Farmers." Press release, November 28, 2006. Online: http://news.starbucks.com/news/starbucks-and-the-ethiopian-government-agree-to-work-together-toward-a-solu (accessed May 1, 2014).

Stefania, Fabrizio, Denis Igan and Ashoka Mody. "The Dynamics of Product Quality and International Competitiveness." Washington, DC: IMF Working Paper, no. WP/07/97. 1997.

Steger, Manfred B. *Globalization: A Very Short Introduction.* New York: Oxford University Press, 2003.

Stiglitz, Joseph E. *La grande désillusion.* Paris: Fayard, 2002.

————. *Pour un autre monde: Contre le fanatisme du marché.* Paris: Fayard, 2006.

————. "The Overselling of Globalization." In *Globalization: What's New?,* edited by Michael M. Weinstein, 228–61. New York: Columbia University Press, 2005.

————. *The Roaring Nineties: A New History of the World's Most Prosperous Decade.* New York: W. W. Norton, 2003.

————. "Some Lessons from the East Asian Miracle." *World Bank Research Observer* 11, no. 2 (1996): 151–77.

Stiglitz, Joseph E., and Andrew Charlton. *Pour un commerce mondial plus juste.* Paris: Fayard, 2007.

Stiglitz, Joseph E., and Bruce Greenwald. *Towards a New Paradigm in Monetary Economics.* Raffaele Mattioli Lectures. Cambridge: Cambridge University Press, 2003.

Stiglitz, Joseph E., and Jason Furman. "Economic Crises: Evidence and Insights from East Asia." *Brookings Papers on Economic Activity,* no. 2 (1998): 1–135.

Stoleru, Lionel. "Rapport au Président de la République: L'accès des PME aux marchés publics." Unpublished report, 2007.

Strauss-Kahn, Dominique. "The Case for a Targeted Fiscal Boost." *Financial Times,* January 30, 2008.

Subramanian, Arvind, and Devesh Roy. "Who Can Explain the Mauritian Miracle? Meade, Romer, Sachs, or Rodrik?" In *In Search of Prosperity: Analytic Narratives on Economic Growth,* edited by Dani Rodrik. Princeton, NJ: Princeton University Press, 2003.

Sullivan, Ruth. "Africa Sees Investor Confidence Grow." *Financial Times,* Companies and Markets, August 13, 2007, 3.

Tax Justice Network – Africa and Action Aid International, *Tax Competition in East Africa: A Race to the Bottom?* Nairobi/Johannesburg, April 2012. Online: http://www.taxjusticeafrica.net/sites/default/files/Tax%20competition%20in%20East%20Africa.pdf (accessed May 1, 2014).

Tchundjang Pouemi, Joseph. *Monnaie, servitude et liberté: La répression monétaire de l'Afrique,* 2nd edition. Yaoundé: MENAIBUC, 1979.

Tenou, Kossi. "La règle de Taylor: Un exemple de règle de politique monétaire appliquée au cas de la BCEAO." Dakar: Documents d'études et de recherche de la BCEAO no. 523, March 2002.

Thompson, Leonard. *A History of South Africa.* New Haven, CT: Yale Nota Bene, 2001.

Thurlow, James. *Trade Liberalization and Pro-poor Growth in South Africa.* Trade and Poverty Project, Southern Africa Labour and Development Research Unit, University of Cape Town, 2006.

Tiryakian, Edward A. "Le travail chez Emile Durkheim." In *Le travail dans l'histoire de la pensée occidentale,* edited by Daniel Mercure and Jan Spurk, 229–50. Quebec: Les Presses de l'Université Laval, 2003.

Trichet, Jean-Claude. "Some Lessons from the Financial Market Correction." Speech delivered at the European Banker of the Year 2007 award ceremony, Frankfurt, September 30, 2008. Online: http://www.ecb.int/press/key/date/2008/html/sp080930_1.en.html (accessed 11 April 2014).

Tricornot, Adrien de. "Euro: Le rêve d'une dépréciation compétitive." *Le Monde*, Economie supplement, July 3, 2007, 2.

Tsafack Nanfosso, Roger. "Pour une réforme budgétaire au Cameroun." In *Budget et politique économique en Afrique*, edited by Roger Tsafack Nanfosso, 109–29. Yaoundé: Editions Clé, 2007.

Tuquoi, Jean-Pierre. "Les Nations Unies réorientent leur politique d'achat des produits agricoles vers les pays pauvres." *Le Monde*, October 16, 2008.

Tunisian Republic. *Le Dixième Plan de développement, 2002–2006*. Tunis, 2000.

_____. *Le XIème Plan de développement 2007–11*. Tunis, 2005.

République tunisienne, Ministère du développement et de la coopération internationale. *Bref aperçu sur le Dixième Plan de développement 2002–2006: Ganger le défi de l'emploi, asseoir l'économie du savoir et consolider la compétitivité*. Online: www.tunisieinfo.com/xemeplan.pdf (accessed February 5, 2007).

_____. *Budget économique 2005*. November 2004.

United Nations Conference on Trade and Development. *Economic Development in Africa: Doubling Aid; Making the "Big Push" Work*. Report no. UNCTAD/GDS/AFRICA/2006/1. Geneva: United Nations, 2006.

United Nations Millennium Project. *Investing in Development: A Practical Plan to Achieve the Millennium Development Goals*. New York: United Nations, 2005.

_____. *Generalized System of Preferences: Handbook on the Scheme of the European Community* (INT/97/A06). UNCTAD Technical Cooperation Project on Market Access, Trade Laws and Preferences. New York: United Nations, December 2002.

_____. *Generalized System of Preferences: List of Beneficiary Countries*. New York: United Nations, 2005.

_____. *Trade and Development Report 2006: Global Partnership and National Policies for Development*. New York: United Nations, 2006.

_____. *Trade and Development Report 2013: Adjusting to the Changing Dynamics of the World Economy*. New York: United Nations, 2013.

_____. "Trade Capacity Development for Africa: Policy Issues for African Countries in Multilateral and Regional Trade Negotiations." Geneva: Trade Negotiations and Africa Series, no. 3, 2006.

_____. *UNCTAD GSP Newsletter*, no. 8. UNCTAD/DITC/TNCD/Misc/2005/7, December 2005.

United Nations Conference on Trade and Development. *Development and Globalization: Facts and Figures*. Geneva: UNCTAD, 2008. Online: http://unctad.org/es/Docs/gdscsir20071_en.pdf (accessed May1, 2014).

US Small Business Administration. *Strategic Plan: Fiscal Years 2008–2013* (Washington, DC: SBA, 2007).

Vamvakidis, A. "Trade Openness and Economic Growth Reconsidered." Mimeo, Harvard University, Department of Economics, 1996.

Vital, Lys. *Les organisations non gouvernementales dans la régulation de l'économie mondiale*. Paris: L'Harmattan, 2008.

Wade, Abdoulaye. "Europe-Afrique: La coopération en panne; Les nouveaux accords commerciaux proposés par l'Union européenne sont inacceptables et ne favorisent pas un vrai partenariat." *Le Monde*, November 16, 2007.

Wallis, William. "Donor Bank for Africa to Meet in Shanghai." *Financial Times*, February 1, 2007.

Webber, Jude, and Richard Lapper. "It Won't Be Easy … No Tears for the IMF as a Feisty Argentina Awaits Its Next Evita." *Financial Times*, October 26, 2007.

Weber, Max. *L'éthique protestante et l'esprit du capitalisme*. Paris: Agora, 1990.

White, David. "Oil Companies Urged to Soften Import Blow to Africa." *Financial Times*, November 14, 2005.

Williamson, Hugh. "G8 Heads Put $25bn Africa Aid in Doubt." *Financial Times*, June 30, 2008.
_____. "G8 Split Over Africa Aid Pledges." *Financial Times*, June 5, 2007.
Williamson, John. "What Should the World Bank Think about the Washington Consensus?" *World Bank Research Observer* 15, no. 2 (August 2000): 251–64.
Winters, L. Alan, Neil McCulloch and Andrew McKay. "Trade Liberalization and Poverty: The Evidence So Far." *Journal of Economic Literature* 42 (March 2004): 71–115.
Woerth, Eric. Interview in *Les cahiers de la compétitivité*, no. 1 (April 2008).
Wolf, Martin. "IMF's Ancien Régime Must Give Up Privileges." *Financial Times*, September 19, 2006.
_____. "Un nouveau Bretton Woods? Un impératif vital." *Le Monde*, Economie supplement, November 11, 2008.
World Bank. *Economic Growth in the 1990s: Learning from a Decade of Reform*. Washington, DC: World Bank, 2005.
_____. *Global Monitoring Report: MDGs and the Environment; Agenda for Inclusive and Sustainable Development*. Washington, DC: International Bank for Reconstruction and Development / World Bank, 2008. Online: http://siteresources.worldbank.org/INTPROSPECTS/Resources/334934-1327948020811/8401693-1327957281774/8402501-1328643991240/8944_Web_PDF.pdf (accessed May 1, 2014).
_____. "Governance Matters V: Governance Indicators for 1996–2005." 2006. Online: http://info.worldbank.org/governance/kkz2005/pdf/2005kkdata.xls.
_____. *Republic of Senegal Joint IDA–IMF Staff Advisory Note of the Second Poverty Reduction Strategy Paper*. World Bank report no. 38131-SN, December 20, 2006. Online: http://www-wds.worldbank.org/external/default/WDSContentServer/WDSP/IB/2007/06/15/000112742_20070615155946/Rendered/PDF/381310File0replacement0IDA1SecM200710010.pdf (accessed 10 April 2014).
_____. *World Development Indicators*. Washington, DC: World Bank, 2008.
_____. *World Development Report 2004: Making Services Work for Poor People*. Washington, DC: World Bank/Oxford University Press, 2003.
World Bank Independent Evaluation Group. *Assessing World Bank Support for Trade, 1987–2004*. IEG Evaluation Report no. 35921. Washington, DC: World Bank, 2006. Online: http://www-wds.worldbank.org/external/default/WDSContentServer/WDSP/IB/2006/04/20/000012009_20060420132512/Rendered/PDF/359210PAPER0As101OFFICIAL0USE0ONLY1.pdf (accessed May 1, 2014)
World Bank and International Monetary Fund. *2005 Review of the PRS Approach: Balancing Accountabilities and Scaling Up Results*. Washington, DC: World Bank/IMF, August 19, 2005.
World Commission on the Social Dimension of Globalization. *A Fair Globalization: Create Opportunities for All*. ILO: Geneva, February 2004.
World Trade Organization. *International Trade Statistics* (Geneva: WTO, 2008). http://www.wto.org/english/res_e/statis_e/its2008_e/its2008_e.pdf (accessed May 1, 2014)
Zhang, Yanhong, Hui S. Chang and Jean Gauger. "The Threshold Effect of Exchange Rate Volatility on Trade Volume: Evidence from G-7 Countries." *International Economic Journal* 20, no. 4 (December 2006): 461–76.

INDEX

Lightning Source UK Ltd.
Milton Keynes UK
UKOW04n0233180717
305522UK00006B/75/P